How to Profit from the Coming Russian Boom

The Insider's Guide to Business Opportunities
and Survival on the Frontiers of Capitalism

Richard Poe

McGraw-Hill, Inc.

New York San Francisco Washington, D.C. Auckland Bogotá
Caracas Lisbon London Madrid Mexico City Milan
Montreal New Delhi San Juan Singapore
Sydney Tokyo Toronto

Library of Congress Cataloging-in-Publication Data

Poe, Richard, [date]
   How to profit from the coming Russian boom : the insider's guide
to business opportunities and survival on the frontiers of
capitalism / Richard Poe.
      p.   cm.
   Includes bibliographical references and index.
   ISBN 0-07-050450-4 :
   1. Investments, Foreign—Former Soviet republics. 2. Business
enterprises. Foreign—Former Soviet republics. 3. Former Soviet
republics—Economic conditions.   I. Title.
HG5572.P64   1993   93-10524
332.6'73'D947—dc20   CIP

1 2 3 4 5 6 7 8 9 0   DOC/DOC   9 9 8 7 6 5 4 3

ISBN 0-07-050450-4

*The sponsoring editor for this book was David Conti, the editing supervisor was
Fred Dahl, and the production supervisor was Suzanne W. Babeuf. It was set in
Baskerville by Inkwell Publishing Services.*

Printed and bound by R. R. Donnelley & Sons Company.

This book is printed on recycled, acid-free paper containing a
minimum of 50% recycled de-inked fiber.

The author wishes to thank *Moscow Magazine* for permission to reprint
substantial portions of its City Guide in Appendices A and B.

This publication is designed to provide accurate and authoritative
information in regard to the subject matter covered. It is sold with the
understanding that the publisher is not engaged in rendering legal,
accounting, or other professional service. If legal advice or other expert
assistance is required, the services of a competent professional person
should be sought.
      *—From a declaration of principles jointly adopted by a committee of the
                  American Bar Association and a committee of publishers*

To my parents,
Alfred and Lillian Poe

Contents

9. CHOOSING YOUR RUSSIAN PARTNER
How to Tell the Shysters from the Players

154

12. MONEY, MONEY, MONEY
Russia's Banking and Currency Crisis Is Your Opportunity   189

13. YOU'RE NOT IN KANSAS ANYMORE
A Beginner's Guide to Russian Culture and Etiquette   197

Appendix B. Your Ready-Made Rolodex:
A Complete Directory of Essential Business Contacts   **268**

Appendix C. Resources   **286**

Foreword

I have been conditioned since birth to think of Russia as a vast, mysterious, threatening yet exciting place that for years lay hidden behind an impenetrable iron curtain. In my childhood, I was taught to fear Russia's military strength and its imperialistic designs. As a young adult, I was trained by the Marine Corps to confront Russia's forces in the land, on the sea, and in the air. As I began my career in international law and business, the world within which I functioned specifically excluded the formidable land masses comprising Russia, China, and the other countries of the former Soviet Union and Warsaw Pact nations.

It was "us" against "them"—two nations pitted in a seemingly eternal struggle for the hearts and minds of the Earth's people. I had no expectation that the struggle would ever end or that the Iron Curtain that separated us would be withdrawn one day.

All of that has changed in the last decade. First China and then the former Soviet Union resolved to move their economic systems toward free market concepts and away from central control; not because they suddenly became converts in a religious sense to the ideologies of the West, but because their systems were falling behind the systems of the West at an ever-increasing rate. It was not ideology that ultimately prompted the conversion. It was food, technology, jobs, VCRs, telephones, PCs, and hula hoops. Ultimately, the barriers were pierced, not by intercontinental ballistic missiles but by consumer demands. As a consequence, the movement toward free markets is irreversible, despite the current turmoil. It is driven by necessity, not by doctrine. Western businesses in Russia and the former Soviet Union now have the most extraordinary and exciting business opportunities that I have witnessed in my lifetime. These opportunities are available to any who will take the time to understand them—understand the risks, the emerging political and economic systems, and the individual Russian people who hold the keys to entry. In this book, Richard Poe provides insight into each of these issues.

Those of us who spend a great deal of time in Russia have come to appreciate the Russian spirit. We recognize the great affinity of Russians toward Americans and the great desire in Russia to join forces with Westerners (Americans, in particular) in order to enjoy business success in this new economic frontier. Richard points out, in the most persuasive way, that those American business pioneers who dare to be first in the Russian market have the opportunity to experience both financial success and a wonderful adventure which will be beneficial to all of us in the long run.

These pioneers will not be alone in their efforts to achieve business success in Russia. Every significant Western democracy is making a heroic effort to assure that the Russian transition succeeds and that the Western ventures there prosper. The odds are high that the transitions will succeed and Russia's vast resources and markets will become readily accessible to Westerners. When that happens, those Westerners who got there first will be the first to benefit. Richard's book is truly a bridge between two great peoples who, for too long, have been isolated from one another.

In the meantime, Russia is not to be trifled with. It still controls one of the world's largest and most powerful armies. It still asserts mastery over the world's largest fleet of tactical and strategic nuclear warheads (a large portion of which remain targeted on U.S. cities). It can become a formidable ally and business partner or a fearsome foe and competitor. We have felt its sting as an adversary. We are only beginning to understand its potential as an ally and business partner.

On the plus side, Russia has a highly skilled work force and an awesome intellectual elite, as well as more land, raw materials, timber, and other valued resources than any other nation on Earth. It promises a vast, new market to Western companies that are fresh out of new markets. It also promised access to some technologies coveted in the West. Yet, Russia remains, in many respects, a Third World nation.

I have traveled extensively through Russia and have visited villages in which people still draw their drinking water from centrally located faucets placed strategically throughout the village. I have been to cities in which hot water is a luxury accessible only two or three times per week. I have been in executive offices, remote from Moscow, in which an advance reservation of 24 hours or more is required to make a telephone call within the country. But on those same trips, I have visited factories which manufacture MIG-29s and Sukhoy 27s (two of the most capable fighter aircraft in the world) and I have seen avionics, jet engine, airframe, and metallurgical facilities as good as any in the West. I have seen Russia's best and worst, and I have met with some of the brightest and best entrepreneurs and policymakers in the new Russia.

I have sat in the Kremlin office of then Soviet Deputy Prime Minister Leonid Abalkin to hear him declare his "shame" that a country so richly blessed as Russia should be so short of money and so long on problems. I have worked with the Russian economist Shatalin as part of a task force developing data and recommendations for his revolutionary "500-day" plan to convert the Russian economic system. I have exchanged ideas in private meetings with key Russian economic advisors such as Abel Aganbegyan in Moscow and Jeffrey Sachs in Cambridge—all of whom have lamented Russia's sorry economic health as they attempted to devise relatively painless cures. Through these meetings, I have developed a sense of confidence that the long-term future of Russia is at least as bright as the current situation is troubled.

Despite all of its shortcomings, Russia is undeniably a land of enormous opportunity. Russia's existing problems actually represent opportunities for those with vision. Russia's existing turmoil actually represents a bargaining chip to those who understand that the higher risks in Russia permit a good negotiator to structure a modest, expandable deal where a small, up-front downpayment can reserve an extraordinary opportunity for the more stable times ahead. The problems and turmoil represent barriers only to those who do not understand.

A wise Westerner will recognize Russia for what it is—a vast, mysterious, exciting country which offers opportunities unprecedented in the twentieth century. In exploring the opportunities now available in Russia, and the obvious problems confronting business people in Russia, some see only a half empty glass. In my view, the Russian glass is half *full* and filling quickly.

Richard Poe, in this extraordinarily useful book, describes the fullness of the Russian glass. His research has been extensive and the information he provides is vital to anyone exploring the possibility of doing business in Russia.

Richard debunks the theory that Russia's extraordinary opportunities are available only to highly trained and highly financed technical specialists, as he points to the numerous success stories involving aggressive, foresighted, and energetic Western entrepreneurs in Russia.

With a wealth of charts, graphs, tables, and statistics, Richard helps the reader understand that much of what is happening in Russia and much of what is valuable in Russia never finds its way into the Western press or into the official reports published by the Russian government itself. But Richard isn't content simply to provide statistics. He also gives specific suggestions on how to get things done in Russia. He examines closely a large number of actual ventures in Russia and walks the reader through the processes which were involved in identifying, structuring, negotiating, implementing, managing, and operating these ventures successfully.

Finally, Richard includes a wonderful directory of resources which are available to business people interested in opportunities in Russia. This is not a book which you read and leave at home. This is a book which you put in your briefcase and take with you on your trips to Russia so that when you get off the plane at Sheremetyevo in Moscow you know where to stay, how to get a cab, where to get an interpreter, where to get your laundry done, where to get a haircut, how to get medical care, where to buy food, where to dine, where to buy a pencil or a pen and some stationery, where to pick a souvenir for the folks back home, where to eat out for rubles rather than dollars (the difference is between a $5 meal and a $50 meal), and where one might take an international phone call, send a fax, send or receive a mail or packages by courier, obtain office space, change money or engage in a wide range of activities which we here in the West take for granted.

For all these many useful features, however, I believe the quality which I most appreciate in this book is its style. The book is wonderfully readable. The stories are both informative and entertaining. The process of doing business in Russia requires a certain elan on the part of the entrepreneurs who go there and succeed. Richard captures that spirit of excitement and adventure in a style that is both educational and entertaining.

The observations in *How to Profit from the Coming Russian Boom* gain credibility from Richard's long personal experience in Russia. He speaks the language very capably (although not fluently, he insists), and, since 1988, has reported extensively on Soviet-American business for *Success* magazine and other publications, making numerous trips to Russia for that purpose. He has also undertaken entrepreneurial activities in Russia, including a publication venture and the production of a Russian-language television special on America which was viewed by over 75 million Russians in June of 1992.

It is Richard's firsthand experience which gives this book its force and usefulness, providing him a rare insight into the nitty-gritty (and not always savory) aspects of dealing with Russia's corrupt and often violent system. Perhaps I like Richard's book so much because I can identify with almost every word in every chapter. Like Richard himself, and like many of the entrepreneurs described in this book, I have had some successes in Russia, and have made more than my share of mistakes along the way. It is my hope and belief that you, the reader, can benefit from Richard's wonderful, readable accounts of those experiences, mistakes, and successes so that your success will be more certain.

Anyone who wishes to engage in business in this exciting, tumultuous, blossoming new market must read this book and must take it with them as they enter this new and exciting frontier.

John Morton
Senior Partner, Hale and Dorr

Preface

As this book goes to press, Boris Yeltsin's fate hangs in the balance. Newspapers question the future of reform in Russia. Network newscasts serve up grim footage of goose-stepping Russian troops. Worried friends and colleagues call me to ask how "all this" will affect my upcoming book.

Most are confounded by my reply. "These developments only accentuate the desperate need for my book," I tell them. Americans are starved for objective information about Russia. Time and again, ignorance has bred false fears. When Gorbachev began his reforms in 1985, many Americans suspected a trick. Surely, this wily career Communist was just trying to catch us off guard, perhaps to launch a nuclear first strike! As reforms progressed, the skeptics decided that, while Gorbachev might be sincere, he would soon be overthrown by "hard-liners." Later, when Gorbachev cracked down on separatists in the Baltics, the pessimists exclaimed, "This is the end of reform!" Not so long ago, it was assumed that Gorbachev's fall would herald a return to Communism. Somewhat later, "experts" assured us that everything depended on Yegor Gaidar remaining in office. Most recently, Boris Yeltsin has been dubbed the last hope of free enterprise in Russia. Don't believe any of it.

Throughout the turbulent events of the last eight years, only three things have remained constant. Each year, the business climate in Russia has improved. Each year, foreign investment has accelerated (see chart on page 12). And, each year, media coverage of Russia has remained relentlessly downbeat.

There are two sorts of people now watching events unfold in the former Soviet states—insiders and outsiders. The insiders are bankers, multinational CEOs, wildcat commodity traders, savvy consultants, and small business owners with a thirst for adventure. The outsiders include average readers of newspapers, viewers of network news, and, alas, journalists themselves. The insiders are mostly optimistic. The outsiders are uniformly glum. Both cannot be right.

That's why Americans need *Russian Boom*. Whether or not you have any intention of personally doing business in Russia, this book will help you to understand the remarkable age in which fate has placed you. Armed with *Russian Boom*, you will scrutinize those alarming news reports with a cooler, more objective eye. Moreover, you will discover the courage, strength, and genius of the Russian people, which for too long have been concealed from American eyes.

Those who actually intend to do business in Russia will, of course, find much more. While *Russian Boom* will probably not make you an instant insider, it will:

- Brief you on the innate strengths and fundamental trends which virtually guarantee an explosion of growth and opportunity in Russia before the decade ends.

- Reveal little-known details about the hottest industries, markets, and regions of opportunity in the former Soviet states.

- Tell you how to find and manage good Russian partners and employees.

- Teach you to structure deals with Russian companies for minimum risk and maximum profitability.

- Prepare you psychologically for certain inevitable and traumatic cultural shocks.

- Take you inside Russia's little-understood banking and legal systems.

- Initiate you into the Byzantine rites of intrigue, deceit and intimidation which all too often comprise Russian negotiating tactics.

- Provide nearly 50 pages of directories, including every name, number, and business service you need to get started now! That includes a complete guide to living, working, and traveling in Russia, a "Ready-Made-Rolodex" of essential business contacts, full listings of books, publications, databases, and consultancies . . . information that might take you *years* to compile on your own!

Some will no doubt complain that *Russian Boom* overemphasizes the role of small business in Russia. After all, multinational corporations like Tambrands, GE, McDonald's, and Bristol-Myers Squibb seem to be the real movers and shakers over there. This might be true, but it is equally true that the skills you'll need to survive and thrive in the Russian marketplace are primarily *entrepreneurial*. Far from the corporate home office, all but cut off from international phone calls and stripped down to a starvation budget, *Fortune*

500 vice presidents in Russia are forced to fall back on their native cunning, stamina, and ingenuity for everything from ferreting out good partners to foraging for a decent meal. I believe that the best teachers of such entrepreneurial skills are the entrepreneurs themselves.

If *Russian Boom* does not move you to risk your money in Russia just yet, I hope that it will at least inspire more Americans to pay a visit to that marvelous land. I first traveled to Russia in 1978, spending a summer session at Leningrad State University. Like so many Americans who crossed the Iron Curtain at that time, I experienced a jolting paradigm shift. Many of us don't like to talk about it because it's a little embarrassing. But I'll give it a shot.

For me, it happened about two weeks after I arrived in Leningrad. For days, it had been building up inside me, a vague, mounting anxiety without apparent cause. Then one day, as I walked along Nevsky Prospekt, it hit me. Two weeks worth of cognitive dissonance exploded in a flash of realization. I looked around at the crowded sidewalks, the shuffling *babushki* with their string bags, the young soldiers bearing armloads of flowers to their sweethearts, the unshaven old veterans with their soiled jackets full of medals, the pretty girls who always managed to look fresh and stylish with the little they had, and I realized with an almost physical shock that *the Russians were people too.*

Times may have already changed sufficiently that this no longer seems a profound revelation. Indeed, it never really should have been, especially not for me. For one thing, my paternal grandparents were themselves Russian Jews. I had studied the language for years, avidly devoured books on Russian history since I was 12 years old. More than most Americans, I should have felt some human connection with these people that transcended media imagery. But the engines of propaganda work subtly in our minds, silent, unobserved, beyond reason or analysis. We should never underestimate their invisible power.

When I returned to America, the real Russia receded from my thoughts, supplanted once again by the *official* Russia of dissident trials, Jewish refuseniks, and high-level arms treaties. But Russia—the real Russia—had cast her spell upon me, and I would never again be free.

If my book can jar loose even a few of the prejudices that have long kept our peoples apart, it will have served the best and highest purpose for which I could have hoped. We *must* draw closer to the Russians, for both our sakes. Unless we become partners in trade, unless we join forces to advance science and develop resources, the logic of power and scarcity will force us once more into deadly confrontation. For this shrinking earth will not sustain in peace two such mighty competitors. Not without an equally mighty effort, at any rate.

Happily, for readers of this book, this is one noble cause which requires no selfless donations of time, money, and energy. The rewards will be rich for those who invest now. And the adventure will be incomparable. Welcome to the greatest opportunity since the Age of Exploration. Be sure to pause and take a deep breath before plunging into these pages. You may never be the same again.

Richard Poe

Acknowledgments

First and foremost, I want to thank my wife and fellow Russia-preneur Marie. Her love and moral support was no less important in completing this book than the far more tangible assistance she rendered, ranging from copying, faxing, and conducting phone interviews to combing through months' worth of newspapers for every minute reference to Russia. Without Marie's tough direction and management of our single successful television venture in Moscow, the program would have flopped, depriving this book of much firsthand insight and many amusing and horrific anecdotes. In addition, much of the research for this book was done during our Moscow honeymoon in 1991, in the dark and drizzly month of November, for which Marie deserves some sort of ultimate Good Sport award. I simply couldn't have done it without her.

My tireless and hard-bargaining literary agent, Richard Karz, deserves endless thanks for getting this book off the ground, and praise for his own heroic, entrepreneurial forays into the Russian marketplace, both those which have involved me and those which have not. I thank David C. Johnson at PlanEcon for patiently suffering my endless questions on the minutiae of Russian exchange rates and production statistics; Paul R. Surovell at Interflo for his constant service at all hours as a human encyclopedia on the Russian economy; John Morton at Hale and Dorr for his deep knowledge, wide experience, and generous donation of both; and Len Blavatnik, Stepan Pachikov, Bruce Macdonald, Jeffrey Zeiger, Paul Zane Pilzer, Geoffrey Carr-Harris, and all the other Russia insiders too numerous to mention—both Russian and American—who have opened their little-known world to me and shown me the ropes.

Special thanks go to *Moscow Magazine* for kindly allowing me to reprint large sections of their City Guide in Appendices A and B, thus making this material available to an American public which cannot yet find this excellent publication even on the newsstands of major cities. I am indebted also to the U.S. Commerce Department, PlanEcon, Inc., Interflo, and to the Central Intelligence Agency for the wide use I made of their publicly available research.

On the editorial end, I am most thankful to David Conti, my editor at McGraw-Hill, for taking a chance on such a boldly counterintuitive book as this. To Duncan Maxwell Anderson, my old colleague and fellow Senior Editor at *Success* magazine, I owe all my present knowledge of the manly craft of self-help writing which figured so importantly in the writing of this book. Scott DeGarmo, Editor-in-Chief and Publisher of *Success*, has earned a very special thank you for his early vision for the Russian marketplace, for sending me to Moscow several times in the last few years, and for his invaluable support in the genesis of this book.

Many thanks and warmest regards to our dear friends Stanislav and Lena Lykov, to whose familiar kitchen we unfailingly resort in Moscow and whose friendship is a welcome beacon in a strange and distant land where we lack both kith and kin. To Victor Kosov and Sasha, my faithful interpreter and driver respectively, during many difficult journalistic expeditions to Moscow, I extend a heartfelt thank you.

Finally, there are no words to express my gratitude to my beloved parents, Alfred and Lillian Poe, to whom this book is dedicated. They never stopped believing in me. At a time when the financial and other pressures of raising six children made their own dreams of travel a distant fantasy, they scraped up the plane fare, tuition, and room and board to give me an unforgettable summer at Leningrad State University, an educational experience whose impact continues to bless and shape my life today. For this, and so much more, I am forever grateful.

1

Why Do Business in Russia?

Untold Riches for Those Who Dare

Scott Klososky was nobody special. He owned two computer stores in Tulsa, Oklahoma and a small ranch. But Klososky had something the chairman of IBM didn't. In fact, nobody in the Western world had what Scott Klososky had. No wonder he walked with a bit of a swagger when he strode into the 1989 Comdex computer show in Las Vegas.

Klososky marched right up to the vice president of one of the largest international computer companies in the world. "I have a text recognition system that can read cursive handwriting," said Klososky. "It's fast, accurate, practical and uses very little memory. I can show you right now on my laptop."

The man looked at Klososky like he was crazy. Klososky was describing something out of science fiction. Silicon Valley's best programmers had tried for 20 years to develop *pen-based computing* which allowed users to write text and commands directly onto the screen with an *electronic pen*, instead of a keyboard. But to read handwritten words required cutting-edge artificial intelligence software that had yet to be invented. In 1989, the best American programs were hard put to decipher carefully drawn block letters. Even then, they did it slowly and painfully, one letter at a time. Now here was this 28-year-old punk claiming he had beaten IBM, Apple, and Microsoft to the punch. Who did he think he was anyway?

Klososky whipped out his laptop and began scrawling words, not in neat block letters, but in wild, messy script, the way real people write. In seconds, the computer "read" every word with no mistakes. The astonished vice president tried it himself. Klososky's little laptop read *his* unique scrawl as well.

"He was shocked," recalls Klososky. "He ran and got the president of the company. I just told my story to each one of them, and every time I told it, they would go get someone else. Soon the whole Board of Directors was there looking over my shoulder."

Klososky had found his magic software package in Russia. A Russian company called ParaGraph had produced it, headed by a brilliant computer scientist named Stepan Pachikov.

"They just couldn't believe what I had," he laughs. "They kept saying, 'A *Soviet* wrote that? That came from a *Soviet* company?' In their minds, they had this idea that the Soviets couldn't program anything."

But the Soviets could. In a single bound, that one software package launched this two-bit PC huckster from Tulsa into the big leagues of the computer business. After months of intensive bargaining with the top names in the industry, Klososky and his Russian partner Pachikov signed multimillion-dollar development contracts with Apple Computer, Digital Equipment, and Sun Microsystems.

How Did He Do It?

How did Klososky gain such a jump on the computer industry's heaviest hitters? Why were the polished executives from Silicon Valley so ignorant about the level of software development in the world's largest country? Indeed, *why hadn't they gone to Russia first?*

The most likely answer is that they'd read so many frightening and discouraging tales about the Russian economy in *The Wall Street Journal, Fortune, Barron's* and other leading business publications that they'd long since written off that marketplace as a hopeless black hole.

A Typical Scare Story

The *Christian Science Monitor* reported on March 31, 1992 that a study conducted by Fordham University Business School professor Vladimir Kvint showed that only eight out of 100 U.S. joint ventures surveyed had succeeded in the former Soviet states. A 92 percent failure rate! Coming five years after Gorbachev welcomed the first U.S. joint ventures, this study seemed to cast a pall over the whole program.

But it needn't have. Probably only a few readers of this article realized that even a new business in *America* has a 90.2 percent chance of failing in the first ten years, according to the Small Business Administration.

When placed in proper context, Kvint's study suggests that launching a business in Russia may be only *twice* as risky as starting one in your own hometown—certainly not an inordinate or unexpected degree of danger.

Russia's Riches: The World's Best-Kept Secret

Scare stories in the press play right into the hands of the *Russia insiders*, that small, select crowd of Western businessmen who are rapidly getting rich from their Russian ventures, even as you sit reading this page. The scare stories, after all, are what keeps the competition away!

Take it from me. As a journalist, I've been reporting on Soviet-American business since 1988. Recently, I've become involved in some Russian business ventures of my own. One thing I've learned is that those Westerners who are making money in Russia tend to be a secretive and clique-ish lot. They don't like talking to reporters and when they do, *they often deliberately pretend that conditions are worse than they actually are.* They play their cards close to the vest. And they don't want you peeking.

"Don't quote me!" demanded a certain Wall Street investment banker whom I interviewed for this book. "Don't mention my name or the name of my firm. Okay?"

Practically hissing into the phone, as if wary of hidden eavesdroppers, the man began to talk. I assumed that he was about to divulge the missing link in the BCCI scandal, at the very least. But the information he "leaked" proved to be of even greater sensitivity.

"You want to know about opportunities for American banks in Russia? I'll tell you. The opportunities are *tremendous*, unbelievable. You're not quoting me, are you? I can trust you, right? The market is volatile, but it's the turmoil and volatility that creates the opportunities. Some will lose their shirts, some will make fortunes. My own firm is involved. That's something I don't want to talk about. We're involved, just leave it at that. You're not going to quote me, right?"

Although this man's behavior was extreme, his attitude was typical. Only in the Russian marketplace is the very *existence* of a market treated as a commercial secret!

Make no mistake. There are Americans in the Commonwealth of Independent States (CIS) right now making a lot of money, most of them *people you've never even heard about.* They're the insiders. They're the pioneers. They're what this book is all about.

What Do the Insiders Know
That You Don't?

Billionaire shipping magnate Aristotle Onassis once observed that, "The secret of business is to know something that nobody else knows." What do the Scott Klososkys of this world know that you don't? Whether you're an entrepreneur or a corporate executive, whether you're presently involved in the Russian marketplace or just daydreaming about it, you owe it to yourself to find out the answer to this question *now*.

Is Russia's Economy Growing
Faster than America's?

Some readers might be wondering why they should risk their time and money in an unstable foreign market when their business is barely making it here at home. The reason is that many American businesses have found it *far more profitable* to penetrate the Russian market than to slug it out in America's overcrowded, stagnant economy today.

"Russia was a Godsend to us," says Earl Worsham, an Atlanta real estate developer. His joint venture, Perestroika, acquires decrepit buildings in Russia and transforms them into ultra- modern office complexes for Western corporations. "Working in Russia has been extremely beneficial for us. Here in the states, our business contracted dramatically over the last three years, almost 50 percent. Now we're just inventorying land in America, waiting for the economy to change. But during those same years in Russia, business has grown 500 percent. Our Russian business today is five times our American business. There are good opportunities and good projects everywhere we look. We just can't do enough over there."

As this book went to press, Worsham disclosed that an ongoing business dispute with his Russian partner will probably result in the breakup of the company. Nevertheless, he is eager to find a new partner and keep the ball rolling. "It's still a dynamite opportunity," he says, "if you can find a partner you can trust."

Russian emigres Michael Tseytin, Lenny Pollak, and Boris Kogan thought they had found the American dream once they got their successful Computerland franchise up and running in Secaucus, New Jersey. But then they decided to take a bigger risk. In 1990, they opened a Computerland franchise in Moscow. Business grew *exponentially*. Today, they own 21 Computerland centers; 14 in the former Soviet states, 5 in Romania, and 3 in Bulgaria. And what about their old store in Secaucus? They sold it back to the parent company. Who needs a store in Secaucus when you're making millions in Moscow?

"I'm not going to tell you our sales figures. But I will tell you we accounted for 13 percent of all U.S. exports of computer equipment to the former Soviet republics last year and the year before," claims Eileen Exeter, vice president of marketing for MBL Corporation—the umbrella firm for the partners' Computerland franchises. Total U.S. exports of computer equipment to the CIS and Baltic states were $75.5 million, according to the U.S. Commerce Department. That would put MBL's sales in the $10 million range.

"Our sales are growing 100 percent each year," says Exeter. "And our staff in Russia has more than doubled over the last year. We're hiring while companies in the United States are laying people off."

Why Does the Press Say Russia's Economy is Shrinking?

Insiders agree that Russia's private sector is growing at an explosive rate. So why do we read in the press that Russia's GNP declined 20-25 percent in 1992? The reason is that Russia's official statisticians have no reliable mechanism for measuring the growth of *private industry*. So they just leave it out of the picture entirely.

Those disastrous figures you read in the newspaper refer only to the *state-owned industries*, most of them military in nature. These decrepit state monopolies have been going down the tubes since the mid-1970s. We are now seeing the final, long- awaited crash at the end of that 15-year freefall. It's not a pretty sight. But it's nothing to cry about either.

Remember that it was the rapid and terminal decline of Soviet state industries which forced Gorbachev to implement his reforms in the first place. If these industries were still humming along at high speed, the world today would be a far grimmer place for you and me.

For one thing, a reformer like Gorbachev would never have been allowed to attain power in a successful, productive Soviet Union. You don't reform something that already works. If the state economy worked, the Communist bureaucracy would still be sitting high in the saddle. The state planners would still be marching relentlessly towards Khrushchev's long-promised goal of "burying" us economically. Afghanistan and half of Europe would still be Soviet satellites. And Russia would be our primary commercial competitor. In fact, judging by America's current lackluster performance, Russia would probably have beaten us hands down by now in every category from cars to microchips.

Thank God, things have worked out otherwise. The Soviet state and its moribund industries have collapsed. This is good news for all who love liberty. It's also good news for those who love free enterprise. Because, from the very ashes of Soviet state industry, a thriving private sector has arisen. Rude, undisciplined, bereft of capital, innocent of MBAs, and invisible to our mass media these rising new entrepreneurs are forging a prosperous, middle-class society before our very eyes. And they're doing it at lightning speed.

Just How Fast *Is* Russia's Private Sector Growing?

Nobody really knows. One online service called RusDataDialine guesses that only 5 percent of total production volume now comes from the private sector. That seems a ridiculous underestimate, but the Russian government says it's even lower—only 4 percent. John Morton, however, Senior Editor of *East-West Executive Guide* and a leading consultant to major corporations in the CIS thinks that the actual figure may be closer to 30 or even 50 percent.

"Half the economy may be free enterprise by now," he says. "It depends on how you calculate it. A lot of private business is in the black market or illegal area."

Most Russia insiders I've spoken to side with Morton, based on their own business experience and everyday observation. In any case, by the time you read this book, the question will probably be moot. Starting in January 1993, virtually every state industry is scheduled to be placed on the auction block and offered to private investors. Shares of stock will be traded publicly, and foreign buyers are more than welcome. The state industrial conglomerates—which have formed the backbone of Soviet power since the 1930s—will finally revert to private hands.

When that process is complete, it will mark the *real* fall of Communism, an event of far greater import than the mere razing of the Berlin Wall.

Even if we confine our analysis to Russia's "on-the-books," official production figures, the picture is far rosier than most Americans realize. While production is clearly plummeting, knowledgeable analysts predict that the end of the tunnel is near at hand.

According to PlanEcon, a Washington research firm, Russia's falling GNP is due to bottom out at about $684.1 billion in 1994. That's when the recovery will begin. PlanEcon prognosticators see a steadily rising GNP hitting $755 billion by 1996. See Fig. 1.1.

The Gold Rush Is On

Knowledgbale observers say there has been a dramatic rise over the last year in the level of American business involvement in the CIS. "In the last few months, our business has increased fivefold," says Randall Morgan,

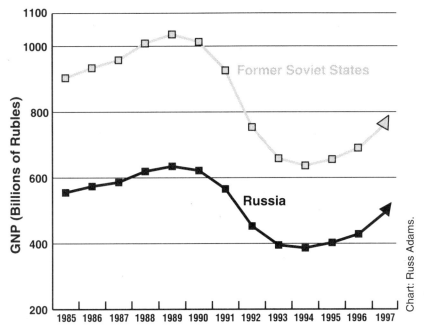

Figure 1.1. The recovery will start in 1995, after bottoming out in 1994, experts say.

president of ASET Consultants in Washington. "It's a greater influx of business than we've seen in the previous two years combined. It really started in the summer of 1992. We started getting calls from a lot of companies who wanted to research the marketplace, a lot of companies who have been postponing major plans but who are now committing to going forward with their projects. "

This past year, Paul Richardson saw a 150 percent surge in sales of his handbook, *The Russia Business Survival Guide,* sold primarily to foreign businessmen on bookstands in Moscow. He calls this trend the "1992 rush on Russia."

"We've been at this for three years," says Richardson. "Last year, we sold 2000 copies. Then there was a dropoff right after the coup. But in January, something just happened. Our sales took off. We'll sell 5000 books this year, easy."

An Economic Refugee

Magazine publisher Richard Karz was hit hard by the recession. After four profitable years, Karz's glossy city magazine, *Manhattan Catalog,* was suddenly on the skids. Advertising vanished. Bills piled up. Before he knew it, Karz was out of business. The trouble hadn't just hit Karz's particular advertising niche. The entire magazine industry was reeling. American companies just didn't have money to advertise anymore. Karz started wondering where his next rent check would come from.

In desperation, Karz flew to Russia. The next 10 days were a grueling round of dawn-to-dusk vodka drinking and head-to-head negotiations as Karz hawked his idea to every major Russian newspaper. But it paid off. In the end, Karz flew home with a dream contract.

Komsomolskaya Pravda, a Russian daily with over 19 million readers, had agreed to publish his new magazine. *America, America*, as it was called, would be distributed as a supplement to one million of the newspaper's subscribers, making it the largest, Russian-language American magazine in the then-Soviet Union. Moreover, the Russians would pay all costs for printing and circulation. Karz would supply the editorial and—most important of all—the ads from Western corporations.

Karz could hardly believe his good fortune, as he sat, dazed, in his one-bedroom apartment on Manhattan's Upper West Side, being photographed for *The New York Times* business section.

Persistence Pays Off

But Karz was to learn that Russia doesn't yield up her favors quite so easily. Only savage determination and monumental persistence unlock the door to her treasure trove.

After a few months—during which this author was briefly appointed Editor of *America, America*—the magazine deal fell through. Ad sales proved slim and printing costs unexpectedly high. Once again, Karz was staring defeat in the face. At that point, he might have ended up like so many embittered dabblers in the Russian marketplace, forever cursing that day he'd set foot in Sheremetyevo Airport. But in the brief few days Karz had circulated around Moscow, he had smelled something in the air. Opportunity. Freedom. Wide-open spaces. Something decidedly lacking in his recession-racked hometown of New York City.

Karz decided to give it one more shot. This time he hit paydirt.

Everyone Can Be a Star

Television provided the magic formula. Karz discovered that Russia's major networks were starved for just the sort of quality programming that an enterprising American like himself could provide. Airtime could be bought for a song, then sold at a profit to American advertisers. And the audiences were phenomenal. One primetime special might reach 180 million viewers—numbers unheard of in America since the advent of cable TV.

In short, Karz became a TV producer. Since early 1992, he has placed a number of documentary specials on Russian television, mainly consisting of existing programs bought on the cheap in America. In startling contrast to their slashing of advertising budgets in the United States, Karz found major multinational corporations more than eager to buy airtime in Russia.

"The Russian market has been very good to me," concludes Karz (who, incidentally, was also my literary agent for this book). "I never could have done this in America."

A New Attitude

Like so many other American businessmen in Russia, Karz has noticed a distinct change in the atmosphere since 1992. Interest in the Russian marketplace has increased dramatically among U.S. advertisers.

"In the spring of 1992, there was still a lot of hesitation," Karz recalls. "Few companies were willing to commit money. Many companies were totally rejecting the possibility of doing any marketing or advertising in Russia at all. But in 1993, I've seen a change in attitude. Many of those same companies are coming back to me and saying they're ready to talk business. They have more confidence now in Russia's long-term prospects. They see that the political situation has stabilized. And they see that their competitors are getting in, so they really have no choice."

Why the Surge? Why Now?

Consultant Randall Morgan believes the surge has been caused by an increase in the "comfort level" of doing business in Russia.

"There's been bad press coming out about Russia for the last five years. Every month there are new stories why the market economy won't work or there's going to be a military coup or whatever. But things just keep getting better. Now we've got IMF money coming in, and OPIC insurance, a lot of government assistance programs. That's made a big difference. I think people are just getting comfortable with the level of risk.

"The forerunners have already gone in, the pioneers. The companies that wanted to hang back and watch what happens to the early birds are now realizing they can go in too and start to get their feet wet."

Bruce Macdonald, head of BBDO Marketing in Moscow puts it in slightly more urgent terms. "Today, every manufacturer in the world has reason to fear that if they're not here, their competition soon will be."

Get in Before It's Too Late

In an article in the *Journal of Commerce* (March, 17, 1992), Steptoe and Johnson partner Sarah Carey warned that the window of maximum opportunity is closing rapidly in Russia. With interest growing among major corporations, Russia's wide-open market will soon be a thing of the past. Those who enter the market in future years will meet ferocious competition from major multinational corporations.

Some oldtimers in the Russian marketplace might snicker at this warning. As Professor Marshall Goldman of the Russian Research Center at Harvard puts it, "The Russians have been saying ever since the 1970s, if you do not come in now you are going to lose your shirt.

"We should remember that for a long time we were being told the Germans were moving in and taking advantage of all these opportunities while the Americans were just sitting back. Well, it is true. The Germans did move in and took care of the 'opportunities,' but they ended up with enormous bank debt which they are now writing off just as the United States had to write off substantial debts in Latin America."

In short, the "over-cautious" Americans knew what they were doing all along. After letting the Germans, Japanese, and Koreans break the ice and make the mistakes, U.S. corporations now command a position of strength. They are moving rapidly to exploit that advantage. Don't mistake the 1990s for the previous two decades. The long-predicted Gold Rush has begun. And this time it's for real.

A Land for Entrepreneurs

Without a doubt, major corporations like AT&T, Tambrands and Bristol-Myers Squibb will shape the Russian marketplace in the years ahead. But for now, the chaotic conditions in Russia lend themselves most readily to the entrepreneur.

Goldman offers this advice to executives of large corporations: "What I would do is put my foot in the door with a small effort. I would not involve senior executives. The senior executives like to be involved—it's exciting, it's romantic—but they most often go home not having accomplished anything and having lost good opportunities elsewhere. I would put in some younger people (even giving them a small stake in the enterprise) and say 'go out and try to do it.' I would give them a firm budget and considerable flexibility. There are opportunities. But if you invest too much, you may later have to answer to those who ask, 'Who was the idiot who authorized that waste of money?'"

For the most part, the *Fortune 500* have followed Goldman's advice. While the list of large corporations with a presence in Russia grows daily, most are still hedging their bets, limiting investment to a few million dollars. This presents a window of opportunity for the entrepreneur. In this unique corner of the world, for this brief moment in history, you can compete on a level playing field with meganational companies who would eat you alive in your home market.

New Business Starts Are Accelerating

Just how fast is Western business penetrating the Russian market? Accurate statistics are difficult to obtain. However, since joint ventures were virtually the only legal means for foreigners to invest in Russia between January 13, 1987 and July 4, 1991, the number of registered joint ventures ought to give us some indication of the trend.

During the first four years of Gorbachev's "Joint Venture Law," only 2905 foreign firms signed deals with the Soviets. Then in the single year from January 1, 1991 to January 1, 1992, that number skyrocketed to 4208. Three months later, it had reached 6381 and by January 1993 it was a phenomenal 13,262. Remember that since July 4, 1991, a new Russian law has allowed foreign companies to form wholly owned subsidiaries, not just joint ventures. Since most foreigners now prefer to form these "joint stock companies" rather than joint ventures, we can safely assume that the remarkable growth in joint ventures over this last year amounts to only a fraction of the growth in other types of foreign-owned businesses which have not been recorded.

The trend is obvious. The Gold Rush is on. The first wave (i.e., the early pioneers of the "joint venture era" is already past. The second wave is well underway. Don't wait for the third wave. The competition will be murder. (See Fig. 1.2.)

A New Maturity

"The business atmosphere has gotten much better," says John Nicolopoulos, a consultant who has lived in Moscow since the 1970s. "It's getting wilder on the surface, but less wild institutionally. In the street, you see a

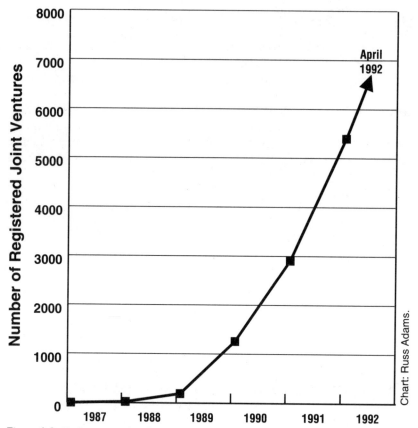

Figure 1.2. Explosive growth in foreign business activity. Despite gloomy press reports, foreign ventures in the former Soviet states have multiplied exponentially in the last four years. *(Note: Figures shown here after 1990 are reliable United Nations estimates. Official statistics from the ex-USSR after 1990 cannot be trusted.)*

lot of Mafia types running around monopolizing products like Marlboro cigarettes. But in the government, in the economic, financial and regulatory institutions, the atmosphere is getting better. People just know more about business. They're not so naive as in early years."

As an example, Nicolopoulos points to an associate of his, Armen Kazarian, an Armenian commodities trader who has just hooked up a nationwide computer network linking hundreds of commodity exchanges across the country.

"Now, if you want to buy some urea in Novorossisk, you can just bring it up on the screen and find a broker that's offering it. This is the kind of sophistication we're seeing now. Such a thing was totally unthinkable in the early days. Now we're seeing all kinds of complex financial deals, takeover bids, deals using promissory notes and other such instruments which were unheard of a few years ago."

Russia's "Secret" Middle Class

"There's a lot of prosperity in Russia," says John Francis, director of overseas operations for The Barbers International. "You don't read about that in the American press. But there's an amazing number of very well-to-do people."

Francis' company just opened a two-story, chi-chi hairstyling salon two blocks from Red Square. Demand is so great, you have to make an appointment weeks in advance to get a perm.

"There are probably 30 percent more private cars on the road today than there were last year," Bruce Macdonald told me in November 1991. Now that number has grown even larger. When General Motors opened its Trinity Motors dealership in Moscow in May of 1992, it sold 151 cars in the first 31 days. The most popular model is the Chevrolet Caprice, which goes for $23,500. Trinity Motors partner Jim Lyle estimates there are some 300,000 hard-currency car buyers in Russia.

Who are these people? Some are no doubt members of Russia's genuinely wealthy nouveau riche society. Commodity trader Artyom Tarasov, for example, is rumored to have a personal fortune in excess of $30 million—a respectable sum by any standard in the world. But the vast majority of Russia's new wealth seems to lie in the hands of people who can only be called a *new middle class*. These are the owners of private businesses, their employees, and the swelling ranks of professionals who are using their skills to earn hard currency.

"I would say that the Russian middle class is growing by about 15 to 20 percent per year," says Len Blavatnik. Inveterate insider that he is, Blavatnik reveals little about his Russian commodities business which takes him on frequent trips to mysterious factory sites in Siberia. But he does admit revenues have been growing 500 percent each year, reaching a figure in the "tens of millions" for fiscal 1992.

Blavatnik knows a lot about Russia's rising middle class. He's helped to create it. "There's actually a labor shortage now for highly qualified people," Blavatnik laments. "For a good accountant, I have to pay 15,000 -20,000 rubles per month [about $100] and in addition $500 to $600 in hard currency. We paid for graphics work recently from some private outfit, for logos, stationery, that sort of thing. We paid them a few thousand dollars. And we're just one of their many clients.

"The time of the illegal millionaires is over. It's no longer the black marketeers and the party apparatchiks with their hand in the till. Now most of the people you see with money have earned it legally."

The Russians Have Money, Lots of It!

I spent my honeymoon in Moscow back in November 1991. It was cold, dark, and wet. I'm afraid it wasn't the most idyllic vacation retreat to which I might have whisked my new bride Marie. But I was working on a story for *Success* magazine, and Moscow was where the action was at.

Food shortages were making daily headlines in the American press at that time, so we were concerned whether we'd find enough to eat. Our fears proved groundless. Just a few blocks from our rented apartment we discovered a fullscale, fully stocked Western supermarket run by an Irish company called Aerianta. Everything was priced in dollars. In the old days, that would have meant that only foreigners and black marketeers would have been able to shop there. But the store was full of Russians, night and day! There were so many Russians, you had to wait in line to get in, something which would have been unthinkable at a hard currency store in the old days.

In the aisles, we were jostled by hordes of Russian women filling up shopping carts, not with wholesome bread and cheese to stave off starvation, but with every kind of silly luxury item, from imported liqueurs to chocolate bon-bons. At the cash register, shoppers chattered brightly with the Russian checkout girls, whipping out fat rolls of American $20 bills with a casual insouciance shocking to those like myself who still remembered when Russians used to horde their dollars secretly like precious, forbidden gems, ever fearful of the KGB's covetous eyes.

Nowhere did we spy the telltale athletic jumpsuits and black leather jackets of Russian "mafia" hoods. These were families with children. They were normal, middle class people who had so many dollars to spare they could afford to buy Dutch chocolates with them.

We soon found out that this scene was being repeated all over the city at other hard currency supermarkets and stores. Since that time, the number of such stores has skyrocketed, but no one has yet found the limits to the Russian hard currency market.

Where Are the Russians Getting All Those Dollars?

Later that week, I chatted with Bruce Macdonald, head of the Moscow office for BBDO advertising agency. Macdonald is perhaps one of the most "inside" of all of Russia's insiders. His client list includes Pepsico, Visa, Avon, GE, Wrigley's and many more in the same vein. I asked him what was going on.

"Nobody knows," said Macdonald. "Nobody knows how they're getting the money. Some are getting it by working for Western companies. Others perhaps are getting it from friends who have gone to the West and brought back more products than they needed, then resold them to commercial stores or to other friends for hard currency. But no one has really tracked it.

"Six months ago, the people who had hard currency fell into three categories: they were taxi drivers, prostitutes, or workers in private co-ops and foreign joint ventures. Today you can make no such distinction. Russians in all walks of life are obtaining and spending hard currency on a regular basis. The spread of hard currency in this country is enormous, much bigger than anybody ever perceived, and *it's growing exponentially*. Just in the last 30 days, we've had to revise all our projections."

A Little-Known Lesson from Pizza Hut

Macdonald pointed out that more and more Russians were now eating on the hard currency side of Pizza Hut. Like many foreign-owned eateries in Moscow, Pizza Hut has both a "ruble side" where Russians line up around the block to get in, and a "hard currency side," where you can usually get a table immediately.

"Six months ago, I noticed a rising number of Russians eating in the hard currency side of Pizza Hut," he said. "Do you realize what this means? Up till then, the conventional wisdom was that Russians would save their dollars for major purchases. But here were Russians making an impulse decision that they would rather spend $30 to $40 on a pizza, which they will eat and it's gone in half an hour, than to wait 40 minutes in line and buy it for rubles."

That conversation took place over a year ago. Since then, hard currency spending has continued to grow unabated, causing major American manufacturers like Wrigley's and Avon to rethink their earlier "all-ruble sales" strategies. Now they're selling some products for dollars too in an effort to comb out those unexpected reserves of greenbacks.

At the time of this writing, Russians are routinely paying $20,000-$40,000 for run-of-the-mill 3-room apartments in Moscow. There are no mortgages. They pay in cash, in American dollars. And it's a very active market.

It's Not About Dollars, It's About People

Don't get me wrong. Russia's future should not depend upon converting to a dollar economy, and believe me, it won't. The Russian government has been threatening for over a year to *outlaw* all transactions in foreign coin, and may even have done it by the time this book is published. This is a healthy and positive step, indicative of Russia's newfound maturity. No sovereign state worthy of the name should have somebody else's currency competing with its own on its mother soil.

However, the prevalence of hard currency today does say a great deal about the resourcefulness of Russia's people who have managed to thrive and prosper despite the most dreadful obstacles. Their talent and resilience indicates a bright future for the Russian economy.

An Entrepreneurial Tradition

"The degree of ingenuity and entrepreneurship that goes into finding the necessities of life (in Russia), and the practices of barter in gray markets that all citizens deal with everyday, have encouraged behavior that will, when legalized in the normal market conditions, produce surplus for other consumers."
GRAHAM ALLISON AND
GRIGORY YAVLINKSY,
1991 Report to the G-7 Nations

Learned pundits in Western newspapers often remark that Russia's "lack of an entrepreneurial tradition" puts it at a distinct disadvantage vis-à-vis other Westernizing nations such as Poland, Hungary, and even China, which only became Communist in the 1940s. This is nonsense. The people who are making a difference in all these countries are not ancient pensioners harking back to some dimly remembered pre-Revolutionary past. They are the very young, people who were born since the 1940s and who have never known any other system than Communism. This is as true in Prague or Warsaw as it is in Moscow. In Russia, they're people like Mikhail Hodorkovsky, the 27-year-old chairman of Menatep Financial Group, one of Russia's leading commercial banks with 800 employees and several overseas affiliates. Or they're people like 24-year-old Vladislav Vasnev, whose chain of street kiosks employs 400 people and sells everything from boots and parkas to blenders and stereo recorders to Moscow's rising middle class.

These bright young Russians learned entrepreneurship not from the tales of their grandparents, but from the harsh necessity of daily living under the Communist regime. Survival alone dictated that every Soviet citizen become a wheeler dealer. Even during the grimmest years of the Brezhnev "stagnation," certain black marketeers made colossal fortunes selling clothing, cars, appliances, computers—activities which would have earned them an honest living in the West.

And it wasn't just black marketeers. Under Communism, every citizen played his part in the shadow economy. The shopkeepers selling marked-up furniture out the back door, the motorists siphoning gasoline on the highway, the cement mixers pouring unauthorized porches and patios on their downtime, and the collective farmers lovingly tending their private plots all provided an unbroken chain of entrepreneurial tradition, handed down since the days of the Stroganoffs—that mighty trading family which opened the Siberian frontier.

"At this point, I see a lot more of an entrepreneurial spirit among the Russians than I do in Eastern Europe," says Karz. "I'm talking to major television networks in Poland, Czechoslovakia and Hungary. The bureaucratic restrictions in those countries are incredible. In Russia, it's much more an attitude of anything goes. Everybody is hustling. Everybody's out to make a deal."

Free Enterprise:
An Unstoppable Force

People like myself who visited the Soviet Union during the depths of the Brezhnev era can never be swayed by all the pessimism in the American press. Unless you've seen for yourself what it was like "before" and "after," there's no way to describe how drastically and fundamentally things have changed since the Soviet era. Free enterprise is a tangible, violent force in Russia. You can smell it in the air. You can feel it as you move through the crowds. This dangerous genie will never again be corked in its bottle. It will kill before it submits.

When I studied at Leningrad State University in the summer of 1978, the Soviet Union was a gray and somber place. The only "ads" I ever saw were the ubiquitous block letters protruding from the tops of buildings and bridges which spelled out such forbidding slogans as "The Soviet Working Class Heartily Approves the Decisions of the 25th Party Congress."

I will never forget arriving at the Ukraina Hotel in April 1990—my first trip back to Russia in 12 years—flipping on the TV in my hotel room and staring in amazement at a leather- clad rock songstress undulating through a heavy-metal ballad, while ad copy for a car leasing agency rolled across the screen.

Like a Boomtown in
the Klondike

Anything goes in the new Russia. Moscow has taken on the honky- tonk air of a boomtown in the Klondike. A friend of mine, Sergei Lisovsky, runs one of the hottest nightspots in town, a makeshift dance club called Ulissa, which he creates every Friday and Saturday night on the hockey rink at Olimpisky Stadium. There, thousands of Russians dance their frustrations away till the wee hours of the morning, accompanied by the clangor of slot machines, the cries of roulette croupiers, and the gyrations of topless "erotic dancers." Burly bouncers patrol the dance floor, ever on the lookout for weapons, drugs, or other unwelcome signs of "Mafia" presence. Not even the New York club scene at its decadent height in the 1980s had anything to compare.

. Commerce has invaded every corner of Russian society in its most lawless and naked form. Russian whores boldly proffer their wares door to door in even the fanciest hotels. Every cab driver in the city seems to be running a mobile currency exchange from his taxi. And for every dying, state-owned store in Moscow with its rows of empty shelves, a thousand little private kiosks have sprung up on the sidewalks, hawking everything from books, perfume, champagne, lingerie, and shoes to children's clothing.

And then, of course, there are the Americans. You can see the bright logos of Coca-Cola and Pepsico looming over Pushkin Square and the glamorous facade of Estee Lauder gracing Gorky Street. Everywhere you find Americans making deals, speaking in hushed tones over drinks about Siberian oil fields and gold mines in Uzbekistan.

"This country is wide open," says Fred Harrison, "editor of the Moscow-based newsletter *Russian Business Reports*. "A small-time entrepreneur can play with millions in devalued rubles. It's like India at the turn of the century, an exotic, mysterious land, ripe with opportunity."

The Last Frontier

In Chap. 8, I will spell out in great detail the vast mineral, human, energy, and industrial wealth available in the former Soviet states. Suffice it to say here that the frequent comparisons one hears between Russia and the old American West are more than just a tired metaphor. Russia truly is a frontier of civilization, one of the last remaining on this earth.

Its vast forest, the Taiga, stretches across six time zones. A 30-minute drive from Moscow will put you in the midst of virgin woodland with 60-foot birches, teeming with elk and other wild game. In Siberia's unsettled reaches roam bear, tigers, snow leopards, boar, and wild wolves so numerous they are regarded as a major pest (rather than an endangered species, as in America).

It is estimated that Russia's untapped oil reserves exceed those of the Middle East, that its gold fields dwarf those of South Africa. Across the great expanse of Siberia lie tracts of land untrod by human feet nor ever seen by human eyes.

"You don't realize how wild Russia really is until you drive on the highways," says George Capsis, a consultant to American corporations in Russia for 20 years. "It's not like here where you leave the city and you see farms and little towns and McDonald's stops every few miles. When you drive outside a Russian city, all of a sudden, you're in the middle of nowhere, the wilderness. There's absolutely *nothing*.

"If you were to stand on the banks of the Mississippi back in the 1850s and look towards the West, what would you see? A huge wilderness, with no law, no money, no railroads, no towns, no investment insurance, nothing except infinite opportunity, a chance for those tough enough and brave enough to go out and make something of it. That's what Russia is today."

Beacon to the World

Strange as it seems, Russia has become a kind of last bastion of free enterprise, in a world where state regulation and "industrial policy" have dampened the fires of entrepreneurship in many countries.

"For me, Russia is the best place to do business," says Moscow impresario Sergei Lisovsky. "It's not so interesting to work in the West. When I went to Germany, I found that the whole country is divided up into several regions, and if I produce concerts in Cologne or Frankfurt, I'm not allowed to produce in Berlin or some other city. If you're at one level in the business, it's very hard to climb to another level. But here in Russia, I'm not restricted to this or that city. I go wherever I like and no one tells me how high I can go."

Long ago, it was just this sort of spirit that made America great. In the years ahead, it is certain to work miracles in Russia. Act now, and you can be part of that revolution.

2
The Russian Threat

We Can Choose to Be Russia's Partners or Her Victims

On the day Hitler invaded Russia, Joseph Goebbels threw a party. The sharp-tongued maestro of propaganda amused his guests by taking funny jabs at the barbaric, oafish "Slavs" who were at that moment being pulverized by German bombers. With utter confidence, Goebbels predicted that Russia would be conquered in "only eight weeks."

The ebullient Reich Minister then turned to film star Olga Tschechowa, who happened to be the niece of the great Russian playright Anton Chekhov. "We have a Russian expert here," teased Goebbels. Then he asked her, "Will we be in Moscow by Christmas?"

The lady stared at him icily. Finally, she said, "You know Russia, the endless land. Even Napoleon had to retreat."

A deathly silence descended. Goebbels' only reply was a mumbled, "So." Ten minutes later, his adjutant "invited" Madame Tschechowa to leave the party. The rest, as they say, is history.

I often wonder if Goebbels remembered his flippant remarks four years later as he cowered in his underground bunker, handing out cyanide tablets to his wife and children as the guns and bombs of the oafish Slavs thundered overhead.

Beware the Goebbels Syndrome

Americans love to make fun of Russians. We mock them for being morose ("Nobody ever *smiles* in Moscow!"), we scold them for being freemarket naifs ("Haven't they ever heard of *supply* and *demand*?"), we accuse them of dishonesty ("Their word means nothing. *Nothing*!"), we lash them for being lazy ("Only in Russia would they close a restaurant for lunch break!"), we snicker at their lapses in fashion sense ("Did you *see* what that woman was wearing?") and smirk at their childish consumerism ("Just take them on a trip to Disneyland. Then they'll sign anything.").

Of course, a little humor now and then—even at someone else's expense—is probably inevitable and usually harmless, as long as we don't start believing our own jokes. But I fear many Americans have actually convinced themselves that the Russians are nothing more than silly, incompetent boobs. Such arrogance can cripple our judgment, as Goebbels discovered.

Is the Emperor Naked?

Few things are more terrifying to us than the threat of being despised by our peers. That's why all the Emperor's subjects in the old fable pretended they could see his new robes, when, in fact, he was buck naked as the day he was born.

Today, there are many "experts" circulating around who will not hesitate to brand you as stupid or uninformed if you dare to exhibit an overly optimistic view of Russia's prospects. The same held true in 1941 Berlin. As you can see, just because "all" the experts say something doesn't make it true.

Is Russia the Next Japan?

The only nation in history to endure nuclear attack, Japan suffered devastation in World War II unparalleled in the annals of the industrialized world. By 1945, two atomic bombs and massive incendiary attacks had reduced Japan's cities and factories to "charred wastelands . . . depressing heaps of blackened remains. . ." in the words of Sony chairman Akio Morita, writing in his recent memoirs. Japanese were parcelling out rice to their children "a single grain at a time," recalls Morita. "Most people had difficulty even *getting* rice."

Japan in 1945 possessed none of the natural advantages which Russia flaunts today in such extravagant abundance. It lacked Russia's limitless energy and mineral resources, her forests, gold mines, fertile farmlands, and her huge domestic consumer market. In one respect and one respect alone, post-war Japan equalled today's Russia—it had a highly skilled, superbly educated populace, determined at any cost to redeem its crippled motherland.

This proved to be enough. Japanese exports became world- competitive in many categories within 10 to 15 years. What Japan did in the 1940s,

Russia might well duplicate in the 1990s. There's no objective reason to suppose that she couldn't, unless, of course, we accept the common "wisdom" that Russians are just too "stupid," "lazy," "disorganized," and "corrupt" to work together for their common salvation. Russian history suggests quite the opposite.

Victory from the Jaws of Catastrophe

Time and again, Russia has displayed a remarkable penchant for snatching victory from the jaws of disaster. When the Germans attacked in World War II, over 1200 Soviet aircraft and thousands of trucks, tanks, artillery pieces, and other weaponry were destroyed within the first few hours. It was an unprecedented disaster. The German high command predicted, with very good reason, that Soviet industry could never replace this equipment in time and that Soviet troops would soon be armed with stones and spears.

These hard, economic facts "proved" that the Soviet Union had already lost the war. However, in a frantic, round-the-clock effort—working in the very shadow of the advancing *Wehrmacht*—Soviet work crews packed up the entire military-industrial complex of European Russia and shipped it to remote regions of the Ural Mountains. There, far from Hitler's bombers, the Soviet factories were reassembled almost overnight.

For the next four years, they churned out the machinery of war—deadly Katyusha rocket launchers, Ilyushin fighter planes, and the famous T-34 tanks which even the haughty Germans acknowledged to be the best in the world.

It is reported that, when Hitler's Army Intelligence Service informed him in 1942 that the Russian factories were spewing out 600 to 700 tanks per month, the Fuhrer pounded his fist on the table and cried that it was impossible. The Russians were "dead!" But, of course, they were far from dead.

More than any other factor, it was this astonishing resilience of Soviet industry which confounded, intimidated, and ultimately defeated the Germans.

A Fighting Spirit

Like the Japanese, the Russians have long prided themselves on their indomitable, warlike spirit. Japan successfully transformed her samurai ethic into a near-fanatical quest for business excellence. A similar metamorphosis may sweep Russia in the years ahead.

Westerners have marvelled for centuries at the stoic perseverance of Russia's warriors. One of the first Westerners to observe Russian troops in the 16th century remarked, "How justly may this barbarous and rude Rus condemn the daintiness . . . of our captains who, living in a soil and air much more temperate, yet commonly use furred boots and cloaks. . . . I pray you, amongst all our boasting warriors how many should we find to endure the field with them but one month?" Another traveller wrote that the Russian soldiers "bore cold and hunger without a murmur, died in their thousands on the earthworks, and never gave in till the last extremity."

"Rude" and "barbarous" they might seem, but the Russians have a reputation for fighting hard and winning. Time and again, they have rebounded from unspeakable catastrophe. Their fighting spirit may stand them in good stead on the commercial battlefields of the 1990s.

It's Not That Far Off

Some Americans snort that the threat of Russian competition is so distant as to fall within the realm of science fiction. "Yes," they admit, "perhaps the Russians may recover someday. But not in this generation."

In fact, Russia has already begun to take major competitive bites out of America's global pie. For example, in 1992, Russia's aluminum exports more than doubled, as a direct result of which the world price for aluminum was cut in half. Go tell ALCOA, Alcan, Reynolds Metals, and Kaiser Aluminum that the "Russian threat" is a joke.

Russia has the capacity *now* to wreak similar havoc in half a dozen other strategic metal categories, not to mention such vital commodities as oil and gas. In the last year, the U.S. Department of Commerce has already investigated charges of uranium and ferrosilicon "dumping" on the part of Russia and other CIS states.

Some may dismiss the dumping of raw materials as a crude and pathetic attempt to scare up capital. Indeed, the Russian government imposed strict export controls on many raw materials in 1992, in order to stanch what it regards as an unhealthy bleeding of its natural wealth. Nevertheless, what began as a stopgap measure to raise quick cash may reappear tomorrow as a conscious global strategy. We should remember that John D. Rockefeller built America's mighty oil industry in large part by undercutting competitors in foreign markets, even when it meant slashing his prices below market rate.

Not all of Russia's low commodities prices can be attributed to dumping. After Russian uranium suppliers captured 20 percent of the U.S. market in 1992, the U.S. government cried "Dumping!" and slapped on a 116 percent duty on enriched uranium. In fact, the Russians' low prices were perfectly legitimate. The problem was that American producers were using obsolete diffusion technology to refine their uranium, while the Russians used low-cost, state-of-the-art centrifugal methods.

The second area where Russian competition will hit America hard is agriculture. Before the Revolution, Russia was the number one exporter of food in the world. There's no reason to think that land reform and modern agrotechnology will not put her right back in first place and soon.

Bulgaria, which had a slight head start in agricultural reform, has already experienced a 16.5 percent increase in food production over the last year, according to PlanEcon. Armenia has reportedly upped its harvest by 50 percent. Similar increases on the part of Russia and the Ukraine would take a huge and immediate bite out of the billions of dollars in grain purchases which these countries make annually from the United States. Such a sudden and overwhelming incursion into our global market share will hit the U.S. farm belt hard, creating a ripple effect through many layers of our economy, starting with our banking sector and its billions in outstanding farm loans. That's not even taking into account what will happen when Russia starts *exporting* food.

Russia's Hidden Strength

Contrary to many cocktail-party jests, Russia is no Third World country. We cannot expect that her exports will forever be confined to food and minerals. A common misperception holds that the only manufactures Russia can export are caviar, vodka, fur hats, and *matryoshka* dolls. We've all heard about the shoddy TV sets that blow up and the rickety "washer-dryers" that spew out dingy clothes dripping with rinse-water.

However, what should be far more interesting to business pioneers like yourself is that estimated 25 percent of Russian industry which has proven hugely successful by every world standard, the defense sector. Following the German reunification, the Federal Republic inherited 24 Russian-built MIG-29A jet fighters from the East German Air Force. Authorities who examined the plane marvelled at its capabilities, pronouncing it "the best fighter aircraft in the Luftwaffe." It is this sort of quality which has made Russia the number one rival of America in the global arms market.

Back in pre-Gorbachev days, East-West trade consultant Samuel Pisar observed that military production comprised "the only sector of the Soviet economy which operates like a market economy." He meant that, just as in the West, Soviet military "customers" would ruthlessly reject any item which fell below quality standards.

The Soviet Union's Defense Ministry long maintained a nationwide system of "closed" factories staffed by the most highly qualified workers, earning top pay and enjoying first priority to computers, automated production systems, and raw materials. For that reason, it is fair to say that military production represents the only area where Russians and Americans have competed on a level playing field. It is therefore significant that the Russians have performed so well at it, managing to achieve a super-power status which Japan and Germany have yet to equal.

Perhaps a glimmering of trade wars to come may be seen in the intensive lobbying now being conducted by U.S. helicopter manufacturers, fearful that the Russians may start "dumping" Mi-26 heavylift helicopters. These Russian choppers can lift twice the cargo of the largest American-built model. American suppliers have been strident in their demands for government protection.

Swords into Plowshares

Until now, Russia has never known a balanced or peaceful economy. Pressed by enemies on all sides since the days of Genghis Khan, she has squandered her resources and ingenuity on war. Indeed, at the height of Soviet power in the late 1980s, some Western observers estimated that 25 percent of Soviet production was devoted to defense, as opposed to only 8 percent in the United States. It is believed that, until recently, one in four Russians were employed in military industries.

Now, some 9 million highly skilled scientists, engineers, and technicians are looking for peaceful work. They represent collectively Russia's single greatest resource, a deep, untapped reservoir of knowledge and skills long dammed up behind barbed wire, surveillance cameras, and security checkpoints. When these floodwaters of talent finally burst into the civilian economy, Russian industry will be electrified.

"In many areas, the Russians have a real technological edge," says John Morton, senior editor of *East-West Executive Guide*. "In the aerospace industry, they have rocket boosters which dwarf everything we have in the West. They have a permanent space station, the biggest transport plane in the world, the biggest helicopter. Their Sukhoi 27 and MIG 29 jet fighters outperform the best American line fighter planes. They hold the records in altitude and speed. They have very advanced composite materials technology, laser and fiber optic technology. They pioneered eye surgery techniques to cure near-sightedness. These are the industries with the real long-term prospects in Russia.

Partners or Victims?

As we've established, history has not treated kindly those, like Hitler and Napoleon, who underestimated Russia's fearsome potential. We should learn from their sobering example. If indeed Russia is destined to become a commercial superpower, the course of action we choose today will determine whether we reign by her side as partners or cringe beneath her onslaught in every industry from software to civil aviation.

3

Why Communism Will Never Return

Your Investments Are at Least as Safe in Russia as They Are in Chile

Will some future hardline clique confiscate your property? Freeze your bank account? Outlaw your business? Imprison your employees? Embargo your imports? *In short, will Communism come back?*

Questions like these continue to keep those Americans with investments in Russia tossing in their sleep. At this late date, most of us don't expect the old Kremlin guard to come charging out with guns blazing. But the American press continues to fret about something *Time* magazine called a "creeping coup." This is a scenario in which Bolshevik diehards subtly undermine freemarket reforms from within. Supposedly, it's going on right now, as you read this page. But is it? Really?

Will the Real Hard-Liners Please Stand Up?

The problem with the "creeping coup" theory is that there's no one left in Russia with sufficient motive to perpetrate such a thing. I don't mean that Boris Yeltsin lacks rivals. Indeed, he may already be history by the time this book is printed. But does Yeltsin's ouster spell the "end of reform?" Those of us with long-term memories going back to mid-1991 will recall the whirlwind of panicky articles painting Gorbachev as the last, best, and only hope for free enterprise. More recently, Prime Minister

Yegor Gaidar was accorded that status. Yet, his ouster in December 1992 has already vanished into the bottomless cistern of forgotten Kremlin trivia.

The real question is not, "Can Yeltsin hold out?" It is, "Who will replace him?" I fail to see among Yeltsin's many credible successors *anyone* who answers to the description of Communist "hard-liner."

"Either We Will Live Like the Rest of the World, or We Shall Live Like Pigs"

Take the political group Civic Union, which is often trotted out as one of the more ominous up-and-comers on the horizon. Who are these people, really? One of them is Yeltsin's own vice-president, Alexander Rutskoi, who expressed his thoughts on socialism most eloquently in 1991, when he said, "Either we shall live like the rest of the world, or we shall continue to call ourselves the 'Socialist Choice' and the 'Communist Prospect' and live like pigs." Hardly the most ringing endorsement I've ever heard of proletarian dictatorship.

Then we have Arkady Volsky, leader of Russia's so-called "industrialists" (i.e., state-appointed managers of giant, government-owned factories). Volsky and his lobbying group—The Union of Industrialists and Entrepreneurs—correspond ideologically to America's top corporate CEOs. Much like our own captains of industry, these Russian "industrialists" use their political clout to lobby shamelessly for government loan guarantees, price supports, tariff barriers and other forms of "corporate welfare."

So what? Admittedly, Volsky and his crew are hardly paragons of entrepreneurial derring-do. But if we label their program "hardline" Communist, then we must, for the sake of consistency, regard our *own* corporate boardrooms as hotbeds of Bolshevist treason.

Let us remember that Russia's state-owned factories experienced a 20 percent decline in production during 1992. Not only are these industries utterly dependent upon Western capital and technology to survive, but the managers themselves—Mr. Volsky not excepted—have been lobbying like crazy for over a year to make sure that they personally get a big chunk of the equity when the shares of those enterprises are divvied up in 1993 and 1994. In other words, these "hardliners" have a *personal, vested stake* in the success of privatization.

How many of my readers, I wonder, are willing to believe that these men would deliberately sabotage a process which has been engineered, from beginning to end, to line their own pockets?

The Pinochet Solution

"We may also see the emergence (in Russia)
of a kind of pro-market authoritarian
government like that of Pinochet in Chile."
                                    HENRY KISSINGER
                                    February, 1993

Of course, we should not forget that there is a third alternative for Russia, not so apocalyptic as Leninist dictatorship, but neither so benign as liberal democracy. This is the much-vaunted "Pinochet Solution."

When Marxist president Salvador Allende came to power in 1970, it was widely feared that Chile would degenerate into a Cuban-style Soviet satellite—a fear which only grew when quadruple-digit inflation ravaged its economy, militant workers seized 600 Chilean companies, and Allende's government expropriated Anaconda Copper.

Chile's dalliance with socialism came to an abrupt end in 1973, when General Augusto Pinochet seized power. For the next 17 years, the general's secret police murdered more than 2025 people. At the same time, he flung wide the doors for foreign investment, returned confiscated companies to their owners and lowered trade barriers.

Pinochet's death squads seem to have retired with him in 1989, but the general's economic legacy lives on. In the last 20 years, Chile's GNP has more than doubled, inflation has slowed to 12.7 percent, and Chile's economy has become the fastest-growing in Latin America.

Of course, none of this justifies the years of terror. In my opinion, it is both wicked and hypocritical to advocate for someone else's country a form of government which you would never tolerate in your own. Until we're ready to surrender our own civil liberties, we have no business preaching such a course to others. For this reason, I blanch at the growing tendency of some American journalists to speak of "pro-market" dictatorships like those of Red China and Singapore as "models" for the developing world. I find the "Pinochet Solution" as repugnant in Moscow as it would be on Main Street, USA.

Nevertheless, I don't believe that either we or the Russians have much to fear from this would-be "wave of the future." Even should some Slavic Pinochet arise in Moscow (and one very well might), his regime would breed within it the germ of its own destruction. For the very hustle and bustle of entrepreneurs in a free market conjures forth democratic pressures which no tyrant can long suppress.

Why Don't the Russians
Seem Scared?

On the first day of the August 1991 coup, the conspirators called a press conference. One nervy Russian journalist asked junta-member Gennadi Yanaev whether he had sought "any suggestion or advice through General Pinochet." Before Yanaev could answer, the room erupted into laughter.

Both the question and the laughter were revealing. It is hard to imagine a Chilean reporter daring to use such sarcasm against Pinochet himself during the height of *his* coup. While the Russians hold few delusions about the grim state of their politics, they also seem to harbor surprisingly little fear.

I believe their confidence arises from their own experience of the last eight years. During that time, the Russians have watched in amazement as a tiny subculture of beleaguered entrepreneurs, fighting for survival on the fringes of the law, have multiplied like a mutant fungus, infiltrated every corner of society, and boldly compelled Gorbachev to move beyond his original, tepid reforms.

Russia's Entrepreneurs Are
the Real Power

The real power in Russia lies in the private sector, among the stockbrokers, commodity traders, commercial bankers, and small business owners. While Russia's state industries hurtle down a precipitous sinkhole to oblivion, all available indicators show that the entrepreneurs are in rapid ascent. They are the power brokers of tomorrow. Some faint foreshadowing of their political muscle was provided during the three days of the coup.

The Untold Story of the Coup

Two months after the coup, I went to Moscow to find out how my entrepreneurial friends had weathered the crisis. To my surprise, I discovered that many of them had played crucial and heroic roles in fighting the junta. In fact, Moscow's business community proved a decisive factor in that struggle—a fact overlooked by most Western media.

"The people supporting Yeltsin were the new business people," says Geoffrey Carr-Harris, a Toronto businessman who witnessed the coup and the siege of the White House. Carr-Harris has been doing business in Russia since the 1970s.

"It was this new middle class," he says, "this small group of *nouveau riche* Muscovites who look to America as their hope. They were the ones defending Yeltsin at the White House. The masses were not there. The masses were sitting at home, wondering what was going on."

According to *Foreign Affairs*, fewer than 1 percent of Russia's population actively resisted the coup. When Boris Yeltsin stood atop an armored personnel carrier and called for a general strike, Russia's workers ignored him entirely. There was no general strike. It was the entrepreneurs who answered the call to arms. They fought back hard and they won.

"The Donald Trump of Russia"

On the morning of August 19, 1991, Andrei Stroyev was at the peak of his success and power. Over the last year, fame had overtaken him in rapid strides. His picture had adorned the cover of *Newsweek*. He had appeared on *Good Morning America*. A prominent German magazine had dubbed him "The Donald Trump of the Soviet Union."

In 1988, he had formed a joint venture with Atlanta real estate developer Earl Worsham. Christened "Perestroika" in honor of Gorbachev's reforms, the new company acquired decrepit buildings in Moscow and converted them to sleek, modern office complexes suitable for Western corporations.

In a city where office shortages forced senior executives from IBM and Sony to work in shirtsleeves from their hotel rooms, Perestroika's ultramodern office suites proved an instant hit. Tenants like Ciba-Geigy, Monsanto, and Dupont Corporation filled up Stroyev's buildings. The fledgling company made $1.6 million profit in its very first year—*in hard currency*, not rubles. A month before the coup, Stroyev had begun building a $170 million hotel complex for Hilton International. The future looked very bright indeed for "The Donald Trump of Russia," as the morning of August 19, 1991 dawned over Moscow.

"I Thought I Would Never See Him Again"

"I don't think you want to get on that plane."

Stroyev and his American partner Earl Worsham were in Istanbul airport, preparing to board their plane to Moscow, when a strange American buttonholed them at the boarding gate.

"Don't you know what's happening?" he asked. "Gorbachev's been overthrown."

"I said to Andrei, 'Don't you even think about getting on that plane,'" remembers Worsham. "I told him I'd get him a flight to Switzerland with his wife. But Andrei said he had to go back. He acted without a second thought, never wavered for a second. When he got on that plane, I thought I would never see him again."

A Day for Everyone to Decide

Back in his Moscow office, Stroyev faced some hard choices. "It was a day for everybody here to make his decision which way to go," he recalls. The new military governor of Moscow had commanded Stroyev to keep his employees from demonstrating in the streets. But Stroyev had other plans.

In addition to his real estate business, Stroyev was general director of MosInzhStroy, a state firm with 35,000 employees, which supervised all construction and repairs on Moscow's sewer lines, water mains, streets, bridges and canals. Stroyev commanded a fleet of some 10,000 trucks, cranes, steamshovels, bulldozers, and other heavy equipment. He now ordered these vehicles to converge on the Russian Parliament building— the "White House"— to help defend Yeltsin.

Bulldozers soon blocked every approach. While the crowd cheered, cranes hoisted immense prefabricated concrete blocks into place to form barriers and tank traps. Stroyev was on the scene, personally supervising the deployment of his equipment. "I saw the spirit of people who are ready to fight," Stroyev recalls. "So strong. Ready to fight for their freedom, for something they believe in."

That same day, Stroyev attended a meeting of the Board for the Association of Joint Ventures of the Soviet Union which represented about 2600 joint ventures. The Board members drafted and signed a letter of support for Yeltsin, typed it on official stationery and faxed it to the White House. That letter was soon rolling out of fax machines all over the Soviet Union, alerting people that Moscow's business community stood solidly behind democracy.

"In this country," says Stroyev, "to put your signature on a political document like that means a lot. We understood that if the coup succeeded, the best we could hope for was prison."

Give Me Free Enterprise
or Give Me Death

At the height of the coup, stockbrokers and commodity traders left work en masse to help defend the White House. Commercial bankers delivered suitcases full of cash. And Pizza Hut worked overtime, distributing thousands of free slices to the beleaguered defenders.

At the same time, Moscow's lucrative real estate auctions continued unabated all across the city, with apartments moving like hotcakes for

$9000 and up. One private real estate firm called Housing Initiative auctioned off a dozen apartments while tanks patrolled the streets outside.

"It was a very successful auction," Housing Initiative's deputy director Igor O. Dobryakov later told *The New York Times*, "because people trusted that what was happening in the streets that day was reversible."

Another real estate firm called Banso achieved a delicate balance between business and subversion. "We too held an auction on the day when the coup was at its height," said Banso director Grigory V. Ivanov. "But first we spent some time at the barricades defending Yeltsin . . . . We were there everyday, for we are the new businessmen, and we understood best what was at stake . . . ."

Computer Nerds for Freedom

When he first heard about the coup, Stepan Pachikov thought, "They'll never pull it off. They'll never last more than a week or two." But he was anxious nonetheless. All his dreams—and the dreams of his 140 employees—hung in the balance. Pachikov had worked hard to build his company from nothing. Now ParaGraph—a Soviet-American computer software company— had become a magnet for the best and brightest among the Soviet intelligentsia.

Pachikov's chairman of the board was none other than Abel Aganbegyan, Gorbachev's top economist. World chess champion Gary Kasparov and renowned mathematician Valeri Makarov were his vice presidents. And both the Academy of the National Economy and the Central Economics Institute of the Soviet Academy of Sciences owned shares in Pachikov's company.

In the last year, Pachikov had grown used to the life of a global executive. He traveled constantly between Moscow and the United States, where he hobnobbed routinely with the likes of Bill Gates of Microsoft, Lotus founder Mitch Kapor, and Bill Joy of Sun Microsystems. He had an American driver's license, a slew of credit cards, an AT&T calling card, and a hefty frequent flyer's account with United Airlines. At the time of the coup, Pachikov was deep in negotiations with Apple Computer, which would later sign an historic multimillion-dollar licensing agreement for Pachikov's ground-breaking handwriting recognition software.

But that was still in the future. Now, Pachikov was worried. The first and second nights of the coup, he stayed in his office till 5 a.m., making frantic phone calls and E-mail transmissions to every big name in Silicon Valley.

"I called everybody I knew in the United States," he remembers. "I called Apple, I called *Byte* magazine. I told them don't worry, don't stop our contract, don't stop relations with the Soviet Union, with ParaGraph, with anybody. This is nothing. These people have no chance to win."

Pachikov set up a small command center in his office. Every few minutes, a fax would come in from Yeltsin's people at the White House. Pachikov's people relayed them out to every fax number they knew, then printed out hard copies on the laser printer and distributed them in the streets.

"For three days, no work got done," grouses Pachikov. "I was very unhappy. But at the end, everything's okay. The bandits are gone."

Rock'n Roll Hero

Sergei Lisovsky was used to being on the wrong side of the law. As one of Russia's leading underground impresarios, he had seen many rock concerts broken up by the militia and many of his friends and colleagues thrown in prison for ill-defined "economic crimes." But none of this prepared him for the shock of the coup. Many of Lisovsky's friends and colleagues had long since defected to the West. But Lisovsky was a patriot. He always maintained that he would never leave Russia. "But when I first heard about the coup," he says, "I had a feeling that I should have gone with them after all."

As an administrator in Komsomol—the Young Communist League— back in the early 1980s, Lisovsky's job was to provide recreational activities for Moscow's young people. The options were limited. Lisovsky watched with interest Gorbachev's evolving reforms, especially the new laws allowing Soviet citizens to form private companies called "cooperatives." In 1987, he formed a company to promote pop concerts.

Lisovsky rapidly overtook the big state concert promoters—Goskonsert and Roskonsert. In his first year, he organized 30 successful pop concerts, while the state agencies succeeded in staging only three.

Adding insult to injury, Lisovsky acquired a reputation for being a better employer than the state. He paid his people more and treated them better. Artists, roadies and stadium managers naturally preferred working with him. Little did Lisovsky realize that the noose was already closing around his neck.

"The first thing they did was to start forbidding singers to work with me," says Lisovsky. "These artists had contracts with the state concert organizations, so they had to obey." Soon, city officials began hinting that they suspected Lisovsky of illegal, black market dealings. How else could he afford to pay his people so well?

"I tried to explain to them that my employees worked 10 to 12 hours a day, with no days off, and that's why we were succeeding. But it was useless."

"From Each According to His Means . . ."

For a year and a half, inspectors from four different government agencies scrutinized Lisovsky's company, but found nothing they could pin on the upstart impresario. Then, in November 1988, Lisovsky was hauled before a special committee of the District Soviet of the Communist Party. The district procurator seemed a fair man. After listening to the case, he announced that he saw nothing at all illegal in Lisovsky's activities.

Then one of the inspectors announced Lisovsky's salary to the group. That year, Lisovsky had made 100,000 rubles, an enormous sum at the time. The highest-paid official in that room made only 5000 rubles. Lisovsky could feel every pair of eyes in the room boring into him with cold hatred.

"As soon as they heard that figure, it was all over," says Lisovsky. "They didn't want to discuss the matter any longer."

All assets of Lisovsky's company were seized immediately, including a one- million-ruble bank account, hundreds of rubles worth of equipment and an old mansion which Lisovsky had purchased in the center of Moscow. He was penniless, with no way to pay his 46 employees and no equipment to do his work.

"I considered myself lucky," says Lisovsky, "because at least they didn't send me to prison."

Never Give Up

Many would have despaired in like circumstances. But Lisovsky was undaunted. "They thought I was finished," he says. "They thought that without my money and property I could never continue my business. What they didn't understand was that they could never confiscate my knowledge and my ability to work. This was just another obstacle I had to face." Lisovsky faced it bravely. He started a new company from the ground floor, and called it LIS'S (pronounced lees-ESS).

Now all the relationships he'd cultivated so meticulously over the past year and a half paid off. A core group of eight people—the "cream" of Lisovsky's management team—agreed to stay with him and work for nothing. They worked out of their apartments and borrowed money from friends.

Lisovsky had been blacklisted. Frightened stadium managers confided to him that they'd been warned not to work with him. Many made excuses and went along with it. But others swallowed their fear and boldly worked with Lisovsky anyway.

"I had always treated these people well. I never stood them up," said Lisovsky. "That's why they came through for me. Besides, so many of the big managers had been threatened by the police themselves, interrogated by the state inspection office or even done time in prison. So they understood clearly what was happening to me and my company. That's why they helped me."

"I'm a Professional"

When Lisovsky told me this story, sitting in his office in Luzhniki Stadium, I asked him how he ever mustered the courage to keep going in the face of such odds. He looked at me blandly and shrugged. "I'm a professional," he replied. "It's my work, so it's natural."

For the first two months, nobody in LIS'S was paid a single kopeck. They put on one concert the first month and reinvested all the profits in a second concert. By the third month, they were back in the black, and everyone was on salary. By August 1991, LIS'S was organizing 75 percent of all major shows in Moscow and Leningrad, many with teen idol Alexander Malinin, a leading pop star in Russia. They even did a concert with American heavy metal stars AC-DC. Revenues for fiscal 1991 topped 200 million rubles.

At the age of 31, almost exactly one year after his "trial," Lisovsky was back in the driver's seat. That's when he got news of the coup.

A Blast from the Past

On the second day of the crisis, with Yeltsin a virtual prisoner in the White House, with wild rumors flying about tank columns and KGB special forces advancing on the city, Lisovsky received an unwelcome, but not unexpected phone call.

The sound of that hated voice caused Lisovsky to wince, his heart to race uncontrollably. It was one of the same government inspectors who had been tormenting Lisovsky since 1987, a man Lisovsky knew only as Ivan Ivanovich. "I just wanted you to know," said Ivan Ivanovich, his voice slippery with glee, "that *we've decided to reopen your case*."

A Profound Shift in Power

As we know, the threat proved idle. Within 24 hours, the coup had fizzled. Nobody reopened anyone's "case." Lisovsky organized a mass rock concert on the steps of the White House, featuring Alexander Malinin. There, with the barricades still in place, and the blood hardly dried from the nearby street where three demonstrators had died, Russia's new generation danced and cavorted to the strains of rock and roll.

A profound shift in power had occurred during those three days of the coup, a change which came dramatically home to Lisovsky only a few weeks later, when he got a call from yet *another* of his former persecutors. There was no threat or bravado this time. The man wanted a favor.

"He asked me for a job," says Lisovsky. Needless to say, LIS'S was fresh out of vacancies at the moment.

I Knew It All Along

Although you may accuse me of 20/20 hindsight, I nevertheless insist that I've known for almost 15 years that Soviet power was doomed. I can even tell you the exact moment when I realized it. It was at approximately 7:30 p.m., July 4, 1978.

At that time, I was a student in the summer program at Leningrad State University run by CIEE (the Center for International Educational Exchange). Quite by chance, I wandered into Palace Square—that immense open courtyard in front of the Winter Palace which was filmed so beautifully in the movie *Reds*—at the exact moment that a rare civil disturbance was brewing.

Legendary impresario Bill Graham had arranged to stage a free, open-air rock concert in Palace Square featuring Santana, Joan Baez, and The Beach Boys. In those days, this was a highly unusual event, to say the least. Few expected that it would really happen.

Not surprisingly, when 5000 young Leningraders showed up for the event, the only thing they found was a battalion of gray-uniformed militiamen blocking the square and a monotonous voice intoning over and over again on a PA system, "Comrade Leningraders, you are blocking traffic. Please disperse to your homes."

For the next six hours, those 5000 young people absolutely refused to disperse. They whistled and mocked the police. They kicked the sides of paddy wagons as they wheeled by on the street. A few bottles were thrown.

No More Jackboots

Now here's the amazing part. Throughout the entire incident, the militia treated that crowd with kid gloves. They could have cleared the streets in minutes. But they seemed to completely lack the will to use force.

"Young people, please . . ." said one *militsionyer*, looking a little hurt as he gently tried to shoo the kids off to a side street.

Needless to say, this is not the image of the Soviet police which most Americans held back in 1978. Before that evening, I would have expected that any such open defiance from a Russian crowd would have been quickly and ruthlessly crushed by truncheon, jackboot, and tank treads. But the Soviet authorities apparently no longer had that kind of license. They had grown soft, unsure of themselves, afraid to alienate their own people.

Sixties Mania

All that summer, I met young Russians my age who loved America with unquestioning abandon. Even in those days, the allure of Levis and Pink Floyd for Russia's youth was a standing joke among Americans. But I discovered that summer that their passion for American Pop didn't stop with rock bands. They evinced a surprising taste for our pop politics as well. My Russian friends grilled me intensively about the hippie counterculture, the race riots, and the antiwar movement of the 1960s. They were obsessed with the subject. Many were deeply shocked to learn that American college students in 1978 considered the Sixties passe.

All of this was going through my mind as I mingled with the crowd that night in Palace Square. I think it was about 7:30 p.m. when I suddenly caught sight of a pretty, blonde young girl, neatly scrubbed and groomed, her hair in two thick braids, standing quietly and gazing across the square at the ranks of *militsionyeri*. From all around came screams, shouts, and harsh laughter, the crackle of loudspeakers, the padding of thousands of feet, the angry beeping of car horns. But around this girl hovered a quiet aura of peace. A tiny smile played about her lips, and she breathed the long, slow breaths of someone waking from a deep and pleasant sleep. It was her eyes, though, that told me everything, gray-blue eyes that shone with the hardness of raw steel, eyes that glittered with courage, pride, and strength. I'll never know for sure, but I have a feeling that that girl was thinking the exact same thing that I suddenly thought the moment I saw her.

I think she realized that evening, perhaps in that very instant, that her generation was destined to be free.

Why Soviet Power Was Doomed

Stepan Pachikov is another person who has known for years that Soviet power was doomed, although for much more practical and scientific reasons than mine. "It was computerization that destroyed Communism," says Pachikov, "The Communists had to choose between being a totalitarian, Third World state with outdated weapons, or remaining a great power by assuming normal, democratic principles of life.

"Today, military force depends on microprocessors and software. They depend now on scientists having a free flow of information. If you cut off information, then scientists can't work, and you can't have high technology."

Communism vs. the Information Age

Soviet industry functioned a lot like U.S. Steel. Gigantic factories with thousands of workers cranked out huge numbers of identical widgets. The more widgets you made, the more bonuses and medals you received. That system works best when you're making raw steel or pumping crude petroleum—two fortes of Soviet industry in past years. But it doesn't work at all when you're trying to keep up with Silicon Valley.

By 1983—two years before Gorbachev took power—a deep "computer gap" had grown between the superpowers. At that time, the Soviets had only 22,000 personal computers—that's 80 PCs for every one million people—while the United States flaunted over a million of them (i.e., 4273 PCs for every million people). While America's budding computer geniuses sat at home by the hour inventing programs, talking to one another on electronic bulletin boards, and mischievously invading other peoples' databases, Russia's programmers were kept out in the cold. The only time most of them got a chance to go near a computer was during those precious moments at work when they would be allowed to enter the locked and guarded computing center at their firm to perform some specific task.

The "computer gap" played a decisive role in the fall of Communism. It remains just as decisive today in the international battle for the emerging Russian marketplace. Here's why.

The Miniaturization of Business

The last ten years have seen an extraordinary shrinkage in the average size of companies in the Western world. This is a direct result of computerization. A small firm with computers can do things which in the past only large corporations could afford to do. For example, by installing computerized inventory controls, a convenience mart can outsell a nearby supermarket. One person with the right direct-mail software can get rich combing out splinter markets, while a major catalog house goes broke saturating the same region with glossy, four-color brochures. The same principle holds true for clothing factories, garbage removal companies, bioengineering firms, architectural design houses, and steel mills.

The Small Business Revolution

As a direct result of computerization, America underwent an entrepreneurial explosion that devastated her oversized corporations. The average firm size shrank dramatically during the 1980s.

Between 1985 and 1990, 30 percent of America's *Fortune 500* companies vanished—a five-year attrition rate equal to that of the previous 25 years. While 3.5 million jobs were disappearing from corporate America, small, entrepreneurial firms were busily creating 21 million new jobs to replace them. If you took the 5 percent of America's companies which accounted for 77 percent of all new jobs in 1990, you would find that *two-thirds* of those fast-growing new companies had fewer than 19 employees.

These small, new firms proved better able to meet rapidly changing consumer tastes. They were agile kayaks compared to the lumbering battleships of the *Fortune 500*, and they led the nation in profitability.

The "Entrepreneurship Gap"

What was devastating enough for our *Fortune 500* proved as lethal as nerve gas for the Soviet state monopolies. Giant Soviet companies were buffeted by the same international market pressures as their American counterparts. But there were no rising young entrepreneurs in Russia to take up the slack. Even if the laws had permitted such a thing, there were no computers for those entrepreneurs to use. The Soviet Union rapidly lost international market share in every manufacturing category.

Like a Third World country, Russia now exported mainly raw materials. Having been the eleventh largest exporter of manufactured goods in 1973, the Soviet Union plunged to fifteenth place by 1985, lagging behind Taiwan, South Korea, Hong Kong, and Switzerland.

It was about this time that President Ronald Reagan launched the Star Wars effort in earnest. The bureaucrats in the Kremlin knew that this time they were licked. It was time to make peace with the enemy.

The Drive for Computerization

Closing the "computer gap" was the primary purpose of Gorbachev's 1987 "Joint Venture Law" allowing direct foreign investment in Russia. Early pioneers in the Soviet marketplace were struck by the rapacious hunger of their Russian partners for high-tech equipment of all kinds. During the early years of the "joint venture" period, importing computers to the Soviet Union proved a shockingly lucrative business. Cheap AT clones sold for 80,000 rubles. Foreign computer importers would use their ruble earnings to buy raw copper, aluminum, and manganese at ridiculously low state prices, then sell those materials in the West, ending up with $130,000 or more for a PC which had cost them less than $1500 at wholesale in Taiwan or Singapore. *A 3000 percent markup.*

The Communist bureaucrats were only dimly aware that all this influx of high-tech hardware carried with it a social revolution. But the rising generation of computer users, like Stepan Pachikov, saw clearly what was coming.

Information Control Equals
People Control

Ever since the invention of the photocopier, Soviet authorities had waged war against the Information Age. Until 1991, every photocopying machine in the country was strictly quarantined, as if laced with some deadly contagion. You needed a special permit to install one in your office. By law, you had to seal it up behind a steel door equipped with an alarm system. Anyone who wished to make a copy was required to fill out a form indicating the material to be copied, the number of copies, and to whom they would be distributed. Then you had to wait days or even weeks for the copy department to deliver. And often they never did.

There were good reasons for all this fuss. The Communists recognized that the free flow of information would destroy them. But so would falling behind in the Computerization Race!

Thus were sown the seeds of Communism's demise. As Pachikov wrote in the October 1989 issue of *Personal Computer World*, "The first PCs began to find their way into our country in 1984 through 1985. The customs officials who were on the look-out to prevent any photocopier technology being brought in, were in the main ignorant of the true significance of such product descriptions as 'printer' and 'home computer.'" Not to mention the significance of such words as "modem" or "fax!"

If anyone in authority feared the subversive potential of computers, they feared much more the thought of someday facing "electronic battlefields" aswarm with Stinger and Exocet missiles, killer satellites, and computerized cockpit controls, without a single decent microchip to call their own.

Entrepreneurs Unite!

By 1991, there were some 350,000 private "co-ops" and small companies operating in the Soviet Union, the most glamorous and successful being in the high-tech sector. This growing computer subculture rapidly attracted the most talented minds in the country. The new entrepreneurs had an insatiable hunger for imported computers, dollars with which to buy computers, and *political freedom* with which to use them. They wanted freedom to travel, to trade, to bargain, to network and to converse at will with their colleagues at home and abroad. The authorities meekly let them have it. What else could they do? This was the only way they could catch up with the developed world, as Gorbachev himself realized.

"The genius of Mikhail Gorbachev," writes economist Paul Zane Pilzer in *Unlimited Wealth*, "may lie in his realization that in order to have *perestroika* . . . he first needed *glasnost*."

It is for this reason, says Pilzer, that Gorbachev relaxed censorship over the media (*glasnost*) a full year before implementing his most fundamental economic reforms (*perestroika*). He recognized the relationship between free speech and technological advancement.

But even Gorbachev failed to understand the colossal force he was unleashing when he gave Russians the right to buy, sell, and work for themselves. The genie he uncorked has swept through the land with a hurricane's force. It swept Gorbachev himself from power. And it will change the face of Russian life forever before this century ends.

The Disobedient Technocrat

Pachikov knows better than most the liberating power of entrepreneurship. Free enterprise literally freed him from the clutches of the KGB. Had Pachikov behaved himself when he was younger, he might have enjoyed the easy life of a talented, Soviet technocrat. His father was a high-ranking Air Force officer, and Pachikov himself a child prodigy. After winning a competition in math and physics at the age of 13, Pachikov was packed off to a special school in Novosibirsk, where he was groomed for a life of privilege in the Soviet Union's scientific elite.

But in college, Pachikov fell afoul of the police state. It was 1968. He and a friend wrote graffiti protesting the Soviet invasion of Czechoslovakia. The KGB suspected Pachikov. Although they lacked evidence to press charges, they had other means of getting to him.

"It's very subtle," says Pachikov. "The KGB talks to your professors, and then when you go in for your oral exams, suddenly the professor tells you you know nothing and he flunks you." The sympathetic Director of his department took Pachikov aside and warned him that his exams had been rigged. There was no point in taking them.

Through an influential friend, Pachikov was able to transfer to the University of Tbilisi in the Georgian Republic. He taught himself the Georgian language and soon excelled in his studies. But one month before his final graduation exams, the KGB caught up with him. They called the university director and sent down Pachikov's dossier. Once more, Pachikov was advised not to bother with his finals.

Slipping Through the Cracks

Had the KGB been an efficient, high-tech organization, Pachikov would have been doomed. But the inefficiency of the secret police allowed him to slip through the cracks. For many years, he lived an in-and-out twilight existence on the fringe of Soviet society.

"You must understand," he explains, "the KGB is not so smart. That's the one thing that made life tolerable under Communism."

Pachikov "hid" for six years on a collective farm, where he was put in charge of automating machinery to control greenhouse temperatures. Later, he pulled some strings and obtained a permit to move to Moscow. Enrolling in Moscow University, Pachikov eventually finished all his degrees, earning a doctorate in mathematics in 1986.

The Life of a Dissident

But Pachikov knew there was a permanent glass ceiling over his head. In Soviet society, you were judged by loyalty, not merit. And disloyalty to the Communist system emanated from Pachikov's every pore.

"Whenever you spoke with official people, they could see it in your eyes," says Pachikov. "They knew that I wasn't one of them. I could not conceal it."

Having despaired of finding happiness in his work, Pachikov did what millions of Russians have done from time immemorial. He looked inward. "I didn't try to make a career. I preferred just to stay home and read books."

"Kitchen Talk"

Under Communism, Russians maintained a private circle of intimates with whom they could speak freely while sitting around the kitchen table after dinner, far from the prying ears of the KGB. Pachikov expanded this principal of "kitchen talk" by holding regular discussion groups at his apartment with a few trusted associates. With no political agenda or subversive intent, they simply conversed on any subject they chose, from art, history, and philosophy to information science. Harmless as it may seem, Pachikov's hosting of this little group was a criminal act under Soviet law. In addition, many of Pachikov's guests were foreigners, a fact which in and of itself was enough to end any hope of a career.

Subversive Activities

Today, the word *samizdat*—"self-publishing"—usually refers to desktop publishing. But in the days before *glasnost*, when state censors controlled all publishing with an iron fist, it referred to the subversive practice of handcopying or xeroxing forbidden books and circulating them by hand. Pachikov became heavily involved in this literary underground.

"I used the photocopier at work to make copies of Solzhenitsyn's *Gulag Archipelago*. Three thousand people have read that book from my hands."

"I Had Never Seen a Personal Computer Before"

Financial necessity finally drove Pachikov from his shell. He had secured a job at the Academy of Sciences doing projections for the oil industry. But Pachikov discovered he could not subsist on his pitiful salary. "My second child had been born," he says. "I didn't have enough money."

Pachikov took a part-time job as a *dezhurny*, or concierge at a hotel for foreign employees working in Moscow. The foreign residents quickly discovered Pachikov's genius for things electronic. They brought him broken tape recorders, TVs, and other appliances to fix.

One fateful day, a Finnish resident brought his Commodore 64 to Pachikov, saying he had just bought it and couldn't figure out how to use it. "I had never seen a personal computer before," says Pachikov. "I asked him for the manual and taught myself. In two weeks, I had written a program using Russian fonts on the screen."

While poring over the instruction manual for that Commodore computer, Pachikov experienced an epiphany. "Suddenly I felt I understood my place in life. I knew I could do something in this field."

The Finn asked Pachikov what he wanted to be paid.

"Computer magazines!" Pachikov replied.

Before long, Pachikov had become the resident computer repairman, programmer, and systems consultant. His apartment filled up with the spoils of his new business—back issues of *Byte*, *Computer World*, and other forbidden literature.

After one particularly grueling job tutoring a Dutchman in software arcana, Pachikov announced that he wanted a personal computer as payment. The man produced an Amstrad 6228, a popular British home PC. Without realizing it, Pachikov had enlisted in a revolution which was destined to overthrow the Soviet state.

Brave New World

Things began to change rapidly for Pachikov. As a computer expert, he had suddenly become invaluable to the state. Pachikov fell in with the charmed circle that was forming around Yevgeny Velikhov, Director of the Academy of Science's powerful Atomic Institute and the man charged with computerizing the Soviet Union.

In some ways, the intensely visionary atmosphere around Velikhov, and the passionate, all-night discussions on computers and information science reminded Pachikov of the old meetings "in the kitchen" with his dissident friends gathered around the table over vodka, salami, and cheese. Except this time it was sanctioned by the highest levels of the government.

Still, Pachikov feared it was too good to be true. Any ill wind from the Kremlin, any shift in Party politics could end *glasnost* in an instant.

In 1987, Gorbachev legalized direct foreign investment in the Soviet economy for the first time since the 1920s. Moscow was aswarm with foreign businessmen. The words "joint venture" were on everyone's lips. Pachikov realized what he had to do. His only hope for freedom lay in entrepreneurship.

Learning the Ropes

Pachikov dreamed of pulling together the top Soviet programmers under one roof so they could work together in an atmosphere of collegiality to produce world-class software for export. So he started a "cooperative"—a highly regulated partnership arrangement which at that time was the only form of private business Russians were allowed to form. His company consisted of one room with two computers, a secretary, and four programmers. Software sales took off immediately. Pachikov's company performed the amazing feat of covering his first month's rent and payroll out of cash flow from his software sales.

But he needed more. Only a joint venture with foreign partners would gain Pachikov the access he needed to Western capital, travel, and international communication. He began making the rounds of foreign computer firms but quickly discovered that companies like Atari and MCI were not exactly champing at the bit to beat a path to his door. "They wanted me to prove myself before they invested," he says.

Pachikov had a whole line of quality software products ready to go on sale, and he knew that soon he would have a breakthrough handwriting-recognition program unlike anything the West had seen. But the big computer companies wanted hard commitments for $100s of millions in sales. When Pachikov told them honestly he had no ability to predict such sales, they suggested he get his business up and running and come back to talk to them in five years.

Foreign Opportunist to the Rescue

That's when Pachikov met Scott Klososky. "When I showed up on the scene," says Klososky, "Stepan was ready to do the deal with the first person who was ready to act seriously."

Klososky was a 28-year-old enterpreneur from Oklahoma. He owned a ranch and two computer stores in Tulsa. Unlike Pachikov, Klososky was unmoved by idealism. He had come to Russia to make money.

"It was a calculated business decision," he says. "After two years in business, my computer stores were making $5 million in sales. I wanted to expand, go international. I looked at India and a lot of different countries. I decided the Soviet Union had the most potential, even though it would be the hardest."

Klososky made a whirlwind tour of Leningrad, Moscow, and Kiev looking at some 20 different project proposals. Then an American attorney working in Moscow introduced him to Pachikov. One look at his handwriting recognition software, and Klososky knew he had a winner.

"Stepan was a big name in the USSR," says Klososky, "and he had all the top programmers working for him."

A Fateful Deal

"I told Scott I can't wait five years for an investor," recounts Pachikov. "I told him I would go with those who were first." They struck a deal. But Klososky didn't have the money. Jetting back to the States, he rounded up $250,000 in investments from a group of businessmen in Boulder, Colorado. The Soviet Academy of Sciences weighed in with 200,000 rubles, which bought them a 25 percent share. By the time the dust cleared on June 28, 1989, Klososky owned 50 percent of a new joint venture called ParaGraph. He hadn't put in a cent of his own money.

The Sweetest Fruit

Today, Pachikov is well on his way to becoming an extremely wealthy man, having signed major deals with Apple, Digital Equipment, and Sun Microsystems. But for him, the sweetest fruit of entrepreneurship is his own personal liberty. For the first time since 1968, he feels free from the influence of the KGB.

"To understand the power of the KGB in the past, " says Pachikov, "you have to understand that there were no laws which gave them power. There was no law even that they could fire you from your job. All their power rested in one thing. If I did something KGB didn't like, they would go to my director at the Institute where I work and say, 'We have information that this Pachikov is not reliable. That phone call alone would be enough for my director next day to fire me. If he doesn't fire me, the same thing will happen to him."

"But look, now I have my own company. What can KGB do? Do they go to my American partner and tell him to fire me? As soon as people in our society saw that they can go to work for a joint venture, a coop, a private company, in one moment, the power of KGB disappeared. People recognized suddenly that there is a life outside of KGB control, a chance to find a job, to buy an apartment, to put your children in a private kindergarten, without anyone's permission. How can they stop you now? There's no one for them to call."

Strike a Blow for Liberty

On top of all the excellent reasons I've given you so far for investing in the former Soviet states, I would like to add another. By participating in Russia's fledgling free market, you strike a powerful blow for the cause of liberty.

4

Do You Have
What It Takes?

The Seven Essential Virtues of the "Russia-preneur"

*"At this point, a person must be real
confident, real crazy, or incredibly wired to
invest here."*

MICHAEL ADAMS, CHAIRMAN
Young & Rubicam/Sovero

"Anyone working here in Moscow has got to be interesting," observes Tracy
Kwiker, an employee of a Russian- American real estate venture. "Just the
fact that they made it over here shows they have a certain chutzpah."

The Western business crowd in Russia are a special breed. While some
are corporate vice presidents by profession, all are entrepreneurs by
nature. They are drawn to danger and chaos. Yet they work day and night
to build a stable order amid the wreckage. Flexible and creative, they are
poised to switch gears at the slightest tremor of the market. Yet no force
on earth can wrest their iron grip from their goals.

I call them *Russia-preneurs*. They're the sort of people who, five
centuries ago, might have taken to the sea in search of new continents.
Indeed, it's striking how often Western business executives in Russia liken
themselves to the oldtime explorers.

"This office may not look like much," one American T-shirt maker told
me in his basement office in Moscow, "but neither did the *Nina*, the *Pinta*,
or the *Santa Maria!*"

Like the explorers of old, the Russia-preneurs hail from all walks of life.
Some are corporate CEOs and attorneys, others stockbrokers, shopkeep-

ers and CPAs. Some are former U-2 pilots and retired intelligence analysts. Others are peaceniks, environmentalists, holistic healing savants, and Christian evangelists.

The Russia-preneurs are a mixed bag, to be sure. But all have one thing in common. *Making money is not the real reason they decided to do business in Russia.* It's just the excuse.

Why Do They Do It?

Few remember today the names of three ships which set sail from England in the year 1553. Their voyage has been all but forgotten among so many more important and famous in that Age of Exploration. In search of a "back door" to China—the legendary "Northeast Passage"—these three brave crews planned to sail north, round the arctic coast of Scandinavia, and then south to what they thought would be the Pacific Ocean. Little did they suspect that between them and their goal lay the impassable reaches of Great Russia.

For weeks, the explorers pushed north. A terrible storm broke up the fleet, forcing two ships to take shelter on an island off the Lapland coast. There the unhappy adventurers languished for five months, waiting in vain for the wind to change, while first the frost, then the snow descended. The days grew shorter and at last the terrified crews were plunged into the six-month night of arctic winter. Huddled together for warmth, they died to the last man, their frozen bodies only discovered a year later, "platter in hand and spoon in mouth," as one contemporary writer recorded.

But the third ship, the *Edward Bonaventure*, was luckier. Under the command of Richard Chancellor, the ship pushed on ever northward toward latitudes no Englishman had ever seen. Chancellor sailed so far that, in the words of one chronicler, "he came at last to where he found no night at all, but a continual light and brightness of the sun shining clearly upon the huge and mighty sea." Chancellor was the first Englishman to see the endless daylight of arctic summer.

When finally he landed at the mouth of the Northern Dvina, Chancellor met bearded fishermen who "prostrated themselves before him, offering to kiss his feet." Chancellor had not reached Cathay, but, quite by accident, he had "discovered" one of the most powerful and wealthy nations on earth—Russia.

Like Pizarro in the Inca treasure rooms, Chancellor marvelled at the splendor of Ivan the Terrible's court, where gold and precious stones seemed as abundant as pebbles. "I could scarce believe it," he wrote. "(The Tsar's) pavilion is covered with cloth of gold and so set with stones that it is wonderful to see. I have seen the Kings Majesties of England and the

French Kings' pavilions, which are fair, yet not like unto his." Thanks to Chancellor's boldness, England set up a lucrative trade monopoly with Russia which enriched the British nation for many years.

A Purpose Higher Than Yourself

Long ago, schoolchildren were taught to admire men like Richard Chancellor. We looked upon the great explorers as giants of vision and courage. Nowadays, we're supposed to regard them as greedy mercenaries, "racists," and mass murderers. But I will never believe that Christopher Columbus, Vasco da Gama, Richard Chancellor, and others of their ilk could ever have accomplished what they did, were power and gain their sole motive.

To achieve great things, you must have *a goal higher than yourself.* Only the purest idealism could have kept Chancellor headed northward in his tiny wooden ship, in spite of storm, death, cold, and fearful uncertainty.

The same holds true today for the new breed of explorers. The qualities you'll need to navigate Russia's treacherous economic waters are not unlike those which kept Columbus true on his course in 1492 or Genghis Khan riding doggedly westward across the icy steppes in 1223, searching for that rich and mysterious land called "Europe." Like these great trailblazers of history, you must love the danger, the thrill, the romance, the adventure far more than you love the booty. Above all, you must believe that your cause is just, your struggle noble, and your ultimate success a gain for humanity—not just for yourself.

If you lack these convictions, I don't recommend that you waste your time in Russia. There are so many easier ways to make a buck.

The Russia-preneur's Code of Ethics

Of course, there are plenty of Americans who have gone over to Russia for the wrong reasons, and some of them have made a lot of money. But this book was not written for them. It was not written for the "carpetbaggers" who swindle Russia out of her dwindling cash reserves and who pilfer her strategic resources for pennies on the black market. Nor was it written for bloodless marketing executives with Lotus spreadsheets for emotions, who think that "diversifying" into Russia will somehow preserve their shrinking "global market share."

By all means *prosper* in Russia! Build your global market share. But when you pack up your bags and return home, please remember to leave behind you a legacy of gratitude, not resentment. As a Russia-preneur, you are an apostle of free enterprise, for good or ill. Your business should be a beacon of hope, your profit margins a paean to liberty. Let your activities bring employment to the Russian people. Let your conduct bring honor to America.

What Does it Take to Become a "Russia-preneur"?

Before you commit to doing business in Russia, step back and take a long, hard look at yourself. *Do you really have what it takes?*

The American West was settled primarily by thrifty, hardworking folk, rather than outlaws and adventurers. Yet, even the most ordinary pioneer family had to know how to use a gun, how to mount a posse, build a house, nurse a horse, hold an election, and stage a hangin'. They had to know how to dream and plan for the future, and how to bring those dreams to life, starting with nothing. Frontier living means being able to *rely on yourself* in all situations, on your own energy, ingenuity, and resourcefulness.

That takes a special type of person, with certain distinctive strengths. Let's call those strengths the *seven essential virtues of the Russia-preneur.* They are as follows.

Virtue Number One:
A Powerful Vision

I have yet to meet a successful American in Russia who did not possess a powerful vision for good. It's remarkable how many have told me that their original purpose for doing business there was to "reach out" to the Russian people or to "open up lines of communication." What's even more remarkable is how, time after time, such selfless visions as these have been rewarded with vast and unexpected wealth!

Joel Schatz is what some people might call a "space cadet." He lives in San Francisco, sports granny glasses, and flaunts an enormous mane of salt-and-pepper hair with an even more luxurious beard. "If I had a million dollars," he once said in the pages of *Mother Jones* magazine, "I'd build neighborhood observatories all over the world. And at each one I'd have good conga drums, so people could drum together as well as observe."

Spacey he may be, but Schatz is no flake. He turned his longing for world peace into one of the most successful of all Russian-American joint ventures. His firm, San Francisco/Moscow Teleport (SFMT) today carries 99 percent of all electronic mail traffic between Russia and the United

States. He maintains permanent offices in Moscow and he's backed by big Wall Street money. Schatz's satellite E-mail service has become the medium of choice for major corporations like Citibank, ABB/Combustion Engineering, and Bechtel Corporation who were fed up with the Russians' unreliable international phone system.

Back in 1983, Schatz was in a better position than most to appreciate the dangers of the Cold War. He'd served for a number of years as an intelligence analyst for the U.S. Army. During the 1970s, Schatz became energy advisor to the governor of Oregon and later traveled the world, from Sweden to Latin America, advising governments and international organizations on the use and conservation of Earth's dwindling resources. Schatz's work gave him a powerful feel for the potential of international cooperation. And his intelligence background gave him a chilling insight into the unpleasant alternatives to cooperation.

"Rhetoric between Moscow and Washington was very gloomy at that time," recalls Schatz. "There were constant threats of nuclear war."

After they spent a few days together on a speaking tour, Schatz began sharing his thoughts with Robert Muller, a United Nations official. The two men realized that they shared many views on how to achieve world peace. Both believed that Russians and Americans needed to build communications lines at the grass roots. Only such "citizens' diplomacy," they felt, could bypass the grim politics of confrontation. Before they realized it, the two had resolved to make a "factfinding trip" to Russia to seek out opportunities for doing just that.

Virtue Number Two:
An Eye for Anomalies

Most great business ideas start by recognizing an anomaly in the marketplace, some curious set of facts that just don't add up. A good entrepreneur recognizes these anomalies as opportunities and knows how to exploit them.

After Schatz and his wife Diane returned from their factfinding trip, they discovered that it was extraordinarily difficult to communicate with their new Russian friends. "We'd met all kinds of interesting people there," says Schatz, "scientists, filmmakers, political people, journalists, faith healers, religious leaders, teachers. But it was very hard to stay in touch with them."

Telex was expensive and inaccessible. Mail took over a month to arrive and was often lost in transit. Long-distance phone calls were often blocked by busy trunk lines, and when you finally got through, you might be cut off in the middle of the call.

Schatz detected an important *anomaly*. How could the two largest nations on earth, with two of the largest economies, be so poorly wired for intercommunication? As Schatz researched the matter further, he learned that there were only 35 phone circuits connecting the United States and the Soviet Union , compared with 600 between the Dominican Republic and the United States. He also discovered that Russian phone lines and switching systems hadn't been modernized since 1917! "It was frightening that a country with such potential for destruction should be operating with such poor communications," Schatz remarks.

Schatz had heard about a new technology called *electronic mail*, or *E-mail*, which allowed people to type out messages over phone lines using personal computers. Why not set up such a computer link with Russia and bypass the traditional communication lines?

Virtue Number Three:
Dogged Persistence

Starting any business requires extraordinary perseverance. But starting one in Russia requires 100 times more than usual.

Schatz sent over 30 telexes to Russia before he finally got a response on his proposal, in the form of an invitation from Yevgeny Velikhov, vice president of the USSR Academy of Sciences. Thus began a five-year runaround, during which Schatz made over 30 back-and-forth trips to Russia. At the end of it all, Schatz had a thriving telecommunications business. But he paid for it with five years of sweat, frustration, sleepless nights, and senseless, Kafkaesque struggles with Soviet and American bureaucrats alike.

Culture Shock.   Through Velikhov, Schatz was introduced into the highest levels of Soviet science. Soon he was working with people like Boris Raushenbakh, who had directed the historic Soviet satellite mission which took the first pictures of the dark side of the moon.

At first, the Soviets hardly knew what to make of this unruly Aquarian Conspirator. Schatz tells how he showed up for one meeting 20 minutes late, barging into the conference room with fogged-up glasses and a snow-covered beard. He was dressed in jeans, a white sheepskin coat and a rainbow-colored ski cap. As Schatz stood panting in the doorway, clutching a computer in a purple cloth case, he realized that the six top-ranking Soviet officials, all dressed in somber blue suits, were staring at him in horror from their seats around the conference table.

There's no telling how long that deathly silence might have continued had not one scientist broken the ice by rising from his chair, throwing his arms wide, and crying, "Ah, a Californian!"

Death by Committee.   The meetings went on interminably, one after an-other. Schatz had discovered the subtle Soviet art of inflicting "death by committee" on all projects of dubious ideological soundness. Communism might be dead, but "death by committee" remains very much alive in Russia's moribund state monopolies and government ministries. As soon as Schatz received tentative approval from one set of officials, another would step in and raise objections. The first time he tried to hook up a modem in Moscow, Schatz spent two full weeks lobbying for official clearance.

"The Soviets didn't know what it was," he recalls. "They looked at it. Took it apart. Everytime I connected the modem, I needed to get permission all over again."

Even two years later, when Schatz's network was already up and running, bureaucratic disturbances continued threatening the project's existence at regular intervals. When the head of the Academy of Sciences suddenly retired, the ensuing power struggle sent Schatz's erstwhile partners into hiding.

"All the organizations that answered to the Academy went into shutdown mode," says Schatz. "All the rules changed. They didn't want to take chances. For the first time, after two years, I couldn't even get into the building. I couldn't get through on the phone, couldn't get through on E-mail."

Finally, Joel got a telex through to his partner Oleg Smirnov, director of the Institute for Automated Systems (IAS). The power struggle was over. Everything was back to normal. In response to Schatz's outraged demands to explain his behavior, Smirnov could only advise him not to take it personally.

"It's not us against you," said Smirnov sadly. "It's just the way it is."

Don't Take *Nyet* for an Answer.   Back in early 1985, Schatz thought he was nearing the end of the tunnel. He'd lobbied all the right ministries and gotten the green light from high officials. But then Raushenbakh informed Schatz that Communist Party General Secretary Konstantin Chernenko was dying of emphysema. No one could make a move until they knew what his successor's policy would be.

"The only thing that kept me going through all of this was stubbornness," says Schatz. " I just didn't like when people said *nyet*. To me, that was just a challenge to get them to say *da*."

Schatz's stubbornness paid off. In March 1985, 10 days after Gorbachev took office, Schatz suddenly received four telexes asking him to return to Russia. The stalemate was over. The E- mail network could proceed ahead. Schatz sent the first electronic mail message from his kitchen phone in June, using a Tandy laptop computer.

"The first time I sent a message through and got a response in my kitchen," says Schatz, "my wife and I looked at each other in disbelief. We did it. We felt like we had witnessed some strange historic event. We'd sent an E-mail message to Russia on four AA batteries, a laptop computer, and our kitchen phone."

Virtue Number Four: Decisiveness

H. Ross Perot's executives use a riddle to train their people in decisiveness. They ask trainees, "What should you do if you see a snake in the road?" Some say walk around it. Others say get a stick and push it away. But the correct answer is ... *kick it!* After that, you have about half a second in which to decide how to kill the snake before it kills you. The decision you make in that half-second may not be the right one. But it will certainly be quick and unequivocal.

When you do business in Russia, obstacles, questions and complexities— *especially of the legal variety*—seem to multiply by the second. And the legal snafus don't always originate on the Russian side. If you insist on resolving each question or ambiguity completely before going on, you may find yourself at a standstill for years. Remember, this is virgin territory. Nobody really knows what the rules are until somebody goes ahead and tries to break them. It might as well be you. Therefore, whenever possible, adopt the "Damn-the- torpedoes! Full-speed-ahead!" approach.

Damn the Torpedoes.   Schatz had cleared his project in advance with the State Department. But officials there warned him he might have problems with the Department of Commerce. "They advised me not to ask the Commerce Department," says Schatz. "They said to just start doing it and ask permission later. It's easier to say no than yes."

In other words, they advised Schatz to *kick the snake*. He followed their advice. It didn't take long for the "snake" to strike back. Soon after Schatz sent that first E-mail message from his kitchen, the U.S. Commerce Department ordered him to shut down his operation.

"They just couldn't believe it was legal," says Schatz. "They had no basis for thinking that. They just intuitively felt that it must violate some law."

Schatz marched down to the export administration with attorneys in tow, demanding to know what law he was violating. The Commerce Department stalled for two weeks, unable to locate any such law. At length, they backed down. Schatz was allowed to proceed. Fortunately for him, he had hardly missed a step. His network was already tested, debugged and ready to roll, because Schatz had acted decisively in the moment of doubt.

Virtue Number Five: Showmanship

Positive publicity can lead directly to lucrative corporate accounts and can even attract investors. That's good news for Russia-preneurs. Any kind of business in Russia carries an innate potential for monstrous publicity. Of course, there are certain businesses which thrive on secrecy. But most can only benefit from extensive press clips, radio and TV interviews.

You've got to be a showman to attract media attention. Schatz proved remarkably skillful at self-promotion. Within days after receiving his final go-ahead from the Commerce Department, Schatz staged a "ribbon-cutting ceremony" for his new E-mail system.

In fact, Schatz's was hardly the first such network. Scientists and academics in the United Stated had been quietly logging on to private computer networks for years in order to exchange data with Soviet colleagues. But you never would have known it from the heady atmosphere at Berkeley's Trinity United Methodist Church, on November 8, 1985. Schatz assembled 320 scientists, professors, and business leaders for what he told them was an historic step forward in U.S.-Soviet relations. With a bravado worthy of Stephen Jobs, Schatz dramatically phoned his contacts in the Soviet Union, while the audience held its breath. The phone rang for several minutes. Suddenly, Schatz remembered it was a national holiday in Russia, the anniversary of the Bolshevik Revolution. There was no one in the office to take his call!

The crowd loved it anyway. The room thundered with applause. Schatz snipped away a blue ribbon wrapped around the computer. He had originally planned to break a champagne bottle as well, but decided that would ruin his Macintosh.

In the months ahead, Schatz made sure his bearded face was never long absent from the printed page. His most effective gimmick was to rig up a makeshift "videophone" using a common video camera, a TV monitor, a two-line Panasonic telephone, his laptop computer, and a mysterious little "black box." Russians and Americans could converse from half a world away, while watching a succession of "slow-scan" still photos of one another in real-time. Schatz staged videophone events in which American and Russian mayors, reporters in newsrooms, and other opinion leaders would greet one another "face-to-face" across the Iron Curtain. Once he threw a "New Year's Party," in which some 150 miscellaneous VIPs ranging from Nobel laureate physicist Glenn Seaborg to astronaut Rusty Schweikart and poet Michael McClure gathered together in a San Francisco office, drank champagne, and attempted to transmit messages ranging from poetry recitals to recorded whale noises to an equally weighty roster of Russian dignitaries on the other end. They failed to make a successful connection. But once again, the press didn't seem to mind. The event was splayed across the front page of *The Los Angeles Times* and Reuters news reported approvingly, "The revellers sipped wine, nibbled hors d'oeuvres and talked of peace."

Silly as it all may seem, the waves of publicity helped Schatz establish a presence. His network grew rapidly. Early users included oil mogul

Armand Hammer, Carl Sagan's Planetary Society in Pasadena, and Dr. Robert Peter Gale of UCLA who logged on with Soviet doctors to plan emergency medical relief for Chernobyl victims in 1986.

Schatz could see where all this was leading. Up till that point, he had run the project on a non-profit basis, with foundation funding. But suddenly, Schatz's "citizen's diplomacy" was starting to look more and more like a business. In February 1988, he incorporated as San Francisco-Moscow Teleport (SFMT).

Virtue Number Six: Flexibility

To succeed in Russia, you must respond rapidly to changing circumstances and seize new opportunities as they arise. Schatz was troubled by the fact that his E-mail transmissions had to pass through Radio Austria by way of Vienna. The Austrians slapped on huge tariffs, and the connections were not always reliable. Surely there must be a better way, he thought, even if no one else had thought of it yet.

Schatz was right. He learned that for a reasonable fee, he could bounce his signals off the Intelsat communications satellite. No one had ever hooked up a computer network to Russia in this way. It meant pioneering a whole new business, just when he was starting to get comfortable with the old one. But Schatz knew that a business which doesn't move forward is doomed to fade away.

The satellite link—which went on line in 1989—vastly increased the speed, volume, and quality of transmissions. It proved the turning point for Schatz's business. For the first time, customers could economically transfer massive amounts of software and technical data quickly and cheaply to Russia. Even more astonishing, the Russians could transfer data *back*! This had been strictly *verboten* in the past by a Soviet government afraid that its scientists might export state secrets via modem. But once again, Schatz's stubbornness had won the day. The East-West "data highway" had become a two-way street.

Prestigious scientific institutes, major corporations, and computer hackers on both sides flocked to sign up for the service. Schatz was in ecstasy. His dream of do-it-yourself detente was taking hold. The Iron Curtain was melting away in a blur of telecommunications. But for Schatz, the real victory was yet to come.

**Virtue Number Seven:
A Maverick Spirit**

Without exception, the real winners in the Russian marketplace have been mavericks in their industries, independent spirits with thick skins and strong opinions. Whether entrepreneurs or corporate executives, they tend to be people who strike out on their own and buck the trends.

One day, Schatz was introduced to a prospective customer named George Soros. The man needed reliable communications between his New York and Moscow offices. Soros complained of all the usual problems with Russian phone lines. But he was far from your usual customer. For one thing, Soros was reputed to be one of the richest men in the world.

Soros was a rebel. "We start with the assumption that the stock market is always wrong," he once told *The Wall Street Journal*. "So if you copy everybody else on Wall Street, you're doomed to do poorly."

Soros ignored the advice of Wall Street investment "experts" and shunned fancy econometric models, relying instead on his own deep study of social, political and technological trends. Soros's eerily prescient investments had marked him as the man to watch on Wall Street.

When Soros bought up oil drilling and equipment stocks in 1972, everyone thought he was crazy. But the Arab oil embargo came only a year later, forcing oil prices through the roof. Nobody ever heard of an "automated battlefield" back in 1975. But Soros invested heavily that year in "smart" bombs, laser-directed artillery shells, and computerized missiles—the same weapons which crushed Saddam Hussein 15 years later. More recently, Soros is reported to have reaped over *$1.5 billion* from the 1992 European currency crisis that had everyone else losing their shirts.

Although Schatz didn't know it when he showed up for his meeting at Soros' New York office, the world's largest money trader had already decided where he was going to place his next bet.

Vindicated!   Soros wasted no time in getting down to business. "He told me right away," Schatz recalls. "He wanted to invest in my company. It was a huge amount of money. I was speechless. All I could say was okay."

Schatz won't divulge the amount, but sources say that Soros and an associate Alan Slifka invested about $1.5 million in SFMT. "I was ecstatic," remembers Schatz. "You work hard, you make 30 trips back and forth to Moscow, you work day and night, you push, push push, just to get to the point of being stable. And suddenly, you realize you've won."

Schatz had won *bigtime*. With names like Soros behind him, corporate America began to treat him with new respect. In short order, AT&T signed a co-venture deal with him to install international fiber-optic lines in Soviet hotels that would increase capacity fivefold. GTE weighed in with a $6.5 million joint project to build an international digital phone system for Moscow. And in August 1991, the British firm Cable & Wireless bought a 33 percent stake in Schatz's venture.

"I feel *vindicated*," says Schatz. "When I first started this project, people told me I was out of my mind," he recalls. "They said it was a ridiculous waste of my time. Even my friends, even people who had done other projects with the USSR, they all said the KGB or the Department of Defense would shoot me down. It's good to know after all those years, that I was right. I wasn't as crazy as I thought I was. I hadn't wasted my time by trying to do something impossible."

In George Soros, Schatz found more than a financial backer. He found a new soulmate. A Hungarian emigré, Soros shared Schatz's vision of uniting East and West. His Soros Foundation has given millions to promote democracy and free enterprise in the former Soviet Bloc, and to nurture friendship between the erstwhile foes.

"He's not just a businessman," says Schatz. "He has a terrific vision for the future of the planet. He's a very large-scale thinker."

In a sense, Schatz has come full circle, returning to the humanitarian womb which first spawned him. All those years that he wandered in the desert of commercial struggle and survival, Schatz kept his focus and never wavered from his goals. Now his selfless toil has earned him riches and rewards beyond every dream or expectation.

You Can Do It Too

There's nothing really special about Joel Schatz. You don't have to be born with some rare gift or talent which marks you as a Russia-preneur. I believe that most of us possess every one of the seven virtues detailed in this chapter, though they might be hidden away more deeply in some than in others. The trick is to let them come out. Necessity, after all, is the mother of all achievement and innovation. And there's no necessity more stimulating than the clammy terror of actually trying to launch a business in Russia. So roll up your sleeves, take a deep breath, and *get involved.*

5
Get a Guide

**Russia Is No Place for Amateurs—
You Need a Seasoned Consultant**

So you've got what it takes. You've looked deep within yourself and determined that indeed, you possess all seven virtues of the Russia-preneur. What's the next step? Buy a ticket on the next Delta Airlines nonstop to Moscow? NO!

Don't even think about going to Russia without seeking expert guidance first. You need a seasoned consultant, someone who's spent a lot of time on the ground in Russia and who has a *track record for making money*. If you try to go it alone, the consequences could be severe.

"Thousands of people come over to Russia every year," says Geoffrey Carr-Harris, president of Phargo Consulting in Toronto. "They take a look around and say, 'Hey, they don't have any good dry cleaners. I'll start a dry cleaning store!' Or they see that Intourist isn't doing a good job, so they say, 'Hey, I'll start a travel service to compete with Intourist!' You can be sure that any idea you come up with the first week or two you're in Moscow, a hundred other people have already thought of it, tried to do something with it, and have gone nowhere." Only a consultant with experience can show you where the hidden boobytraps lie.

Without a Guide, You're Just Another Sucker

Back in America, Paul Zane Pilzer thought he was a pretty savvy guy. He became the youngest vice president of Citibank in his mid-20s, was appointed an advisor to Presidents Reagan and Bush, made a fortune in real estate, and wrote popular business books such as *Other People's*

Money and *Unlimited Wealth*. Many consider Pilzer an economic and financial genius. But when he set foot in Moscow, Pilzer discovered that he was *just another sucker.*

"From 1986 to 1990, my company spent over $2 million out of pocket on lawyers' fees, documents, plane tickets, hotels, on what I call worthless things," says Pilzer, "all because we thought we were going to make millions in Russian real estate."

On the surface it looked great. Pilzer was wined and dined by high officials. Accords were signed. Sites were inspected. Tenants were signed up.

"We would have these beautiful financing deals," says Pilzer, "where the tenants were so desperate for office space, they'd agree to pay a year's rent in advance at $100 per square foot, and we'd arrange to build the building for $80 per square foot using all foreign labor and materials. Nice deal, huh? You never had to go to a bank. It's a real estate developer's dream. You can't believe the euphoria in my company as I'd come home with these deals one after another." But the euphoria quickly faded. Every single one of Pilzer's deals fell through.

"The pattern was always the same," he recalls. "We'd get the deal done, we'd sign the deal, I'd pay $50,000 to the lawyer, and then the Russians would come back to me and say, 'Paul, the Germans have offered us a better deal. It was always the Germans, for some reason."

The Russians would typically demand a greater split of the profits. If Pilzer offered them a 30 percent split, they would say that "the Germans" had offered them 38 percent. If Pilzer offered them 50 percent, "the Germans" would counter with 55 percent. Of course, in reality, there were no Germans. It was all a trick.

"I would say, 'You don't understand, we already signed this deal.' But the Russians would just say, 'Well, yes, we signed, but it still needs someone else's approval.' They would just make something up and then they'd tell me, 'If you don't do this right now, the deal is off.' Every deal died in this way."

It was only after losing $2 million and five years of his time that Pilzer caught on. The Russians were just stringing him along, pumping him for fancy dinners, trips to America and other perks. They were never serious about the deal in the first place.

"The Russians were just playing chicken with me," Pilzer concludes. "If only I knew then what I know now."

Many have concluded from such horror tales that the best solution is to stay away from Russians entirely. But that's drawing the wrong lesson. In fact, many Western developers have successfully concluded precisely the sorts of "dream" real estate deals that slipped through Pilzer's hands. The difference is that they had expert advice from consultants with *real, inside knowledge and connections.*

Don't Just Pick Any Consultant

Of course, you don't just want *any* consultant. There are a lot of bad ones out there. One *Fortune 500* company learned that lesson the hard way. "We blew over half a million dollars over a 10-month period," laments an executive of that company, who insists that both he and the corporation remain anonymous. When this company decided in May 1991 to scout out the Russian marketplace, they brought in a consultant to help them do it.

"Our vice president knew this guy from somewhere and recommended him. But there was something about him that bothered me from the start. When I watched him sell, he sold like an insurance man, putting all the brochures out on the table. He just didn't seem to have the kind of sophistication that a consultant at our level should have."

Nevertheless, the man claimed he had top-drawer connections and vast knowledge of the Russian market. A simple background check would have punched holes in that story. At one time, he had tried unsuccessfully to import cars from Mercedes-Benz, then wine from Austria. Before that, he had been a door-to-door insurance salesman. But no one found that out until later.

The company started pouring money and time into the Russian project, rotating two or three executives almost constantly in Moscow. They were looking for large institutional clients who would be interested in purchasing high-end desktop publishing and printing systems. The consultant was supposed to produce top-level officials with access to hard currency. But months and months went by with no clients materializing at all. The man spent more time with his Russian mistress than trying to cadge business for the company. When he was working, he was more often than not pursuing his own personal projects, while continuing to draw on his client's expense account. Eventually, the company concluded that he was incompetent.

Our anonymous executive attempted to save the situation, swooping in, and rounding up clients himself. For the first time in months, things started to move. He found four good accounts right away. But it was already too late. Too much money had been spent, too many targets missed. The president of the division was afraid of getting heat from his own boss. He pulled the plug on all further Russian operations.

"The fact that a company of our stature fell for this guy is embarassing," admits the executive. "Thank God I had no part in hiring him. The vice president who brought him in has been outplaced. There were some heads that rolled over this thing."

"It's a shame," he adds. "If we went back in now with the connections I've made, we could do a good job. But we wasted too much time waiting around for this guy to do something."

Our unnamed executive says that if he had it to do over, he would use a more mainstream consulting firm. "Later we hired a big accounting firm in New York which had good internal information on Russia," he says. "Had we done that originally, we would have saved all our money. We could have used their resources to check out this guy and they would have told us they'd never heard of him and that he'd never done anything in Russia. They also turned out to have good information on some of the potential Russian customers whom this consultant had brought us, much more than our consultant had ever gotten on them.

"For $9000 to $10,000 they would put together a full report on a Russian company and its CEO. It was expensive but it was worth it."

Eight Ways to Tell a Good Consultant from a Bad One

How do you separate the chaff from the grain? How do you find the right consultant for you? The rules are pretty much the same as they would be for finding a consultant in any industry. But there are a few points specific to the Russian marketplace.

Rule One: Hire an American

This may sound chauvinistic, but you need at least one bona fide American citizen on your consulting team. There are plenty of smart, talented Russian consultants in Moscow and St. Petersburg who dress sharply, speak perfect English, and throw around business jargon like they were born to it. But ultimately you'll find there are definite limits to their ability to fully comprehend your needs as a Western businessman. By all means, hire Russian consultants. But do so *in addition* to your American consultant, not instead of him.

Rule Two: Pay a Personal Visit to the Consultant's Office

When interviewing a new consultant, don't let him wine and dine you at a fancy restaurant. Go see where he works. The size and condition of his office will tell you a lot. Obviously, if your consultant shares seedy, cramped office space with a collection agency and a bail bondsman or two, you can deduce that his consultancy is not thriving. Probably his clients aren't either.

Rule Three: Make Sure He Speaks Russian

In a large consultancy or law firm with an extensive staff and a high degree of compartmentalization, it's not necessary for your key advisor to speak Russian. He probably has plenty of people on staff to do that for him. However, when dealing with smaller firms, in which one or two key individuals will be representing you to Russian nationals, you'd better make sure they speak Russian and speak it *fluently*. The success or failure of a negotiation can depend upon precise knowledge of the language, and you can't always rely on interpreters. Arrange for your prospective consultant to converse with a native speaker, and later ask that native speaker privately to assess the consultant's level of skill.

Rule Four: Get References

Ask for the names of at least 10 clients whom the consultant has helped to launch a successful business in Russia. Then call up every single one of them, not just one or two. When you speak with past clients, don't ask general questions such as, "Did you get your money's worth from this guy?" Often, people will hesitate, out of pride or politeness, to admit that they were taken for a ride.

Ask highly specific questions, such as "What type of support did Consultant X give you?" "What high-level Russian contacts did he provide?" "Tell me about a tense or difficult situation which he helped you work through." "How much did you earn in your new business venture during your first year? Your second year?" "How much did you invest?" "How much of a percentage of your earnings went to pay consultants' fees?"

Rule Five: Do a Background Check

Treat your consultant as you would any important prospective business partner. Check him out! It probably won't hurt to run a Lexis/Nexis search to see whether he's turned up in the media for any reason, favorable or otherwise. Check his TRW credit history. Do a pending litigation search through Prentice Hall Legal & Financial Service or Equifax, to see if any unhappy clients have taken him to court. It's probably a good idea to run his name past relevant trade groups.

Rule Six: Beware the Consultant with Rose-Tinted Glasses

You're hiring this guy to tell you the truth. If your prospective consultant lavishes praise on each and every business idea you throw out on the table, he's not helping you. Let's face it. Most of your ideas are idiotic and completely unsuitable for the Russian marketplace. Your consultant should hasten to warn you of this fact and should be prepared to explain why they won't work.

Rule Seven: Does the Meter Start Ticking on Your First Phone Call?

You want a consultant who is willing to invest his time in your business. If he starts nickel and dime-ing you from your very first phone call, he's probably in the business of chatting rather than doing.

Rule Eight: What Resources Does He Have?

One of the most important things your consultant can do for you is to obtain information. That means background information on prospective Russian partners, reliable and up-to- date market research data, who's who in the government bureaucracy, the latest laws and regulations. Any consultant worth his salt will be able to obtain all of the above.

One caveat. Your consultant might be getting his information *from another consultant.* If this is the case, maybe you should go right to the horse's mouth, instead of paying premiums to a middleman.

Your consultant should also be able to provide top-notch legal and accounting services, either in-house or through trustworthy referrals.

Who Are the "Name Brands?"

There are a lot of good consultants out there, some large, some small, some polished and professional, others wild and woolly. Some unconventional entrepreneurs may actually prefer working with the Lone Rangers and the wildmen, for reasons of budget and temperament. You'll find a wide selection of recommendations in the "Ready-Made Rolodex" in App. B.

In general, you're going to be better off going with a "name brand." Several major law firms and accounting firms have been heavily involved in the Russian marketplace for years, many of them maintaining full-time staff in Moscow and other Russian cities. You can't go wrong with such familiar names as Hale & Dorr; Steptoe & Johnson; Arnold & Porter; Baker & McKenzie; Chadbourne & Parke; Cole, Corette & Abrutyn; Coudert Brothers; Arthur Andersen; Ernst & Young; and Price Waterhouse.

What Should a Consultant Do for You?

When you interview a prospective consultant, it helps to know what the industry standards are, so you can determine whether he's offering true world-class service. A *Fortune 100* vice president who expects state-of-the-art service will go to someone like John Morton, co-chair of the CIS Practice Group for Hale & Dorr. This prestigious law firm has nine attorneys working exclusively on the former Soviet states, including one stationed full-time in Moscow. If you're a small company, you may shrink from Morton's fees, but his methodology will provide a good standard by which you can judge the level of service you obtain from other consultancies.

Step One: Set Goals

Morton begins by listening to your "wishlist" and advising you on which goals seem realistic and which don't.

Step Two: Research the Market

The next step is to do detailed market research. How big is your potential market in Russia and who are your customers? Where are the choice properties, who owns them, and how much do they cost? You would never launch a business in America without getting answers to such basic questions. Don't settle for anything less in Russia.

I wish I had a penny for every time during my research for this book that some consultant, economist, or businessman assured me that it was "absolutely impossible" to obtain reliable data on the Russian marketplace. If any consultant tries to snow you with this flimsy excuse, don't waste another second of your time talking to him.

You should expect and demand the same level of detailed information on people, properties, and industries in Russia as you would on those in the United States. True, there's no Dun & Bradstreet in Russia, but the same type of business information can be found in institutional records, ministries, and other sources. All it takes is someone with the energy, the know-how, and the resources to go and get it.

"We are able to get information with great detail and accuracy from any part of the former Soviet Union, including Uzbekistan and areas even more remote," says John Morton. "We can find out any and all financial and accounting information about a particular entity. With regard to any person in business or government in the CIS, we can find out their background, education, their employment record, how they fit into the system, whether they are liberal or conservative." Don't bother to ask Morton *how* he finds all this out. It's a secret.

For $15,000 to $30,000, Morton will produce a 200-plus- page "briefing book" on your particular industry. The research for these reports can be quite elaborate. "It can take up to a month of intensive effort. We turn people loose all over Russia, as many as necessary. At times we've sent people to very remote areas by airplane, and kept them there for a week. They've been very effective."

How effective? Morton says that one report he completed recently for the oil and gas industry includes such details as "a list of all existing prospecting teams by name in the region in question; a description of their management structure; names of all enterprises operating in the region; who's in charge—their names, phone numbers, and personal profiles; their alignment with political forces in the region; the areas over which they have control; which superagencies they report to; and which entities they are affiliated with. It tells which geographic areas haven't yet been fully prospected; where the suspected oil and gas reserves are; what access is there to roads, seaports, and refinery capabilities; what ancillary industries are there in the region which use oil-based products like plastics; what are the local political conditions; what conflicts are there with the central authorities; what disputes exist over control of the resources; who are the relevant central, regional, and local authorities; which agencies need to be informed about your activities; which people in the bureaucracy do you need to approach; and how much weight do you need to give to each of them?"

Whew! Have you got all that? The moral of the story is don't listen to anyone who tells you there's no reliable market information in Russia. You can find out *anything* you need to know about Russia, her people, her markets, and her industries. *For a price.*

Step Three: Do a Reality Check

Morton next reviews your "wishlist" and helps you revise it, based on the realities uncovered in his market research.

Step Four: Identify Specific Entities and Individuals

For any business, you will need to find reliable Russian partners as well as business entities which you may choose to purchase outright or form joint ventures with. One of the biggest challenges for American businessmen is finding out whether the Russian manager or official you're talking to really has the legal authority to negotiate with you. You might buy a factory or apartment house only to find out later that the person who "sold" it to you doesn't really "own" it. Morton uses his extensive investigative resources to nip these problems in the bud.

"Another thing you have to watch out for," warns Morton, "is that there are thousands of Russian factory managers coming out of the defense sector saying they're qualified to produce, let's say, consumer electronics. But many of them lack the appropriate technical know-how. The products they turn out prove to be very unworthy. We know how to get reliable information on who has the real skills that you need."

Before you make your first trip to Russia, Morton will give you a list of prime properties and reliable potential partners. This information alone is worth its weight in gold.

Step Five: Evaluate Assets

How much is a Russian factory really worth? You'd better have a clear idea before you sit down and negotiate the question over multiple vodkas. Morton can help you with this.

Russians tend to vastly overrate the value of their hard assets. Most Russian industries are so structured as to be almost worthless to an American investor. The equipment is antiquated, the suppliers unreliable, the workforce inefficient, and the budget padded with things like kindergartens, schools, housing, health clinics, and swimming pools for workers.

Another question mark is the state of supplier relationships. A sweater factory which has run smoothly every year since the Revolution may depend entirely on wool from Uzbekistan, which is suddenly no longer available. Such hidden information is critical in evaluating the true worth of a Russian enterprise.

Morton likens a Russian industrial facility to a stack of coins, with each coin representing another facet of its vast, vertically integrated network of interlocking supplier relationships. The "higher" the stack of coins, the more unstable is the whole edifice. The trick is to identify only those "coins" that you can really use and separate them out from the rest of the ungainly stack. Morton's team of investigators provides you with all the information you need to make such delicate judgments.

Step Six: Kick the Tires

Now you're ready for your first actual visit to Russia. Morton or one of his associates personally escorts you to Russia and oversees your entire visit to make sure you are provided with first-class travel accommodations, interpreters, drivers, international telecommunications, and more. He introduces you to prospective partners, suppliers, and customers.

This is your chance to physically inspect the assets you've targeted. If you're in the energy or mineral field, you can conduct assays of minerals in the ground or make surveys. If you're looking at a plant, you'll want to examine the machinery, the layout of the shop floor, the management team, and the work habits of the people. A picture is worth a thousand words.

Step Seven: Negotiate and Sign a Protocol

This is usually done at the conclusion of the first trip, provided everything meets with your satisfaction. A protocol is a short document stating the intention of the parties to continue negotiating a business arrangement. It frequently stipulates timetables and deadlines, as well as such key conditions as exclusivity and secrecy agreements. The Russians will need this signed letter to initiate the long series of bureaucratic procedures needed to obtain official approval for setting up your business. Morton and his team will assist with the negotiation.

Step Eight: Above and Beyond the Call of Duty

Morton often uses his high-level contacts to render services far beyond the normal call of duty. At times, he has lobbied Russian legislators for laws favorable to his clients, and has met with considerable success. In cases where a client's project can benefit from improvements in the infrastructure—such as extending railways or roads, and creating seaports—Morton has proven adept at pushing forward such public projects.

"We can help to bring in IMF funds and other types of grants which have been set aside for infrastructural development and bring them to bear to support a particular project in Russia," Morton states. Now *that's* service!

There's a Consultant for Everyone

As you shop around, you'll find that most of the major law firms and accountancies offer a level of sophistication similar to that described previously. If you can afford their price tag, congratulations! But even if your budget forces you to settle for something less, you're better off hiring a second stringer than trying to go it alone.

Even after all this, some independent souls will still decide that they can buck the system, and do it by the seat of their pants. Far be it from me ever to suggest that anything is impossible to a determined and committed spirit. Many Americans have built successful businesses in Russia entirely without the help of consultants. You may be among the fortunate few who manages to pull it off.

Nevertheless, it won't kill you to spend just an hour or two chatting with a consultant before you make your move. Who knows? You might even learn something.

6

Get 'Em While
They're Hot!

Russian Securities Are the Biggest Game in Town

Ninety years ago, Russian stocks and bonds were the hottest investments in the world. By 1914, foreign capital accounted for fully one third of all money invested in Russia. Foreigners sank billions into Russian bonds, many with maturity dates *80 years or more* in the future. One issue of Tsarist bonds floated in 1913 didn't come due until 1992, which should give some idea of the degree of confidence foreigners felt in Russia's future back then.

Then came the Bolsheviks. In 1917, they siezed foreign assets, shut down the stock exchange, and repudiated all foreign debts. France—which had placed one fourth of all its foreign holdings in Russia—was plunged immediately into the worst banking crisis of its history. Other nations announced an immediate boycott against the renegade state.

Deprived of capital, the Russian economy promptly crashed through the floor. For the next 60 years, foreign investment was forbidden by law. And everyone forgot there had ever been such a thing as Russian stocks and bonds.

A Silent Revolution

In what can only be described as a silent revolution, Russian securities are making an historic comeback. And this time, they're here to stay. Quietly, but swiftly, Russia is laying down the infrastructure to accommodate an unprecedented influx of foreign capital. As far back as 1990, a new law freed Russian companies to sell ownership shares and to issue corporate bonds. Russian and foreign stocks have been traded on the Moscow Central Stock Exchange since March 1991, as well as on a host of other commodities exchanges in Russia. And Bear Stearns' chief economist Lawrence Kudlow predicts that Russia can raise up to $50 billion in bond issues abroad. The New York investment firm has already submitted a proposal to Boris Yeltsin offering to conduct a $500 million bond offering in the West.

Take a tip from me. This is where the action is. Insiders point to startling opportunities in Russia's emerging capital markets in the years ahead. Indeed, the next two years promise to see an explosion of interest in Russian securities unlike anything seen since 1917.

"The Biggest Game in Town"

"Just between you and me," says Bruce Macdonald, head of BBDO Marketing in Moscow, "privatization is the biggest game in town."

In Russia, privatization is *everything*. It's not just big business, it's probably one of the biggest businesses that ever existed. Or ever *will* exist!

Figure it out for yourself. The Russian government has promised to privatize *100 percent* of all small business, housing, and most of its defense plants by 1994, and up to 70 percent of its other large state enterprises by 1995. Some 7000 factories—including world-class chemical refineries, aircraft assembly plants, sophisticated microelectronics factories, television networks, and more—will thus be put up for grabs at bargain basement prices.

As you know, the very essence of investment is to buy cheap and sell dear. Now here's Russia putting on the auction block the *largest store of undervalued stocks* ever marketed in history. Prices have hit rock bottom. They have no place to go but up.

Half of Russia's Industries May Be Sold Off in Bankruptcy Auctions

While we're on the subject of undervalued stocks, consider the little-known fact that over 50 percent of Russia's state industries are now technically insolvent and perhaps 70 percent on the brink. A decree issued by Boris Yeltsin on June 14, 1992 orders that all state enterprises which fail to meet their debt payments for three consecutive months can be forced into bankruptcy by government order. They will be turned over to the State Committee for the Management of State and Municipal Property and auctioned off to the highest bidder.

Already, 30,000 factories employing some 30 million people are considered eligible for bankruptcy by the Russian government.

How Far Could Russian Stock Prices Rise in the Future?

Of course, this is impossible to predict. However, we can get some idea of Russia's potential growth by considering the state of Russian agriculture. Even under Communism, Russia's collective farmers were allowed to keep small, private plots which they could cultivate in their spare time. Naturally, the farmers lavished all their tender loving care on their own little plots and neglected the state fields. They also personally brought their produce to market in the city and hawked it themselves from sidewalk vegetable stands or in rented stalls at the farmer's market. Meanwhile, the state-produced goods were left to rot on provincial loading docks, waiting weeks and weeks for trains or trucks that never arrived.

As a result, that one percent of farmland in Russia which is privately owned has typically produced 27 percent of the total national farm output. In other words, the private plots are *40 times* more productive than state land.

The "Privatization Factor"

If we were to apply that same multiple to the entire state-owned sector of Russia's economy (accepting PlanEcon's conservative estimate that Russia's 1993 GNP will amount to $699.5 billion, and conceding the Russian government's unlikely claim that 96 percent of Russian production comes from state-owned enterprises), it would escalate Russia's GNP to a staggering $26.8 *trillion*.

Obviously, that figure is absurd. But, just as obviously, privatization is certain to work a magic on Russia's manufacturing and retail sectors as potent as that which has enriched its private farm plots for decades. While the precise increase in production is impossible to predict, the trend is clear. We can expect phenomenal growth in the value of Russia's assets as private ownership takes hold.

Won't the Russians Just Take My Money and Run?

"But wait a minute," you say. "If I invest in Russian securities, how do I know that the Russians won't just take my money and run?" Well, you don't.

That's one of the many reasons why it's risky. However, historical precedent suggests that the risk may be less than you think.

Oil mogul Armand Hammer got his start doing business with Russia during the 1920s when Lenin's "New Economic Policy" temporarily opened the doors to foreigners. Business was good.

But by 1930, the party was over. Lenin was dead, his "New Economic Policy" forgotten. The new boy in town, Joseph Stalin, was whipping up hatred and paranoia against "parasitical" foreign capitalists. Western businessmen stampeded to liquidate their Russian assets and flee the country. In railroad depots and seaports throughout Europe, entrepreneurs with bitter expressions on their faces clutched suitcases bulging with worthless Soviet promissory notes. For years, they had naively traded goods and services for these notes, trusting Lenin's personal guarantee to make good on them. But now no one expected to see a penny of it. No one, that is, except Armand Hammer.

In many ways, Hammer was in the same boat as all the others. He too had been driven out by Stalin's crackdown and he held as much "bad" Soviet debt as anyone else. Like his embittered colleagues, Hammer was painfully aware of the Bolsheviks' sad track record vis-à-vis their foreign creditors. After all, wasn't this the same regime which had defaulted on hundreds of millions of dollars worth of Tsarist bonds in 1917?

What Goes Down Must Come Up

But unlike his colleagues, Hammer had developed an uncanny feel for Russia's historical ups and downs. He was able to assess the situation with a cool head.

"My attitude toward the Soviets was based upon my business experience," he wrote in his autobiography. "I had invariably found that whenever a company supplying me had gone bust, been liquidated, and then re-formed, the new management always paid its debts promptly and in full, being desperate to establish a good name with its customers."

Hammer was convinced that Stalin would soon attempt to restore his country's good standing in Western business circles. Risking everything on this hunch, Hammer began buying up every Soviet promissory note he could find. His colleagues were more than happy to unload the "worthless paper," even at an extremely disadvantageous rate. The Nervous Nellies lived to regret their decision. As Hammer expected, the Soviets made good on all their debts. Within three years, Hammer's profits soared into the millions.

Similar opportunities exist today for those, like Hammer, who are willing to bet their money on the Russians' *desperate need to reestablish their credit.*

How Does Privatization Work?

Most state enterprises in Russia have had the theoretical right to "go private" since July 1991. The management of the firm can submit an application to the government, which then conducts an auction or closed bid for all or part of the shares in that company.

Some 46,000 state and city-owned businesses were privatized in this way by January 1993—most of them shops, restaurants, and other service businesses. Nearly 10,000 additional state enterprises have already been converted to joint stock companies. This means that they now have the legal right to sell up to 15 percent of their total equity without restriction. With permission from the government, they may sell 50 percent or more.

But converting to a joint stock company is only the first step toward going private. Up till now, bureaucratic inertia has kept most Russian firms from taking the plunge. That's why the Russian government has stepped in with a program for massive, state- mandated privatization in 1993.

Russia's First Full-Scale Securities Market

On October 1, 1992, the Russian government distributed to each of its 150 million citizens a "voucher" worth 10,000 rubles towards the purchase of shares in a state enterprise. Starting in December 1992, Russians were allowed to trade in those vouchers for equity shares in a company of their choice. The total value of the vouchers now in circulation is estimated at about $4.5 billion.

There is no set number of shares which a voucher can buy. In a typical privatization offering, the total number of vouchers submitted by the public is simply divided by the number of shares being offered. The more vouchers submitted, the less shares are given for each one.

These vouchers comprise, in effect, the first significant market in *tradeable Russian securities* since 1917. The law permits you to buy and sell vouchers to whomever you wish, in *any quantity*, at *any price* the market will bear. Foreigners are more than welcome to participate.

A Growing, Over-the-Counter Market

A lively, over-the-counter market in vouchers has rapidly taken shape in Russia. Shortly after the first vouchers were issued, they began trading for about 4000 rubles, or $10 by the exchange rate at the time. By December 1992, the price had risen to 7000 rubles, and jumped to 8000 when the first state companies were put up for auction under the voucher plan.

Just like securities markets in the West, the voucher market responds sharply to political developments. When Boris Yeltsin came under fire from the Congress of People's Deputies early in December, the price of vouchers dropped temporarily down to 6000 rubles.

The Role of Russia's Stock and Commodities Exchanges

Much of the present trade in vouchers is strictly informal. Some entrepreneurs are reported to be hawking them in the streets and subway stations. Rumor has it that Russian prostitutes—notoriously conservative in financial matters—are readily accepting vouchers in return for their favors.

But such trade has limits. When a Russian on the street sells his voucher to another Russian, the seller doesn't have enough information handy to price his voucher accurately. He might end up selling it for 20,000 rubles, when yet another Russian further down the street would have been more than willing to pay five times that amount. Only a centralized exchange can ensure that all buyers and sellers have rapid access to accurate and up-to-date prices.

Happily, Russia's organized stock and commodities exchanges have moved decisively to fill this need, leaping into the voucher game with furious abandon.

The Infrastructure Is Already in Place

An extensive network has already formed in Russia for trading such commodities as metals, food, minerals and manufactured goods. That infrastructure is now being adapted to move stocks, bonds, futures, and other sophisticated investment instruments.

The most prominent *birzha* (i.e., commodity exchange) in Russia is the Moscow Commodity Exchange, which held its first trading session in October 1990. It's a far cry from the Chicago Merc. Ted Kowalyk, a New York commodities trader who visited the Moscow *Birzha*, describes the trading floor as a large room filled with tables. At the beginning of each session, the exchange workers lay out lists on the tables, containing the names and phone numbers of individuals or enterprises who are interested in buying or selling certain items.

The brokers rush in at the beginning of the day, rifle through the lists for promising offers, copy them down, then rush to the phone to start calling their clients. For the most part, clients are looking for barter arrangements. A factory manager, for example, might offer to trade machine parts for jeans so that he can offer those jeans at discount as a perk to his employees. The broker will undertake to track down the jeans for him.

The system is far from perfect. In America, commodity exchanges guarantee timely delivery of their products, be it pork bellies or gold ingots. They maintain elaborate warehousing and distribution facilities for this purpose. But in Russia, the broker is on his own to figure out how to ship, say, 10 tons of nickel from a seller in Siberia to a buyer in Murmansk.

Payments are another problem. In a country where nobody accepts checks and bank-to-bank wire transfers can take weeks, brokers often take their lives into their hands lugging suitcases filled with millions of rubles in cash, in order to close deals. And there's no guarantee during any phase of the process that either buyer or seller may not suddenly back out of the deal entirely, leaving the hapless broker holding the bag. "I've heard that one in five trades goes bad," says Kowalyk.

For all these problems, commodity trading in Russia has proven extraordinarily lucrative, and over 1000 independent *birzhi* have sprung up around the country.

The Shakeout Has Arrived

In 1992, a major shakeout began decimating the ranks of Russia's commodity exchanges. When it's over, only the best and brightest will be left. Many of these will form the vanguard of Russia's burgeoning financial industry.

Among the strongest survivors are the Russian Commodities and Raw Materials Exchange (RCRME), the Moscow Central Stock Exchange (MCSE), the International Commodities Exchange, the Moscow International Stock Exchange, the Siberian Stock Exchange, the Nizhny Novgorod Stock Exchange, the Asian Stock Exchange, and the St. Petersburg Stock Exchange.

We shouldn't waste any tears on those *birzhi* which are dying out. The losers are those which made their money primarily by exploiting temporary weaknesses in the Communist system. For example, before 1992, many brokers made overnight fortunes by purchasing huge quantities of goods at ludicrously low state prices and then selling them for wildly inflated "commercial" prices. However, the price reforms enacted in January 1992 have already eliminated much of the artificial difference between state and "market" prices, and with it the opportunity for such lucrative "arbitrage."

Another doomed trading strategy is the widespread practice of bribing factory managers to steal state property and sell it on the exchanges. This is a holdover from the old Communist system, in which employees regarded company property as a limitless reservoir for supplying their own personal black market activities. A recent CIA report speculates that the rapid decline in production figures for Russian state industries may actually be an illusion created by fraudulent underreporting on the part of crooked plant managers. The managers simply report that their production declined 10 percent over the last month, then take that unreported 10 percent surplus and sell it out the back door to commodity traders. President Nazarbayev of Kazakhstan recently complained that unscrupulous brokers had illegally exported 7000 tons of copper and over 350,000 tons of oil in a single year.

When Russia's major industries pass into private hands—as most of them will during the next couple of years—their new owners will crack down hard on this sort of pilferage. Brokers who owe their profits to criminal corruption will be quickly winnowed out of the market.

A New Professionalism

As the wildmen and wheeler-dealers slowly fade from the picture, a new breed of ultra-sophisticated Russian trader is making the jump to high-tech, global finance. According to *Forbes*, two of the biggest names in Russian commodities trading—German Sterligov and Artem Tarasov—are now raising $12 million to launch a worldwide computerized trading network. Sterligov's company Alysa (a network of 32 commodities exchanges), has offices on Wall Street, as well as in London, Taipei, Geneva, Milan, and Hanoi. Alysa is just one of many similar computerized exchanges springing up across the CIS.

Many of Russia's rough-and-tumble commodities traders are already experimenting with sophisticated investment products. For example, in October 1992, the Moscow Commodity Exchange—better known for its dealings in surplus cement and Siberian timber—began a brisk trade in currency futures for both rubles and hard currency. Trading in dollar futures has roughly doubled each week, as Russia's neophyte currency traders experiment with this new method for turning hyperinflation into profit.

The Revolution of 1993

Up till now, trade in Russian securities has been one of the least glamorous of all Russian businesses, largely due to the paucity of attractive buys. The bestselling stocks have tended to be those issued by the major commodity exchanges themselves. In addition, investors could buy shares in a handful of commercial banks, investment firms, and safe but boring blue-chip manufacturers like the KAMAZ truck factory. Less than 2 percent of

Russian savings were invested in securities as of May 1992, according to the Russian Federation State Statistical Committee.

However, the introduction of vouchers has revolutionized Russia's financial industry. Spearheaded by the St. Petersburg Commodity Exchange, the Moscow Central Commodity Exchange (MCCE) and the Russian Raw Materials Exchange (RCRME), formalized trade in vouchers has reached three million rubles per day and is rising fast.

How Will Capital Markets Help Russia?

For one thing, a thriving securities market will allocate capital far more widely and democratically than Russia's current economy allows. Let's say I'm an entrepreneur trying to start a urea factory to compete with a state conglomerate called Consolidated Bolshevik Processing. If I go to the bank for a loan, I might unknowingly find myself sitting across the desk from Consolidated Bolshevik's own banker. Not only does this banker have a vested interest in protecting Consolidated Bolshevik from competition due to the *100 million* rubles they owe his bank, but he also happens to be an old Communist Party comrade of the general director of Consolidated Bolshevik!

In a highly centralized system like Russia's, conflicts like these abound. Your options are limited by everything from the overall scarcity of capital to the shadowy designs of the Communist old-boy network which still controls most of the available credit.

But in a country with developed capital markets, an entrepreneur can always hold a public offering or issue bonds. If he has a good offer, the money will flow in freely from foreign and domestic sources alike, unimpeded by bureaucratic whims or hidden agendas.

Capital Markets Will Fuel an Explosion of Growth

Even more important, when the market for Russian stocks and bonds takes off in earnest, the sudden influx of foreign capital will ignite an unprecedented explosion of growth.

Ninety years ago, when Russia-mania was raging through European investment circles, Russia's economy took off like a rocket. Her growth actually *exceeded America's* in certain key industries between the years 1900 and 1914. Russian coal production rose 124 percent during those years, iron and steel production 51 percent. Russian petroleum exports competed neck and neck with Standard Oil. Thousands of miles of railroads were laid at record-breaking speed. Living standards skyrocketed. Grain exports reached number one in the world.

There's no reason why a new infusion of foreign wealth won't trigger a similar quantum leap in the 1990s.

The Next Two Years Are Crucial

Without a doubt, the rash of privatizations scheduled for the next two years will provide the missing catalyst in establishing a full-scale trade in Russian securities. It's important to get in now, while most Westerners aren't even aware it's happening.

How to Invest

Russia's securities markets are still in their embryonic stages. The rules are changing everyday. The waters are filled with sharks and barracudas. You need expert guidance to find secure and sensible opportunities for your Russian investment portfolio.

Many American brokerage firms and investment banks are reported to be working in this area, but most are extraordinarily close- mouthed about their operations. Your best bet is to seek advice from a major law or accounting firm, such as those listed in App. B.

Opportunities in Mutual Funds

Adventurous financiers may wish to take a lesson from Viktor Kozeny, the 28-year-old investment banker who made a killing in Czech vouchers in 1992. When Czechoslovakia introduced a voucher program similar to Russia's in February of that year, a multitude of private investment funds sprang up to help people dispose of their vouchers. Viktor Kozeny smelled opportunity. Kozeny's Czech parents had brought him to America when he was a teenager. Now a Harvard graduate with some brief experience at a London investment bank, Kozeny saw a chance to make it big in the old country. Backed by family money and guarantees from New York banks, Kozeny offered, in a TV ad blitz, a 10 to 1 return on investment *within one year* for any vouchers invested in his new mutual funds. Kozeny also hired an Amway-like, part-time sales force of 22,000 to get the message out. It is reported that Kozeny's Harvard Capital and Consulting Corporation now controls some 20 percent of all vouchers sold to Czech citizens.

The jury is still out on whether Kozeny will fulfill his 10 to 1 promise to Czech investors. But the abundance of valuable real estate and industrial facilities available in the Czech and Slovak republics today makes Kozeny's horde of vouchers a significant prize in itself, of great interest to Western corporations and financiers.

Russian Investment Funds Are on the Way!

Russia seems to be following the Czech model. Private investment funds are taking form to help Russians dispose of their vouchers. An organization called the Joint Conference of Investment Funds was created to coordinate new funds as they arise. Anatoly Chubays, who, as chairman of the Russian State Committee for Management of State Property, could be considered Russia's privatization "tsar," predicts that "hundreds of thousands" of these funds will be formed. But so far, I've heard of only three: the Moscow Investment Fund, the Bolshev Investment Fund, and the fund at Consortium Metropolis.

How to Find Investment Information

Most Americans will shrink from high-risk schemes like that of Viktor Kozeny. For them, privatization mainly offers a chance to make a direct investment in a particular Russian company of their choice and to *keep* it there.

A number of Russian firms are in the business of helping foreigners like you spot promising properties among the thousands of firms available for privatization. You'll find these consultancies listed in App. B.

"We are preparing a whole complex of measures to provide information to foreign investors," Chubays told Russian Television in August 1992. "A computerized database will be compiled containing key indices about the enterprises to be privatized. We will flesh out this data base with the most practical information, such as the addresses, telephone numbers, and the names of those people who should be approached. This database will be distributed via the Russian trade missions throughout the world."

"Controlled Adventure": A Whole New Dimension for American Investors

When Russia's securities markets are finally up and running at full speed, Americans who aren't so inclined will no longer have to get their hands dirty wrestling with the aggravating details of hands-on operations in

Russia. From the comfort of your stateside office, you'll be able to dabble in such exotic instruments as Russian corporate bonds and ruble futures. You might still lose your shirt. But at least you'll be lending a helping hand to freedom and democracy. And maybe, just maybe, you'll walk away with a handsome profit.

7

The Franchise Advantage

Your Secret Formula for Market Dominance

Geoffrey Carr-Harris is one of the most successful Western entrepreneurs in Russia. His $20 million empire includes real estate ventures, computer imports, sheepskin production, ultrasound technology, gallium arsenide chips, book publishing, a circus, a string quartet, and a rock band. But the bedrock of Carr-Harris's success lies in *franchising*. He started out with two Alpha-Graphics Printshops and two MicroAge computer franchises in Moscow.

"Franchises give us our core dollar business," explains the 40-year-old Toronto businessman. "That frees us up to make other, riskier investments."

What Is Franchising?

Back in 1955, White Castle, with only 27 outlets, was the leading hamburger chain in the United States. McDonald's was nothing but an unknown roadside burger stand in California. Thirty years later, McDonald's boasted an incredible 8278 outlets, while White Castle trailed behind at 167 stores.

What was the difference between these two companies? Simple. McDonald's was a franchise and White Castle was not.

White Castle's restaurants were all wholly owned branches of the parent company. Each time White Castle wanted to add a store, it had to invest its own money. That meant hiring managers and employees, paying for all opening costs and carrying the new store's operating expenses until it became profitable. White Castle's rate of growth was therefore limited by its available cash.

McDonald's, on the other hand, licensed its locations to independent entrepreneurs. These entrepreneurs—or *franchisees*, as they're called in the business—would pay all expenses from their own pockets. They would also pay a hefty licensing fee for the right to use the McDonald's trademark and operating system. And, they paid a monthly *royalty* (a percentage of gross sales) to the parent company (the *franchisor*) for the rest of their business lives.

Think about it. Slow growth financed out of your own pocket. Or lightning growth financed by other people. That's the franchise difference.

Franchising Cuts Risk

Franchising also benefits the individual franchisee. Buying a franchise is probably the least risky method for becoming a business owner.

According to the Small Business Association, a full 23.7 percent of new businesses fail after two years. By the sixth year, 62.2 percent have failed. But almost 85 percent of new franchises *are still up and running* after five years. Why the difference? Most business failures are caused by inexperience. You have to be a kind of genius to invent and execute a really successful new business concept. Not only must you have basic technical knowledge of your chosen industry, but you must have an organizational flair for reducing your business to efficient systems and procedures, marketing talent for seeking out and winning customers, financial ability for managing cash flow. Failure in any one of these areas can result in rapid bankruptcy.

Buying a franchise gives you a shortcut through most of these obstacles. You're buying a proven concept which has been perfected and debugged by many who've come before. You gain a recognizable trademark, access to an existing distribution system, collective buying power for supplies and advertising through the parent company and the network of franchisees, tried and true management procedures and principles. If you run into unexpected difficulties—as you inevitably will in any new business—you can always get on the phone and call the home office or a more experienced franchisee for advice.

An Economic Revolution

In the last three decades, a *franchising revolution* has swept America. Virtually every type of retail business from accounting firms and temp agencies to health clinics, real estate firms, beauty salons, doctor's offices, and body shops have begun to use franchising. American franchises today account for an astonishing 34 percent of all retail sales in the United States. That is $757.8 billion annually. And the number grows every year.

American Franchises in Russia

It is a little-noted fact that a disproportionate number of the most success-
ful American businesses in Russia use some form of franchising. Pepsico
got its feet wet back in the 1970s selling franchised bottling plants to the
Soviets. Now Pepsi is opening Pizza Hut locations all over the country.
Other franchise companies in Russia include McDonald's, AlphaGraphics,
MicroAge, BaskinRobbins, City Looks, the Radisson Hotel, and Com-
puterland. It is reported that Dairy Queen, ServiceMaster, and Subway
Sandwiches and Salads will soon join the feeding frenzy.

So far, only AlphaGraphics, MicroAge, and Computerland have opened
real franchises in Russia. That means their Russian outlets are owned and
operated by *independent franchisees*. The other companies named here
have elected to start with company-owned stores wholly controlled by the
parent company or franchisor.

Nevertheless, even in the case of company-owned stores like those which
McDonald's and Baskin-Robbins maintain in Moscow, it is still the turnkey
franchise system which largely accounts for their success. And all of these
companies have stated their intention to sell real franchises as soon as their
infrastructure is firmly established in Russia.

Your Key to the Russian Market

Before embarking upon any venture in Russia, you ought to give serious
thought to franchising. This remarkable distribution method can be
adapted to virtually any type of business.

The story of Geoffrey Carr-Harris reveals how franchising overcomes
many of the unique challenges of the Russian marketplace. Following are
the 12 steps Carr-Harris took to build his franchise empire.

Step One: Select a Franchise Concept

By 1988, Geoffrey Carr-Harris was ready to give up. For three years, he'd
beaten his head against the wall trying to sell computers to the Soviets.
But he just couldn't find the right formula. Cold War export restrictions
and meddlesome Russian bureaucrats blocked him at every turn. It seemed
to take months to get the right pencil pushers to sign off on a simple trade
deal. No matter how hard Carr-Harris tried, he just couldn't seem to make
any money. Then an associate told Carr-Harris about something called
franchising.

"Of course, I knew about McDonald's and all that," says Carr-Harris,
"but I'd never given much thought to what a franchise was or how it

worked." Carr-Harris's associate had seen a magazine ad for a company called AlphaGraphics Printshops of the Future based in Tucson. Much more than a printshop, AlphaGraphics was really a ready-made international telecommunications and computing center. It offered state-of-the-art desktop publishing, fax service, and a satellite network called Alpha-Link that could beam camera-ready graphics instantly to any AlphaGraphics store in the world.

In a country like the Soviet Union, where international phone calls could take days to get through and Xerox machines were as rare as particle accelerators, AlphaGraphics seemed tailor-made to make a splash.

Step Two: Sell Your Idea
to the Franchisor

Not every franchisor will jump at the chance to enter the Russian marketplace. You'll have to sell yourself and your business plan.

AlphaGraphics founder and CEO Rodger Ford was dead set against Carr-Harris' plan. "I didn't want to do it," he admits. At that time, perestroika was in its infancy. Private printing and copying were flat-out illegal in the Soviet Union. To Ford, Carr-Harris's plan was a pipe dream. He ordered his staff not to waste any more company time talking to the wild man from Toronto.

Step Three: Win Allies
in Middle Management

When you can't get a fair hearing at the top, try to win over middle managers who will plead your case to the boss. Carr-Harris quickly discovered that he had one friend at AlphaGraphics. Mary Pat Sloane, the Vice President of Sales and Development, had studied Eastern European markets as a graduate student. She was intrigued by Carr-Harris's "pipe dream."

"She was a fireball," recalls Ford. "She wouldn't take no for an answer. I finally said to her that AlphaGraphics owned her between 6 a.m. and 10 p.m. If she wanted to do this deal with Russia, she could work on it on her own time." That's precisely what Sloane did.

Step Four: Negotiate
a Franchise Agreement

Most franchises have a cookie-cutter franchise agreement with set fees, royalties, and other requirements. However, when you set up a franchise in a foreign country—and especially a country as exotic as Russia—flexibility is crucial. You should negotiate a franchise agreement which fits the unique challenges of the Russian marketplace.

Carr-Harris initially tried to pressure AlphaGraphics into selling him the "master license" for the entire Soviet Union. That means that he would reserve the right to build every AlphaGraphics franchise that would ever be opened in that country. He also argued that, due to the extraordinary risks involved, AlphaGraphics should not require him to pay monthly royalties.

"They kept telling us we'd make up for it in all the free PR we would get," laughs Sloane. "But we're not in this business for publicity. We're in it for royalty money."

Eventually, the two sides reached a compromise. AlphaGraphics offered an option for two stores, at the same price it would have cost to open one store in the United States. It also offered Carr-Harris an option to buy the master license for the whole country by a given deadline. Carr-Harris could secure the master license for nothing and then pay a separate fee per store as he expanded. AlphaGraphics even agreed to waive the normal royalty.

"We couldn't take rubles and getting dollars out of the country was tough," says Sloane. "So we crafted a technology transfer fee to cover ongoing support and update of equipment. We charged a fixed amount, not a percentage of sales."

Even so, the two sides had a Mexican standoff over the initial fee. Normally, prospective AlphaGraphics franchisees are asked to pay a $5000 deposit to seal a franchise agreement. But Ford decided to make the starry-eyed buccaneer from Toronto jump through a few extra hoops. He asked for *$10,000* upfront, plus the cost of flying Sloane to Moscow for a fact-finding trip.

The deal hung in the balance right up until the very last minute, on the Friday afternoon before Sloane was scheduled to leave for Moscow. If the parties failed to close that day, the trip—and probably the whole deal—was off. Carr-Harris gave in. He faxed a signed option agreement and a confirmation from his bank stating that $10,000 was being wired into AlphaGraphics' account.

"I was thrilled!" says Sloane. "Even if the deal didn't go through, I knew at that point that I was still going to Moscow."

Step Five: Find a Russian Partner

For the next year, Carr-Harris met with 32 potential Soviet partners. Negotiations were tough. Most seemed interested only in getting their hands on the store's laser typesetters and four-color presses for their own projects. Others demanded too much control.

But at last, a year and a half after starting his search, Carr-Harris found what he was looking for. A state publishing firm called Kniga Publishing

House seemed to offer the right mix. It was a powerful government-owned enterprise, which could push its weight around in the bureaucracy. And it brought to the table a prime retail space on Moscow's famous Gorky Street—the heart of the business and shopping district.

Carr-Harris agreed to contribute $300,000 for 49 percent of a new joint venture called Kniga Printshop. The Soviets paid all local costs of the start-up and obtained a 20-year lease for the shop.

Step Six: Think Small

One of the most reliable rules for doing business in Russia is to *keep your investment small*. The modest size of most franchise investments keeps them precisely within the optimum range.

"If I set up a company for $200,000 in working capital and I put in $300,000 in equipment, and then my $200,000 is repaid over the first couple of years, my total exposure then is just $300,000," says Carr-Harris. "Whatever happens, I don't care. Even if the equipment rots in the shop, we still have another 18 years of leasehold of storefront on Gorky Street, which is probably worth $100,000 rent tomorrow if I want to rent it."

Step Seven: Sell the Russians
on Franchising

Even Americans have trouble understanding how franchising works. Unless you're dealing with an unusually sophisticated Russian, you'll probably have to exert a lot of energy explaining why he should pay good money for something as intangible as a "licensing agreement."

"They couldn't understand why they should pay money to use somebody else's name," says Carr-Harris. "They thought AlphaGraphics should pay *them* for advertising the company!"

During one crucial meeting with the Russians, Carr-Harris and Sloane compared AlphaGraphics' proprietary system to military secrets. That seemed to light a few bulbs in their heads, but the doubts lingered for many months.

Even today, many Russians retain a Marxist prejudice according to which only hard products like boot soles and aluminum extrusion slugs have "real" value. Carr-Harris overcame these notions by emphasizing the concrete advantages of franchising: training programs, software, built-in management systems.

"He learned to explain franchising in terms Soviets could understand," says Nikita Kozmiriouk, a former official for Kniga Publishing.

Step Eight: Abide By the Law . . .
Within Reason

If Carr-Harris had paid too much attention to the existing laws, he never would have gotten to square one. When he opened his shop in March 1989, he literally didn't know if the police would show up at any moment and shut him down.

"Every day the shop was open, 37 different Soviet laws were being broken," he says. "Just to open our doors, we had to get a special exemption for each law. And the day we opened, we were still in violation of a few of them."

For one thing, it was against the law to run a printing press without special state authorization. It was also illegal for a private company to make photocopies. Having presses in the basement was a health violation, ostensibly because there was insufficient ventilation. It was also illegal to keep a photocopier in a room that didn't have a metal door and bars on the windows.

"We just crossed our fingers and opened up anyway," says Carr-Harris. "As a result, when the laws finally changed, we were already up and running."

AlphaGraphics proved fantastically successful. While most joint ventures in Russia were losing money hand over fist, "Kniga Printshop"—the name of the new venture—racked up dollar profits of $100,000 and over 500,000 in ruble profits in its first year. Revenues were $400,000 and 4 million rubles respectively.

Step Nine: Train Your Employees

The cookie-cutter format and rigid operating procedures of a franchise provide precisely the sort of rigorous training regimen the Russians need most.

For Geoffrey Carr-Harris, franchising supplies what Russian management lacks. "The Russians don't understand how to run a sophisticated business," he says. "They run out of supplies because they don't order in time. They have no sense of urgency to increase sales. They don't market. They don't do special offers, don't have a sales force pounding the pavement. They just assume people will come in to shop." But franchising puts the system over the individual.

"Despite our many problems with Russian managers," says Carr-Harris, "the system still works. The procedures, the manuals, the training is all in place. People know that every day you start at 6 a.m. They know that when customers come in, you smile."

"We need franchising," says Nikita Kozmiriouk, now a Russian investment counselor for Carr-Harris's company, Phargo Ltd. "We need the guidance, the standardized systems. On our own, it would take us years to learn how to set up a business."

Franchising also provides a safe management school for those Soviets with potential. "We have a lot of clever, entrepreneurial Soviets working for us. They have a lot to contribute, but right now, they're too wild, too inexperienced, too undisciplined. Through franchising, we can train them to operate the right way."

Of course, just because the proper procedures are listed in the operating manual doesn't mean your Russian partner will comply. Franchising has an answer to this problem. Most franchise agreements contain a clause permitting the franchisor to withdraw the franchise rights should a franchise owner fail to comply with quality standards and proper procedures. This looming threat gives an American franchisee a great deal of bargaining power over an uncooperative Russian partner.

Step Ten: Establish Your Infrastructure

The power of franchising lies in *economies of scale*. Once you have a single unit up and running, and you've mastered its operation, you can then duplicate that success quickly and cheaply on a massive scale, either by opening more franchises yourself, or through subfranchising—selling franchises to others within the geographic area you control.

The infrastructure you establish to serve your original unit will then serve your satellites as they multiply. Thus the gigantic food processing plants which McDonald's built in Russia will someday serve a regional network of hundreds or even thousands of McDonald's outlets. Ditto for the Baskin-Robbins ice cream plant. From a single printing plant, Carr-Harris could serve a number of AlphaGraphics outlets.

Step Eleven: Sell Picks and Shovels

The weakness of most foreign businesses in Russia is that they have no steady hard-currency income. Carr-Harris realized that franchises like AlphaGraphics printshop could provide a core business from which he could expand into other more speculative and interesting ventures.

Inspired by his success, Carr-Harris opened two MicroAge computer franchises in Moscow in May 1990. He holds exclusive development rights for MicroAge and AlphaGraphics throughout the former Soviet states and Eastern Europe, and expects to open at least 20 more franchised outlets over the next two years.

Carr-Harris's business strategy pivots on serving other businesses in Eastern Europe.

"We figured out a long time ago," says Carr-Harris, "the only way to make money in the gold rush is to sell the shovels and picks, to provide services to the prospectors. Trying to find gold yourself is too risky."

The prospectors are flocking to Carr-Harris's trading post. McDonald's orders millions of tray liners from AlphaGraphics. *The Los Angeles Times* beams over a daily Moscow edition via AlphaLink, which Carr-Harris prints and delivers to Muscovite readers hours before it hits the stands in Los Angeles. Carr-Harris also leverages his long experience in Russia by providing consulting services to other foreign business travellers, helping them do everything from chasing down hotel reservations to finding reliable Russian partners.

But, as it was from the beginning, the key source of revenue for Carr-Harris comes from his franchised outlets, low-risk, proven, turnkey businesses targeted directly toward the business customer.

Step Twelve: Recycle Your Rubles

Most Western businessmen eat, sleep, and breathe hard currency. Many even pack up and go home when they find how hard it is to squeeze dollars from the Russian economy. But Carr-Harris has become a master at reinvesting rubles.

"This country is filled with brainpower, skilled people, equipment and facilities," says Carr-Harris, "much of which can be bought for rubles."

Building from the secure base of his franchise operations, Carr-Harris has taken his millions of rubles in earnings and set up a spidery network of highly speculative—and often highly lucrative—deals across the former Soviet states.

Carr-Harris tells how one military factory in Minsk, devastated by defense cutbacks, was forced to go into consumer products. "These guys had worked on the Soviet space shuttle," says Carr-Harris. "They didn't want to make ironing boards and toasters for a living."

Carr-Harris gave the managers an attractive alternative. He offered half a million rubles worth of equipment, if they would develop and produce computer plotters, ink-jet printers, and other high-tech hardware for the Russian market. They jumped at the chance. Revenues are already pouring in from national sales.

"Companies like this, that already have experience with Western marketing and management, will make ideal partners later on for foreign corporations," says Carr-Harris. "We'll be able to sell shares for millions of dollars. Every ruble we invest here today will be worth $10 a few years from now."

"This is the sort of project I really live for," says Carr-Harris. "I couldn't frankly care less about running a printshop. But these little franchised businesses give me a secure base from which I can do more interesting sorts of things."

Franchising: The Secret Engine of Privatization

Russia is still a profoundly bureaucratic country, where your ability to win over powerful officials to your cause can often spell the difference between success and failure. Ordinarily, purveyors of consumer goods and services take a back seat in Russia's scale of national priorities to importers of sexier, high-tech materiel. But whether you choose to enter Russia as a franchisor or a franchisee, you may find it advantageous to point out to relevent officials the extraordinary solution which franchising brings to one of Russia's biggest political headaches—privatization.

So says franchise attorney Phillip Zeidman, a partner in the Washington law firm, Brownstein, Zeidman and Lore. Zeidman has worked intensively with international organizations like East Europe Law, the U.S. Agency for International Development (AID) and the Organization for Economic Cooperation and Development (OECD) to push the franchise solution in Russia and other former East Bloc countries.

Below, Zeidman details some of the key benefits of franchising for Russia's developing economy. For more information on franchising in Russia, see App. B.

Advantage One: Provides a Training Ground for Fledgling Entrepreneurs

"Franchising is the perfect psychological solution for the new breed of Russian businessman who wants to own shops but is fearful of losing his savings in a shifting economy," says Zeidman. "Many of them are ready to go into business, but not yet ready for full independence."

As a franchisee, Russia's business neophytes will get help with shop design, reliable access to supplies, services, advertising, as well as to bank loans. Being attached to a major Western company gives them a much-needed feeling of security, as well as a golden opportunity to learn Western sales, marketing and management standards.

Many in Eastern Europe apparently understand the importance of thse advantages. When McDonald's advertised its intention to sell franchises to Hungarian citizens, hundreds of offers jammed the phone lines. Many said they were prepared to fork over the entire franchise fee of 4.3 million forints ($57,000) on the spot. Most U.S. franchisors would keel over from shock if a single advertisement generated so many attractive offers in the States.

Advantage Two: Provides a Safety
Net for Dying State Enterprises

Perhaps the worst nightmare of privatization officials in Russia is that nobody will show up for the firesale, when the state industries are placed on the auction block. Franchising provides a means of dividing up the gigantic "pie" of state-owned enterprises into small, bite-sized chunks, which can be more easily disposed of.

"Many of the existing state enterprises, such as hotel chains, tourism companies, and distribution facilities are already structured and managed in a way that is not very different from the franchise concept," says Zeidman. "They share the same trade name and operate under a common system. These enterprises can be privatized by selling them outright in their present centralized form, or they could be privatized by selling the individual units as franchises within a network."

Consider, for example, the Russian savings bank, Sberbank, with over 25,000 branch offices. That's more than twice the number of McDonald's franchises in the world. Such unwieldy national networks could be divided up among managers and employees, thus reducing the disastrous unemployment which is expected to accompany privatization. This would be superior to the standard stock ownership plans being implemented by many Russian organizations, for it would put many employees in charge of their own individual businesses, in many cases dealing with jobs similar to what they had been trained to do in the past.

Advantage Three: Provides a
Distribution Infrastructure

"For foreign companies, the franchise format provides the best way to bypass Russia's broken-down distribution system," says Zeidman. "Franchising increases the speed and efficiency by which goods are distributed. With its own network and its own shops, a company can be sure that its products actually get on the shelves."

Such ready-made distribution systems make it financially viable for Western investors to build large-scale factories for making consumer goods. Thus, existing plans for a nationwide network of efficient retail outlets helped McDonald's and Baskin-Robbins executives justify their plans to build expensive hamburger and bun factories and ice cream processing plants.

Advantage Four: Provides a Support
System for Existing Private Businesses

Many of the shops and service businesses which have already been privatized are struggling for want of distribution support. *Retro-franchis-*

ing—the practice of converting an existing retail business into a franchise—
could save many of them from bankruptcy.

Advantage Five: Lightning Speed

Perhaps the most compelling advantage of franchising is the incredible
speed with which a good franchise concept can spread across the nation.

"In the period of franchising's greatest growth in the United States,"
says Zeidman, "systems often went from zero franchised units to double
or sometimes even triple digit numbers of units within a year. The scope
of what has to be accomplished in the former Soviet republics makes speed
an imperative."

A Worldwide Movement

Franchising is far more than a peculiar medicine for the sick nations of
Eastern Europe and the CIS. It is truly a worldwide movement, which
promises to have a profound impact upon the global economy of the
twenty-first century.

Major corporations are even now experimenting with franchised distribution systems for products which they have traditionally dispensed
through wholly owned outlets. Governments in many regions of the world
are examining the possibility of privatizing state-supplied services through
franchising. Even in America, fast-growing franchises like Mail Boxes Etc.
have begun to provide serious competition for the U.S. Post Office.

To a far greater extent than most of us realize, the world of tomorrow
will be a *franchised* world. Business pioneers like yourself can ride that
crest of opportunity to unimaginable riches simply by helping Russia wake
up to the exciting possibilities of franchising.

8

What's Hot, What's Not

Regions of Opportunity

In this chapter, I will identify the hottest industries and the hungriest markets in Russia. I will describe the cornucopia of opportunities found in different regions of Russia as well as in the other former Soviet states.

Why Talk About the Non-Russian Republics?

Strictly speaking, this book focuses only on the *Russian* boom. However, you'll discover that it's hard to draw a sharp line between Russia and the other republics, once you actually start doing business over there.

Before the coup, Soviet planners enforced an artificial division of labor between republics to prevent any one republic from becoming too self-sufficient. Uzbekistan was turned into a vast cotton farm but was unable to feed or clothe its own people. While energy-poor southern Kazakhstan drew its electricity from Kyrgyzstan, energy-rich northern Kazakhstan supplied electricity to Siberia. There was often no rhyme or reason for these interlocking arrangements. They seemed to be set up simply to prevent republics from breaking away.

Today, the republics love to trumpet their "independence." But they remain welded to one another by indissoluble commercial links. A factory in the Urals might have its best customers in Kazakhstan and its key suppliers in Belarus. A Russian retail chain might use a Ukrainian trucking company, while an electrolytic metal refining plant in Tajikistan imports its engineers from Vladivostok. Every nationality seems to migrate freely back and forth across republican borders for work and trade.

Interrepublican Trade in Chaos

Even before the breakup of the Soviet Union in December 1991, trade between the republics had started to break down. Official CIS statistics show that the volume of consumer goods traded between republics dropped 50 percent during the first nine months of 1991 as compared to the same period in 1990. Deliveries of coal went down 30 percent, shipments of trucks, buses, passenger cars, and tractors dropped 40 percent, and the trade in metal-cutting machine tools was reduced by half.

Some of these dropoffs are the results of mini-"trade wars" which the republics have unleashed upon one another, as they jockey for advantage with wild price increases and draconian import and export restrictions. Technical problems such as difficulties in making payments across republican borders and questions about exchange rates for new local currencies also contribute to the problem.

Nevertheless, the republics will continue to trade heavily with one another as they have for centuries. Indeed, the private sector may already be taking the bull by the horns. The flourishing black market trade between republics probably makes up already for much of the dropoff in official trade statistics.

The Winners: Azerbaijan, Turkmenistan, and Kazakhstan

Certain republics will benefit from the breakdown in trade with Russia. Chief among these, according to PlanEcon analysts, are Kazakhstan (with its oil, natural gas, and metals), oil-rich Azerbaijan, Turkmenistan (with its natural gas), and Uzbekistan (with its gold and cotton). In the past, these republics had a raw deal, trading their valuable resources to Russia for disadvantageous ruble prices. Now they can sell to any country in the world for hard currency.

Money from energy and raw materials exports may soon allow these republics to greatly increase their imports of items from abroad which they could never before afford.

The Losers: Moldova, Belarus, and the Baltic Republics

Hard times will hit those republics which have been most dependent on Russian trade. Poor in natural resources, the republics of Moldova, Belarus, and the Baltics have traditionally traded manufactured goods for oil, gas, and raw materials from Russia and the other republics.

Now these republics have to pay world market prices for these raw materials. But how can they afford them? Their low-quality manufactures cannot be sold in the West for hard currency. So these republics are caught in a squeeze.

Each of these fledgling nations is searching for its own solution, with varying degrees of success. But until their factories learn to produce Western-quality goods, they are in for a rough time.

The Russian Uni-Culture

The ties between republics run much deeper than commerce. Centuries of common history unite them. Universal schooling in the Russian language has forged a mass culture which changes little from Smolensk to Samarkand. Moreover, generations of intermarriage have woven dense webs of blood relations across republican borders. Such intimate bonds will not be sundered easily. So if you want to do business in Russia, you should resign yourself to eventually dealing with her sister republics as well.

Where Are Foreigners Investing?

Of all the republics, Russia is by far the most popular target for foreign investors, for reasons which will be made clear in the following discussions. Indeed, the city of Moscow itself has drawn a hugely disproportionate number of foreign ventures, as shown in Fig. 8.1.

Which Republic Is Right for You?

Some business pioneers may have specific reasons for being interested in the non-Russian republics, whether these be personal ethnic ties or the availability of a particular natural resource. You must exercise shrewd judgment before making your move. Table 8.1, assembled by researchers at PlanEcon, will help you gain a feel for the relative strengths and weaknesses of the former Soviet republics.

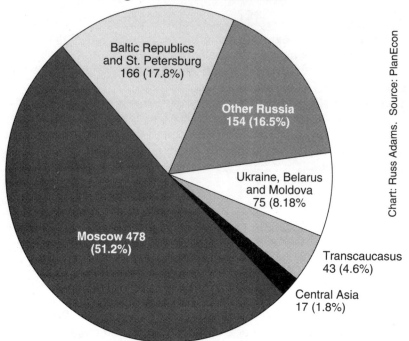

Moscow is the Mecca for Foreign Business Pioneers

Baltic Republics and St. Petersburg 166 (17.8%)

Other Russia 154 (16.5%)

Ukraine, Belarus and Moldova 75 (8.18%

Moscow 478 (51.2%)

Transcaucasus 43 (4.6%)

Central Asia 17 (1.8%)

Chart: Russ Adams.   Source: PlanEcon

Figure 8.1. Geographic distribution of foreign joint ventures as of October 1, 1989—the last date for which such data is available. *(Source: PlanEcon.)*

The following discussion is an overview of the 15 former Soviet republics including the 11 constituent republics of the CIS and the "breakaway republics" of Estonia, Latvia, Lithuania, and Georgia, giving some idea of the size and nature of their economies, and the opportunities contained therein. Statistical and other data on these pages was drawn from PlanEcon, the CIA, the U.S. Department of Commerce, the International Monetary Fund, the 1992 Europa Yearbook, and other sources. The economic "prognoses" for each republic are largely adapted from forecasts in *PlanEcon Report*, as are the tables of imports and exports for each republic. (For further information, see App. C.) We'll begin with Russia itself.

Russia

Size of Economy (Projected 1993 GNP). $699.5 billion or 60 percent of the total for all former Soviet republics.

Table 8.1. Relative Attractiveness to Foreign Investors of the Former Soviet Republics *(Source: PlanEcon)*

(A = Outstanding prospects; C = Average; F = Dismal Prospects)

	Russia	Ukraine	Belarus	Lith.	Latvia	Estonia	Moldova	Georgia
Overall	B	C	C	B	B	B	F	D
Reform prospects	B	C	D	B	A	A	F	D
Market size	A	B	C	D	D	F	F	D
Natural resource endowment	A	B	D	F	F	D	F	C
Infrastructure	B	B	B	A	A	A	C	C
Receptivity to foreign investment	C	C	C	B	B	B	D	D
Foreign aid prospects	A	C	C	A	A	A	D	D
Education/labor skills	B	B	B	B	A	A	D	F
Work ethic/discipline	C	C	C	B	A	A	D	B
Geographic location	B	B	C	A	A	A	C	C
Foreign policy problems	B	C	A	C	C	C	F	D
Political stability	C	C	A	B	B	B	F	F

	Azerbaijan	Armenia	Kazakhstan	Uzbekistan	Kyrgyzstan	Tajikistan	Turkmenistan
Overall	D	C	B	D	D	F	C
Reform prospects	D	A	C	F	C	F	C
Market size	D	D	C	C	F	F	D
Natural resource endowment	C	F	B	C	D	D	C
Infrastructure	D	D	D	F	F	F	D
Receptivity to foreign investment	C	A	B	C	D	D	C
Foreign aid prospects	D	B	C	F	C	C	C
Education/labor skills	D	B	D	F	F	F	F
Work ethic/discipline	D	B	C	D	D	D	D
Geographic location	C	F	D	D	D	F	D
Foreign policy problems	F	F	B	C	C	D	B
Political stability	F	B	B	C	C	F	A

Population.   148.5 million people or 51.2 percent of the total ex-Soviet population. 82 percent Russians, four percent Tatars, three percent Ukrainians.

Land Area.   6.6 million square miles or 76.7 percent of ex-Soviet territory.

Three Russias, Not One

There are really *three Russias,* not just one. Students of Romanov trivia (and probably no one else) will recall that the formal titles of the Tsar used to begin with the phrase, "Emperor and Autocrat of *all the Russias.*" This was a reference to the three traditional "Russias," called Great Russia, Little Russia and White Russia, or, as we know them today, Russia, Ukraine and Belarus (pronounced byel-uh-ROOS). In centuries past, the three Russias were also sometimes referred to respectively as Black, Red and White Russia. "Belarus" simply means "White Russia," while "Ukraine" comes from the Russian word *okraina,* meaning "borderland" or "frontier."

Strange as it may seem, the Ukrainians are really the *original* Russians. A thousand years ago, the Russian state was called the *Rus,* and had its capital in Kiev, now the capital of *Ukraine.* In other words, Ukraine and Russia were *one and the same.* At that time, all Russians everywhere spoke the same language.

The Origin of Russia

How did we end up with three different "Russias" out of one? Here's what happened. Starting from the middle of the 11th century, wave after wave of invaders poured into Russia (or "Ukraine," if you prefer). First came the Polovtsy from the East, then the Mongols. Later, from the West, came Poles and Lithuanians.

These conquests and partitions divided the Russian "family" into three isolated parts. Over the centuries, their styles of speech veered ever farther apart, until at last they grew as unintelligible to one another as Spaniards are to Italians. However, to this day, scholars still debate whether Russian, Ukrainian and Byelorussian should be called separate languages or merely dialects of a single tongue. On a more dangerous note, passions continue to fly as white-hot as if the Polovtsy had ravaged only yesterday over the question of whether these scattered "Russian" peoples ought to be one nation or three.

"Our people came to be divided into three branches by the terrible calamity of the Mongol invasion, and by Polish colonization," lamented Alexander Solzhenitsyn in an impassioned 1990 essay. "All the talk of a separate Ukrainian people . . . is a recently invented falsehood."

All this notwithstanding, I will hereafter concede to popular usage, according to which only the northern or "Great" Russians are to be called "Russian."

The Russian Colossus

Russia is not only the largest of the republics (encompassing one-sixth of the earth's surface) and the most populous (with over twice as many people as Germany), but it is by far the richest in natural resources and the most heavily industrialized. No other republic comes close to rivalling Russia's overwhelming economic power. (See Fig. 8.2.)

The Russian Land

Encompassing more than three-fourths of the land area of the CIS, Russia's terrain varies from the flat Russian plain, to the towering Ural mountains which separate Europe from Asia. Siberia is a gigantic plateau, or "steppe,"

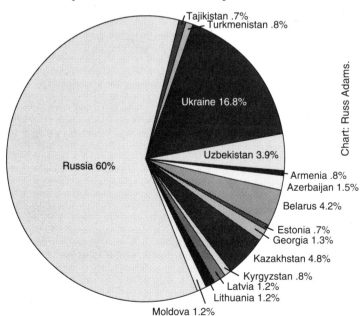

Russia Dominates the Other Republics Economically

Tajikistan .7%
Turkmenistan .8%
Ukraine 16.8%
Uzbekistan 3.9%
Russia 60%
Armenia .8%
Azerbaijan 1.5%
Belarus 4.2%
Estonia .7%
Georgia 1.3%
Kazakhstan 4.8%
Kyrgyzstan .8%
Latvia 1.2%
Lithuania 1.2%
Moldova 1.2%

Chart: Russ Adams.

Figure 8.2. Comparative size of economics of the former Soviet republics, shown as percentage of total projected 1993 GNP. (*Source: PlanEcon.*)

covered with forests in the south and with barren permafrost in the north. The eastern and southern extremities of Siberia are ringed with mountains, while the Kamchatka peninsula lying at the extreme Eastern rim of Russia is a sparsely inhabited forest zone, interspersed with hot-water geysers and volcanoes.

Russia's Natural Resources

Russia's natural wealth staggers the imagination, although most of that wealth is concentrated in Siberia, where a hostile climate makes it difficult to recover. Russia contains *nearly half the coal, oil, and natural gas reserves of the entire world*. Although most of the oil is in Siberia, the oil deposits between the Volga and Ural rivers north of Kazakhstan are so rich, that the region is called the "second Baku," after the famous oil fields of the Caucasus.

Russia's great forest, the Taiga, stretches across more than 2 million square miles of Siberia. It is larger than either the Amazon jungle or America's lower 48 states. In that dense, virgin wilderness of birches and pines live tigers, giant brown bears, moose, elk, sable, roe deer, and wolves. It contains over a third of the world's timber. Russia's forests yield the richest source of prime furs in the world, many of them trapped by Udegei tribesmen who dwell in log cabins in the Taiga's depths.

Russia's coastal waters offer an unlimited abundance of cod, salmon, and herring.

Russia has gold and diamond reserves that may well dwarf those of South Africa. She also has enormous untapped stores of uranium, asbestos, mercury, platinum, rhodium, palladium, copper, tin, bauxite, potash, magnesium, vanadium, lignite, nickel, zinc, phosphates, sulfur, pyrites, molybdenum, tungsten, mica, cobalt, iron ore, manganese, salt, and precious gems, as well as a river system which provides enormous hydroelectric power. Locations of Russia's principal natural resources can be found on the map of "Natural Resources and Transport" in Fig. 8.3, on page 104.

Agriculture in Russia

Russia contains some of the richest farmland in the world—yielding large crops of oats, rye, wheat, potatoes, and flax—and accounting for about 48 percent of the total agricultural *net material product* (NMP) of the former Soviet states.

The wheat fields of the Caspian plain, near Krasnodar and Stavropol are renowned for their fertility. Russia's farmers also produce dairy products. Although Russia remains a net importer of food, due to her inefficient collectivized farm system, land reform is expected to restore Russia soon to her past position as a food exporter. It is to be noted that Armenia's land reform resulted in a 50 percent increase in agricultural output in the first year. An increase on that scale would restore Russia almost immediately to food self-sufficiency.

Russia's long winters and scorching summers are a terror to farmers, and almost half of her lands lie in the permafrost zone. *Permafrost* is a layer of earth which remains permanently frozen all year round. In parts of Siberia, it can extend as deep as 1000 feet or more. However, the top few feet do thaw in the summer and Siberians manage to raise wheat, oats, cabbage, and other crops. Siberian tomatoes are grown in hothouses.

By May 1991, as many as 20,144 private farms had been established, but most were only about 41 hectares in area. Land reform has been proceeding slowly since late 1990, but political pressures are building for a more rapid privatization of Russia's farms. Such a development could transform Russia quickly into a major food exporter.

Distribution is a major problem for Russian agriculture because of the extreme shortage of large-scale, food storage facilities within easy distance of its farms. Food must be transported hundreds of miles to storage, and often never makes it because of the shortage of trucks and freight trains. Food distribution is therefore a prime target for foreign investors.

Agricultural output of Russia is broken down by region, opposite the map of "Economic Regions of Russia" in Fig. 8.4 on page 108.

Russia's Leading Industries

Russia accounts for about 61.9 percent of the total industrial capacity of the former Soviet Union, measured in net material product (NMP). Its principal strength lies in such "extractive" industries as the recovery and refining of petroleum, natural gas, gold, uranium, palladium, platinum, rhodium, and other strategic metals. Russia also produces formidable quantities of crude steel, copper, aluminum, as well as industrial chemicals such as processed sulfur, anhydrous ammonia, potassium chloride, and urea.

Russia has a well-developed light industrial sector, producing cotton and woolen textiles and consumer goods. But it also produces large amounts of machine building equipment, construction materials, and food processing equipment, as well as cars, trucks, tractors and other heavy vehicles.

Among its many famous factories are the world-renowned Kamaz Heavy Trucks factory, located on the Kama River, about 120 miles east of Kazan. American, British, German, and Italian firms built the plant in the early 1970s. It is now considered the largest truck factory in the world, producing some 120,000 trucks per year. Kamaz became one of the first Soviet

Figure 8.3a. Natural resources and transport. *(Sources: CIA, Hammond Atlas.)*

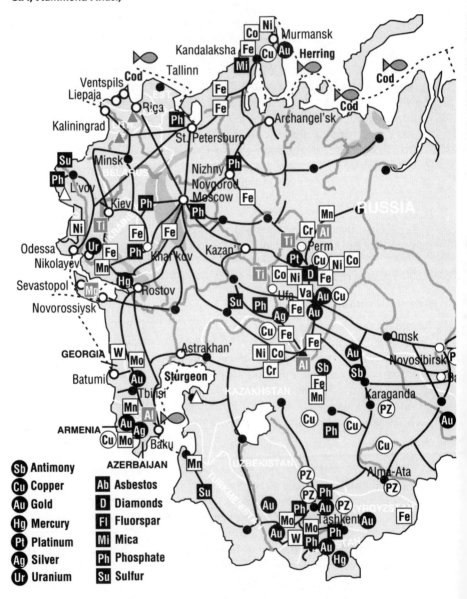

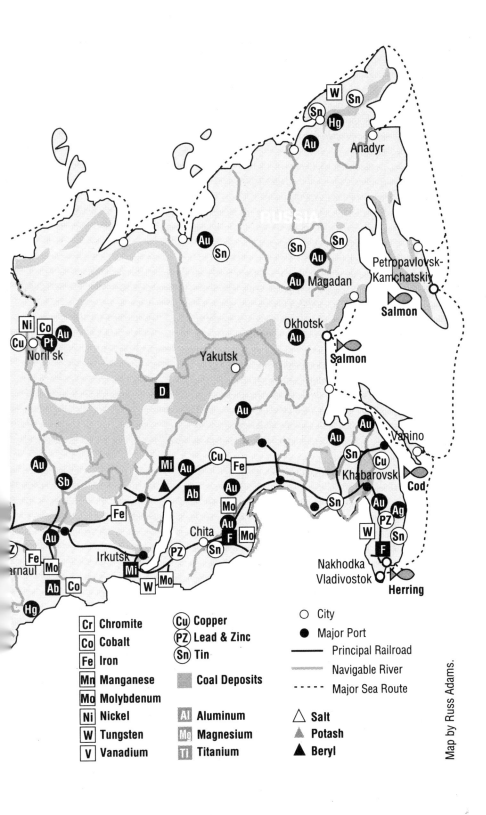

Anadyr

RUSSIA

W · Sn
Sn · Hg
Au

Petropavlovsk-
Kamchatskiy

Au · Sn
Sn · Au
Au · Magadan

Okhotsk
Au

Salmon

Salmon

Ni · Co · Au
Cu · Pt
Noril'sk

Yakutsk

D

Au

Au

Au

Vanino

Au

Au · Sn · Cu
Khabarovsk

Cod

Au
Sb

Mi · Au
▲
Ab

Cu · Fe

Au

Mo

Sn

Au · Ag
PZ
W · Sn

Fe

Au · F
Chita   Sn   Mo

Au
PZ

Nakhodka
Vladivostok

F

Au
Fe
Mo
arnaul

Mi
W · Mo

Irkutsk

Herring

Ab · Co

Hg

Cr	Chromite	Cu	Copper
Co	Cobalt	PZ	Lead & Zinc
Fe	Iron	Sn	Tin
Mn	Manganese		
Mo	Molybdenum	▨	Coal Deposits
Ni	Nickel		
W	Tungsten	Al	Aluminum
V	Vanadium	Mg	Magnesium
		Ti	Titanium

○ City
● Major Port
── Principal Railroad
～～ Navigable River
---- Major Sea Route

△ Salt
▲ Potash
▲ Beryl

Map by Russ Adams.

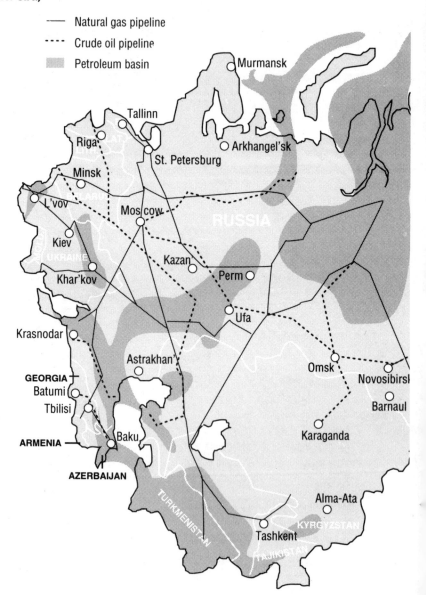

Figure 8.3b. Petroleum deposits in the former Soviet States. (*Source: CIA.*)

Legend:
- —— Natural gas pipeline
- ---- Crude oil pipeline
- ▨ Petroleum basin

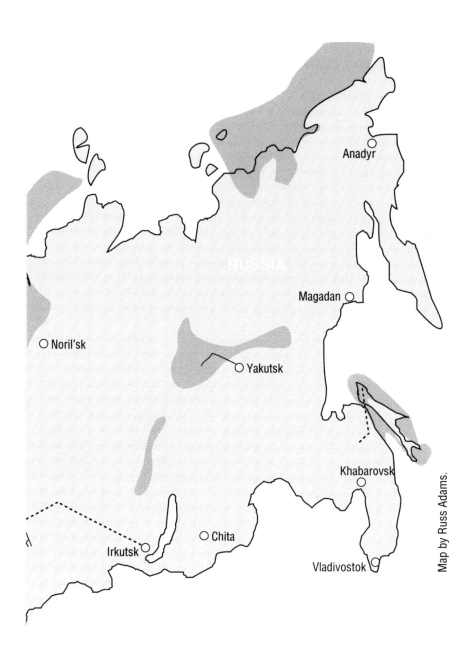

Map by Russ Adams.

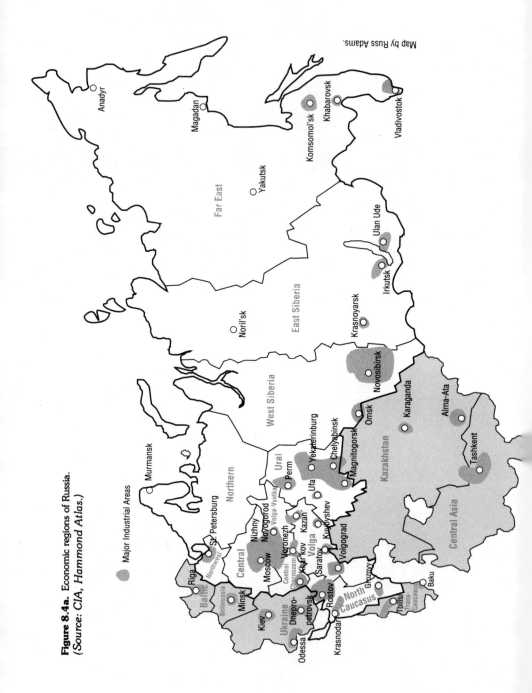

Figure 8.4a. Economic regions of Russia. *(Source: CIA, Hammond Atlas.)*

Map by Russ Adams.

● Major Industrial Areas

Anadyr
Magadan
Far East
Komsomol'sk
Khabarovsk
Vladivostok
Yakutsk
Ulan Ude
Irkutsk
Noril'sk
East Siberia
Krasnoyarsk
West Siberia
Novosibirsk
Karaganda
Alma-Ata
Omsk
Ekaterinburg
Chelyabinsk
Kazakhstan
Tashkent
Ural
Magnitogorsk
Perm
Central Asia
Ufa
Murmansk
Kuybyshev
Volga-Vyatka
Kazan'
Nizhny Novgorod
Voronezh
Volga
Saratov
St. Petersburg
Northern
Khar'kov
Volgograd
Central
Moscow
Central Chernozem
Riga
Northwest
Grozny
Baku
Rostov
Trans-Caucasus
Baltic
Minsk
Belorussia
North Caucasus
Tbilisi
Kiev
Ukraine
Dnepro-petrovsk
Krasnodar
Odessa

108

Concentration of Industry, by Region

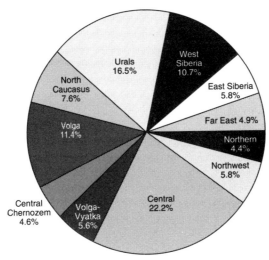

Figure 8.4b. Industrial output is shown as a percentage of Russia's total industrial Net Material Product (NMP) in 1985—the last year for which such data is available.

Concentration of Agriculture, by Region

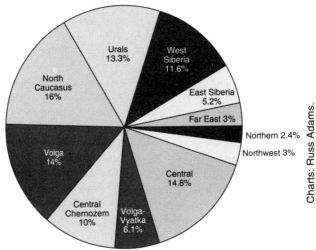

Figure 8.4c. Agrigultural output is shown as a percentage of Russia's total agricultural Net Material Product (NMP) in 1985—the last year for which such data is available. *(Source: Plan Econ.)*

Figure 8.4d. Land use in the former Soviet states. (CIA.)

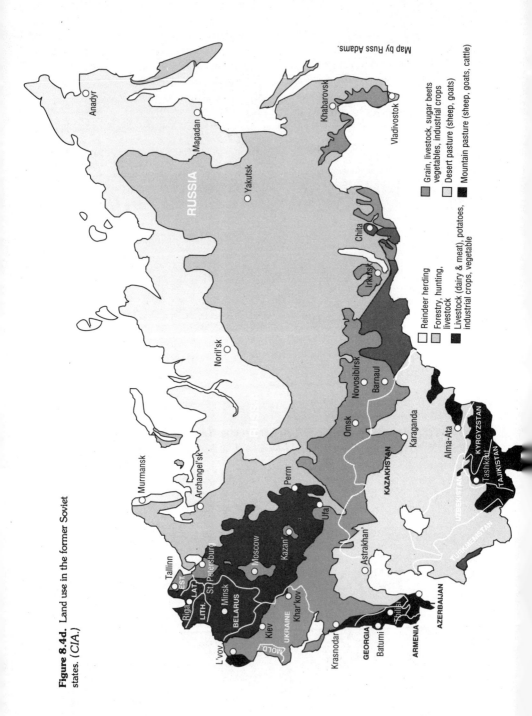

Legend:

- Reindeer herding
- Forestry, hunting, livestock
- Livestock (dairy & meat), potatoes, industrial crops, vegetable
- Grain, livestock, sugar beets vegetables, industrial crops
- Desert pasture (sheep, goats)
- Mountain pasture (sheep, goats, cattle)

Map by Russ Adams.

industries to "go private" in June 1990, selling about 30 percent of its authorized stock to 1200 suppliers and major customers and the rest to its 170,000 workers. About 50 percent of the stock has been retained by governmental entities.

The town of Togliatti on the Volga is the site of the famous Italian-Soviet Fiat Volga Auto Works (VAZ), which makes about 700,000 cars per year (70 percent of the total produced in the former Soviet states). Fiat attempted to buy a 30 percent ownership stake in February 1992, but offered only $1 billion against the $4 billion asking price. The outcome is unknown as of this writing.

Russia is also a world leader in the manufacture and export of arms, and her burgeoning R&D sector promises that, in the future, Russia will become a global powerhouse in such areas as medicine, aerospace, advanced materials production, metallurgy, computer software, as well as laser and fiber optic technology.

Russia is a net exporter of electricity, generated through its extensive hydroelectric, fossil and nuclear plants.

Major Industrial Regions

Accounting for 22.2 percent of all industrial output, the "Central Economic Region" around Moscow is clearly the primary manufacturing hub for the entire former Soviet states, followed by the Urals and the Donets Basin in the Ukraine. Other major manufacturing regions of the CIS can be found around St. Petersburg, Riga (in Latvia), the Kuznetsk Basin, Volga Valley, as well as parts of Siberia, Belarus, Lithuania, and northern Kazakhstan.

The major industrial regions of Russia and of the other former Soviet states are shown on the map in Fig. 8.4 on pages 108 to 110, while the map in Fig. 8.5, "Industries of the Former Soviet States" on page 112, gives the locations of specific industries.

Russia's Foreign Trade

Russia does a significant amount of trade with America, to which it sells mostly metals and chemicals, along with alcoholic beverages, furs, fish and tractors. Other important Western trade partners are Germany and the Scandinavian countries.

Russia's leading trade partners are still its fellow CIS republics, but Russia is far more self-sufficient than any of the rest. Only about 18 percent of Russia's NMP comes from exports to other republics, and about 8.6 percent from exports to other countries. (See Figs. 8.6 and 8.7.)

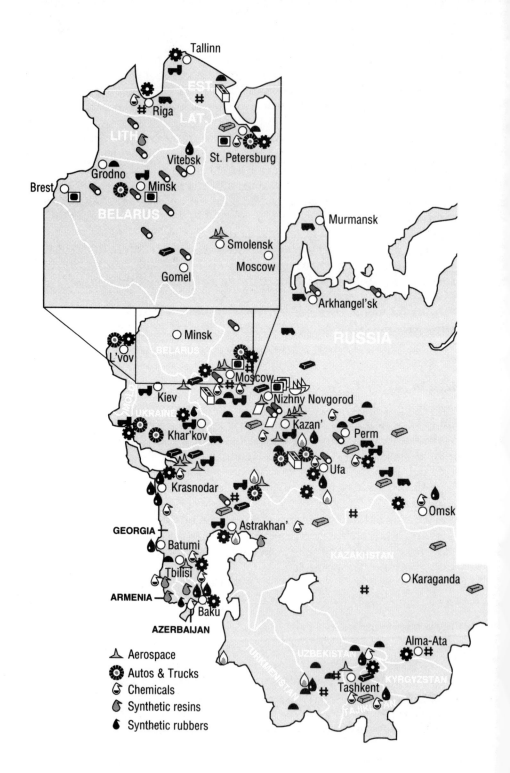

Tallinn

Riga

St. Petersburg

Vitebsk

Grodno

Brest

Minsk

BELARUS

LITH.

LAT.

EST.

Murmansk

Smolensk

Moscow

Gomel

Arkhangel'sk

RUSSIA

Minsk

BELARUS

L'vov

Kiev

UKRAINE

Moscow

Nizhny Novgorod

Kazan'

Perm

Khar'kov

Ufa

Krasnodar

Omsk

Astrakhan'

KAZAKHSTAN

GEORGIA

Batumi

Karaganda

Tbilisi

ARMENIA

Baku

Alma-Ata

AZERBAIJAN

UZBEKISTAN

KYRGYZSTAN

TURKMENISTAN

Tashkent

TAJIKISTAN

Aerospace

Autos & Trucks

Chemicals

Synthetic resins

Synthetic rubbers

112

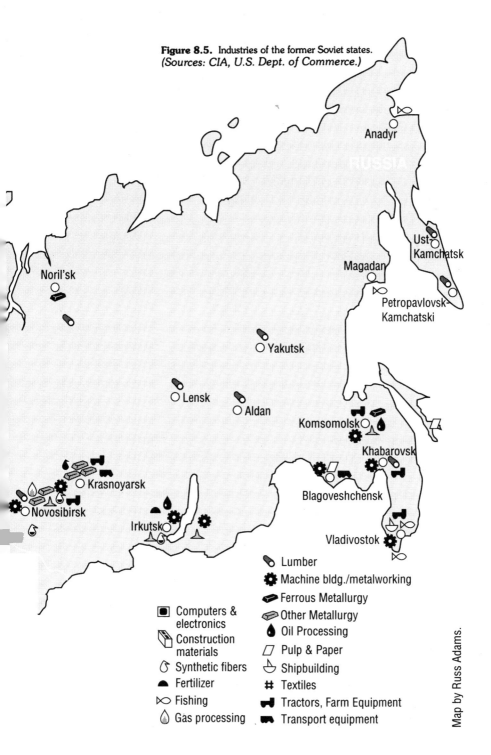

Figure 8.5. Industries of the former Soviet states. (Sources: CIA, U.S. Dept. of Commerce.)

RUSSIA

Anadyr

Noril'sk

Ust-Kamchatsk

Magadan

Petropavlovsk-Kamchatski

Yakutsk

Lensk

Aldan

Komsomolsk

Khabarovsk

Krasnoyarsk

Blagoveshchensk

Novosibirsk

Irkutsk

Vladivostok

Lumber

Machine bldg./metalworking

Ferrous Metallurgy

Computers & electronics

Other Metallurgy

Oil Processing

Construction materials

Pulp & Paper

Synthetic fibers

Shipbuilding

Fertilizer

Textiles

Fishing

Tractors, Farm Equipment

Gas processing

Transport equipment

Map by Russ Adams.

113

Principal Russian Exports (1991)

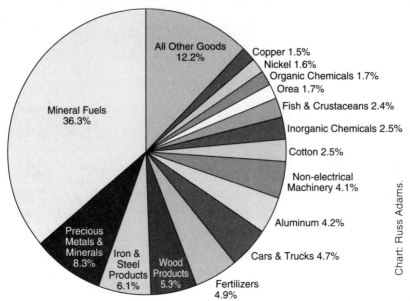

Figure 8.6. Russia's total exports to non-Soviet countries came to $36.9 billion in 1991. *(Source: PlanEcon.)*

Russia's Arms Exports

Weapons have traditionally been Russia's second-largest export, after oil and gas, acccounting for 15.2 percent of total exports from the Soviet Union in 1989. Although defense spending has dropped sharply since 1988, Russia continues exporting large quantities of arms from diesel submarines to advanced aircraft, tanks, and air defense missile systems, primarily to Third World countries, such as Iran and India. In 1992, Yeltsin authorized the sale of 1600 military aircraft. Russia's black market weapons dealers have found a lucrative market for small arms, artillery and armored vehicles in the wartorn areas of the Caucasus and Moldova.

Nevertheless, arms exports appear insignificant on recent official trade figures. In 1991, for example, the Russians claimed to have exported only 29 million rubles worth of weapons—a ridiculously small figure. PlanEcon analysts believe the Russians are camouflaging arms exports under such innocuous- sounding categories as "machinery," "iron and steel products," or even "cars and trucks." In fact, Russia's weapons exports probably accounted for up to 7.5 percent of its exports in 1991, say PlanEcon researchers.

Principal Russian Imports (1991)

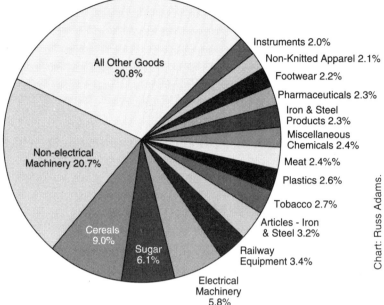

Figure 8.7. Russia's total imports from non-Soviet countries came to $25.7 billion in 1991. *(Source: PlanEcon.)*

Work "From the Outside In"

Experienced insiders advise American business pioneers to "work from the outside in." This means you should develop markets around the periphery of the country before delving deep into Russia's interior. Much like an invading army wary of overextending its supply lines, business pioneers who "work from the outside in," retain critical access to neighboring foreign countries, where they can find supplies, services, hard-currency customers and other logistical support.

For example, the Primorsky Krai, an extension of land on Russia's Pacific coast containing the major ports of Nakhodka and Vladivostok, is only hours away from Japan and Korea by boat, or 30 minutes by plane. Its proximity to these highly developed markets suggests business opportunities that would be unthinkable in Siberia's deep interior. For example, some entrepreneurs have undertaken to provide dirt cheap transhipment points, satellite stations, storage facilities, hotels and conference centers to serve Japanese businesses, who are notoriously cramped for space on their own tiny island.

Similarly, St. Petersburg and Kaliningrad, both major ports on the Baltic Sea, provide immediate access to Scandinavia and Western Europe.

The "Finnish Window"

Many foreign firms have found it easier to enter the Russian market via the *Finnish window.* They form partnerships with Finnish companies in order to gain the advantage of the Finns' unique experience, contacts and rapport with the Russians.

"By taking advantage of the Finnish window, U.S. firms can save a lot of time and money," advised international management consultant Robert J. Radway in an editorial in *The Wall Street Journal.*

Zones of Hard Currency Saturation

As in every republic, sellers of consumer goods in Russia will find the greatest opportunities in those major cities and tourist centers where a high density of foreigners has created zones of hard-currency saturation. Areas rich in natural resources, such as oil, gold, diamonds, and natural gas, also tend to have high concentrations of foreign currency.

Free Economic Zones (FEZs)

To encourage foreign investment, the Russian government has set up *free trade zones* (FTZs) or *free economic zones* (FEZs) around certain cities. Originally, 11 cities were designated, but only three seem to have moved forward to implement Yeltsin's plan. The three are Kaliningrad, Nakhodka and Vyborg. Other designated FEZs, like St. Petersburg, Sakhalin, Chita, Altay, Kemerovo, and Novgorod have temporarily dropped out of the program due to bureaucratic infighting.

All of these zones offer tax breaks of some sort. Many place a cap or maximum limit on the overall tax burden for an enterprise. Most will exempt from taxation all profits reinvested in the local economy. In addition, free trade zones reduce or entirely eliminate import and export duties, and greatly simplify the paperwork of foreign trade by eliminating quotas and licensing requirements.

Local authorities in FTZs are given unusual autonomy in registering foreign enterprises, setting tax rates and negotiating leases of state property.

Nizhny Novgorod: Model Freemarket City

Nizhny Novgorod, a veritable Silicon Valley of high-tech Russian industries, has become one of the hottest investment targets for foreign business thanks to an experimental privatization program launched by the International Finance Corporation (IFC), a World Bank affiliate.

Beginning in January 1992, the IFC began implementing plans to auction off some 3000 state-owned retail businesses in the city. Over 800 were sold by September 1, 1992. Most properties have been selling for 20 to 30 times the asking price of the government, with four to five bidders vying for each property.

Formerly known as Gorky, Nizhny Novgorod was long a "closed" city, forbidden to foreign travelers because of its extensive defense-related industries. The very existence of top-secret facilities like the Krasnoe Sormovo Submarine Plant, the Mikoyan Design Bureau (which makes MiG fighter aircraft), and the Scientific Research Institute of Measuring Systems (which makes computers, semiconductors, and automated control systems) was once a closely guarded secret. Now these and other firms have flung wide their doors to foreign investment.

Thanks largely to the efforts of such reformers as Boris Nemtsov, the dynamic 32-year-old governor of the region, mayor Dmitri Bednyakov, and regional council chairman Yevgeny Krestianinov, the IFC experiment has proven a brilliant success. Nizhny Novgorod's rapid privatization program and plethora of prosperous local entrepreneurs has made Russia's third largest city (population 1.4 million) an unusually fertile soil for foreign investment.

A similar IFC program is planned for the city of Volgograd and for a third, as-yet-unannounced, municipality.

Siberia: The Final Frontier

In 1581, a cossack named Yermak Timofeyevich crossed the Ural Mountains into Asia with a band of 150 men. No Russian had ever set foot there before. Armed with the newest muskets, Yermak and his band of 150 cossacks made quick work of the Tatars who lived on the other side. Yermak returned to Moscow and presented his conquest to the Tsar. It was a country of birch forests and mighty rivers which the Tatars called "Sibir" or "The Sleeping Land." Thus began the 100-year conquest of Siberia. The unsettled East became to the Russians what the Western territories once were to Americans—the frontier. For the next century, Russian settlers rolled relentlessly eastward, lured by furs, gold, timber, and fertile farmland for the taking. Like the American West, Siberia became a magnet for freebooters and adventurers, a wild, lawless land of brawlers and braggarts.

There's only one difference between Siberia and our own Wild West. Siberia *still remains* largely untamed, its vast wealth hardly tapped. Most insiders point to Siberia as the real land of opportunity for foreign investors.

Land Without Limits

Siberia stretches 3400 miles from the Urals to the Pacific Ocean. The whole of Western Europe could easily fit inside of it, or the whole of the United States with half of Canada as well. Yet, in all that vast expanse, Siberia's population is less than 30 million, with most people clustered around the slender thread of the TransSiberian railroad running along the southern border. It is the longest railroad in the world.

There is more natural gas under the ground in Western Siberia than in the whole United States. Siberia contains 90 percent of all bituminous coal in the former Soviet states, 75 percent of the iron ore, 80 percent of the timber, and 80 percent of its water power. Siberia also abounds with gold, silver, and diamonds.

Far Eastern Siberia:
Opportunity Region

Russia is promoting the Far Eastern Economic Region as a special target for foreign investment, offering such lures as a three-year tax holiday for foreign ventures and a profits tax reduced to 10 percent from the normal 35 percent which prevails in the other regions.

For obvious reasons of geography, this region has proven richly appealing to Alaskan companies. Indeed, the Alaska University Center for International Business estimates that there are 87 Alaskan-Siberian joint ventures, including Autogenesis Inc., a firm which makes and rents automated orthopedic devices developed by Russian physician Dr. Gavriil Ilizarov, and Indian Valley Meats, an Anchorage firm which has set up "reindeer sausage" processing plants in the Russian Far East. Indian Valley sells the sausage for rubles in Russia, then earns hard currency by shipping the reindeer antlers to South Korea, where they are valued for medicinal and aphrodisiac qualities.

The Russian Far East is rich in mineral and forestry resources, and is advantageous for its proximity to the rich markets of the Asian Rim.

Prognosis for Russia

Russia's prodigious energy, mineral, and other natural resources make it a good candidate for economic recovery in 1994 through 1995, according to PlanEcon analysts. Like Azerbaijan, Turkmenistan, and Kazakhstan, Russia will gain huge, hard-currency windfalls from exports to Western countries, while sacrificing less-profitable trade with the other republics. Ukraine, Belarus, Moldova, and the three Baltic Republics will be the big losers in this arrangement, losing access to supplies of Russian energy and raw materials whose low price they will never be able to match on world markets.

"Such an economic policy (on Russia's part) would devastate most other republics," concludes *PlanEcon Report*, "and it would assure collapse of the CIS."

Nevertheless, Russia will almost certainly emerge from the fray as a leading world energy supplier on the scale of Saudi Arabia.

Ukraine

Size of Economy (Projected 1993 GNP). $195.4 billion, or 16.8 percent of the total for the former Soviet states.

Land Area.   233,000 square miles, or 2.7 percent of total ex-Soviet territory.

Population.   52 million, or 17.9 percent of total ex-Soviet population. 73 percent Ukrainians, 22 percent Russians.

Natural Resources.   Ukraine's huge Donbass coalfields are among the richest in the world. It also has high-grade iron ore, manganese, lignite, peat, mercury, and titanium. Ukraine's temperate climate gives it an advantage over Russia, most of whose minerals are located in the harsh Siberian wilderness.

Agriculture.   The Ukraine accounts for 17.1 percent of the total agricultural net material product (NMP) of the former Soviet states. Its humus-rich black earth, the famous *chernozem*, is some of the richest in the world. Major crops include wheat, potatoes, sugar beets, cotton, flax, tobacco, soybeans, fruit and vegetables. Cattle and pig breeding are also practiced.

Industry.   Ukraine is a heavily industrialized region, accounting for 16.7 percent of the total CIS industrial NMP, and more than 25 percent of all machine production in the former Soviet states. Its factories produce aircraft, locomotives, railway equipment, tractors and other heavy vehicles, cars, machine tools, chemical equipment, large electrical transformers, agricultural machinery, computers, televisions, and tape recorders. Coal mining and steelmaking are major industries, as is production of petrochemicals, acids, soda, alkaline dyes, and chemical fertilizers.

Principal Ukrainian Exports (to Non-Soviet Countries)

Machinery and equipment (including instruments and
apparatus, and transport equipment) . . . . 28.5 percent

Iron	21.2 percent
Iron and steel products	14.3 percent
Food	6.1 percent
Chemicals	4.4 percent
Fertilizers	3.6 percent
Other	21.9 percent
Total 1991 Exports	$4.8 billion

Note. Ukraine trades heavily with other CIS states. Its exports to other former Soviet republics account for about 39.1 percent of its NMP as compared with only 7.4 percent from exports to other countries.

Principal Imports of Ukraine (from Non-Soviet Countries)

Machinery and equipment (including instruments and apparatus, and transport equipment)	55.2 percent
Textiles, apparel and shoes	18 percent
Essential oils, perfumes and cosmetics	3.8 percent
Pharmaceuticals	2.6 percent
Chemicals	3.4 percent
Food	3.9 percent
Energy	.6 percent
Other	12.5 percent
Total 1991 Imports	$6.7 billion

Note. Ukraine's petroleum and natural gas has traditionally come from Russia, but Iran will probably be an important energy supplier in the future.

Prognosis. Ukraine will face major difficulties in the next few years. The loss of cheap Russian energy and raw materials will hit hard at an economy whose two major resources, food and coal, are unlikely to find good prices or open markets in the developed world. Near-term prospects for Ukraine are, therefore, "not good," according to PlanEcon.

Republic of Belarus

Size of Economy. (Projected 1993 GNP). $48.8 billion rubles, or 4.2 percent of total GNP of the former Soviet states.

Population.   10.2 million people, or 3.5 percent of total ex-Soviet population. 78 percent Byelorussian, 13 percent Russian, 4 percent Polish.

Land Area.   80,000 square miles, or .9 percent of ex-Soviet territory.

Natural Resources.   Belarus has small deposits of petroleum, coal and potassium, but is otherwise poor in natural resources. Its most important resource is peat, which provides fuel for Belarus's electrical power plants.

Agriculture.   About 4.9 percent of the total agricultural NMP of the former Soviet states comes from Belarus. Agriculture yields 23 percent of Belarus's NMP and employs 10 percent of its labor force. About 60 percent of Belarus's agricultural output comes from animal husbandry, with meat, milk and eggs being important products. Belarus also raises such crops as potatoes, barley, rye, flax, wheat, oats, sugar beets, tobacco, buckwheat and vegetables. Land reform is moving slowly, but shows great promise. Private production from the tiny personal plots of collective farmers yields about a quarter of Belarus's total output. Much of Belarus's land is still radioactive from the Chernobyl disaster and cannot be safely cultivated.

Industry.   Industry produces 51 percent of Belarus's total NMP (about 4 percent of the total industrial NMP for the former Soviet states) and employs 31 percent of its workforce. Belarus has long been known for its sophisticated military industries, and is especially strong in radio engineering, electronics, machine building, metalworking, chemical production, agricultural machinery such as fodder harvesting combines, metal-cutting machine tools, and prefabricated construction materials. Byelorussian factories also produce cars, tractors, and other heavy vehicles, refrigerators, furniture and radios. Light industry concentrates on textiles such as silk and woolen fabrics, and consumer goods.

Minsk has long been a top-secret "closed" city where high-tech military production is carried out. The sudden drop in demand for Belarus's military products has left the republic desperate to convert its former defense industries to civilian use, and many foreign businesses have found opportunities in this area.

Principal Imports of Belarus (from Non-Soviet Countries)

Machinery and equipment (nuclear reactors,
boilers, etc.) . . . . 57.2 percent

Chemical products . . . . 8.3 percent

Pharmaceuticals . . . . 4 percent

Plastics and plastic products . . . . 2.8 percent

Textile products . . . .   8.7 percent

Food . . . .   7.7 percent

Other . . . .   11.3 percent

Total 1991 Imports . . . . $2 billion

Note.   Belarus is heavily dependent upon interrepublican trade, mainly with Russia, Ukraine and the Baltics. It imports over 70 percent of its industrial raw materials from these republics, and sells them about 40 percent of its output. Over 90 percent of Belarus's energy or (of about $5 billion worth) is imported.

Principal Exports of Belarus (to Non-Soviet Countries)

Road transport equipment . . . .   36.4 percent

Other machinery and equipment . . . .   20.6 percent

Textile products . . . .   8.2 percent

Organic chemicals . . . .   5.1 percent

Fertilizers . . . .   5 percent

Food . . . .   4.7 percent

Other chemicals . . . .   4.2 percent

Other . . . .   15.8 percent

Total 1991 Exports . . . . $1.6 billion

Note.   About 69.6 percent of Belarus's NMP comes from exports to other former Soviet republics—a higher proportion than for any other republic. Only 6.5 percent of Belarus's NMP comes from exports to countries outside the former USSR.

Prognosis.   Like the Ukraine, Belarus will suffer from the loss of cheap Russian energy and raw materials. Moreover, heavy reliance on vanishing Russian military contracts has already resulted in major disruption of Byelorussian industry. Nevertheless, PlanEcon forecasters are "more up-beat" about Belarus than the Ukraine, largely because of its greater political stability and friendly relations with Russia, ensuring better trade deals with the eastern Goliath.

The Baltic States

The "Baltic" republics of Lithuania, Latvia, and Estonia offer a unique corridor by which foreign investors may enter Russia "through the back door." By far the most "Western" of all former Soviet republics, the Baltic states were once a showcase for Soviet propagandists. They have always been more prosperous than the rest of the republics, their populations better educated, their industry more sophisticated, and their stores better stocked.

It was in the Baltics that Soviet planners placed their most sophisticated industries, including computer production, production of military equipment, of precision medical and electronic instruments, of mini-vans, locomotives, radios, TVs and 80 percent of the pharmaceutical drugs used in Soviet hospitals.

What the Baltics offer to foreigners is a close proximity to major sea lanes and trade routes of Western Europe, with a host of good harbors; a highly developed manufacturing base, with a highly-educated population; and independent governments from which Communists have been thoroughly purged, and which have implemented full-fledged freemarket reforms.

Republic of Lithuania

Size of Economy (Projected 1993 GNP). $14 billion, or 1.2 percent of total GNP for former Soviet states.

Land Area.   25,170 square miles, or .3 percent of total ex-Soviet territory.

Population.   3.8 million, or 1.3 percent of total ex-Soviet population. 80 percent Lithuanians, 9 percent Russians, 7 percent Polish.

Natural Resources.   None to speak of.

Agriculture.   Agriculture accounts for about 29.6 percent of Lithuania's Net Material Product (NMP) and employs about 30 percent of its workforce. Animal husbandry is the major agricultural activity, yielding almost 66 percent of total agricultural production. Lithuania's main crops are cereals, flax, sugar beets, potatoes, and vegetables. Land reform was implemented in 1991, but so far, less than half a percent of cultivated land is in private hands. Meat, eggs, and dairy products are also important.

Industry.   About 35.9 percent of Lithuania's NMP comes from industrial production, of which 39.7 percent came from consumer goods. Major industries are machine-building and metal working (25.7 percent of industrial output), food processing (21.9 percent) and light industry (20.8 percent). Minicomputers, electronics and machine tools are also important manufactures.

Principal Exports of Lithuania (to Non-Soviet Countries)

Machinery and equipment	42 percent
Oil and gas	18 percent
Food products	16 percent
Forestry, wood, paper	8 percent
Light industrial products	8 percent
Other fuels	1 percent
Building materials	1 percent
Other	2 percent
Total 1990 Exports	$238 million

Principal Imports of Lithuania (to Non-Soviet Countries)

Machinery and equipment	31 percent
Light industrial products	30 percent
Food products	18 percent
Chemicals	9 percent
Agricultural products	7 percent
Other industrial products	2 percent
Forestry, wood, paper	1 percent
Building materials	1 percent
Ferrous metal products	1 percent
Total 1990 Imports	$919.5 million

Note. Although Lithuania has a nuclear reactor at Ignalina and even a few oil wells, it relies upon fuel imports for most of its energy needs, shipping in petroleum, coal, and natural gas.

Prognosis. Lithuania's relations with Russia are poor, its competition from neighboring Belarus keen, and Lithuania lacks strong historical or ethnic ties with Western countries, such as have brought significant Finnish investment to Estonia and German and Scandinavian investment to Latvia. Lithuania doesn't even get along very well with Poland! For all these reasons, PlanEcon forecasters give Lithuania the poorest prospects of any of the three Baltic republics.

Republic of Latvia

Size of Economy (Projected 1993 GNP).　$13.7 billion, or 1.2 percent of total GNP for former Soviet states.

Population.　2.7 million, or .9 percent of total ex-Soviet population. 52 percent Latvian, 34 percent Russian and 5 percent Byelorussian.

Land Area.　24,595 square miles, or .3 percent of total ex-Soviet territory.

Natural Resources.　Peat deposits form Latvia's only significant natural resource.

Agriculture.　Agriculture accounts for 20.4 percent of Latvia's GNP and employs 18.8 percent of its workforce. Dairy farming, pig breeding and fishing are important, while the main crops are cereals, sugar beets, potatoes, and fodder crops.

Industry.　Industrial production accounts for 60.3 percent of GNP and employs 28.4 percent of the workforce. Major industries include machine building, metal working, petrochemical and chemical production, light industry, manufacture of railroad cars and electronics.

Port Cities.　Latvia has the potential to become an important maritime nation, with major ports at Riga (Baltic Sea) Liepaja (Baltic Sea) and Ventspils (Baltic Sea). Riga is the most active port on the Baltic.

Principal Exports of Latvia (to All Countries)

Machinery and equipment	27.9 percent
Food products	21.6 percent
Textiles	17.3 percent
Chemicals	12.4 percent
Forest products	2.6 percent
Agricultural products	2.1 percent
Ferrous metals	1.9 percent
Electricity	1.7 percent
Building materials	1.4 percent
Non-ferrous metals	.2 percent
Fuel	.1 percent
Other	10.9 percent
Total 1990 Exports	$3 billion

Note.   About 64.1 percent of Latvia's total NMP comes from exports to other former Soviet republics, while exports to other countries accounted for only 5.7 percent.

Principal Imports of Latvia (from All Countries)

Machinery and equipment . . . .   31.3 percent

Textiles . . . .   16.3 percent

Chemicals . . . .   11.6 percent

Food products . . . .   9.9 percent

Fuel . . . .   7.6 percent

Ferrous metals . . . .   5.6 percent

Agricultural products . . . .   4.6 percent

Forest products . . . .   2.4 percent

Non-ferrous metals . . . .   2.2 percent

Electricity . . . .   1.8 percent

Building materials . . . .   1.1 percent

Other . . . .   5.6 percent

Total 1990 Imports . . . . $3.6 billion

Prognosis.   Latvia will have a difficult transition, says PlanEcon. Lacking natural resources, Latvia's two major advantages lie in its high-quality labor force and its location on the Baltic Sea, allowing Latvia to serve as a "gateway" between Russia and the West. For example, the most important export point for Russian oil to the West is the Latvian port of Ventspils.

Though largely cut off from its once-critical trade with Russia, sizeable investment from Germans and Scandinavians has softened the blow to Latvia. Historically, Latvia has been considered the third most wealthy republic of the former Soviet Union, after Estonia.

Republic of Estonia

Size of Economy (Projected 1993 GNP). $8.4 billion, or .7 percent of total GNP for former Soviet states.

Population.   1.6 million, or .6 percent of total ex-Soviet population. 62 percent Estonians, 30 percent Russians, 3 percent Ukrainian.

Land Area.   17,413 square miles, or .2 percent of total ex-Soviet territory.

Natural Resources.   Estonia has greater natural riches than any of the other Baltic states, including timber, peat, phosphorite ore, and oil shale deposits comprising about 60 percent of the total reserves of the former Soviet states.

Agriculture.   Agriculture in Estonia is heavily geared to animal husbandry, including livestock breeding, dairy farming, and growing crops for animal fodder. In fact, Estonia produces about 1.4 percent of total meat production in the former Soviet states. Dairy products, cattle feed, vegetables, meat, and potatoes are its principal food products.

Industry.   Estonia has well-developed timber, woodworking and paper industries, which benefit from its extensive forests. Phosphorite ore is refined into phosphates, and oil shale is used to generate electricity. Estonia also has extensive machine-building, furniture, electronics and electrical engineering industries. It processes fish and other food, and manufactures textiles and consumer goods. Estonia was one of the leading producers of consumer durables in the former Soviet Union.

Port Cities.   Tallinn

Principal Exports of Estonia (to Non-Soviet Countries, 1990)

Fish and food products	42.6 percent
Textiles	21.6 percent
Machinery and metal products	8 percent
Lumber, pulp and paper	8.4 percent
Iron and steel	5.1 percent
Chemicals and plastics	3.7 percent
Raw food materials	3.4 percent
Other: (oil shale, building materials, industrial products, etc.	3.4 percent
Total 1990 Exports	$62.7 million

Note.   92 percent of Estonia's exports still go to other former Soviet republics.

Principal Imports of Estonia (from Non-Soviet Countries)

Textiles	37.6 percent
Fish and food products	18.1 percent
Machinery and metal products	7 percent
Raw food materials	11.1 percent
Chemicals and plastics	7.1 percent
Electric power	2.7 percent
Other industrial products	2.1 percent
Iron and steel	1.1 percent
Lumber, pulp and paper	.8 percent
Building materials	.7 percent
Coal	.5 percent
Nonferrous metals	.4 percent
Other	.1 percent
Total 1990 Imports	$222.7 million

Note. Despite its large reserves of oil shale, Estonia is as dependent upon imported fuels as the other Baltic states, and buys large quantities of oil, coal and natural gas from Russia and other former Soviet republics. Estonia is intently pursuing trade with Western countries, especially Finland and other Scandinavian countries. But 82 percent of Estonia's imports still come from other former Soviet republics.

Prognosis. Like the other Baltic republics, Estonia was hard hit by the collapse of trade with Russia in 1991 and 1992. Nevertheless, its strong ethnic and linguistic ties to Finland have brought a disproportionate amount of investment from that country. PlanEcon analysts give Estonia a "high" rating for future economic recovery.

Republic of Moldova

Size of Economy (Projected 1993 GNP). $13.8 billion, or 1.2 percent of total GNP for the former Soviet states.

Population. 4.4 million people, or 1.5 percent of total ex-Soviet population. 64 percent Moldovans, 14 percent Ukrainians, 13 percent Russians.

Land Area.   13,000 square miles, .2 percent of total ex-Soviet territory.

Natural Resources.   None to speak of.

Agriculture.   Agriculture forms the basis of Moldova's economy. Tiny Moldova yields about 1.8 percent of the total agricultural net material product (NMP) of the former Soviet states, accounting for 25 percent of its fruit and vegetables, 23 percent of its tobacco, and 10 percent of its meat. Major crops include fruit, vegetables, tobacco, wheat, and sugar. Grape-growing and wine-making are important industries.

Industry.   Moldova accounts for about 1 percent of the total industrial net material product (NMP) of the former Soviet Union. Most of Moldova's industry centers around its agricultural produce. Wine distilleries, tobacco production and food processing plants churning out such wares as vegetable oil and canned fruit are the chief industries. However, these is some light production of textiles, chemicals, consumer goods, including shoes, clothing, refrigerators, and washing machines.

Principal Moldovan Exports (to Non-Soviet Countries)

Processed foodstuffs	25 percent
Textiles and apparel	18 percent
Machinery and equipment	16 percent
Chemicals	15 percent
Shoes	6 percent
Other	20 percent
Total 1991 Exports	$155.7 million

Note.   About 62.1 percent of Moldova's NMP comes from other former Soviet republics, to whom Moldova exports tobacco, meat, fruits and vegetables. Only 3.4 percent derives from exports to foreign countries. Wine exports are a major source of hard currency.

Principal Moldovan Imports (from Non-Soviet Countries)

Machinery and equipment	39 percent
Textiles and apparel	12 percent
Processed foodstuffs	8 percent
Handicrafts and glassware	8 percent

Other . . . .   33 percent

Total 1991 Imports . . . . $597.6 million

Note.   Moldova is heavily dependent upon energy imports from other former Soviet republics.

Prognosis.   PlanEcon analysts see a grim future for Moldova in the near term, due to political unrest. The ethnic Russian minority living on the left bank of the Dniestr river violently opposes independence. Clashes with Moldovan authorities have resulted in scores of deaths. Eventually, Moldova will probably rejoin its mother country, Romania. "But this sort of embrace," says *PlanEcon Report,* "poor mother embracing destitute daughter, is not likely to do much for Moldova."

The Caucasian Republics

The three republics of the Caucasus—Georgia, Armenia, and Azerbaijan—are among the most promising areas for foreign investment. Despite the interethnic fighting and civil wars which have raged through the Caucasus since 1989, economic reforms have been thorough, and foreign investment strong.

These nations are extremely ancient, with recorded histories dating back 3000 years and more. Legend holds that Georgia is the mythical land of the Colchians, to which Jason and his Argonauts journeyed to recover the Golden Fleece. Armenia is home to Mt. Ararat, where Noah's ark came to rest after the flood. Unfortunately, the fortunes of past wars have now placed that mountain on the Turkish side of the border, along with the bulk of Armenia's ancestral territories. Azerbaijan is reputed to be the ancient land of *Adurbadagan* the "land of flames," where the Persian prophet Zarathustra was born. Azerbaijan's abundance of naturally occurring, burning methane jets supposedly inspired Zarathustra to found a religion of fire worshippers called Zoroastrians.

Since earliest days, the Caucasus has been a crossroads for caravans, merchant ships, and conquering armies. Persians, Romans, Mongols, Arabs, and Turks all had their turn at ruling the Caucasus, before the Russians finally seized it in the eighteenth and nineteenth centuries.

The Caucasian peoples thus became adept at survival. They are shrewd traders, renowned for their skill at commerce. Today, Caucasian peoples are vastly overrepresented among the new breed of *commersanti,* or businessmen, in Russia, to the point where many Russians have come to resent the financial power of these "blacks" from the south—so-called for their swarthy skin and flaring black mustachios.

Republic of Armenia

Size of Economy (Projected 1993 GNP). $9.8 billion, or .8 percent of the total for the former Soviet states.

Population.   3.3 million people, or 1.1 percent of total ex-Soviet population. 93 percent Armenian, 3 percent Azeri, 2 percent Russian.

Land Area.   12,000 square miles, or .1 percent of total ex-Soviet territory.

Natural Resources.   Copper, zinc, aluminum and molybdenum.

Agriculture.   Before its radical land reform, Armenia accounted for about .7 percent of the total agricultural NMP for the former Soviet republics. More recent figures, when they are compiled, will certainly show a significant increase, since Armenia's 1991 harvest showed a 50 percent rise in production over 1990. Major crops include tobacco, vegetables, melons, figs, pomegranates, apricots, peaches, and other fruits. Armenian wines and brandies are renowned.

Industry.   Armenia provides 1.2 percent of total industrial net material product (NMP) for the former Soviet republics. Its leading industries are non-ferrous metallurgy, production of electrical equipment, instruments, machinery, chemicals and computers, trucks, tires, electronics, elevators, synthetic rubber, aluminum foil, textiles, and leather footwear. Much of Armenia's industry is powered by its extensive hydroelectric power complex.

Principal Armenian Exports (to Non-Soviet Countries)

Machinery and equipment	28 percent
Transport equipment	17 percent
Metal products	15 percent
Chemicals	11 percent
Other: (fruits, preserves, wines, etc.)	29 percent
Total 1991 Exports	$68.7 million

Note.   A full 63.7 percent of Armenia's NMP comes from exports to other republics, but only 1.4 percent from exports to other countries.

Principal Armenian Imports (from Non-Soviet Countries)

Prefabricated housing: (and some furniture) . . . . . . 80.3 percent

Machine building . . . . 11 percent

Other: (metals, fuel, etc.) . . . . 8.7 percent

Total 1991 Imports . . . . $794 million

Note. Armenia imports 60 to 70 percent of its food (including 70 percent of its bread and 66 percent of its dairy products) as well as significant proportions of its meat.

Prognosis. Armenia's 1991 imports were heavily distorted by the 1988 earthquake which accounts for the heavy purchases of prefab housing. In addition, Armenia is at war with Azerbaijan over the disputed territory of Nagorno-Karabakh. PlanEcon analysts "can't be upbeat" about the republic's near-term prospects, since they feel it is in danger of turning into another Lebanon.

Nevertheless, this author sees great hope in the involvement of Armenian emigres. The Armenians have proven remarkably adept at leveraging the power of a wealthy and numerous diaspora abroad. Some 66 percent of Armenians now live in other countries, and a high percentage have become quite wealthy. The Armenian Assembly of America (a powerful lobby in Washington) has managed to steer much foreign investment and technical aid to its motherland. For example, of the 421 international long-distance phone lines which AT&T installed in the former Soviet states, 184 went to Armenia. In addition, agricultural and freemarket reforms have been unusually thorough in Armenia. Risk-prone entrepreneurs who don't mind ducking an occasional bullet will find fertile soil for investment, and minimal competition.

Republic of Azerbaijan

Size of Economy (Projected 1993 GNP). $18 billion, or 1.5 percent of the total for the former Soviet states.

Population. 7.1 million people, or 2.4 percent of total ex-Soviet population. 83 percent Azeris, 6 percent Armenians, 6 percent Russians.

Land Area. 33,000 square miles, or .4 percent of total ex-Soviet territory.

Natural Resources. Oil, iron ore, copper.

Agriculture.   Accounts for 2.2 percent of total agricultural net material product (NMP) of the former Soviet states. Azerbaijan is an arid country where most farmland requires irrigation. The lowlands of the extreme southeast are semitropical, and are used for growing tea, tobacco, nuts and other warm-weather crops. Cotton, wheat, fruit, vegetables, and wine grapes are important products. Sheep, cattle and goats are also raised on the grassy steppes.

Industry.   Azerbaijan accounts for 1.7 percent of total industrial net material product (NMP) for the former Soviet states. One of the leading oil-producing areas of the world, most of its industry centers around the extraction and processing of petroleum. Major oilfields are located on the Apsheron Peninsula and near Siyar, Neftechala and Ali-Bayramli. There are major reserves located offshore in the Caspian Sea. Crude petroleum is piped to refineries in Baku and also to Batumi, Georgia. About 60 percent of all extraction and production equipment for the CIS petroleum industry, as well as spare parts, are produced in Azerbaijan, which also has important chemical and petrochemical, construction, mining and machine building industries, powered by its extensive hydroelectric plants. Textiles, food processing and wine making are also important.

Port Cities.   Baku (inland port on the Caspian Sea).

Principal Exports of Azerbaijan (to Non-Soviet Countries)

Crude oil . . . . 56.7 percent

Textile products . . . . 15.5 percent

Chemicals . . . . 10.2 percent

Machinery and equipment . . . .   9 percent

Other: (grapes, fruits, vegetables, etc.) . . . . 8.6 percent

Total Exports (1991) . . . . $320.5 million

Note.   58.7 percent of Azerbaijan's net material product (NMP) comes from exports to other former Soviet republics, and 3.7 percent from exports to other countries.

Principal Imports of Azerbaijan (from Non-Soviet Countries)

Machinery and equipment . . . .   45 percent

Knitted apparel . . . . 24.8 percent

Other textile products . . . . 4.2 percent

Animal husbandry products: (meat, milk, etc.) . . . . .   11 percent

Other: (consumer durables, etc.) . . . .   15 percent

Total 1991 Imports: . . . . $810.3 million

Prognosis. Despite Azerbaijan's ongoing war with neighboring Armenia over who owns Nagorno-Karabakh, PlanEcon prognosticators are "very upbeat" over this Muslim republic's economic prospects. The reason is oil. Azerbaijan contains some of the greatest petroleum deposits of the world, and major western oil companies have high hopes for planned offshore drilling in the Caspian Sea.

Republic of Georgia

Size of Economy (Projected 1993 GNP). 15.7 billion, or 1.3 percent of total GNP for the former Soviet states.

Population. 5.4 million people, or 1.9 percent of total ex-Soviet population. 70 percent Georgian, 8 percent Armenian, 6 percent Russian.

Land Area. 26,000 square miles, .3 percent of total ex-Soviet territory.

Natural Resources. Timber, coal, manganese.

Agriculture. Georgia contributes 2.1 percent of the total agricultural NMP of the former Soviet states. The subtropical climate on the shores of the Black Sea permits cultivation of tea and citrus fruits. Elsewhere, other fruits and berries are grown, as well as wine grapes, flowers, tobacco, almonds, grain, and sugar beets. Animal husbandry is practiced in the mountains, where sheep and goats are pastured. Georgia is famous for its wine and champagne.

Industry. Georgia has a well-developed industrial base, accounting for about 1.4 percent of the total industrial NMP of the former Soviet states. Its extensive coal deposits, coal-powered electric power plants and hydro-electric stations make Georgia self-sufficient in energy. Most industrial activity is spread out across a long, thin belt from Tbilisi to the Black Sea. Chief industries include ferrous metallurgy, machine-building, construction materials, chemical and petrochemical production. Georgia's oil refineries at Batumi process petroleum from the Azerbaijani oilfields at Baku. Petroleum deliveries, however, have suffered from the fighting. Tourism is also important. Sochi and Sukhumi on the Black Sea coast are among the most popular resorts in the former Soviet states. The Caucasus mountains contain magnificent but little-known ski slopes.

Principal Georgian Exports (to Non-Soviet Countries)

Aluminum	35.2 percent
Other metal products: (manganese ore, etc.)	20.8 percent
Raw food materials: (tea, fruits, etc.)	24 percent
Other: (wines, etc.)	20 percent
Total 1991 Exports:	$210.6 million

Note. About 53.7 percent of Georgia's NMP comes from exports to other former Soviet republics, and 3.9 percent from exports to foreign countries.

Principal Georgian Imports (from Non-Soviet Countries)

Machinery and equipment	40 percent
Processed food	12 percent
Transport equipment	9 percent
Textiles and apparel	8 percent
Tobacco	6.6 percent
Other: (including consumer durables, ferrous metals, fuel oil, etc.)	24.4 percent
Total Imports (1991)	$1.5 billion

Prognosis. Georgia has been plunged in a bloody civil war since 1990. Fruit exports to Russia—long a pillar of the Georgian economy—will probably dry up as Russia starts using its oil and gas riches to buy cheaper fruit abroad. Nevertheless, PlanEcon prognosticators see some hope for Georgia's future, provided it focuses on its traditional role as a resort mecca for the Russian elite, "providing warm climate, Black Sea, gambling and other entertainment" to *nouveau riche* Russian oil barons and the like.

The Central Asian Republics

Until the recent breakup of Russia's empire, most Americans never realized there was any such thing as Central Asia. Yet, the nations of this region—bearing such exotic names as Kazakhstan, Kyrgyzstan, Uzbekistan, and Tajikistan—represent an array of business opportunities as limitless as those which greeted Marco Polo's caravans when he first visited those lands in the thirteenth century.

Located on the Old Silk Road between China and the Middle East, the fabled kingdoms of Central Asia have long been a prize, much fought over by successive generations of conquerors. Alexander the Great took Samarkand more than 2000 years ago. Persians, Arabs, Greeks, Mongols, and Turks have all ruled these lands at different times. Only in the nineteenth century did Central Asia come under Russian control.

Most of today's Central Asians belong to that same Mongol-Turkic family of peoples which has been terrorizing Europe since the days of Attila the Hun, Genghis Khan, and the Turkish hordes. Indeed, their languages are all closely related to modern Turkish, with the exception of Tajik, which is closer to Persian. The long historical and ethnic links between these peoples have moved the Turkish government today to attempt a revival of its ancient empire, in the form of a Pan-Turkic trading bloc, orchestrated from Istanbul. So far, the Central Asians have proven cool to this proposal, although the Central Asian republics did form a loose economic bloc between themselves in August 1991 and, in January 1993, declared a Central Asian "League of States" as a stand-by measure, should the CIS dissolve—an event which many in Central Asia seem to expect.

Those American business pioneers who aspire to walk in Marco Polo's shoes will find the Central Asian republics awash in natural resources, laden with well-developed industries and agriculture and aswarm with lively entrepreneurs, some honest, some not. Their remote locations have kept them out of the way of the mainstream of foreign competition, for which reason, they are all the more ripe for the plucking.

Republic of Kazakhstan

Size of Economy (Projected 1993 GNP). $56.2 billion, or 4.8 percent of total for the former Soviet states.

Population.   16.7 million, or 5.8 percent of total ex-Soviet population. 40 percent Kazakhs, 38 percent Russians, 6 percent Germans.

Land Area.   The world's ninth largest country in area, Kazakhstan encompasses 1.05 million square miles, or 12.2 percent of total ex-Soviet territory.

Natural Resources.   Major coal reserves, iron ore, lead, zinc, copper, manganese, chromite, and petroleum. There are also several rare metals and phosphates. The major coalfields are in the Karaganda Turgy, Ekibas-tuz and Maykuben basins, while petroleum and natural gas reserves are found in the Caspian Depression and the Mangyshlak Peninsula. Annual gold production is reckoned at $200 million.

Agriculture.   Kazakhstan's extensive farmlands account for 6.1 percent of total agricultural net material product (NMP) for the former Soviet states. Its principal crops are fruits, sugar beets, vegetables, potatoes, cotton, and, most importantly, grain. The republic produces much of the meat for Central Asia. Sheep breeding is important, as is fishing. Most agriculture is concentrated in the north and the irrigated parts of the southeast.

Industry.   Kazakhstan provides 2.5 percent of total industrial net material product (NMP) for the former Soviet states. Most of Kazakhstan's industry is focused around the extraction and processing of minerals. It includes iron and steel making, the making of chemical fertilizers, fuel, power, chemicals, machine-building, as well as textiles and food-processing. There are major industrial regions in Kazakhstan centered around Alma-Ata and Karaganda in the north.

Principal Exports of Kazakhstan (to Non-Soviet Countries)

Metal products (Iron and steel, including manufactures)	25.2 percent
Fuels and minerals: (Oil, coal, etc.)	16.5 percent
Copper and lead	12.2 percent
Fertilizers	11.8 percent
Inorganic chemicals	8.3 percent
Ores	6.9 percent
Raw hides and skins	6.4 percent
Other: (meat, wool, grain, etc.)	12.7 percent
Total 1991 Exports	$778.4 billion

Note.   About 30.9 percent of Kazakhstan's net material product (NMP) comes from exports to other republics, and about 3 percent from exports to other countries, making it one of the more self-sufficient republics.

Principal Imports of Kazakhstan (from Non-Soviet Countries)

Machinebuilding	33 percent
Textile products	19 percent

Fuels and minerals . . . .   9 percent

Other: (consumer durables, fruits, vegetables, etc.) . .   39 percent

Total 1991 Imports: . . . . $1.7 billion

Prognosis.   Prospects for Kazakhstan are "very good," say PlanEcon analysts, primarily because of this republic's huge energy and mineral resources, and its well-developed agriculture. Another strength is Kazakhstan's unusually friendly relations with Russia, which speak well for its future political stability.

Republic of Kyrgyzstan

Size of Economy (Projected 1993 GNP). $9.7 billion, or .8 percent of the total for the former Soviet states.

Population.   4.4 million people, or 1.5 percent of total ex-Soviet population. 52 percent Kirgiz, 21 percent Russian, 13 percent Uzbek.

Land Area.   77,000 square miles, or .9 percent of total ex-Soviet territory.

Natural Resources.   Uranium, mercury, antimony, coal, petroleum, oil shale, natural gas, lead, zinc, gold, marble.

Agriculture.   Kyrgyzstan provides about 1.2 percent of total agricultural net material product (NMP) for the former Soviet states. Major crops are grains, sugar beets, sugar, fruits, vegetables, tobacco and cotton. Sheep, pig, goat and horse breeding is practiced.

Industry.   Kyrgyzstan accounts for .6 percent of total industrial net material product (NMP) for the former Soviet states. Most industry centers around the extraction and processing of mineral and energy resources, especially coal, petroleum and natural gas, and the mining of non-ferrous metals, as well as generation of electrical power, especially from the republic's extensive hydroelectric plants on the Naryn, Talass, and Chu rivers. Cement and other construction materials are produced, as well as footwear, woolen and other textiles and processed food. There is some manufacturing of livestock equipment, medium-sized electric motors and washing machines.

Principal Exports of Kyrgyzstan (to Non-Soviet Countries)

Chemicals	35 percent
Metal products	27 percent
Machinery and equipment	22 percent
Other: (sugar, wool, fruits, vegetables, flour, livestock equipment, etc.)	16 percent
Total 1991 Exports	$45.8 million

Note. 50.2 percent of Kyrgyzstan's net material product (NMP) comes from exports to other former Soviet republics, and 1.2 percent from exports to other countries.

Principal Imports of Kyrgyzstan (from Non-Soviet Countries)

Machinery and equipment (nuclear reactors, boilers, etc.)	76 percent
Textile products	9 percent
Shoes	7 percent
Other (electricity, fuel, metals, consumer durables, etc.)	8 percent
Total 1991 Imports	$560.7 billion

Prognosis. Although Kyrgyzstan boasts an abundance of hydropower and mineral deposits, it has the misfortune that its primary natural resources are uranium, mercury and antimony, all suffering from low demand on world commodity markets. For this reason, PlanEcon forecasters judge Kyrgyzstan's prospects "not as favorable" as those of its energy-rich neighbors, Kazakhstan and Turkmenistan.

Republic of Tajikistan

Size of Economy (Projected 1993 GNP). $7.8 billion, or .7 percent of the total for the former Soviet states.

Population. 5.2 million people, or 1.8 percent of total ex-Soviet population. 62 percent Tajiks, 24 percent Uzbeks, 8 percent Russians.

Land Area. 55,000 square miles, or .6 percent of total ex-Soviet territory.

Natural Resources.   Gold, copper, uranium, iron, lead, zinc, mercury, tin, coal, as well as small deposits of petroleum and natural gas.

Agriculture.   Tajikistan provides 1.2 percent of total agricultural net material product (NMP) for the former Soviet states. Tajikistan's farmland requires extensive irrigation. Cotton and silk are the major agricultural products. Tajik farmers also grow flowers, dried apricots, nuts, grapes, corn and other grains, fruits and vegetables. Cattle breeding is also practiced.

Industry.   Accounting for .4 percent of total industrial net material product (NMP) for the former Soviet states, most industry in Tajikistan centers around extraction and processing of minerals, such as electrolytic metal refining, aluminum reduction, refining of copper, lead and zinc, electro-chemical manufacturing, metalworking machine tools. Refrigerators are also produced. Some agricultural equipment is produced, as well as machinery for power stations, used in Tajikistan's extensive hydroelectric power plants. There is considerable light industry, producing silk and cotton textiles, carpets and processed food, such as vegetable oil and canned foods. The city of Dushanbe has meat packing plants, a tannery, a textile mill, a tobacco factory and also cement and wine factories. Mining and cotton milling are also important.

Principal Exports of Tajikistan (to Non-Soviet Countries)

Aluminum	60.4 percent
Cotton	22.2 percent
Chemicals	7 percent
Other textile products (silk cloth, etc.)	1.8 percent
Other metal products (machine tools, etc.)	.6 percent
Other (hydroelectric power, dried apricots, nuts, grapes, etc.)	8 percent
Total 1991 Exports	$279.3 million

Notes.   Tajikistan obtains about 41.8 percent of its net material product (NMP) from exports to other republics and about 6.9 percent from exports to other countries.

Principal Imports of Tajikistan (from Non-Soviet Countries)

Machinery and equipment	40.3 percent
Inorganic chemicals	30.5 percent

Textile products . . . . 16.2 percent

Other (transport equipment, consumer durables, etc.) . 13 percent

Total Imports (1991) . . . . $458.3 billion

Prognosis. Like its neighbor, Kyrgyzstan, Tajikistan offers little aside from cheap hydroelectricity. Moreover, it has been wracked by civil war since early 1992. Some 60,000 Tajiks were killed in the last six months of 1992, and, in December, a hardline Communist government siezed control. For all these reasons, PlanEcon gives poor Tajikistan "below average prospects into the 1990s."

Republic of Turkmenistan

Size of Economy (Projected 1993 GNP). $9.5 billion, or .8 percent of the total for the former Soviet states.

Population. 3.6 million people, or 1.2 percent of total ex-Soviet population. 72 percent Turkmen, 9 percent Russians, 9 percent Uzbeks.

Land Area. 189,000 square miles, or 2.2 percent of total ex-Soviet territory.

Natural Resources. Turkmenistan has significant petroleum and gas deposits in the western part of the country and under the Caspian Sea. It also has potassium, sulphur, sodium chloride, mirabilite and magnesium chloride.

Agriculture. Produces 1.2 percent of total agricultural net material product (NMP) for former Soviet states. Most of Turkmenistan is a desert, but the country has extensive river valleys and oases where crops may be grown. Cotton is the main crop. Fruits, melons, vegetables, wine grapes, cereal and fodder crops are also grown. The Turkmen people are masters at breeding Turkoman horses, camels, and the distinctive Karkul sheep, whose soft, curly pelts are used to make Turkmenistan's famous handmade Oriental carpets.

Industry. Accounting for .4 percent of total industrial net material product (NMP) for the former Soviet states, Turkmenistan's industry centers around petroleum and natural gas extraction, petrochemical production and cotton growing. Textile production and cotton-ginning are important, as are food-processing, wine making, traditional glass making and weaving of Oriental carpets.

Principal Exports of Turkmenistan (to Non-Soviet Countries)

Textile products (cotton products, etc.) . . . .   36 percent

Nickel . . . .   11.1 percent

Other metal products . . . .   6.9 percent

Food raw materials (fish, vegetable oil, etc.) . . . .   15 percent

Chemicals . . . .   14 percent

Other (natural gas, etc.) . . . .   17 percent

Total 1991 Exports . . . . $96.1 million

Note. 50.7 percent of Turkmenistan's NMP comes from exports to other former Soviet republics and 4.2 percent from exports to other countries.

Principal Imports of Turkmenistan (from Non-Soviet Countries)

Machinery and equipment . . . .   36.7 percent

Textile products . . . .   25 percent

Plastic and rubber . . . .   2 percent

Other (Grain, potatoes, steel, consumer goods, etc.) . .   21.1 percent

Total 1991 Imports . . . . $401 million

Prognosis. Although unemployment in Turkmenistan is high—up to 40 percent by some estimates—PlanEcon analysts rate the republic as having the "best economic prospects" in the former Soviet states, along with Russia, Azerbaijan and Kazakhstan. The reason is energy. Turkmenistan has traditionally provided up to 72 percent of the natural gas formerly exported by the USSR. Gas exports don't appear significant in the above tables because most have been going to Russia, at below-market ruble rates. These prices are now being renegotiated, whereby Turkmenistan stands to gain a "major windfall."

Republic of Uzbekistan

Size of Economy (Projected 1993 GNP). $44.9 billion, or 3.9 percent of the total for the former Soviet states.

Population. 20.3 million people, or 7.2 percent of total ex-Soviet population. 71 percent Uzbeks, 8 percent Russians, 5 percent Tajiks.

Land Area. 173,000 square miles, or 2 percent of total ex-Soviet territory.

Natural Resources. Uzbekistan is blessed with extraordinary mineral wealth, including huge reserves of natural gas, along with coal, petroleum, gold, uranium, copper, tungsten, lead, zinc, and molybdenum.

Agriculture. Uzbekistan provides 5.2 percent of total agricultural net material product (NMP) for the former Soviet republics. Its "cotton monoculture" is both a blessing and a curse. By turning the republic into a one-crop state, Soviet planners insured Uzbekistan's economic dependency upon the USSR. Today, Uzbekistan is one of the world's leading producers of this important cash crop, but excessive cotton cultivation has exhausted its soil and the Uzbeks wish to diversify into other crops. Crops grown in Uzbekistan include jute, kenaf (a fibrous plant used to make sacking) grain, grapes, other fruits, berries and vegetables. Uzbeks also raise pigs and sheep, which are famous for their "astrakhan" pelts. Silk is also produced in abundance.

Industry. Uzbekistan produces 2.3 percent of total industrial net material product (NMP) for the former Soviet states. Most industry is connected either to the extraction and processing of minerals or to the cotton industry. Uzbekistan has extensive iron and steel industries, as well as chemical industries, which make such products as mineral fertilizers and synthetic fibers. The historic city of Tashkent forms the hub of a major manufacturing region, and Uzbekistan has the largest machine-building industry in Central Asia, producing in its factories excavators, machine-building equipment, chemical production equipment, and equipment for cotton farming. Also important are silk and cotton textiles, cotton-ginning, consumer goods and production of processed foods like vegetable oil and processed vegetables. Uzbekistan is a major producer and exporter of electricity.

Principal Exports of Uzbekistan (to Non-Soviet Countries)

Cotton . . . . 65 percent

Fertilizers . . . . 10.6 percent

Metal products . . . . 7 percent

Other textile products . . . . 3 percent

Chemicals . . . .   2.4 percent

Other . . . .   12 percent

Total 1991 Exports . . . . $650.2 million

Note. Uzbekistan is the world's second-largest exporter of cotton, supplying about 20 percent of the world's total. It ships about 1.13 million tons of cotton to Russia annually. Uzbekistan also exports vegetable oil, vegetables, fruits, natural gas, and chemical equipment. It supplies much of the electricity for other Central Asian republics.

Principal Imports of Uzbekistan (from Non-Soviet Countries)

Electrical machinery and equipment . . . .   33.8 percent

Instruments and apparatus . . . .   10 percent

Textile products . . . .   31 percent

Food raw materials (flour, milk, eggs, meat, etc.) . . . .   10 percent

Chemicals . . . .   7 percent

Other (Coal, petroleum, consumer durables, clothing,
etc.) . . . .   8.2 percent

Total 1991 Imports . . . . $1.3 billion

Note. Uzbekistan imports substantial amounts of grain, wood, construction materials and oil from Russia.

Prognosis. The outlook for Uzbekistan is "not optimistic" in the near term, says PlanEcon. Its main export, cotton, is inferior to Egyptian cotton, making it less attractive to the world market. Most Uzbek cotton goes to Russia. And so far, the Russians have countered every price hike on Uzbek cotton with even worse price hikes for Russian oil, on which the Uzbeks depend. PlanEcon analysts say that gold exports present the best bet for Uzbek prosperity in the near future. A third of all gold produced in the former Soviet states comes from Uzbekistan, but the exact amount of Uzbek gold exports is unknown, since none appear on official trade statistics.

Industries and Markets of Opportunity

It has become something of a cliché to exclaim (usually after a week-long factfinding trip to Moscow) that the Russians "need everything." They are in desperate need of just about every sort of consumer and industrial goods imaginable. But a sensible business plan must be forged with more rigor.

There are certain things that the Russians need far more than others; some of which they need so badly that they're willing to shell out large quantities of their precious hard currency reserves to get them. Others, they don't really need at all. It's important to know these distinctions.

The following is an informal overview of the most pressing needs of the Russian economy, broken down into six industry groupings—Technology, Emergency Social Priorities, Emergency Budgetary Priorities, Physical Infrastructure, Distribution Infrastructure, and Information Infrastructure. These form the hottest targets for foreign investment in Russia.

For each grouping, data is provided on the *Key Priorities* (goods and services in greatest demand) and *Leading Imports* (American products imported in greatest quantity in 1990).

Statistical information in this section was provided by the Russia Desk of the U.S. Commerce Department, and applies to all the former Soviet states as a whole.

How to Interpret These Data

Official compilers of trade statistics have yet to catch up to the Information Age. They still measure international commerce primarily in terms of solid objects which are manufactured in one country and physically shipped to another.

Unfortunately, such data tells us little about the real opportunities which exist in Russia. Only a small portion of Russia's economic potential will be tapped by foreigners importing expensive industrial machinery, plastics, resins, pharmaceuticals, and the like. Far more opportunities exist for those foreigners who can *teach the Russians to supply goods and services to themselves*, in other words, for those who can "sell" *knowledge* of manufacturing, sales and marketing to the Russians, rather than just hardware. Such transfers of knowledge, unfortunately, will not appear on Commerce Department lists.

Broad Areas of High Activity

Unless your company actually makes some of the items listed here, these data will be mainly useful to you as an indicator of *broad areas of high activity*. For example, the fact that the CIS states imported $20 million worth of plastics production machinery in 1990 is obviously of some interest to makers of such machinery. But, far more importantly, it indicates that the Russians are gearing up for a major escalation in domestic production of plastic items. Once those Russian factories are retooled, sales of such machinery will drop rapidly. However, phenomenal opportunities will then open up for foreigners to help individual Russian factories make and market plastic goods of all kinds.

Similarly, the fact that the Commerce Department projects a $20 billion market for cars in the CIS is of interest not only to the Big Three automakers, but also to entrepreneurs who can use this intelligence to envision a plethora of service businesses growing up alongside the new automotive culture, from franchised lube shops and roadside diners to collision insurance.

Category One: Technology

Key Priorities.   Russia intends to recover its status as a global industrial leader. This requires three things. First, the Russians must computerize their factories, installing all the latest automated production and control systems. Second, they must convert existing military factories to production of consumer goods. Finally, they must build up their scientific research and development facilities.

Americans are helping Russians in all three areas. Many high-tech items which Americans were formerly barred from selling to the Russians under COCOM guidelines can now be freely exported. Under the stimulus of these high-tech imports, Russia's computer and software industries, as well as electronics will become major growth areas in the 1990s.

Russia has yet to undergo the Plastics Revolution which struck America in the 1940s and 1950s. Many products now made of metal in Russia will soon be replaced by plastic. The potential for this industry is colossal, given Russia's immense petroleum reserves—the primary ingredient of plastics.

Although Russia is a leading producer of many industrial chemicals, it still needs to import many from abroad. Establishing domestic production of these chemicals is a high priority for Russian industry in the 1990s.

Leading Imports

1. **Computers and Peripherals**
   Total imports (1990): $670 million
   Imports from US (1990): $75.7 million

2. **Computer Software and Services**
   Imports: Data not available
   Application software (projected market): $350 million

Data processing management and maintenance (projected market): $300 million

Programming utility software (projected market): $200 million

3. **Laboratory Scientific Instruments**
   Total imports (1990): $128 million
   Imports from U.S. (1990): $18 million

4. **Electronics Components**
   Imports: Data not available
   Semiconductors (projected market): $450 million
   Capacitors/Resistors/Semiconductor Comp (projected market): $500 million
   Integrated circuits (projected market): $350 million

5. **Process Controls—Industrial**
   Imports: Data not available
   Programmable controllers (projected market): $500 million
   Process monitoring/control equipment (projected market): temperature: $250 million
   Process controls/chemical industry (projected market): $350 million

6. **Electronics Industry Production/Testing Equipment**
   Imports: Data not available
   PCB equipment (projected market): $500 million

7. **Plastics Production Machinery**
   Total imports (1990): $20 million

8. **Plastic Materials and Resins**
   Total imports (1990): $1.6 billion
   Imports from U.S. (1990): $20 million

9. **Industrial Chemicals**
   Imports from U.S. (1990): $50 million

10. **Pollution Control Equipment**
    Imports: Data not available
    Air pollution control equipment (projected market): $40 million
    Water pollution control equipment (projected market): $30 million
    Industrial waste treatment equipment (projected market): $50 million

Category Two: Emergency Social Priorities

Key Priorities. Providing food, health, housing, and clothing to the Russian people is a matter of national security. For example, one of the most worrisome phenomena plaguing Russia's leaders today is their inability to house hundreds of thousands of demobilized troops. Supplying such basic needs will do much to insure civil peace in the years ahead.

As mentioned earlier, Armenia experienced a 50 percent increase in food production after privatizing its farms. Russia may well enjoy a similar food bonanza, but will require a nationwide overhaul of its primitive food storage, processing and packaging industries in order to make sure that the surplus reaches hungry Russian mouths.

Finally, medicine in Russia is a national disgrace. Drugs are so scarce that doctors in emergency rooms will set broken bones without anesthetic, while hypodermic needles are routinely reused without being sterilized. Major opportunities exist for providing medical equipment, pharmaceuticals and health services to the Russians.

Leading Imports

1. **Food Processing and Packaging Equipment**
   Market size (1990): $2.5 billion
   Total imports (1990): $1.8 billion
   Imports from U.S. (1990): $20 million

2. **Agricultural Chemicals**
   Imports from U.S. (1990): $250 million

3. **Agricultural Services**
   Imports: Unknown
   Market projections unavailable

4. **Medical Equipment**
   Market size (1990): $3 billion
   Total imports (1990): $841 million
   Imports from U.S. (1990): $25 million

5. **Drugs and Pharmaceuticals**
   Total imports (1990): $3.2 billion

6. **Textile Machinery and Equipment**
   Market size (1990): $2.24 billion
   Total imports (1990): $1 billion
   Imports from U.S. (1990): $24.3 million

Category Three: Emergency Budgetary Priorities

Key Priorities.   The Russians are in debt up to their ears and need to earn hard currency *fast*. First and foremost, this means selling oil and gas, which now comprise over half of all export earnings for the former Soviet states. Western investment and technology is sorely needed to explore and exploit new reserves, and to build pipelines for getting these resources to market.

Also significant are precious metals and other metals. Here, too, Western money and technology can vastly increase Russia's exports. Russia has the largest virgin forests in the world. She exports over $4 billion worth of wood and paper products annually. However, production methods are primitive and inefficient. Some Russian entrepreneurs have created thriving businesses simply by salvaging the huge amounts of timber which sink to the bottoms of Siberian rivers as they're floated to the sawmills. Western assistance can no doubt ameliorate some of these problems.

Russia will never tap its incredible potential for tourism until it replaces its shabby network of Intourist hotels with Western- style accomodations. The travel and hospitality industries in all their forms are therefore wide-open for foreign investment.

Leading Imports

1. **Oil and Gas Field Machinery and Services**
   Total imports (1990): $152 million
   Imports from U.S. (1990): $60 million

2. **Mining Industry Equipment**
   Total imports (1990): $1.2 billion
   Imports from U.S. (1990): $30 million

3. **Forestry and Woodworking Equipment**
   Estimated total imports (1990): $900 million

4. **Hotel and Restaurant Equipment**
   Imports: Data not available.
   Food preparation equipment/hotel, restaurant (projected market):
      $80 million
   Fast food equipment (projected market): $10 million
   Hotel automation (projected market): $20 million

5. **Travel and Tourism Services**
   Data unavailable

Category Four: Physical Infrastructure

Key Priorities.   Export controls have recently been lifted on much advanced telecommunications technology. This is another national security priority for the Russians, and one where large quantities of hard currency are made available.

Russia's energy grid is in need of a complete overhaul. The abundance of oil and coal in the past encouraged waste. Now they need more efficient power and, of course, much safer nuclear reactors than are currently in place at such sites as Chernobyl.

I consider vehicles like cars, trucks, and aircraft to be part of a country's physical infrastructure, because they form collectively a "transportation grid" of which the whole economy makes use.

In transportation, Russia is clearly headed for an Automotive Revolution, such as we experienced in the 1950s. Today, Russia makes only 1.3 million cars per year. Even with the current cash shortage, Russians are so desperate for cars that they're buying expensive foreign vehicles rather than waiting in line for the scarce Russian models. Look for a major expansion in car-making and highway building.

Civil aviation is also hot. The vast distances people must traverse in Russia make air travel and air freight services essential. Airports will be modernized and expanded, private airlines formed and civilian aircraft manufactured at levels far greater than in the past.

Opportunities in real estate development are unimaginably abundant. Russia's existing structures are falling apart, and there is a critical shortage of housing and office space. Many of the most successful foreign business ventures are in this area.

Leading Imports

1. **Electrical Power Systems**
   Total imports (1990): $1.5 billion
   Imports from U.S. (1990): $6 million

2. **Telecommunications Equipment**
   Imports: Data not available
   Switching/cables (projected market): $400 million
   Cellular telephone equipment (projected market): $50 million
   Fiber Optic Transmission Equipment (projected market):
     $100 million

3. **Construction Equipment**
   Total imports (1990): $900 million
   Imports from U.S. (1990): $1 million

4. **Automobiles and Light Trucks/Vans**
   Imports: Data not available
   Passenger cars (projected market): $20 billion
   Vans (projected market): $1 billion

5. **Avionics and Ground Support Equipment**
   Imports: Data not available
   Air traffic control/NavAids (projected market): $150 million
   Airborne avionics (projected market): $1 billion
   Airport instrumentation and equipment (projected market): $250 million

6. **Aircraft and Parts**
   Imports: Data not available
   Aircraft jet engines (projected market): $750 million
   Commerical passenger/Cargo jet aircraft (projected market): $1.5 billion
   Executive/General Aviation Aircraft (projected market): $250 million

Category Five: Distribution Infrastructure

Key Priorities.   Distribution, of course, is one of Russia's most critical deficiencies. This will change very rapidly in the next few years, since retail and wholesale operations have been given first priority in Russia's privatization program. As Russian stores, warehouses, and shipping companies pass into private hands, we can expect vast improvement in this area, and mega-opportunities for foreign investors.

Much of Russia's new retailing industry will be handled through less conventional channels, such as franchise chains, direct selling operations and multilevel marketing, where independent distributors work on a commission basis for wholesalers.

Leading Imports.   Doesn't apply.

Category Six: Information Infrastructure

Ordinarily, we think of *information businesses* as those which involve high-speed transfers of digital datastreams, as in banking and securities brokerage. However, there is a very real practical and organic link which binds together *all* industries for whom the manipulation and transfer of *knowledge* (i.e. words, figures, sounds, images and ideas) forms the principal engine of *production.*

For one thing, all depend upon *media* to transfer that *knowledge* which is their coin of trade. And all must function within an abstract and invisible *infrastructure* of ideas which exists nowhere except in the human mind.

Thus, a legal services office has no function unless it is surrounded by a large mass of people sharing the same ideas about law and government. Similarly, a line of flimsy but high-fashion women's apparel has little use outside of a wide community of consumers who have been conditioned by fashion magazines, movies, TV shows and advertisements to appreciate and admire the stylishness of the woman who wears them. Such common bodies of belief and know-how form the information infrastructure of a society.

Key Priorities. The collective Russian mind today resembles an enormous, blank computer memory into which the entire mass of laws, styles, financial systems, religious and philosophical beliefs, and product tastes which form Western consumer culture are being relentlessly *downloaded.*

Some of the hottest Russian business opportunities lie in helping to build that invisible *info-structure* in such areas as banking, finance, brokerage, tax and legal services, advertising and marketing, fashion, style, religion, mass media, entertainment, trade shows and exhibitions, education, and training.

In this area, far more than most, Commerce Department trade statistics tell us very little. However, the large quantities of printing and graphic arts equipment imports reported here certainly reveal the escalating needs of a free and unfettered press in Russia. Similarly, sales of packaging equipment point to a new appreciation for the importance of *marketing* products, rather than simply wrapping them in brown paper. As for the $1.1 billion worth of cosmetics and toiletries imports reported here, we may assume that this is merely the tip of a gargantuan fashion iceberg. Look out for a Beauty-and-Style Revolution in Russia, that will sweep many industries, from apparel to mass media.

Leading Imports

1. **Printing and Graphic Arts Equipment**
   Market size (1990): $640 million
   Total imports (1990): $360 million

2. **Packaging Equipment**
   Total imports (1990): $40 million

3. **Cosmetics and Toiletries**
   Total imports (1990): $1.1 billion

Table 8.2 shows the number of operating joint ventures by branch of the national economy as of July 1, 1991—the last date for which such a breakdown is available. The number of *operating* joint ventures is lower than the number of *registered* joint ventures, shown elsewhere in this book.

A Caveat   It is obviously impossible to provide enough detailed data in the space of this chapter to enable you to confidently commit your resources to a particular venture or industry. I can only hope that I have managed to convey the magnitude and scope of opportunities which exist, and that I have stimulated at least some broad strategic ideas in your mind.

Table 8.2. Where's the Action?

	Total	Industrial	Construction	Retail	R&D	Others
Former Soviet States	1572	650	83	120	136	583
Russia	968	432	53	80	93	310
Ukraine	155	67	6	8	18	56
Belarus	78	44	1	4	6	23
Uzbekistan	32	7	1	—	2	22
Kazakhstan	22	15	—	2	1	4
Georgia	31	8	2	—	7	14
Azerbaijan	7	4	—	1	—	2
Lithuania			—— data not available ——			
Moldova	34	6	1	2	1	24
Latvia	114	28	—	2	3	81
Kyrgyzstan	1	1	—	—	—	—
Tajikistan	—	—	—	—	—	—
Armenia	14	4	2	—	5	3
Turkmenistan	—	—	—	—	—	—
Estonia	116	34	17	21	—	44

Source: PlanEcon.

9

Choosing Your Russian Partner

How to Tell the Shysters from the Players

Edward Saad left the conference room in a blind rage. How could he have been such a fool? How could he have let the Russians skin him alive for $250,000? Saad thought he had a sure thing. For months, he'd been arranging to set up a cosmetics factory which would operate out of a major chemical plant in the Ukrainian city of Donetsk. The factory managers kept assuring Saad that there would be "no problem" getting official clearance for their joint venture.

In dribs and drabs, the Russians had slowly milked Saad out of his money. One week, they would need a few thousand to buy new cosmetic manufacturing equipment. The next week it might be architectural work or redesigning parts of their four-story plant. Saad's personal investment inched up gradually to a dizzying quarter-million dollars.

But Saad wasn't worried. Everything seemed to be going on schedule. The factory was being retooled. The Russians had produced a detailed business plan. Only one obstacle remained. Because the chemical plant was state-owned, a certain ministry in Moscow had to rubber-stamp their proposal. Saad's partners assured him it was a mere formality.

But they were lying. At a tense meeting in Moscow, the minister who had authority over the factory informed Saad that he had no intention of rubber-stamping anything. The deal was off. As for the $3 million investment which Saad's prospective partners had promised to put into the new venture, the minister looked at Saad sadly across the conference table and said, "Mr. Saad, these people don't even have three million *rubles* to put up."

Saad was in shock. "I just said, 'Thank you, gentlemen,' got up, and left," he recalls.

Where Did He Go Wrong?

As an experienced cosmetics executive who had worked many years for Faberge, Saad was nobody's fool. He would never have put in so much money had he not had full confidence in his partners. The chemical plant was a leading producer of one of Russia's number one exports—urea. The managers he spoke to were polished professionals. They had shown Saad sensible plans for redesigning the shop floor, ordered just the right sort of equipment, and gone over ideas for packaging the proposed cosmetics products. They had invested a great deal of time haggling at length over the fine points of the deal.

But now Saad had to face the fact that he had simply been talking to the wrong people. They'd never really had the authority to negotiate with him in the first place.

Don't Give Up

Dazed, Saad wandered back down the hallway. Earlier, while waiting for his meeting to start, he'd struck up a conversation with two Russians in the lobby. Saad noticed that they were still there.

"You look a bit perturbed," said the one Russian who spoke English.

"Frankly," Saad replied, "I feel like punching the first person in the mouth I see that's Russian." The two Russians exchanged glances.

"Obviously, you've been sold a bill of goods," said the English-speaking one sympathetically. "Why don't you come to our office tomorrow? We'd like to talk to you. If you're serious about doing business here, I think you'll find that we can produce results."

A million thoughts swam through Saad's head as he took the proffered business card. "At that moment," he remembers, "I had two choices. Do I walk away from all the vast opportunity in Russia, just run away with my tail between my legs? Or do I learn from my mistake, wise up, and try to recapture my money in another deal? Thank God, I chose the latter course."

The Right Partner: Key to Success in Russia

At the very blackest moment of his Russian sojourn, Saad had discovered the perfect partners. The deal they offered him was to catapult Saad to instant prominence on the Russian business scene.

"The best way to make money in Russia is to have a good partner," says Earl Worsham, chairman of one of the most successful real estate ventures in Russia. "If you don't have a good partner, you lose your ass."

Nowadays, foreign businessmen tend to be sceptical of Russian partners. This is a backlash from the "joint venture era" of 1987 through 1990, when foreigners were virtually forced to take on Russian partners in order to gain tax breaks and dodge bureaucratic harassment. Many of these "shotgun partners" turned out to be incompetent or downright dishonest. Yet, foreigners were stuck with them. If you dumped your Russian "partner," the authorities would withdraw your permission to operate in Russia.

Today, the laws are much more lax. Legally, you don't need a Russian partner at all. But if you can find a good one, it still works to your advantage. This is as true in Germany and Singapore as it is in Russia. In every market of the world, smart foreign investors always try to form joint ventures with local business leaders. A native knows the local market in a way that you never will. And a full-fledged partner, with an equity stake in your business, will work harder on your behalf than a mere employee or consultant.

Twelve Ways to Tell the
Shysters from the Players

However, as Edward Saad's experience demonstrates, you need to be careful about whom you climb in bed with. Experienced insiders suggest twelve key criteria for sorting the chaff from the grain, when choosing a Russian partner. They are as follows.

Criterion One: Does He
Seem Too Needy?

If your prospective partner seems too needy, look out! A partner who starts out negotiations by requesting money, equipment, services, or personal perks is probably not seriously interested in doing business with you. This was the case with Saad's ill-fated cosmetics venture.

In the past, state-employed managers became notorious for this sort of behavior. They had no personal stake in concluding a business deal. Joint ventures with Americans represented only additional and thankless work for them. However, by drawing out fruitless negotiations *ad infinitum*, they could milk hopeful Americans for gifts, expensive dinners, or trips to the West.

Nowadays, such behavior is dying out, primarily because managers of state firms can now secure personal stakes in ventures through the new privatization laws. This has made everyone in Russia a lot more serious about doing business. However, Russia still abounds with rapacious "entrepreneurs" who think it far more clever to bilk Americans out of money and services than to invest in long-term relationships based on mutual trust and profit.

You don't need to deal with these sort of people at all. Don't excuse them by saying, "Well, that's just how these Russians are." The real movers and shakers in Russia do not behave this way. In fact, the new Russian businessman has become quite sophisticated. Most have travelled and shopped their fill in the West. They have successful businesses, considerable cash reserves in foreign banks, and they know how to obtain such things as computers and fax machines without leaning on prospective American partners. In short, *they don't really need you for anything*, except, of course, to transact some mutually profitable business! These are the sorts of partners you're looking for.

Criterion Two: Does He Have Impressive Physical Facilities?

It's always wise to go see where your partner "lives." A prospective partner with money and clout should have impressive offices and other facilities to show you. When Saad went to visit the two mysterious Russians from the lobby he discovered that their company, Vimpel, inhabited an impressive edifice in a "high-tech" district of Moscow. Saad was stopped at a security checkpoint as he entered and his passport examined. Finally, he was led upstairs to a plush office with fine, antique furniture, many computers, and a large conference table.

There, Saad was greeted by the two Russians he'd met at the ministry. They were Nikolai Mikhailov and Vasily Bakhar, the General Director and Vice President respectively of Vimpel Corporation.

Quietly, modestly, without boast or bluster, they explained to Saad that Vimpel was a leading defense contractor in Russia. With 20 scientific institutes under its wing and over 80,000 scientists in Russia, Ukraine, and Belarus, Vimpel had been the key organization responsible for creating the Soviet version of Star Wars.

"I didn't know what to think," recalls Saad. "It was scary. These guys were either some very powerful people or the biggest BS-ers I'd ever met."

Criterion Three: Is Your Prospective Partner an Impostor?

Russia has always been a land of secrecy where accurate information is more priceless than gold and more elusive than the Loch Ness monster.

One of your biggest challenges in choosing a partner lies in simply ascertaining that he or she is credible.

In the thick legal haze which still hovers about Russia as heavy as the mists of Avalon, it's all too easy to waste a lot of time negotiating with the wrong people. Just because some Russian factory manager or ministry official waves a piece of paper around doesn't mean that he or she actually has the authority to lease or sell a particular piece of property or even to negotiate with you at all.

Many hapless American investors have spent years hammering out contracts, only to find at the end that the factory or building they just "leased" is really controlled by some unknown ministry. They have to begin negotiations all over again, this time with the *right* people.

In this area, you really need outside help. In any deal where the identity or authority of a prospective partner seems to be in question, you should secure the services of a major law firm or even one of the Western detective firms which have been setting up shop in Russia. You need someone with the pull, the resources, and the expertise to fight through the tangled jungle of Russian documents and regulations and get at the truth. You can find such firms listed in the "Ready-Made Rolodex" in App. B.

Be advised that a few informal inquiries at the American embassy or among the expatriate business community *will not do the job*. All too often, Russians and foreign expatriates alike will deliberately lead you astray, either to protect their own proprietary access to information or to keep you from doing business with their competitors.

Edward Saad's partner, Nikolai Mikhailov, is a case in point. Quite by chance, I crossed paths with Mikhailov several times before I ever learned about Saad's deal. I first met Mikhailov back in 1990 at a banquet when I was participating in a Moscow seminar on entrepreneurship. I later interviewed him for *Success* magazine. In June 1992, when my wife and I were filming a documentary on Russian-American business for broadcast on the Russian Television Network, I proposed interviewing Mikhailov for the show. Our Russian partner in the TV production department looked startled at my suggestion and tried to talk me out of it. "Vimpel is not very big, not an important company at all," he said. "Don't waste your time."

I drew a similar response from an executive of a large, multinational American corporation. This executive had been stationed in Moscow for several years, and, by the nature of his business, would have had to know of a high-tech organization as large and prominent as Vimpel. Yet, he feigned puzzlement. "Vimpel? Vimpel?" said the executive. "I've never heard of them. Are they involved in clothes retailing or something?"

Only later did I discover that this man's company was even then deep in negotiations with Vimpel over an important high-tech R&D venture. But at the time, I was becoming worried that Mikhailov might not be such an important figure after all.

Luckily, I had brought along a few back issues of *Interflo*—a monthly compendium of Western press coverage on business in the former Soviet states. I was able to find a number of articles on Vimpel which confirmed Mikhailov's claims. Had I not brought those *Interflo* issues, I might have been stuck. You can't do a Lexis/Nexis search in the middle of Moscow.

The moral of the story is *don't rely on casual tips and referrals.* You need to do thorough, professional background checks if you want to find out who's who and what's what in Russia.

Criterion Four: Start with Small Deals

Many Americans have found it prudent to test prospective Russian partners by engaging in limited, one-time deals, involving small sums of money. This tests their competence and integrity, while creating little risk for you.

Early in their negotiations, real estate developer Earl Worsham received a disquieting phone call from his prospective Russian partner. Worsham had been negotiating with Andrei Stroyev (whom the press has since dubbed the "Donald Trump of Russia") to develop some Moscow properties. Now, all of a sudden, Stroyev wanted Worsham to wire him $60,000 in cash. Stroyev said he would use the money to buy $60,000 worth of computers which he would then sell to Russian customers for 1.2 million rubles—a 20 to 1 markup, by the exchange rate of those days.

"That's enough money to fund our joint venture for two years," argued Stroyev, "and to pay for all of our employees."

It sounded a little too good to be true to Worsham. "I started asking a bunch of questions and I didn't get very good answers," recalls Worsham.

Under questioning, Stroyev refused to divulge his proposed supplier for these computers. It was just "a friend in the computer business." When Worsham asked him if he was sure the specs of the computers he bought would meet the needs of his intended customers, Stroyev just laughed as if it were a stupid question. "Don't worry, Earl," he said. "It's not a problem. Any kind of computers I buy, I can sell them."

Worsham had been around the block enough times in Russia to hesitate at the words "no problem." Nevertheless, he decided to use Stroyev's unusual request as an opportunity to test the man's mettle. "I went ahead and sent the $60,000 without even a written agreement," says Worsham. "If it didn't work, that was the end. I'd cut off all dealings with Stroyev and save myself a million dollars or more that I might have risked."

But as it turned out, Stroyev proved as good as his word. Within days, Worsham's fledgling real estate venture was 1.2 million rubles richer—money he could use to pay salaries and buy construction materials.

"Right then," says Worsham, "that showed me he was a doer, not a talker." The two partners went on to build one of the most successful real estate development companies in Russia.

In the case of Nikolai Mikhailov, Edward Saad built a long-term relationship with him through a series of minor deals. Saad would sell him consumer products like shoes and shampoo, which Mikhailov then sold to his employees at cost as a perk.

"The trust wasn't immediate, on either side," says Saad. "It built up over months and months. But eventually, we reached a point where I became the man Vimpel would turn to for contacts in Western markets."

Criterion Five: Does Your Partner Have *Blat*?

Under the old Soviet system, *blat*—or "influence"—was the key to success. If you had the right contacts, you could gain power, prestige, luxurious living quarters, foreign travel, and even *money* through sanctioned black market dealings. A person with blat never worried about the law. Police and KGB alike would turn the other way, no matter how flagrant your violations.

Blat is still important in Russia. Even today, bureaucratic obstacles can stop you dead in your tracks, unless you have a powerful ally who can grease the gears for you behind the scenes. Many will tell you that *blat* is a thing of the past, that the almighty dollar speaks louder in Russia today than any high-level connections. That may be true. But unless your partner has *blat*, you'll find yourself coughing up exorbitant quantities of "almighty" bribe money every time you want equipment, supplies, or real estate. A partner with *blat* might be able to get those same goods or services for rubles—or for nothing at all. Mikhailov proved to have the kind of *blat* that you can't buy at any price.

One day, Vimpel's vice president, Vasili Bakhar, told Saad that Vimpel wanted to enter the cellular phone market. Could he provide Western contacts? Saad did some homework and came up with an up-and-coming Naperville, Illinois firm called Plexsys International. The little company grossed only $6 million in 1991, hardly a match for a giant like Vimpel. But Plexsys had certain key advantages.

Plexsys had proprietary technology which allowed it to create profitable networks with only a few hundred subscribers (as opposed to the hundreds of thousands needed to support more orthodox systems). Plexsys's unique technology enabled it to develop rural, Third World markets that major telecommunications firms couldn't afford to go near. What worked in Latin America might just work in Russia as well.

In October 1991, Saad ushered Augie Fabela, Jr. (Plexsys's 26-year-old president) to Moscow. Just 10 days later, Fabela signed a deal with Vimpel which was to shock the giants of telecommunications.

"Pick Russian partners with care," advised *Forbes* magazine after the deal was announced. "U.S. West didn't, and is about to have its lunch eaten by tiny Plexsys Corporation."

U.S. West, the multibillion-dollar "Baby Bell," previously had formed a cellular phone network in partnership with such heavy-hitters as the Moscow City Telephone network and Dr. Svyatoslav Fyodorov, the world-renowned eye surgeon who invented keratotomy surgery for curing near-sightedness. Despite these high-level connections, U.S. West was unable to win major concessions from the Russian Communications Ministry. They were only licensed to use the obsolete "Nordic" system, which operated in the 450 MHz band. Higher frequencies were reserved for military and civil aviation, said the Ministry.

Then along came little Plexsys. It shocked the telecommunications world by announcing that its cellular phone system would use the forbidden 850 MHz range for its transmissions. Plexsys subscribers would have a devastating edge over those of U.S. West. They would be able to use smaller, more compact phones, get clearer, stronger signals, and make larger numbers of calls at the same time.

How did Plexsys do it? Simple. Vimpel tapped a few friendly shoulders at the Defense Ministry and gained special clearance for the restricted frequency. Now *that's blat.*

Criterion Six: Have You Considered Alternatives?

When working in a foreign land—and especially a country as alien as Russia—small achievements seem disproportionately large. All too many Americans will start patting themselves on the back as soon as they locate a plausible Russian partner. Afraid of losing their first, real live Russian, they will make excuses, overlook obvious faults, and otherwise regard their erring partner through rose-colored glasses.

A good cure for this common self-delusion is to simply go out of your way to interview several different candidates before closing any important deal. This way you can test your own perceptions. Are you *really* satisfied with your partner, or just settling for the first warm Russian body you could find?

Before bringing Plexsys over to close the cellular phone deal, Ed Saad interviewed two different Russian firms in addition to Vimpel as possible partners.

"Both of them said, 'Yes, we can get the deal done, but it's going to cost because we'll have to pay off people and do this, that and the other," says Saad. "Vimpel was the only one that didn't ask for bribes and didn't play any Mickey Mouse games. They didn't nickel and dime me, didn't ask for any money up front. There was absolutely no graft involved, no innuendo. A few days after I introduced them to Plexsys, Vimpel just said, 'Let's do it!'"

Criterion Seven: Does Your Prospect Have Good Technical Resources?

An effective Russian partner must have access to the technical resources and skilled personnel you'll need to operate. Vimpel's credentials in this regard were obvious.

In the first few days of negotiation, Plexsys president Augie Fabela, Jr. was bowled over by the degree of technical expertise at Vimpel's disposal. Before they were even close to closing a deal, Vimpel's engineers had worked out a complex plan for placing cellular phone antennae around Moscow—a task involving complex calculations of the effect of buildings and other landmarks on the radio signal.

"A difference of 20 feet in placing an antenna can make all the difference in the world," says Fabela. "Vimpel had already made significant progress in thinking this through."

Fabela was taken on a grand tour of Vimpel's R&D facilities in the Moscow area, including several radio-telecommunications institutes associated with the Academy of Sciences. "They had very clearly thought-out ideas on how to manage their resources. They created a team concept, planning out how they could bring in different elements of these institutes to benefit our joint venture, but in a very streamlined way, bypassing the bureaucracy," says Fabela.

Today, Vimpel has some 35 scientists and engineers and over 100 manufacturing people working full-time on the Plexsys contract. Vimpel is developing a microwave network to complement the existing system. Also, it's now manufacturing its own cellular phone antennae; precision equipment which Euronet (Plexsys's Russian joint venture) would otherwise have had to import from America at much higher cost.

Fabela estimates that before 1993 is out, Euronet should be up and running in every major city of the CIS, thanks largely to the incredible technical prowess of Vimpel.

Criterion Eight: Does Your Prospect Ask the Right Questions?

A sophisticated Russian businessman is no more willing to accept *you* at face value than you *him*. He will question you closely about your track record, your finances, and your experience in international business. A prospective Russian partner who fails to check you out thoroughly displays, at best, excessive naivete and, at worst, desperation for an American partner—*any* American partner. Either way, it augurs ill for your joint venture.

Joseph Francis was approached by a prominent Russian entrepreneur after appearing on Russian television talking about his plans to build a hairstyling salon in Moscow. The Russian, whose name Francis refuses to divulge, was so eager to locate him, that he called Francis' office in Minneapolis and obtained the address in Moscow where Francis was staying.

At 7 a.m. one morning, Francis received two unexpected visitors at the apartment where he was staying. The two middle- aged ladies turned out to be high-placed managers in the hairstyling department of the Soviet Health Ministry. The eager entrepreneur had dispatched them to check Francis out.

While Francis fumbled sleepily for his coffee, the ladies grilled him on technical aspects of hairstyling until they were satisfied that he really knew his business. They asked him detailed questions about his chain of salons back in America and examined brochures and pictures which Francis had brought with him.

Next came a series of personal meetings with the Russian entrepreneur, who had made his fortune in the lumber business. Francis was surprised at the sophisticated questions the man asked.

"He wanted to know how long I'd had my company, what problems I'd run into in business, had I ever gone bankrupt, did I have good banking relationships, did I have international credibility, was I going to be involved in the day-to-day management of our joint venture?" It wasn't until Francis brought the Russians to Minneapolis to see his headquarters that the ice really seemed to break.

"When they saw our facilities, our corporate headquarters, our state-of-the-art equipment, I thought they'd died and gone to heaven," says Francis. The deal was closed shortly after.

Criterion Nine: Be a Detective

As mentioned previously, it is always advisable to obtain professional assistance in checking out a potential Russian partner. However, such services can be quite expensive and may not always be appropriate, especially when you're talking informally to a lot of different Russians about a lot of small deals.

In the States, we have a number of resources for running quick, informal checks on potential partners. You can run a Lexis/Nexis or Equifax search, check with Dun & Bradstreet, TRW, the Better Business Bureau, or with local Chambers of Commerce. "Everybody in America is on some computer disk somewhere," says Francis. "But in Russia, it's not so easy to check someone out." To get the goods on a prospective partner in Russia, you've got to use ingenuity and persistence.

Francis went first to the U.S. Commercial Office at the American embassy to see if they had a dossier on the man. They didn't. Next, Francis made discreet personal inquiries into the man's past professional record. He had apparently once been a high-placed government minister. Over the course of several months and several trips to Moscow, Francis painstakingly pieced together a "trail of friends and associates" of his prospective partner.

Getting a personal bank statement from the man proved unexpectedly difficult. The man refused several times until Francis finally got tough and told him the deal was off. Then he sheepishly produced a statement from a Finnish bank showing that he had hundreds of thousands of dollars in cash safely secreted outside the country.

Francis even managed to have an influential Russian friend run a KGB check on the man. "He came back with a clean slate," says Francis. "They said he was one of the up and coming chargers. In fact, he had performed so well in his job, they thought he should have been in the military."

Criterion Ten: Chemistry

No matter how many references you compile, how many background checks you run, or how closely you scrutinize a prospective partner's balance sheet, there's a limit to what you can learn from such hard facts. At some point, you must let intuition be your guide. Fortunately, Russian negotiating traditions provide ample opportunity for testing the personal chemistry between yourself and your prospective Russian partner.

"There was an awful lot of entertaining," Francis remembers, "a lot of intimate dinners. They'd take me to a room in a hotel and present these fabulous dinners with all kinds of foods, wines, cognac. There was a lot of time for many long talks and cordial banter late into the evenings. It got pretty boring after awhile, but that was their method."

The Russian tradition of mixing business with copious amounts of pleasure affords both partners an excellent chance to size up one another. Francis listened carefully while the man talked at length about himself, his family, his desire to learn from Americans, and to become a successful entrepreneur. Ultimately, he was satisfied that this was the sort of partner he could work with and Francis's "City Looks" salon opened successfully in Moscow in June 1992.

Criterion Eleven: Is Your Partner An
Apparatchik in Disguise?

The worst horror stories about Russian partners come from Americans who unknowingly team up with *apparatchiki* disguised as entrepreneurs. An *apparatchik* is a bureaucrat reared in the old-fashioned Communist tradition. Of course, many of today's most dynamic Russian entrepreneurs started out as *apparatchiki*. But they succeeded in business only because they were young and flexible enough to shed their *apparatchik* mentality. Most Russia insiders learn quickly that it's dangerous dealing with any Russian older than age 45. After that age, there tend to be too many ossified habits baked in by the Stalinist system.

Francis's principal partner was an example of the former—a talented *apparatchik* who managed to make the transition to entrepreneur. However, the two, middle-aged ladies who ended up managing his Moscow salon proved to be classic examples of unrepentant and incurable *apparatchiki*.

When the ladies first showed up on Francis's doorstep at 7 a.m. in the morning, he was impressed by their professional credentials. "These women had hiring and firing power over the managers of 15,000 state hair salons," says Francis. "All of the chain-owned salons in America don't add up to 15,000."

To impress him, the ladies took Francis to their training school in Moscow, where Russian hairstylists were put through a training regimen more rigorous than any American could imagine. "In America, hairstylists train for nine to twelve months," says Francis. "In Russia, they go to school for three years and then enter an apprenticeship program."

The ladies put on a private exhibition for Francis, in which students at the hairstyling academy were required not only to create an original, fantasy hairstyle but also to personally design and sew the elaborate period costumes which the models wore—right down to the last detail of the underwear.

"There were some with their hair weaved onto wire so it looked like they were wearing a crown," says Francis. "They had costumes from the Renaissance era. There must have been 20 different presentations. It took three hours just to watch it. Each one must have taken two days to create. We just don't have that kind of ability in the United States. They put on this whole show just to impress me. I was the only one in the audience. These women were trying to show me the calibre of people that they would hand-select for our stores."

Needless to say, Francis was suitably dazzled. The ladies were brought in as partners, and charged with managing the new, as of yet, unconstructed store.

Their *apparatchik* mentality quickly showed itself. Although it became apparent that the ladies lacked hands-on experience running a salon, they stubbornly insisted on maintaining iron control over every aspect of running the store, from the initial construction on.

"They didn't know how to run a store," says John Francis, Joe Francis's son, who spent eight months in Moscow overseeing the store construction and opening, "They would walk in, go into their office, and sit behind the desk. That's what they do. They don't know how to greet customers, how to deal with staff, do paperwork. Nothing."

After months of bickering, the Francis's prevailed upon the ladies to allow an American manager to run the store so that they could devote their energies to sitting at their desks. But allowing them to preside over the construction and opening had been a costly mistake. The store opened 16 months behind schedule and ended up costing almost eight times the projected startup costs, largely as a result of their mismanagement.

The moral of the story is: Don't judge Russian partners by their high-falutin' bureaucratic titles. In general, work with the younger generation and only with those who've proven their mettle in the private sector.

Criterion Twelve: Is Your Partner a Political Risk?

Political struggle plays a role in every country. But in some, this role is grossly magnified. As long as Russia's leaders remain locked in the present political crisis, some business deals will fall through for reasons that have nothing to do with money, markets, or competence.

In selecting partners, try to get some idea of where your prospective partner stands in the ongoing power struggle. How secure is his position? How powerful are his enemies?

Paul Zane Pilzer thought he had a dream deal. The Dallas entrepreneur had figured out a way to use Russia's Far Eastern region as a transshipment point to move air freight between Japan and the United States. Japan's airport bottleneck is notorious. There just aren't enough landing slots in Tokyo to accommodate the number of arriving cargo planes. A priority shipment to a Japanese factory might wait three days or more just to get clearance to land in Tokyo. It could sit in Japanese customs for three days and then take another day or two to be transported to the appropriate factory by boat.

Russia provided a shortcut. Pilzer calculated that he could fly freight shipments from Los Angeles to the Far Eastern city of Nakhodka in one day, then ship them directly by boat to any part of Japan in 18 hours. He'd never have to go near the Tokyo bottleneck.

Pilzer's idea was so hot that he quickly got four freight companies to book flights in advance. He arranged to purchase 60 Ilyushin-72 cargo planes from a Russian company called ANT. Everything was set. Pilzer saw himself preparing to roll out a billion-dollar-a-year business.

Then Pilzer got a panic-stricken call in the middle of the night from his representative in Moscow. "The head of ANT has been arrested," said the man. "He was caught smuggling tanks out of the country."

Pilzer knew ANT's director, Vladimir Ryasantshev, quite well. He'd spent a lot of time negotiating with him. The company seemed to have impeccable high-level connections. When Pilzer first stepped into ANT's Moscow offices, he was struck by the sleek, Western look of the place.

"I couldn't believe it," recalls Pilzer. "It was wall-to-wall American IBM PCs, clean floors, everything modern. It was like walking into what you'd imagine KGB spy headquarters to look like."

But suddenly Ryasantshev was in jail in what quickly shaped up to be a major national scandal. The Russian press went crazy! ANT had been caught shipping tanks to foreign countries in crates marked as cranes and other heavy equipment. Also, the company was accused of making $700 million worth of illegal exports of strategic metals like nickel, copper, magnesium, and titanium. Pilzer was warned privately by U.S. State Department officials that if he returned to the Soviet Union, he might be arrested by Soviet authorities as a suspected accomplice.

"The whole deal fell through," says Pilzer. "ANT was supposed to deliver my planes in four months. I had my reputation on the line with all these air freight suppliers who'd signed on as clients. But there was nothing I could do. A billion-dollar-a-year business had just gone right down the drain."

Only later did Pilzer learn that the ANT scandal had been an apparent setup by hardliners who had wanted to discredit Gorbachev's reforms. High-level government figures had apparently instructed Ryasantshev to sell weapons and materials abroad in order to raise money to import consumer goods for the Soviet people. When Ryasantshev did as he was told, he was nabbed as a "criminal." His case aired in the Congress of People's Deputies as an example of rapacious capitalism. Numerous government figures were implicated. A shadow of suspicion even fell on Soviet Prime Minister Nikolai Ryzhkov. The timing of the scandal, too, seemed uncanny, coming in the midst of Gorbachev's 1990 campaign for the presidency of the Soviet Union.

A Calculated Risk

Ultimately, choosing a Russian partner will be a gamble, as it is in any country of the world. But if you take these sensible precautions, you can make it a sober, calculated risk rather than a blind crap shoot. Choose correctly and you may gain access to incalculable skills and resources that would never be available to a Lone American Wolf.

10
Build a Team

**The Russian Workforce Can Be
Your Greatest Asset**

In 1991, *The New York Times* ran a story about a new breed of immigrants. These immigrants were highly educated, hardworking go-getters, willing to work for slave wages. In fact, these newcomers were proving so attractive, that employers were beginning to give them preference over the homegrown variety.

Who were these new immigrants? They were Russians. And the country they were migrating to was Poland. Seeking greater opportunities in Poland's rapidly reforming economy, Russians had quickly acquired a reputation as the best workers to hire.

"They work for much less money," said one Polish employer. "They don't need vodka, and they work without supervision."

Even in our own country, Russian immigrants have adapted so quickly as to create a formidable and wholly unexpected threat to native workers in certain high-paying fields. For example, many Russians have discovered that computer programming is an ideal job for someone who doesn't speak English. They sign up for computer courses almost as soon as they clear customs at Kennedy Airport. As a result, so many Russian programmers have flooded Wall Street brokerages houses that some managers have been quietly told not to look at any more resumes with Slavic surnames.

"I've worked in companies where almost all the programmers were Russian," says one programmer. "Everybody is speaking Russian to each other all the time. It makes the Americans insecure. They start feeling dominated, that there are too many of us."

Change the System and You
Change the People

These stories fly in the face of common "wisdom," which holds that Russians are by nature lazy, slovenly, unresourceful, and slipshod in their work. How do we account for the discrepancy?

The answer is that Russians are the most diligent and hardworking of all employees once they're taken out of the demotivating environment of the typical Russian workplace. It's true that 70 years of socialism have wrought a *homo sovieticus* in Russia who answers to many of the most unsavory descriptions of the critics. But precisely the same problems appear among the East German workforce, despite the fact that German workers have been renowned for generations for their ant-like diligence and pride of craftmanship.

The lesson is: Change the system and you'll change the people.

The Russian Workforce:
Your Greatest Asset

If you know how to use it, the Russian work force can prove to be your greatest asset. The Russians yearn for a chance to excel—exactly the sort of chance an American entrepreneur can give them. Talented Russians are so starved for achievement, they'll practically pay *you* to let them work. And they'll work till they drop.

At one point, David Kelley considered pulling the plug on Spantek, his printed T-shirt venture in Moscow. "Sales were very slow. I was ready to pack it in," he says. "Then two of my Russian workers just sat me down and said, 'Look, David, we're going to make this work. If we have to come in and *work for nothing*, we'll do it. We're not going to give up.'"

Ira Kitova was one of them. Asked why she was willing to work for nothing, she explained, "This company is our baby. We can't just abandon it. We have to pull together and fight for our existence."

You'll search a long time before you find such dedication among American workers. But in Russia, employment at an American firm is more than just a job. For many Russians, such work is prized on a par with life itself.

Certainly, that's the case with Kitova. At 26, she now earns more money than her father ever dreamed of. Every day, she goes to work in a world he could never imagine, a world she never thought herself privileged to enter. "It's up to the young generation now," she says. "This is our time to act, to build a new life for ourselves."

A Team of Superstars

By popular accolade, Joint Venture Dialogue is recognized as the Apple Computer of Russia's Silicon Revolution, a flame that consistently attracts the brightest stars from the ranks of Russia's high-tech innovators. Formed in November 1987, Dialogue was one of the earliest of the joint ventures. Indeed, it was only the *second* Soviet-American partnership registered under Gorbachev's 1987 joint venture law. While other joint ventures took years to get off the ground (those which managed to get started at all), Dialogue distributorships spread like wildfire across the whole breadth of the Soviet Union. By the end of Dialogue's first full year of operation, the company had netted 90 million rubles and $3 million. By the end of its second year, with over 38 offices throughout the Soviet Union, Dialogue's trademark could be found from Nakhodka on the Pacific Coast to Minsk, Leningrad, and Prague. Today, Dialogue has over 100 offices in the former Soviet states and Eastern Europe. It has become a name to conjure with, practically synonymous with the *success* of Russia's freemarket reform.

Initially a computer reseller and software house, Dialogue's range of ancillary businesses has expanded to include bioengineering, tourism, real estate, land development, construction, timber, telecommunications, banking, legal services, consulting, and an on-line business information database called RusData Dialine. Dialogue has also become one of the major manufacturers of computer hardware in the former Soviet states, operating assembly plants in Minsk and outside of Moscow. Its DialogBank is a fast-rising force in Russian finance.

Perhaps the most remarkable thing about Dialogue is that it built its success on *Russian* talent. Its American founder, Joseph Ritchie, believes fervently in the rich potential of Russia's talented people, and he has forged a unique network for finding and harvesting that talent wherever it lies.

A master teambuilder with an unorthodox approach to management, Ritchie and his company deserve close study by any American wishing to build a similar team of Russian *superstars*.

A Magic Kingdom of Achievement

Joseph Ritchie once called Walt Disney "my hero for the twentieth century." Like Disney, Ritchie has built his company into a Magic Kingdom of achievement where only the best, brightest, and most talented may gather, as around King Arthur's Round Table.

Now 46 years old, Joseph Ritchie was born and raised by American parents in Afghanistan. He attended three years of Bible college in Oregon before going on to earn a philosophy degree at Wheaton College. A rebel at heart, Ritchie spent years trying to "find himself," working at various times as a bus driver and a deputy county sheriff. But at last, in 1977, the young Bible student cum philosopher found his true calling—options and futures trading.

With $200,000 scraped together between them, Ritchie and a few friends started a new firm called Chicago Research and Trading (CRT). Ritchie was 30 years old. Dressed at the time in a borrowed business suit, Ritchie presided over strategy sessions from behind a "desk" that was really a door laid across two boxes.

Ritchie is reputed to be a mathematical genius. According to *The Wall Street Journal,* he once solved the famous Rubik's Cube puzzle by examining the cube from different angles and calculating the algorithm which underlay it. When Ritchie turned his powerful talent to commodities trading, it quickly made him one of the world's richest men.

Mind Power, Team Power

The heart and soul of CRT was *mind power.* Armed with little more than PCs and hand-held calculators, Ritchie and his team brainstormed a secret computer program which put them years ahead of established trading firms. CRT's computers now scour world commodity markets from Buenos Aires to Indonesia, searching out tiny, evanescent differences between options and futures prices and executing lightning deals during those split seconds of opportunity. It's profit margins are often infinitesimal. But they are *guaranteed* by the laws of mathematics.

In its first 10 years, CRT grew to become the largest options trading company in the world, executing $2.5 billion in trades each day and amassing over $225 million in capital, accounting at any given time for up to *40 percent* of total trading volume in global options markets.

Build a Mystique

To attract the best minds and the most committed workers, Ritchie consciously built a mystique around his company not unlike the aura which once glittered about his idol's Walt Disney Productions.

CRT recruits ran a gauntlet of highly personal interviews and were put through a battery of sophisticated psychological tests. Likely candidates were then challenged to take a pay cut when they were hired, in order to prove they were motivated not by money but by some nebulous higher ideals—a rigorous enough test in a profession as money-mad as commodities trading.

Once on the team, traders found an incentive structure that encouraged cooperation rather than competition between team members. The CRT acolytes were urged to think of themselves as a "family," a mood encouraged by the casual atmosphere of the office where slacks and golf shirts prevailed over "power ties" and suspenders. Ritchie kept five chefs on staff so employees could relax together over free meals. This was the corporate culture which Ritchie brought to Russia in 1987.

Nine Ways to Build and Motivate a Winning Team of Russians

Ritchie's uniquely effective approach to teambuilding in Russia can be broken down roughly into nine techniques. They are as follows.

Technique One:
Form High-Level Alliances

Russia is, and always has been, a highly centralized land of inside connections where a few power brokers pull the strings for everyone else. You will have trouble identifying, contacting, and winning over the most talented Russians unless you first gain access to the intimate Rolodexes of powerful individuals and organizations. This especially holds true for the military-industrial sector, where Russia's foremost talent is invariably concentrated.

Ritchie went right to the top in making his initial business contacts in Russia. On a 1986 trip to the Soviet Union, Ritchie formed an alliance with Pyotr Zrelov, who was, at the time, director of Management Information Systems (MIS) for KAMAZ—the largest truck factory in the world.

Zrelov pitched Ritchie on an idea to form a Soviet-American computer company. Their ensuing joint venture immediately attracted some of Russia's top industrial organizations and think tanks as partners. Among them were KAMAZ itself, Moscow State University, the Computer Center of the Russian Academy of Sciences, and the Central Institute of Economics and Applied Mathematics.

Three things helped Ritchie win this kind of high-level support. First, the stature and contacts of his initial partner, Pyotr Zrelov. Second, his own stated willingness to invest a large sum of money ($5 million to start). And finally, Ritchie was helped by his choice of industry. By offering to develop affordable computer hardware and software for the Soviet market, Ritchie meshed his business plan perfectly with the highest priorities of the Soviet government, which equated rapid computerization with national survival.

Technique Two: Provide a Vision

When my wife and I were in Moscow filming a documentary about Russian-American relations, I wrote a reference into the script to Russia and the United States as "the two greatest powers in the world." Our Russian script editor was appalled at such bombast. He told us the passage was completely unsuitable for the Russian television audience for whom we intended it.

"This kind of inflated language—it's the sort of thing Brezhnev would have said 20 years ago," he complained. "Russians don't think about their country as a great power anymore."

Our interpreter later told us that he didn't quite agree with the script editor's criticism. Yes, it was true that most Russians would be disgusted to hear such cant out of *another Russian*, but our interpreter thought that as long as the audience understood it was *coming from an American*, it would be all right. "Russians don't care anymore about idealistic things," he said. "But we understand that Americans still think this way."

One of the greatest gifts Americans can bring to the Russian people today is good old Yankee optimism. For 70 years, the Russians cringed beneath the peppy slogans of Communist workmasters, who pestered them night and day with visions of some far-off Utopia. Now, anyone who sounds too idealistic is treated as a fool. To appear sophisticated and worldly, a Russian must now affect the blackest pessimism and make wry jests about squeezing money from foreigners.

Don't believe the pose. A cynic in any culture is just a disappointed optimist crying out for help. Russians are as much in need of a higher goal as the rest of us. And despite their extravagant shows of cynicism, they yearn for some reason to feel pride in their people, their country, and themselves. An American businessman is in a unique position to provide all three.

When manager Bob Clough told a group of Russian employees back in 1989 that Dialogue intended to manufacture the first Soviet personal computer suitable for export, the whole room erupted in laughter. "Their attitude was, 'Give me a break. Sell Soviet computers in the West? We can't do it. It's never going to happen.' And they really believed that. So part of our task is getting the Russians to believe in themselves."

The way to do that was to show them results. As Dialogue slowly began developing software packages and selling them in the West, Clough saw the Russians' self-image improve almost daily. Dialogue started assembling PCs from imported components at a plant in Minsk and in a new 100,000 square foot factory it opened outside of Moscow. More and more programmers and engineers were put to work on the new, all-Russian PC. Dialogue hardware now sells briskly within the former Soviet states. And although the new, exportable PC has yet to be released, the laughter and catcalls have given way to quiet determination and feverish work.

"It's clear in their eyes," said Bob Clough when I interviewed him in 1990. "They're starting to believe in themselves. There's no question they can do it."

As in any venture anywhere in the world, you must provide leadership. State a clear vision, a lofty goal to which your Russian team may aspire. Then show them how to attain it practically.

Stepan Pachikov, director of ParaGraph, has built a team of Russian programmers on a par with any software house in the West. His style of leadership plays upon that delicate balance of hope and despair which stalks the Slavic soul.

"From the beginning, I used a little psychological trick," he explains. "I gave them a picture, an image of our company a little better and brighter than the reality. That gave them a direction. They tried to make themselves in accordance with this image. But the image couldn't be *too* much brighter than reality, not 10 times or a 100 times, because then they wouldn't see any real chance to attain it. The difference had to be reasonable. But every time I moved the frontier further and further, higher and higher. So now I can tell them that someday we will be one of the best computer companies in the world. And they believe it."

Technique Three: Delegate Authority

In a famous experiment, American psychologist Martin E.P. Seligman took two groups of dogs and subjected them to electrical shocks. One group could stop the shock simply by pushing a panel with its nose. The second group also had a nose panel, but no matter how many times the dogs pushed, the shocks would keep coming. A third group, or the "control" group, was never shocked at all.

After being conditioned in this way, the dogs were placed in boxes with two adjacent compartments. One compartment had a metal floor through which shocks were administered. A normal dog would soon learn that it could escape the shocks by jumping over the low partition into the adjoining compartment.

Within seconds after being placed in the "shock box," the first group of dogs—those who had learned to stop the shocks by pushing a panel—jumped to safety. So did the "control" group, who had received no shocks at all. However, the third group simply lay down on the metal floor and whimpered. They made no attempt to escape the repeated shocks.

Seligman concluded that the whimpering dogs had "learned helplessness." Because they had been taught earlier that shocks would keep coming no matter how many times they pushed the nose panel, they had concluded that pain was inescapable, and that there was no point in trying to get away from it.

Humans too can "learn helplessness" when they are repeatedly thwarted in every attempt to better themselves. After awhile, they just lie down and whimper. The Soviet past is still recent enough that most talented Russians you'll meet have already been thoroughly abused by the state bureaucracy. In Soviet state companies, top managers guarded their fiefdoms jealously against ambitious up and comers. No matter how hard you tried, personal advancement was nearly impossible. Therefore, most Russians "learned helplessness" at an early stage in their careers.

Your task will be to break these destructive presumptions in your employees. As with dogs, you must employ *counter-conditioning* techniques. Your Russian employees learned to be passive and helpless after repeatedly taking action and getting no results. Now you must *force them to act* and *reward their initiative* with *immediate results*.

Dialogue's "nonhierarchical" structure provides a perfect vehicle for such counter-conditioning. Corporate titles are kept to minimum. Employees are encouraged to take on whatever projects or problems present themselves for solution, and not to worry about authorization.

"The basic guideline that was given to me when I came to work for Dialogue," says former manager Virginia Clough, "is that you have to *make decisions*. If you don't have the technical background or the business acumen, just do what *feels good*. If you need to go out and buy something, do it. If it gets to be a problem five months down the line, we'll talk about it then. But until then, don't bother to get approval. We're always told that we have the authority to do our job and the authority to do whatever it takes to get that job done."

In accordance with this philosophy, new employees at Dialogue—both American and Russian—are often immediately thrown into positions of responsibility where they must "sink or swim."

When Nikolai Lyubovny was hired in 1989, Dialogue had just signed an agreement with AutoCad to distribute their CAD (computer-assisted design) software in Russia. Lyubovny immediately was put in charge of the entire sales and marketing program for AutoCad products—areas in which he had absolutely no expertise. In his old job at a state research institute, Lyubovny had been a mere programmer.

"I felt like a small person at my old job," says Lyubovny. "But at Dialogue, I was allowed to have my own voice. I could give my opinion, argue with the boss, talk to the General Director, with anyone, and fight for my opinion. In my previous job, no one wanted to hear my opinion."

But Dialogue expected more out of Lyubovny than just talk. "I was responsible for everything, for advertising, signing agreements with end-users, all negotiations," marvels Lyubovny.

It was all new to Lyubovny, but he dove into the task with gusto. "I had to call AutoCad and find out all the information myself," he remembers. "I spent a lot of time trying to understand the financial arrangements, how much money to charge, where to send the money, how to get products delivered, what discounts to charge for end-users, the conditions for licensing." Five months after starting work at Dialogue, Lyubovny was sent without supervision to the important CAD show in Birmingham, England. His only instructions were to schmooze his way around and make a few deals. Amazingly, he closed a distribution deal with a British freight company to deliver AutoCad products to Russia by truck.

"Nikolai increased the sales and developed a very good distribution network," says Virginia Clough. "He went from being a one-man show to having 25 people working for him. He became a middle manager."

Technique Four: Reward Those Who Take the Initiative

In the old Soviet system, employees were often punished for taking initiative. That's why cynical Soviet bureaucrats used to quip that, "The only safe decision is a decision you don't make."

You must counter this attitude by rewarding initiative in clear and obvious ways. The greatest reward of all is advancement. It's the chance to rise up the ladder and "play with the big boys."

After his great success marketing AutoCad products, Lyubovny was given the crucial job of "localizing" Microsoft products. That meant translating the manuals to Russian, changing the software specifications to conform to Russian standards, adapting the software to Cyrillic characters, as well as developing and implementing a marketing plan.

When the new product line was finally ready to roll, Lyubovny and his group attended a victory banquet hosted by none other than Microsoft founder Bill Gates. Lyubovny could hardly contain himself.

"It was very exciting for us," he remembers. "We'd been working almost two years on the project. Microsoft thought it was very good. I was tired at that point, but very proud."

Lyubovny felt that he had arrived at last. At 42, he was no longer a nameless Soviet programmer slaving away in some back office. He had joined the international fraternity of computer professionals. As he talked with the legendary billionaire Bill Gates, Lyubovny was surprised to find that he and Gates were made of pretty much the same stuff.

"Bill Gates is an interesting person," says Lyubovny. "He's not a businessman, but a programmer. When he first appeared at the dinner, he seemed bored by the whole thing. But as soon as we started to talk about computers, he changed. He was a new man. I was surprised that in his position, he knows everything. You can talk to him about all technical details. He spent the main part of the dinner with the programmers."

Technique Five: Create a
Work-Friendly Environment

The old Soviet worker traditionally regarded his workplace as hostile and alien territory. People put in their time grudgingly like prisoners on a chain gang, escaping at the first opportunity. They played cat and mouse games with the boss, covering for one anothers' frequent absences. In order to avoid "wasting" too much time sitting at their desks, Soviet employees used their worktime to call around, trading shopping tips with their friends. If someone got a tip about a late-breaking shipment of children's shoes or sausage at a nearby store, that was it for the day. The employee would bolt work immediately to stand in line.

Dialogue set out to create a work-friendly environment, similar to the "family" atmosphere enforced in the Chicago offices of Joe Ritchie's CRT Group. Dialogue's touchy-feely work culture would be unusual even in America. Children roam the corridors freely, climbing into programmers' laps as they work. Employees vacation together, play Ping-Pong between meetings, or strum guitars. Beer blasts are held every Friday afternoon in an uncanny echo of Apple Computer's early days. In Dialogue's early days, an in-house cafeteria served three free meals a day, with coffee, tea, and snacks available at any time. As the company grew, that became too expensive. But on-site cafeterias still provide hearty and inexpensive fare at each of Dialogue's Moscow facilities.

"It makes sense from a business perspective," says Virginia Clough, "because otherwise our employees would be out two hours every day trying to find food. If they could find food. Here, they can get together over snacks and tea in the cafeteria, they can bring guests, talk about their projects, and not have to worry about daily survival."

"People actually enjoy hanging out at Dialogue," says Clough. "Their kids hang out at Dialogue. They're there all the time. We sometimes feel guilty going home at eight o'clock at night because people are still there."

Marat Ishnev was amazed to discover that he was allowed to stay up all night and work on the computers at Dialogue. Even as an MIS manager at the advanced KAMAZ truck plant, he needed special permission anytime he wished to work at odd hours.

"You punched in at a checkpoint," he remembers. "You came in at 8 a.m. and left at 6 p.m. That's not good for a programmer. Sometimes you'd rather work late at night and come in at noon. At Dialogue, you have the freedom to do that."

"The computer nerd mentality is the same the world over," says Virginia Clough. "We have people who will work for 36 to 48 hours straight. They have bleary eyes and pale skin, because they haven't seen the sun for days, and they just sit there and eat junk food. We have one programmer who always gets a big stack of candy bars before he starts a project, and he just stares at the computer screen for hours and hours and then at the end of this marathon session, the candy bars are done and so is the program."

Technique Six: Screen for Personality

Potential Dialogue recruits are subjected to rigorous psychological screening similar to that imposed on job candidates at Ritchie's Chicago Research and Trading Group. As at CRT, candidates whose primary goal seems to be immediate financial gain are mercilessly screened out. The quest is to find true believers who will buy into the vision and commit their lives to the company. Much of the screening is accomplished through an unorthodox interview process which focuses on personality and downplays job history.

"It's not the piece of paper the person carries, it's not the degree or the expertise," says Virginia Clough. "It's their quality as a person. Is that person interesting? Is that person interested in developing something here? Is that person interested in fulfilling their own personal potential and in doing it in a group setting?"

Clough tells of Russian job candidates who were taken aback when Dialogue interviewers began probing into their family and childhood backgrounds. "Sometimes they say they're just not comfortable talking about such personal things," she says. "One Russian guy told us that we were trying to find out if he could be our friend, and that it was impossible to find this out in a 15-minute interview. Then there was a woman we interviewed once who said that she thought our egalitarian style of management was Communist, and that we should have learned by now that Communism didn't work. We didn't end up hiring those people."

"When we hire people here," says Marat Ishnev, "we must be able to have fun together, to be friends. You look for character, you hang out with them, go to a restaurant in the evening, have good communication. That way we know we can all work together and we don't waste time fighting."

Technique Seven: Build a Rapid Response Mechanism

The power of franchising was discussed in Chap. 7. In the strictest sense, Dialogue's network of semi-independent distributors is too loosely organized to qualify as a true franchise. It requires no strict business format such as a Baskin-Robbins or a Pizza Hut would demand. Indeed, the free-and-easy requirements of a Dialogue "affiliate" agreement don't even stipulate that distributors be in the computer business at all!

Nevertheless, Dialogue's ingenious system of licensed "affiliates" brings to bear many of the same strengths as would a full-fledged franchise program.

It provides a framework by which talented Russians in any part of the country can use the prestigious Dialogue trademark for a fee, as well as the training and infrastructure of Dialogue to support their fledgling businesses. At the same time, the individual affiliates nurture and perfect their local Dialogue distributorships with the kind of passion and creative abandon which comes only from a committed owner-operator.

Only three years after it was founded, Dialogue had become a major national presence, with a full-time staff of 750, as well as 35 *representatives*, 25 *dealers* and 15 *affiliates*—terms which describe Dialogue's graduated system of distributorships in which a *representation* is the lowest *pre-affiliate* stage. The skilled scientists and engineers employed by or affiliated with all these far-flung offices number in the thousands.

The loose conditions of Dialogue's licensing agreement allow its affiliates to pursue essentially any sort of business they choose, under the Dialogue banner. That's a risky proposition, as any Russia veteran knows who's had some feckless Russian partner waste money on unauthorized, hare-brained "business" schemes. But by choosing its affiliates judiciously and reining in their wilder excesses, Dialogue has been able to strike a delicate balance between creativity and wackiness.

"We always stressed that they should develop the unique strength of their region, their people," says Virginia Clough, who has since left Dialogue, and now co-heads the Nantucket Corporation's Moscow office with her above-mentioned husband, Bob. "So our Tallinn affiliate is involved in microbiology, developing enzymes. If that's what they're good at, let them do it, and we'll support them as best we can, whether that means providing them with computers for their offices or whatever. Then we have an affiliate in Nakhodka who's working in forestry and tourism." The trick is to provide a framework responsive to creative pressures from below, which at the same time possesses enough inner strength not to break apart over those same pressures.

Technique Eight: Scour the Provinces

One of the key benefits of Dialogue's affiliate system was to provide "eyes and ears" in Russia's outlying provinces, to glean those pockets of talent hidden far from the nerve center of Moscow. Many Western businessmen focus their recruiting efforts too exclusively around major urban centers like Moscow and St. Petersburg. While these cities are both prominent industrial centers, they are neither the largest nor the most important.

In fact, during the Soviet era, many Russians deliberately chose to work far from the capital. What the provinces lacked in creature comforts, they more than made up for in greater political freedom. Many of the most forward-thinking inventors, theorists, and innovators therefore can be found in places like Siberia and the Caucasus.

Dialogue's network of affiliates keep the home office informed of new "discoveries" out in the Russian heartland, and a constant stream of fresh talent flows to Moscow from these frontier posts.

"What's important to Joe Ritchie is not that we have an astounding profit every year," says Virginia Clough. "It's that we've identified people that we want to work with. If the computer business fails, if there's a law passed tomorrow saying that no Westerners can sell computers, that's okay, because we've found the people that we want to work with and it doesn't matter what the business is. The investment is in the people."

Technique Nine: Train, Train, Train

Training is crucial for any business anywhere. But in Russia, its importance is magnified a hundredfold. Dialogue requires its software and hardware suppliers to provide sales training for its people. It maintains extensive training facilities in Russia and frequently sends people to the States for training programs. Training is especially important in the areas of sales, marketing, and advertising

Back in 1990, I participated in a week-long seminar on how to start your own business, co-sponsored by Miami-based Businesship International and the Young Communist League or "Komsomol." For the first few days, the Russian attendees—who ranged in age from high school students to middle-aged industrial managers—seemed bored. Many complained that they were learning nothing new. But on the day we covered marketing, something electric seemed to crackle through the seminar. Every corridor of the conference center was filled with Russians chattering excitedly about *marketink*, as if the subject were a latebreaking news report.

I asked one participating coed from the Moscow Aviation Institute what all the excitement was about. She explained, "Before today, I always assumed that I would end up working for a state organization after I graduated. I never imagined I could really start my own business. But when I heard the lesson on marketing, all of a sudden, I realized that this is something completely new, something that we never understood before. It is the key to make a successful business. Now I know for sure that I can make a business for myself."

This young lady's love affair with sales and marketing is a widespread Russian phenomenon. They take to sales training like the famished defenders of Leningrad to their first deliveries of post-siege bread. Nikolai Lyubovny still talks about the marketing fundamentals he learned at Dialogue as if they were keys to the secrets of the universe.

"Through joint ventures like Dialogue, Russians are learning what a market is," he says with quiet awe. "Russian computer companies advertise in newspapers or on TV, give an address and phone number, and then they just wait in their office for people to come and knock on the door. It's not sufficient. At Dialogue, we learn that *you* must go out and knock on *their* door. You have to go to the customer's office, find out what he wants, what problems he has in his office, think how you can help him, educate him.

"At Dialogue, after we sign an agreement with Russian dealers, we invite them to our office. We have meetings every two months. The subject is how to sell software products, how to solve the problems of end users, how to demonstrate software and hardware.

"I personally supervise about 20 dealers. Part of my job is to visit them, to solve their problems, help them with advertising, with working with the end-users. I have to teach them to sell. I spent all my life as a programmer. But I got this kind of experience only here at Dialogue."

Ready to Die for their Jobs

Dialogue's main building on the outskirts of Moscow looks as if it were airlifted out of Silicon Valley, a concrete and glass, high-tech bunker which used to be the House of Science for a horticultural institute. But it's not Silicon Valley. As American as they look in their jeans and T-shirts, these young programmers hunched over their keyboards are Russians. Young and old, they carry within them a heritage of terror, bloodshed, and struggle unknown in America. They bring to their workplace a level of seriousness which we can only attempt to understand from afar.

One thing the Russians know is that, even at this late date, the iron fist of the state might yet slam down upon them. When Lenin legalized free enterprise back in the 1920s, he let businesses flourish just long enough to get the economy back on its feet. Then he cracked down. Successful entrepreneurs, called *NEPmen*, were shot or shipped off to Siberia.

When I last spoke with Nikolai Lyubovny, it was May 1990. Gorbachev was still in power and the failed coup was over a year in the future. But Lyubovny's words ring just as relevent today as they did at that time.

"If they tried to turn things back now, I think I would fight," he said thoughtfully. There was no drama or bravado in his voice. But Lyubovny's quiet, deliberate tone suggested that he'd long since thought this through and meant every word of it.

"What happened to the NEP-men in the 1920s, it could happen again. I've thought about this. But I decided for myself that the time I've spent in Dialogue is the happiest time in my life. I have no regrets even if I got sent to Siberia. If the reforms are reversed, I will fight against the conservative forces, with a machine gun, if necessary."

11
How to Structure a Deal

Twelve Ways to Cut Risk and Maximize Profits

Since December 1991, the structuring of deals in Russia has become infinitely more civilized. That's when the infamous joint venture law passed out of existence. Before that date, foreigners were virtually forced to form "joint ventures" with Russians. Gorbachev's 1987 law was really an elaborate trap whereby unwary foreigners were lured into partnerships with Russians so they could be squeezed for high-tech equipment and hard currency. For example, the original law required that Soviet state institutions retain a *controlling share* of the joint venture and that *Soviet managers be placed in charge* of operations—a surefire formula for a double-whammy disaster. Although these draconian conditions were later lightened, the revised joint venture law retained enough Byzantine restrictions to remain a dreadful millstone around the necks of foreign investors until it was finally dissolved in 1991.

Today, foreigners may set up any type of company in Russia that a Russian can. Just as in America, your strategic vision and flair for negotiation now form the only restrictions on how you can structure a deal or partnership. Many foreign companies, weary of battling with their Russian partners, have already taken advantage of this new freedom by simply buying out the Russians, converting erstwhile joint ventures into wholly owned branches or subsidiaries.

Throw Out the Bathwater, But Keep the Baby

Professor Christopher Osakwe, a noted expert on Russian business law, warns Americans not to throw out the baby with the bathwater. He believes

182

Russian partners are still valuable. "I normally tell people that it's advantageous to have a local partner who can go to bat for you," says Osakwe. "It sounds great to be a Lone Ranger, to have complete control through a wholly owned subsidiary, but then when you need to obtain licenses or get the electricity turned on, all of a sudden you find it's not so easy. A good Russian partner with the right connections can take care of such things for you."

The New Joint Ventures

The term *joint venture* is still used in Russian business circles, but it now applies in the same generic sense that it would in the West. It simply means a venture—any venture—between two or more parties. There is no longer any such thing as a special joint venture category for foreigners, carrying unique privileges and incentives like two-year tax holidays and the like.

Joint ventures in Russia today might be structured as *joint stock companies* of the *open* or *closed* variety, a form of business similar to an American corporation. In the open type of joint stock company, individual shareholders are free to sell their shares to third parties. In a closed joint stock company, such transfers of shares must be approved by the other shareholders. Joint ventures may also take the form of limited or general partnerships, which are roughly analogous to partnerships in America.

What Types of Companies Can You Form in Russia?

In all, there are now 12 different types of business structures allowed under Russian law, ranging from small enterprises and concerns to such exotic formats as *closed family enterprises* and *employee-owned enterprises*. It's extremely important when forming a Russian business to choose the right format for your needs since each carries with it dramatically different tax and legal liabilities.

There is no room in this chapter for a detailed description of the various advantages and disadvantages of these business formats. To do so would fill a book. In fact, it already *has* filled a book—Professor Osakwe's groundbreaking *Soviet Business Law*, published in two volumes by Butterworth Legal Publishers, and updated with periodic looseleaf supplements. A good breakdown of Russian business formats also appears in the *Russia Business Survival Guide*. Information on how to order these books can be found in App. C

Free to Negotiate

Having been freed from the joint venture vice-grip, Americans may now wheel and deal with abandon, crafting sensible contracts that maximize their profits, limit their risks, and circumvent the most destructive excesses of their Russian partners. The following are 12 tried and true techniques for structuring Russian deals to your maximum advantage.

Technique One: Work on a Contract Basis as Long as Possible

The first rule of any business deal in Russia is to avoid forming a binding partnership for as long as possible. If the nature of your business permits, test the relationship first with a series of small, one-time deals, such as importing a shipment of Italian suits or exporting a trainload of aluminum pipes. Only after you've concluded a number of such profitable transactions should you think about entering a permanent partnership.

Technique Two: Retain a Controlling Share

If you decide to form a partnership, make sure that you retain *not only a controlling share of the equity*, but also a contractual guarantee that you and *you alone* are the boss.

Joe Francis thought his 60 percent of CL/Moscow—a joint venture which runs a hairstyling salon in downtown Moscow—would assure that his word would be law. But Francis quickly discovered that two of his Russian partners—two middle-aged ladies who had held bureaucratic posts in the state-run Soviet salon business—had other plans. "We've had some very heated arguments about certain issues," says Francis, "but they think they're equal partners and don't have to listen to me."

Even such basic issues as the salaries and size of the staff were effectively out of Francis's control. "Those ladies hired 11 administrative people when we only needed two or three," he complains. "I asked why do you need them, and they said, well, we have people, we have friends who needed jobs, so we gave them jobs. I told them it's got to change, and they said it's not going to change."

"With inflation going up every month, I told them we need to raise prices. They told me they have a moral objection to that. They said they'll feel bad if they make money by gouging their friends."

Francis attempted to solve the problem by sending over a Russian-speaking manager from America. But his "partners" have conspired to undermine the new manager's authority at every turn. "They exclude her from management meetings, won't talk to her, won't listen to her. She really has no power, even though she is my appointed representative. Because I'm 6000 miles away, the only time I can be influential is when I'm standing right there on the spot. That's why next month we're going to have a summit meeting, and either I'm going to buy them out, or they're going to buy me out, because this is not working."

Technique Three: Split the Costs with the Russians

Too many early joint ventures failed because the Russian partners had no personal stake in making them work. Often their sole contribution came in the form of signing their names to bureaucratic documents or handing over a lease to state property which they didn't own in the first place. In most cases, the Russian partners would also provide labor. But the salaries usually amounted to pennies, which came out of institutional coffers anyway.

You should compel the Russians to stick their necks out, just as you would an American business partner. Only by sharing the risk can both partners merit their share of the profit.

Francis's Russian partners provided a three-story space in a choice downtown district of Moscow. They were responsible for gutting and remodeling the crumbling eighteenth-century building at their own expense, paying rent and staff salaries until such time as the salon became profitable on a monthly basis. Francis, on the other hand, was to provide construction materials, haircare supplies, and hairstyling equipment.

One of the biggest concessions Francis wrung from the Russians required no cash outlay at all from them, but nevertheless forced them to stick their necks out for the new business. He forced them to sign a noncompete agreement.

"They fought that hard. They couldn't understand at all why I wouldn't want to train them and then have them open a competing salon across the street. I had to threaten to tear up the contract and end the deal before they would agree to that."

Technique Four: Set a Ceiling on Costs

When the new American Embassy was built in Moscow, it ended up costing $200 million, even though the straight costs by floor space should have run only about $40 million, says one real estate developer who retrieved the information from inside sources. That's because the pre-revolutionary infrastructure in Moscow is so primitive, the construction company had to spend $160 million laying new underground water pipes, gas lines, electrical cables, and other infrastructure needs sufficient to support a modern building complex.

This is just an example of how hidden costs can play havoc with your projections in any kind of Russian deal. It's important to anticipate significant cost overruns and build into your contract a firm ceiling on expenditures.

Francis anticipated that starting up his City Looks salon in Moscow would cost about $80,000, split between the three American partners. As a result of repeated delays and continually escalating demands from his Russian partners on the size and decoration of the store, the American partners ended up shelling out $400,000—of which Francis personally paid $130,000. Francis' share still came short of the $150,000 cost ceiling which Francis had written into the contract. If the Russians had forced him to pay over that mark, Francis would have had the right to take his equipment and go.

Technique Five: Withhold Delivery
Until the Russians Have Paid

On May 11, 1990, only three years into the "joint venture era," the *Journal of Commerce* reported that Russian companies owed more than $120 million to U.S. firms. Today, the total amount of unpaid bills to foreign corporations in Russia is estimated in the $3 billion range. The moral of the story is don't expect the Russians to pay you once you've already delivered the goods. Whenever possible, insist on 100 percent payment in advance of any shipment.

Joe Francis' City Looks hair salon required thousands of dollars worth of expensive equipment. He was expected to provide sinks, chairs, cabinets, haircare products, dryers, and other hairstyling equipment. Francis told his Russian partners that he would withhold delivery until they had completed *their* part of the bargain. That meant finishing the remodeling of a three-story space in a deteriorating eighteenth-century building.

The remodeling was painfully slow and ridden with problems. Construction delays caused the store to open 16 months late, with the opening date rescheduled seven times. For over two years, Francis watched impassably, secure in the knowledge that it was the Russians who were footing the bill for the whole Keystone Cops routine. Francis's investment was sitting safely in company warehouses in the United States. Only when the work was near completion did Francis relent and send the goods.

"They really did a marvelous job," he says. "They made it beautiful. It's probably one of the nicest buildings in Moscow now, with everything in marble, bronze, brass, crystal chandeliers, and elegant draperies."

Technique Six: Set a Deadline for Making Back Your Investment

You should have a built-in escape clause in your contract which allows you to recoup some of your assets if the venture fails to repay your investment by a given deadline. Francis stipulated that his investment in equipment and product should be repaid in five years, at a rate of 20 percent per year. "If revenues were insufficient, we would take our equipment and go somewhere else," says Francis.

Technique Seven: Control the Bank Account

The corporate bank account should always be in your name with payments over a certain limit requiring your personal authorization.

Technique Eight: When Possible, Take Profits in Hard Currency

It's now possible to change large quantities of rubles into dollars on the Moscow Interbank Currency Exchange. Nevertheless, it is still inconvenient and dangerous, in view of rapidly rising inflation, to rely exclusively on a ruble income. Whenever possible, you should take profits in dollars or other hard currency. In the case of Francis's salon, he was offering a service which was prized highly enough to enable him to charge hard currency in exchange for greater convenience. Ruble customers must wait weeks for a hairstyling appointment, while dollar customers may be served immediately.

If your core business doesn't lend itself to dollar sales, there are other ways to convert ruble earnings into exportable currency. These techniques are described in the following sections.

Technique Nine: Sell Products for Rubles and Convert Rubles to Hard Currency Through Separate Deals

Many of the most lucrative businesses in Russia today are simple trade arrangements by which a foreigner brings in consumer goods like computers, VCRs, clothes or processed food, sells them for rubles, then uses the rubles to purchase goods or commodities which can be sold abroad for hard currency. This technique is an easy way of turning rubles into dollars.

**Technique Ten: Invest Ruble
Proceeds in Russia**

Another way to turn rubles into dollars is to make long-term investments in Russia itself. This is obviously more risky, but the rewards will ultimately be greater. Rubles can be invested effectively in construction projects, factory conversions and other startup costs for new businesses. McDonald's, for example, is investing millions of rubles in a new office building in downtown Moscow.

**Technique Eleven: Limit
Your Investment**

Everybody chuckled when Robert Strauss, former U.S. ambassador to Russia, remarked, "If I had $100,000, I'd invest it in Russia. But if I had a million dollars, I'd still invest $100,000 in Russia."

In fact, the ambassador's quip enunciated a valuable tip for American business pioneers. While a few Americans have made successful, large-scale investments in Russia, far more have been burned when they overextended themselves. You're better off not investing more money than you can realistically afford to lose.

Technique Twelve: Use Countertrade

Many of the biggest and most celebrated deals in Russia have used *countertrade* or bartering methods. The classic example would be Pepsico's historic agreement. Twenty years ago, Pepsico agreed to trade its secret Pepsi formula and turnkey bottling franchises in exchange for the rights to sell Stolichnaya Vodka to the West.

Pepsi's Stolichnaya sales have run about $156 million per year, while it sells the ruble equivalent of $750 million in Pepsi annually in Russia. In 1990, Pepsi signed an agreement to take some of the billions of rubles it has amassed and buy 10 Russian cargo ships worth more than $300 million, leasing the ships to Western firms and using the proceeds to finance its new Pizza Hut restaurants in Russia and to double production of Pepsi in the CIS. It's hard to argue with that kind of success. Countertrade works.

Conclusion

These 12 points give only the barest guidelines for negotiating a Russian deal. You should work with an experienced attorney when going nose to nose with your potential partners. Attorneys with solid expertise in closing deals in the CIS can be found in the "Ready-Made Rolodex" in App. B under the heading of "Legal Services."

12

Money, Money, Money

Russia's Banking and Currency Crisis is Your Opportunity

A shock wave rolled through the Western business world in December 1991. Vnesheconombank—the Russian Bank of Foreign Economic Affairs—suddenly announced that it was freezing its $5.3 billion in hard currency deposits. That meant that virtually every foreign company in the Soviet Union was now suddenly denied access to its own corporate accounts.

Foreign companies reacted instantaneously. Many abandoned their plans to enter the Russian marketplace. The press warned of a "cold shower" effect upon future investment. In the eyes of many Westerners, the image of Russia's banking system was forever tarnished. But they were missing the point.

Death of the Old,
Birth of the New

What was really happening was that the old Communist banking system was dying. A new system, based on entrepreneurship and free enterprise, was quietly taking its place. Russia's intrepid new financiers had long since mastered a peculiar brand of alchemy—the art of transforming Russia's perennial banking and currency crises into *profit*. For them, Vnesheconombank's collapse provided just another interesting set of opportunities.

In the months following the Big Freeze, Russian commercial bankers stepped forward offering to buy up frozen accounts for rubles. Others simply paid 80 cents to the dollar. If and when the accounts were unfrozen, these speculators would earn 20 cents profit on each dollar restored—a tidy sum indeed. Many of the speculators were rumored to be acting as proxies for foreign financiers.

The privately owned Inkombank offered a particularly creative swap. It extended a free ruble account in Inkombank to any Vnesheconombank depositor, equal to the dollar deposits he had lost in the Big Freeze—provided the depositor would agree to buy shares in Inkombank equal to 30 percent of his frozen accounts. This was all risky business, to be sure. But it apparently paid off. Vnesheconombank announced after a year that it will start unfreezing hard-currency funds in July 1993.

Is the Glass Half Empty or Half Full?

The lively and optimistic reaction of Russia's private bankers to this crisis suggests that, while the "glass" of Russian banking is obviously half empty, *it is just as obviously half full.*

Even as the financial pundits gasp anew at each lingering death rattle of Russia's sclerotic state banks, forward-looking business pioneers—both Russian and foreign—are working hard to compensate by providing private financial services of all kinds. Runaway inflation is countered with new currency markets in dollars and dollar futures. Credit shortages are attacked with unorthodox third-party financing deals. Indeed, many insiders predict that banking and financial services will prove one of the hottest growth areas in Russia for many years to come.

Russia's Banking Revolution

It's hard to believe that before 1988, there was only one bank in Russia—the aptly named Gosbank or "State Bank." Gosbank did everything. It issued new money, it lent money to state enterprises, it took deposits from savers. There was, of course, no such thing as a checking account or a credit card in those days.

But in 1988, Gorbachev opened a Pandora's box. He legalized independent banks for the first time in Soviet history. Immediately, private companies, state enterprises, government ministries, municipalities, and research institutes stampeded to start their own banks.

By 1992, there were over 2000 commercial banks in the former Soviet states—1500 in Russia and 500 in Moscow alone. And they're growing fast. Total assets and liabilities for all commercial banks in the former Soviet

Union rose sharply from 630 billion rubles on January 1, 1992 to 1.6 trillion rubles five months later, according to *The Economist*. This explosion of banking activity signals the opening of Russia's hottest new business frontier.

Enormous Possibilities

"There are significant opportunities for American bankers in Russia," says an official at a major Wall Street investment bank. "You must be very patient and flexible. But you can do anything you want. There are opportunities available to advise foreign investors, to advise Russians on how to integrate vertically both in and out of the country, to help Russians create and improve their financial markets, and to buy and sell companies. There are also opportunities in commodities, such as improving the trading infrastructure for oil, gas, and metals."

The Pioneers

Despite the risks, the abundance of opportunities in Russian finance has been attracting an ever-more sophisticated crowd of Western adventurers. Perhaps one of the hottest deals to break lately in Russia was the establishment of the Russian-American Investment Bank, a joint venture between insurance mogul Hank Greenberg, Chemical Banking, Primerica's Smith Barney unit, Harris Upham & Company, London-based J. Rothschild, Wolfensohn & Co., and top Russian military-industrial leaders. The bank will invest Western money in energy and real estate projects in Russia.

A noted riskmaster, Greenberg has wowed the insurance industry for years, raking in billions insuring such perilous clients as toxic waste haulers and North Sea oil rigs. His company, American International Group (AIG), cleared $1.6 billion profit on $18 billion in 1992 revenues. Now Greenberg is putting his talent for calculated risktaking to the ultimate test.

Crisis Equals Opportunity

"The opportunities (for banking in Russia) are *tremendous,* unbelievable" says a Wall Street investment banker. "The market is volatile, but it's the turmoil and volatility which creates the opportunity." The turmoil in Russia's money system is well-known. But the opportunities are less well advertised. Some of them follow.

Be a Quasi-Banker

Many Russian businesses can't get loans at all. Ditto for American firms who try to drum up bank credit for risky Russian ventures. Time after time, eager Russians and Americans alike must turn down hot deals because they have no money to take action. Enter the *quasi-bankers*—entrepreneurs who provide third-party financing for risky but lucrative one-shot deals.

One American firm does tens of millions of dollars a year in such deals. Typically, this firm might arrange for a Russian factory to purchase machine-tooling equipment from an American supplier. The quasi-banker will then put up his own money or letter of credit to buy the equipment from the American supplier. He then arranges for the Russian factory to pay it back over time in the form of some goods such as semi-finished copper tubes, which the quasi-banker can easily sell in the West. The quasi-banker absorbs all the risk, but usually makes a tremendous margin on the deal.

As with real banking, you can't just hand money to any Russian off the street. The quasi-banker must have an excellent relationship with both the Russian and American entities, to which he advances credit.

Feast on Runaway Debt

One of the surest formulas for success is to find some cheap, plentiful commodity which nobody else wants but which can easily be processed into a valuable product. In Russia today, no "commodity" is more plentiful than unpaid debt. Indeed, Russia's entire industrial base is riding on a rapidly expanding bubble of debt.

It works like this. Let's say you're a Russian factory director who makes cars, but you can no longer afford the inflated prices which your supplier charges for rubber tires. You go to the rubber tire supplier and say, "Look, give me a shipment of tires on credit and I'll pay you back after I've sold the cars."

In effect, the tire supplier is acting as your bank, making a loan of tires to finance your manufacture of cars. The problem is that you have probably made similar deals with all your other suppliers, who in turn have asked credit from *their* suppliers, and on and on up the production line. In fact, every significant industrial concern in Russia now seems to owe money to every other one. As this page is written, Russia's inter-enterprise debt has already reached a staggering 2.75 *trillion* rubles. It seems highly unlikely that Russia's major enterprises will ever succeed in repaying these debts if left to their own devices. Meanwhile, many of these firms are going private. Foreign investors bidding on them are left wondering whether they will be held accountable for their inter-enterprise debt.

One possible solution to this problem might be *factoring*. A *factor* is really a sort of glorified bill collector. He buys accounts receivable from a manufacturer at a discount, then collects the debts from the manufacturer's customers at the full amount. The factor assumes all the risks of the debt. That may sound like an overly risky proposition in a cash-poor society like Russia's, but remember, you can always collect the debt in the form of equity.

Traditionally, factoring was carried out by independents, many of them shady tough guys from the arm breaking school of bill collection. However, most factoring is now done in a much more civilized manner by the banks themselves. In Russia, Japanese banks have been particularly active in this area.

Factoring ultimately may prove to be a major stimulus to Russia's recovery in the years ahead. It provides a much-needed supply of grease to keep the wheels of Russian commerce spinning—as well as a peculiarly alchemical means for Westerners to transmute the dross of Russian debt into golden profits.

Provide Clearing Services

One of the biggest weaknesses of Russia's burgeoning banking sector is the lack of a modern clearing system. Foreign businessmen in Russia love to swap horror tales of wire transfers which took sixth months or more to complete. In such cases, by the time the money passes from the customer's bank to the seller's, inflation has often turned a profitable deal into a net loss. Until Russia establishes a modern, centralized clearing system, there will be many opportunities for smaller firms to ease the creaking gears of Russian bank transactions.

Ello, Inc., an American trading company based in Secaucus, New Jersey, helps its trading partners facilitate bank transfers. If a particular deal requires a money transfer from a bank in Kazakhstan to one in Moscow, an Ello courier will hand-carry the transfer slip to the Moscow bank, where an Ello executive will then use his influence with high-level bank officials to push the transaction through once it arrives. Thus, transfers which ordinarily might take two months can be completed in a matter of days. Such convenience provides an obvious incentive for trading with Ello over some other competitor.

Cash In on Consumer Credit

Perhaps the most neglected banking customer in Russia is the ordinary consumer. The shortage of banking services has created a voracious seller's market. Most Russian banks charge interest rates of 80 percent and higher on short-term loans, but they have no trouble finding takers. Many require hefty bribes just to open an account. Russian banks routinely turn away all but the very wealthiest institutional customers.

The need for affordable consumer credit is desperate. And enterprising companies, both Russian and Western, are already rising to meet it. VISA and American Express have been active for years providing credit card services to foreigners in Russia. But VISA soon plans to roll out a ruble-based credit card for ordinary Russians.

A Russian company called Ort International has already issued a ruble credit card called the *Ortcard*. It's something less than a true credit card because holders of the Ortcard must deposit twice the amount of their credit line in hard currency with Ortex Trading and Finance—a division of Ort International. The card supposedly allows Russians to make purchases at home or abroad, as well as at any of Ort's nationwide chain of stores which sell Western consumer products in the CIS. Ort, which maintains offices in Irvine, California, hopes to sign up more than 300,000 customers in the first year.

A Cashless Russia?

"We expect that we'll see a lot more interest on the part of banks in setting up plastic payment systems in Russia," says Bruce Macdonald, head of BBDO Marketing in Moscow. BBDO's advertising clients in Russia include VISA International and Sberbank—the preeminent Russian savings bank, with over 25,000 branches throughout the former Soviet states and up to 50 million depositors.

"Basically, you have a country which up till now has been a cash country," he says. "Everything is done in cash. The use of checks is miniscule. Bank transfers are the normal way of buying things."

Macdonald suggests that Russia may move rapidly to a cashless society— that much-talked-about but elusive dream of Western financial leaders. "It takes a major investment to create a check infrastructure," says Macdonald. "If you know you're just going to have to do the same thing a couple of years later for credit cards, why not just jump directly to plastic and skip the check generation? Many banks in Eastern Europe have already made their decision to do just that."

Macdonald points out the added attraction for Russian tax officials of being able to monitor every transaction in the country—a capability which could theoretically bring Russia's black market tradition to a sudden and unceremonious denouement.

Western-Quality Banking:
Just Around the Corner?

Westerners in Russia still have to rough it when it comes to simple matters like cashing checks or wiring money from abroad. But things are changing quickly.

Western banks already have over 70 representative offices in Moscow. None of these are fully functioning branches yet, but they will be soon. Credit Lyonnais has already announced plans to open a full-service Western bank in Russia. Citibank maintains correspondent relations with 10 different Russian commercial banks through which it can render some limited help to Westerners in making hard currency transfers and confirming letters of credit.

The closest thing to a full-service bank in Russia today is the International Moscow Bank (IMB), a joint venture between Russian, German, Italian, and Finnish banks. Founded in 1990, IMB earned more than $6.3 million in profits in 1991. Its business has surged since the breakup of the Soviet Union. Deposits increased rapidly from $800 million in December 1991 to more than $1.6 billion today. With over 400 clients and a daily volume of about 600 transactions per day, IMB is now moving into retail operations and has announced plans to invest $37 million in a new office building. For further information on banking services available in Russia, see the "Ready-Made Rolodex" in App. B under the heading "Banking."

Here Come the Russian Banks

Ultimately, if Russia's financial system is to work, it is the Russians themselves who must pull it off. As yet, Russia's commercial banks fall far short of Western standards. Americans with corporate accounts in Russia recite lengthy laundry lists of banking horror stories.Typically, if you deposit money in a Russian bank, you may not be able to withdraw it the next day. It has already been invested in some high-risk deal. The cashier won't tell you this, of course. She'll probably ask you to fill out a form and come back next Tuesday. But next Tuesday, she'll suddenly discover a "mistake" on your form and ask you to come back next Wednesday. And on it goes. Virtually your only chance to withdraw the money will be to come in on a day when someone else just made a hefty deposit.

"It's a little bit of a Ponzi scheme," John Morton concludes. "There is no FDIC, no insurance, no loan guidelines. We can expect very substantial bank failures over the next year or so. Loans will go sour and banks won't have money to pay depositors."

To some extent, you must use Russian banks. But there are ways to minimize your exposure. For example, if you open an office in Russia, employ full-time people there and conduct business in the country, you're required by law to open a Russian bank account and process your domestic business through it. But many foreigneres get around this requirement by conducting all their business abroad. For example, if you're importing goods to Russia, invite the buyers to your office in New York and close the deal there.

Another way to circumvent the Russian banking system is to pay your Russian employees through an offshore bank. Simply open accounts for them in another country, and pay their salaries into that account. This is legal, under Russian law. However, Morton warns that it is absolutely *illegal* to take advantage of such arrangements to conceal your transactions from Russian tax collectors.

Your best bet is to avoid Russian banks as much as you can," advises Morton. "Use them where the law requires, but stay clear of them when the law permits."

The New Russian Banker

Most agree that these problems are temporary. A new breed of sophisticated Russian banker is coming up fast. A typical example would be Mikhail Hodorkovsky. At 28 years of age, he heads the mighty Menatep Financial Group, comprising 25 commercial banks, insurance, investment, and foreign trade companies with over 800 employees. Menatep's reported turnover of 75 billion rubles in 1991 would make it a smashing success by any standard in the world.

In future years, Russian banks will minister to the needs of sophisticated businessmen, Russian and Western alike, with all the skill and know-how of their Wall Street brethren. Should things continue going as they are, that halcyon future may lie closer at hand than we realize.

13

You're Not in Kansas Anymore

A Beginner's Guide to Russian Culture and Etiquette

One day, as I was riding with a prominent Russian business executive, we passed a construction site outside Moscow where a cluster of charming, Western-style townhouses were being built. "Look," said my host, gesturing with evident pride. "Now we have housing developments just like in America."

I'd traveled in Russia enough times to recognize that fatal combination of words. Whenever you heard the phrase, "*Now we have . . .*" coupled with the phrase, "*just like in America*" or with its common variant, "*just like in the West,*" you knew that you were treading on the dangerous ground of the Russian national ego. But I ignored the alarm bells.

Having read recently that just such a housing development was being built by a well-known Russian-American construction firm, I inquired innocently of my host whether this was the very one I had read about? Instead of answering, he scowled and fell silent. Concentrating on his driving, he smoldered for several minutes with evident ill-humor. When at last he resumed the conversation, my host had completely changed the subject.

What Did I Say Wrong?

That uncomfortable moment needn't have happened at all. The man had obviously been proud of the new townhouses. He had pointed them out specifically as a *Russian* achievement. For my host, the houses were *nash* (ours)—that laconic Russian pronoun which implies so much more than mere ownership, but hauls with it many decades and centuries of nationalistic baggage (as in *nash* victorious Olympic teams, *nash* troops storming Berlin in 1945, *nash* cosmonauts, scientists, and hydroelectric dams).

But I had ignored all that. Instead, I had blithely asked whether American money and know-how might really be responsible. Intentionally or not, I had suggested that perhaps those townhouses were really *nash*! *American*! Suddenly, it was a battle of the *nash's*, my *nash* against his.

And merely by asking the question in the first place, I had implied that I didn't think the Russians were capable of building such nice townhouses on their own. Clearly, it would have been better if I had simply admired the townhouses and left it at that.

The Delicate Art of the Traveler

A wise traveler studies the psychology of the people he meets and learns to offend as seldom as possible. Courtesy and empathy for others has been a basic survival skill since the first Stone Age traders journeyed into another tribe's land. Great merchants and explorers like Marco Polo have always been marked by a rare gift for getting along with strangers. Indeed, the famous Venetian would never have lived to tell his remarkable tale had he not learned to consort just as comfortably with gruff, Afghan warriors around a campfire as with polished courtiers in the palace of Kublai Khan.

In this chapter, I will provide a roadmap to that strange and perplexing psychological maze called the "Russian soul." As a foreigner, you will never really understand the Russian soul, so don't even try. But you can and should at least learn how to duck whenever it threatens to wallop you on the head.

The Sensitive Russian Ego

Let's start with the subject we began the chapter with—the sensitive Russian ego. There are good, practical reasons why you might expect the Russians to feel hypersensitive these days, not the least of which is the fact that they have just lost the Cold War. But Russia's national inferiority complex far precedes her current travails. Indeed, it has festered like an untended sore for centuries.

The Tsar Who Hated Russia

Few peoples in history have thought so ill of themselves so consistently as the Russians. Indeed, Russia's preeminent national hero, Peter the Great, is best remembered for his boundless loathing for his own native culture.

As a young prince, Peter traveled extensively throughout Western Europe, admiring its superior science and culture. All the while, he promised himself that he would someday go home and eradicate the barbarous Russian culture, replacing it with European Enlightenment. Peter finally got his chance when he mounted the throne in 1682.

Immediately, Tsar Peter went to war against everything Russian. He commanded his noblemen to shave off their beards and to trade in their long, Asiatic robes for Western trousers and waistcoats. Scores of Italian architects and engineers were brought in to build a new, Venetian-style capital in the north, complete with canals and Renaissance palazzos. In this new city of St. Petersburg, Peter the Great established a royal court where generations of succeeding tsars would actually grow up speaking French, German, and other foreign tongues among their families and courtiers rather than the hated Russian.

All his life, Peter strove to make Russia the sort of country that he wouldn't have to feel ashamed of anymore.

"Just Like in the West"

To this day, Russians still retain Peter's lifelong, nagging fear that Westerners might be snickering at them behind their backs. The only salve is to become as Western as possible. Every Russian nowadays has evolved into a sort of mini-Peter the Great. In business, in dress, in entertainment, in creature comforts, each strives to build for himself a private way of life "just like in the West."

America Good, Russia Bad

Russian self-hatred has not gone unnoticed on Madison Avenue. For years, Pepsi has been marketing its soft drinks in Russia using a logo rendered into Cyrillic characters. But now BBDO Marketing in Moscow has worked up an entirely new image for the company which plays up Pepsi's *American* origin and uses Latin letters instead of Russian.

"This market has a disrespect for its own products in category after category," explains BBDO Marketing head Bruce Macdonald. "It's a market in which 'Russian' suggests low quality even to the Russians themselves and 'American' suggests the best you can get. So a product which does not avail itself of Latin letters in its presentation, English in its overtones, and Americana in its heritage is losing one its key marketing points."

Don't Blame the Products

Some might point out that Russia's shoddy products usually deserve all the contempt they get. But this is not always true. The Russians' aversion to their own products goes far beyond logic or reason. It borders on the mystical.

In their book *Cutting the Red Tape*, East-West business consultants Mark Tourevski and Eileen Morgan describe how an American consultant tested 200 identical bras on Russian women, 100 of them produced in an American factory and 100 produced in a Russian factory. He deliberately mislabeled 50 of the Russian bras as "American" and 50 of the American ones as "Russian." Not surprisingly, the women came back saying they loved all the "American" bras (even those that were actually Russian) and hated the "Russian" ones (even though 50 of those were made in America). All were of identical material and design. But the bras' actual feel or quality clearly had nothing to do with the women's choice. Their contempt for their own country proved more powerful than their physical senses.

Why Did Russia Lag Behind the West?

At the root of Russians' insecurity lies their fear that Russia is not quite as "civilized" as the West—a notion which has unfortunately been shared for centuries by Westerners. How did Russia come to withdraw from the mainstream of European life? Probably much of the credit can go to a man named Genghis Khan.

In 1187, Genghis Khan (pronounced CHING-iss khahn)was an insignificant nomad chieftain. His people wandered aimlessly across the plains of Mongolia, driving their horses, goats, and sheep in a never-ending quest for fresh pastures.

Historians tell us that the Mongols never numbered more than one million. But they were a powerful and warlike folk. Mongol boys were put in the saddle almost at birth and trained with bow and arrow from the age of 3. When the Mongols rode to war, each man took several horses and rode them in turn, staying on horseback for two days straight and sleeping only when his horses grazed. On campaign, they lived on mare's milk and fresh blood drawn from a horse's vein.

Claiming a special mandate from the Sky God, Mongke Tenggeri, Genghis Khan united all the peoples of the steppes. Keraits, Merkit, Naiman, Uighurs, and Tatars all flocked to his banner. In the past, these tribes had fought only against one another. Now they joined forces and the world trembled.

Before he died, Genghis Khan had conquered vast portions of Russia, China, India, and Afghanistan. His sons and grandsons pushed even farther, until the *entire Asian continent*, Persia, Mesopotamia, and *half of Europe* (including Poland, Hungary, and Russia) had submitted to Mongol dominion. No land empire before or since has ever encompassed such a vast territory. For the next 270 years, Russia lay in thrall to a succession of Asian despots, effectively removed from the flow of European history.

Humiliation Beyond Measure

*"Man's highest joy is in victory: to conquer
one's enemies, to pursue them, to deprive
them of their possessions, to make their
beloved weep, to ride on their horses, and to
embrace their daughters and wives."*
                                    GENGHIS KHAN
                                    1167–1227 A.D.

When the Mongols came thundering across southern Russia in 1223, many thought the fierce horsemen had ridden straight from the mouth of Hell. "They are terrible to look at and indescribable," wrote one Armenian monk. ". . .They give birth to children like snakes and eat like wolves. Death does not appear among them, for they survive for three hundred years."

The Golden Horde—as the invaders called themselves—attacked on horseback in overwhelming numbers. Captives were often slaughtered wholesale: men, women, and children. The Mongols would impale their prisoners on stakes, drive nails or woodsplints under their fingernails, drop burning coals in their boots, or roast them alive. Sometimes they would blind or dismember their captives for sport.

Mongol law required that prisoners of high rank be killed without spilling blood. So they devised imaginative methods for doing just that. In one recorded case, the Mongols laid captive Russian noblemen on the ground, placed boards over them, and held a feast on top of the boards. While the Mongols reveled, the Russian princes were crushed.

"The (Mongols) . . . learn warfare from their youth," wrote a Russian monk. "Therefore, they are stern, fearless, and fierce towards us . . . We cannot oppose them, but humiliate ourselves before them, as Jacob did before Esau."

Why the Word "Slav"
Came to Mean "Slave"

Russia, for centuries, was ruled by the Tatars, fierce vassals of the Mongols. They refer to this dark epoch as the Tatar Conquest. Each Russian prince was compelled to prostrate himself before the Tatar Khan in his new capital of Sarai on the Volga. Cities which refused to submit and pay tribute were put to the torch, their people carried off into slavery. Even centuries later, when many Russian cities had managed to break free of the Khan's grip, Tatar raiding parties continued pillaging their villages and towns, carrying off men, women, and children for the slave marts.

During those years, Russians and other Slavic peoples became the primary source of slaves for the Mediterranean world. Russian women filled the harems of Turkish sultans. Russian men rowed the galleys or worked the fields for Muslim lords, while Russian children brought a good price in slave auctions from Cairo to Baghdad. Even in Christian Europe, Slavic people remained the chattels of choice until African captives replaced them in later centuries. For this reason, the word "Slav" came to mean "slave" in English and in other European languages.

Lest we write off this matter as mere ancient history, it is well to remember that thousands of Russians still living today served as slave laborers in German factories and households during World War II. Hitler justified his forced labor program by painting the Russians as a "race of slaves"—a pointed allusion to their sad history under the Khans.

Half Asian, Half Western

For obvious reasons, the Russians have mingled their blood and customs for centuries with the people of Asia. When Western Europeans first began traveling to Russia in the sixteenth century, they remarked on the peculiarly Asiatic fashion favored by the Russian ladies who were in the habit of plastering their faces, necks, and hands with red and white dyes, painting their eyebrows "black as jet" and even blackening their teeth with mercury. At her wedding, a Russian woman would fall at the bridegroom's feet, "knocking her head upon his shoe in token of her subjection and obedience." And like the Khans and Turkish sultans, Russian noblemen maintained a *terem* in their households—a heavily guarded wing where women were concealed from the world.

Long after the Tatar rule was broken, Asiatic lords blended into the ranks of the Russian gentry, intermarrying with their daughters. Indeed, noble Russian families eagerly sought marriages with descendants of Genghis Khan, for the blood of Mongol royalty was held the purest and finest of all.

The Cult of the Warlord

Today, the high cheekbones and narrow eyes of many Russians mark them as distant descendants of the Khan's lusty horsemen. But the Tatar legacy lies deeper still, surviving in that dark, brutal, and mystical vision of life which we call the "Russian soul." If Russians are noted for one thing, it is their patient resignation in the face of oppression. The Tatars certainly had some hand in this, for they brought to Russia its uniquely Asian brand of despotism. Considered semi-divine beings, the Khans dispensed life or death to their subjects with god-like license. In Joseph Stalin's reign of terror, we saw far more of Tamerlane the Great and Genghis Khan than of Karl Marx.

It is estimated that Stalin murdered upwards of 20 million people and sent another 40 million to the labor camps. Not a single family in Russia escaped his dread hand. Yet, when he died, the Russian people were convulsed with a grief unlike anything imaginable in the West.

Millions poured into Moscow from every province, weeping and screaming as they filed past his open coffin, anguish and horror in their eyes. At one point, the grief-stricken crowd was so siezed by hysteria that thousands were trampled to death in the ensuing riot.

"A shudder moved across the land," writes Gail Sheehy in *The Man Who Changed the World*, "people trembled at the thought of going on without the omnipotent leader. Stalin made the day begin, Stalin made everyone work at night because he worked at night, Stalin made every decision there was to make, Stalin gaveth life and Stalin took it away. Even those who had suffered under Stalinism felt helpless and feared to think of the future."

In his book *The Russians*, Hedrick Smith reports that as recently as the late 1970s, the mere appearance on a Russian table of a bottle of Kinzmarauli (Stalin's favorite Georgian wine) was enough to set off a round of nostalgic toasts to the *krepki khozyain*, the strong master, as Stalin was affectionately termed. And today, Stalin's portrait continues to appear in many antigovernment demonstrations, side by side with pictures of the Tsar.

I am not among those smug Westerners who joke that the Russians "need" a tyrant to "keep them in order." But, clearly, the Russians' strange love affair with their own oppressors finds few parallels in the West. It is not, I think, too fanciful to see in Stalin's "Cult of Personality" some lingering shadow of the Tatar cult of the warlord.

A Nation of "Battered Children?"

Like children of abusive parents, the Russians long ago adopted a cloistered, suspicious attitude toward outsiders. For hundreds of years, foreign visitors have been subjected to extraordinary restrictions and regulations, housed in separate compounds, strictly segregated from casual contact with Russians, and spied upon incessantly, as if the Russians were somehow afraid their dirty family secrets might be discovered by these nosy strangers. This metaphor of an abused family may be more than coincidental.

A Wound That Never Heals

Under Communism, psychiatry was a tool of state oppression. Mental illness was defined as opposition to the status quo. It was "treated" with drugs and by incarceration in insane asylums.

However, Vadim Viazmin was among an illicit underground of self-taught psychoanalysts who ministered to their patients in accordance with the forbidden tenets of Freud and Jung. Now living in New York, Viazmin has developed an unusual theory of Russian history, based on his clinical observations. "Russia is mentally ill," he concludes simply. "It is schizophrenic."

At the root of Russia's problems, Viazmin sees a deeply suppressed *castration complex*—an inordinate fear of genital mutilation dating from infancy, which typically results in wild extremes of personality.

"Such a person usually becomes either a victim or a warrior," says Viazmin, "and usually has elements of both. He has a great feeling of deficiency and insecurity, and is constantly trying to prove himself or to seek punishment. Even when he is successful, his success contains a hidden catastrophe. The more success he develops, the more unhappy and insecure he becomes."

The Russians Are Different

For Viazmin, the Russians' much-vaunted "spirituality" or "mystical" bent is merely a sign of their national illness. I don't know whether this is true. But there is clearly something *different* about the Russians.

Once, when I was having lunch with my Russian business partner in a TV venture, the conversation turned to Siberia. My partner told me that he had once lived on the shores of Lake Baikal, a Siberian lake whose extraordinary depth, peculiar fish, and great antiquity make it something of a geological mystery. Baikal's shores, my partner told me, had been found to emanate a high level of "energy."

"Energy? What kind of energy?" I asked in Russian. He shot me a look as if to chide me for my stupid question.

"*Bio-energyetika*," he replied. Bio-energy. Of course!

Most Russians seem to accept quite matter-of-factly the idea that human beings and other objects emanate an "aura" or "bio-energetic field." Such fields are believed to be instrumental in facilitating telepathic communication and psychic healing. If you listen attentively, you will notice that Russians lace their casual speech with almost as many offhand references to "bio-energetic" phenomena as Americans pepper theirs with such phrases as "anal personality" or "Freudian slip." To many Russians, bio-energy is a proven scientific fact. A person's "aura," they claim, can even be photographed, using the Soviet-invented technique of Kirlian photography.

Of course, many Americans believe in such things as well, and serious scientists do study them. I will not speculate here on whether or not they really exist. However, the point is that such ideas have attained a mass acceptance in Russia unheard-of in the West, where such notions are found mainly among New Age sectarians.

Faith Healers, Flying Saucers, and the Like

When the first reports came in over the TASS newswire in September 1989, journalists all over the world started buzzing. Was it a joke? Some bizarre hoax? What had gotten into the Soviets?

According to TASS—the official Soviet news agency—UFOs had landed near Voronezh, a town located about 300 miles southeast of Moscow. Locals reported seeing nine-foot-tall alien creatures with three eyes, bronze boots, and silver overalls. One 16-year- old boy was reported in good condition after having been zapped by an alien ray gun, which caused him to vanish for a few moments.

Western journalists deluged TASS with phone calls. Was it some kind of gag? Not at all, TASS responded. The reports were 100 percent accurate.

"It is not April Fools' today," sniffed one indignant TASS official.

Since that first shock in 1989, we have almost grown used to the flood of strange reports emanating from Russia describing sightings of abominable snowmen, extraterrestrial visitations, bizarre cults, and popular TV shows by psychic healers. Many in the West have long since concluded that the Russians have gone stark, raving bonkers.

Our pundits have bent over backwards trying to explain why a nation which once prided itself on its "scientific atheism" has suddenly taken such a precipitous nose-dive into la-la land. Most speculate that, having lost their "faith" in Communism, the Russians are now so desperate to "believe in something," that they'll experiment with almost any sort of silliness. Such superficial explanations, however, ignore one of the most fundamental facts about Russia's unique civilization.

Russia Never Left the Middle Ages

During the Dark Ages, Western Europeans embraced the unseen and the supernatural as never before or since. They despised such vain "things of this world" as comfort and wealth. Instead, they sought "heavenly" treasures, such as humility and faith. Thousands became monks or nuns. Great scholars who in another age might have been mathematicians or scientists instead agonized over such metaphysical conundrums as the size, shape, and texture of Satan's penis. Pilgrims and "hermits" wandered the countryside en masse, praying and contemplating heaven while they lived off the charity of others.

In such a world, the delicate curtain which separates spirit from flesh, tangible from intangible, frayed so thin as to almost vanish. Angels, devils, and other celestial beings became an everyday sight. A milkmaid who set off down the road was as likely to run smack into the Virgin Mary as she was to meet a peasant from the next village. Whether you consider such visions "real" or "imaginary" is irrelevant. The point is that in the Dark Ages, many saw them, and all believed in them. Later, as reason, science, gunpowder, and international trade filled European minds with more practical obsessions, the flood of beatific visions subsided.

But far to the East, the phantoms lingered on. Long after Columbus sailed for his New World, long after Newton invented his calculus, Russia kept right on dreaming and slumbering through her endless Dark Age. Locked in mortal combat with the hordes of Asia until well into the eighteenth century, Russia never even noticed the Renaissance.

Holy Men and Castrates

As late as the turn of this century, Russia's country roads still teemed with *startsi* (wandering saints and hermits) in quantities not seen in Western Europe for 700 years or more. Perhaps the best-known *starets* of all was Rasputin. His intimacy with the Tsar's family and his role as their official faith healer reveals the importance which this medieval institution of *starchestvo* still retained at that late date.

All too often, Russia's extravagant religiosity has spilled over into the realm of madness. One prerevolutionary sect called the *skoptsy* or "castrates" fought the sin of lust by—you guessed it—castrating themselves and one another (not always on a voluntary basis).

Another sect, called the *Khlysty*, attained *radenie* or religious ecstasy through wild dancing, after which the worshippers would fall upon one another in an orgy of violent sex, which they called the "love of Christ."

It is reported that in 1897, a peasant named Kovalev, convinced that the Antichrist was coming, buried his entire family alive, along with most of his fellow villagers. What is more shocking, and quintessentially Russian, is that Kovalev's victims *willingly went along with it*, praying and crying out to God even as he shovelled the earth into their living tombs. Such incidents were quite common before 1917, and it is not at all clear that they stopped at that point, though mention of them did vanish from the newspapers.

The Mysterious Russian Soul

Having despaired of ever "catching up" with the West, many Russians throughout the ages decided that Russia has no need of Western civilization. After all, Russia has her *own* unique strengths, say the "Slavophiles."

But what *are* those strengths? Chief among them is something called the mysterious "Russian soul."

It may be awhile before the Russians you meet feel comfortable enough to talk to you about it, but most will admit under questioning that they believe in this "Russian soul." Very much like the storied "soul" of African-Americans, the Russian "soul" can never be understood by outsiders. Any overt attempt by a foreigner to figure it out will be met by laughter and derision.

But what exactly *is* this Russian "soul?" Most Russians will squirm uncomfortably when asked to explain it. They will say that it cannot be put into words. However, emigre Russian psychotherapist Vadim Viazmin manages to sum it up quite neatly. "The Russian soul is that mysterious quality which makes Russians superior to all other people," he explains. "It's complete nonsense, of course."

Moscow: The Center of the World

An extraordinary number of Russians continue to believe that their country has a *special* destiny, mystical, divine, redolent of the blood and soil of Slavs, utterly alien to Western science and reason. When Rome fell to the Gothic hordes in 410 A.D., Europe turned to Constantinople as the "second Rome." It was the new City of God and center of Western learning. But then Constantinople fell to the Muslim Turks in 1453. A new "Rome" was required. Immediately, the Russians stepped forward to volunteer their own capital for the job. Moscow would replace Constantinople as the "Third Rome," they boldly announced.

Many in Europe objected—not the least of whom being the Pope—but the Russians ignored them all. For them, Moscow's preeminence had been decreed by God Almighty.

"(Moscow) alone shines in the whole world brighter than the sun . . ." wrote the Russian monk Filofey in 1510. "Two Romes have fallen, but the third stands and a fourth there will not be."

Ever since, Russians have clung stubbornly to the conviction that they hold a divine mission to enlighten the world. Communist propagandists exploited this belief expertly, firing Russian imaginations with their vision of a World Revolution inspired and orchestrated from the Eternal City of Moscow.

Beware the Russian Who Invented Baseball

Those of us who haven't yet blotted the Cold War completely from our memories may still recall one of that era's most characteristic "types"—the bombastic, Russian blow-hard who could never stop boasting about his country's "achievements." Everything the Americans had done, this arrogant commissar bragged that *his* people had done bigger, better, and *first*. For instance, it was actually claimed at various times that Russians had invented the telephone, the airplane, and baseball.

We no longer see this immodest fellow ridiculed on American variety shows as we did in past years. Most of us imagine that he has passed out of existence altogether. But he hasn't. Deep in the heart of every Russian lurks that same blustering megalomaniac. His overinflated view of himself has survived through the centuries. He knows when to lie low. But he will spring out at you, when you least expect him, and grab you by the throat.

Only Russians Are Allowed to Make Fun of Russia

All this history brings us back to the subject of the fragile Russian ego, and how you should handle it. On a recent business trip, my Russian driver cursed as he ran over another of Moscow's infamous and everpresent potholes.

"God, how I hate this country," he exclaimed. "You Americans should have dropped a hydrogen bomb on this city when you had the chance." I chuckled politely at his joke. However, I wisely did not hasten to agree with him, nor to add my own flippant embellishments. I can assure you, they would not have been appreciated.

The first rule of Russian etiquette is both simple and incredibly unfair. It is that *only Russians may freely make fun of Russia*. In the ceaseless patter of anti-Russian jokes, wisecracks, and subtle slurs with which Russians never tire of pummeling their motherland, foreign participation is not welcome.

Many Americans will rush to object. They will cite numerous instances when some nasty putdown they made of the Russian people has brought forth peals of laughter from their Russian "friends." They will suggest that if you have good rapport with "your" Russians, you don't have to worry about offending them. I would suggest, however, that most of these loose-lipped Americans don't really have quite the rapport they think they have. Many have simply stumbled upon Russians who are far more gracious than they. Others have found Russians who see some economic advantage in keeping their murderous resentment to themselves . . . for the time being.

The Russian Concept of "Face"

Russians have a brittle sense of personal pride which is not so different from the Oriental concept of "saving" or "losing face." Never forget this fact in your dealings with them.

"If you're in a meeting or even one on one and a Russian proposes something," explains Len Blavatnik, president of the trading company Renova, "it would be very American to say, 'Your idea doesn't make sense because of one, two, three, four, and five.' In the States, a person wouldn't take that too personally. But Russians are traditionally insecure, especially with foreigners. They always have to be right. If you point out that a Russian is wrong, in public or in private, he'll be upset at you. He'll take it personally. You'll never know why your deal died, because he'll hide it and never show it."

Status Counts

Shortly after Boris Yeltsin overturned Gorbachev, a Western reporter asked Yeltsin if he felt any resentment toward President George Bush for having refused to meet with him some months before, during Yeltsin's first trip to the United States.

"No," replied Yeltsin bluntly. "President Bush treated me in accordance with my status at the time." As a lifelong Communist apparatchik, Yeltsin had long ago learned to accept both the privileges and the limitations of his bureaucratic status with a heavy-handed fatalism unfamiliar to that Western reporter.

Russia's society, even today, is essentially feudal. Barons and lords, in the guise of government bureaucrats, state factory managers, underworld kingpins, and wealthy entrepreneurs dole out favors and patronage like mafia dons. In such a society, the code of status is taken very seriously. That's why the conspirators in the August 1991 coup wasted so much time fighting over who would take which office in the Kremlin, even while their power slipped away by the minute. That's why Boris Yeltsin confiscated Gorbachev's limousine and ordered his parliamentary rival Ruslan Khasbulatov to give up his personal guards. Such frills and trappings conveyed an aura of status on Yeltsin's rivals which he found excessive.

Honor the Bureaucracy

Of course, in most of your dealings, you will be facing young entrepreneurs of the rising business class for whom the cult of bureaucracy is a weak and fading memory. But even today, you will often find it necessary to deal with officials and organizations in Russia whose mindset is locked in the old ways.

With such people, there are a thousand tiny ways by which you can recognize and honor the status of your negotiating partners, all of which will be noticed and appreciated. Some of them are listed on the following pages.

Pompous Toasts and Speeches

There was a time when virtually every negotiation between Russians and Americans was attended by banquets and fanfair, at which Soviet officials hoisted glasses of vodka and declaimed long, pompous toasts on the theme of "friendship between the superpowers."

That doesn't happen much anymore. But old habits die hard, and many Russian bureaucrats may still be tempted to open meetings and negotiations with flowery, self-important pronouncements. Be patient with these windy procedures. Be prepared to respond in kind should you be invited to do so.

Let the Boss Show His Authority

In a Russian meeting, there's no doubt who's the boss. Usually he sits at the head of the table, with his subordinates arrayed around him in hierarchical symmetry. Protocol for the meeting is simple. The boss does the talking and his subordinates keep their mouths shut. If they speak at all, it is only to echo or gratuitously praise something the boss has said.

If you find all of this a little bit silly, don't let it show. Allow the boss his moment in the sun. Let him play the Big Cheese. Show him the same deference that you would a Tatar Khan surrounded by bodyguards with drawn scimitars.

Never cut him off. *Never* make him lose face in front of his sycophants, even if you disagree with him. If you anticipate differences, work them out in advance of the meeting, either directly with the boss or with his subordinates. The "full-dress" meeting itself is largely ceremonial and should not be spoiled with embarassing confrontations.

Above all, allow the boss to appear in complete control at all times, whether he is or not. Any decisions that are made should appear to be his.

The Business Card Ceremony

Much like the Japanese, Russians will expect you to study their business cards very carefully and attentively for several moments after they are handed to you. Don't just stick the card in your pocket. And you should definitely come to any meeting or introduction prepared with plenty of business cards of your own, enough for everyone at the meeting.

Some old Russia hands say this isn't so important anymore. In the old days, Russian bureaucrats needed to know precisely what hierarchical positions their counterparts occupied in a meeting. You didn't want to lower yourself by meeting with a person of lower status than yourself. A factory director wanted to talk to another factory director, not to an assistant shop manager.

Such distinctions are indeed less vital now than they used to be. More often than not, what's important in a meeting is who has the money or who has an opportunity to offer. Nevertheless, the business card ceremonial seems to linger on intact.

Business Hospitality

In the old days, a foreign executive would be dazzled at almost any business meeting with lavish spreads of cookies, pastries, tea, coffee, hors d'oeuvres, cognac, and vodka. Most meetings would start with more than one bottoms-up toast. Regrettably, this charming custom is now becoming rarer and rarer. The Western practice of keeping things "strictly business" is taking over. Most of this just has to do with time. In the old days, foreign businessmen were a rare species and your visit to a Russian's office a special occasion. Now, foreigners file in and out of Russian offices all day long. Don't take it personally. It just isn't practical anymore to roll out the red carpet for everyone.

Be Punctual

Everyone has heard that the Russians don't keep appointments or that they tend to show up late. This is true quite often. Russians have a leisurely, almost "Mediterranean" approach to their daily schedules. However, you, as an American, will be held to a higher standard. The Russians have high expectations of American punctuality. Especially when you first meet, you should not disillusion them.

"If you don't protect your image as an American," says Blavatnik, "they lose respect, and you lose some advantage. They like dealing with Americans. But if you don't seem like a *typical* American, they may lose interest."

As your relationship develops, you'll find that punctuality becomes less important, especially since your Russian partners will certainly find occasion to be late for meetings time and time again.

Dress for Success

Business dress is the same as it would be in the West. Your image as an American requires that you be nattily attired in your Madison Avenue best.

At one time, there was a great deal of mystification over the subject of Russian fur hats. That's because, in the old days, when Western clothes were hard to come by, the fur hat you wore in the winter was one of the only signs by which you could distinguish yourself from the masses. A high-level Party *apparatchik* wanted to make sure that he was well turned out in a mink or sable hat, rather than a lowly rabbit. One American executive whom I know was actually taken aside by his Russian partner and chided for showing up at a business meeting in a plain lamb's wool hat.

However, as a foreigner, you're generally not expected to know such rules. Besides, the hat game is becoming increasingly passe as Russians turn their attention to other details like shoes and imported suits.

"At one time," says Blavatnik, "you could automatically tell who was a foreigner by their clothes. But not any more. The Russians are dressing very well these days. Russian businessmen, plant managers, they've all been abroad a lot of times now, and have done a lot of shopping."

A Common, Stupid Error

All too many American companies still have it in their heads that Russian businessmen are penniless and naive. This is no longer true. Such outdated and condescending assumptions have resulted in a lot of needless insults and broken deals.

"There's a whole class of Russian businessmen now," says Blavatnik, "who are moving millions of dollars all the time. Yet, many Americans still think every Russian is poor. They try to impress them with very small amounts of money, and the Russians basically just walk away."

Stepan Pachikov, whose software company ParaGraph has made multimillion-dollar licensing deals with Digital Equipment, Sun Microsystems and Apple Computer (see Chap. 3), laughs at the memory of one major American corporation which offered him $5000 to license his software.

"I saw that this is the kind of company that thinks, 'Let's give these stupid Russians a few dollars and a couple of computers and they'll be extremely happy,'" recalls Pachikov.

Still smarting from the $87,000 he had just shelled out on lawyers' fees for his last deal, Pachikov had an idea. "I told him okay, it's a starting price, I can discuss any number," says Pachikov. "I told him I would send four of my lawyers down to discuss some details, and maybe there will be one month of negotiations. As soon as they heard I would hire four lawyers at $250 an hour, they understood that their $5000 would not be enough for me."

Treat the Russians as Equals

"American corporate types tend to talk in paternalistic ways," says Blavatnik. "They talk down to the Russians. That will always rub the Russians the wrong way. It's important that they feel equal. If they feel that you treat them as people of a lower status or from a lower country, they'll really hold a grudge."

Blavatnik recalls one negotiation which broke down because a major American firm overestimated its powers over its Russian negotiating partner. "Even though they gave the Russians the red carpet treatment, private club, executive suites, and all that, still their whole tone was condescending. Their attitude was take it or leave it. They said, 'Without us, you'll be in bad shape. You need our money and know-how.' That's the red flag that will always make the Russians cut it off. These Russians said privately, 'They think we need them? Well, we'll just go and do the deal with someone else.' Which they proceeded to do."

Getting Past Business

When my wife and I first arrived at the office of our Russian partner for our TV production, we were treated to a little performance. Our partner sat bolt upright behind his desk, stiffly shuffled through some papers, then cleared his throat and welcomed us very formally.

"Our project will be a great success," he pronounced. "We will work hard, cooperate with one another, and achieve a successful outcome." Suddenly, he slumped visibly in his chair, letting out an obvious sigh of relief.

"Now," he said weakly. "Enough business for the day. Let's have some vodka." Our partner's little talk—which lasted all of about 60 seconds—did indeed prove to be the last item of business for that day.

"Russians basically feel uncomfortable in business situations," says New York-based consultant George Capsis. "They want to get past that formal business stuff as quickly as possible and just get down to relating to you as a person. What they really want is to touch you, to feel you. They want to know who you really are. That's what's important to them."

Eye to Eye

Americans have a reputation for being the most impersonal businessmen in the world. We like to get right down to business. If a deal can be transacted quickly, by phone, so much the better.

For the Russians, this is all too abrupt. They hate doing anything by phone, and they will resist transacting any business without having adequate time to get to know you face to face.

"When it comes to a real negotiation, a closing, they have to meet you in person," says emigré filmmaker Vladimir Kononenko. "That's the only way they'll do it. They want to look you in the eyes. They want to know what kind of air you're breathing, what you are made of. They like to deal with people who are on the same wavelength."

The Drinking Game

The traditional Russian method for scrutinizing a potential business partner is to get him drunk. "Drinking is still very important," says Blavatnik. "If you can drink with the Russians, it helps. It's the way they do business. Everybody gets drunk, everybody gets loose, then the real conversation starts."

Seven years of temperance propaganda and multiple exposures to health-conscious American executives have caused many Russians to tone down on the pressure to drink. Many Russians have learned to drink moderately or not at all when Westerners are around. However, don't be fooled by all this apparent good behavior. Russia has been a bibulous society for many centuries, and it remains so today.

Many Russians will still pressure you to drink heavily. In some cases, they do it simply because they feel like having a drink themselves and would like a partner. But more often, it is a real test of your character. Many Russians believe that only when you're drunk can they find out what you're really like and what you really think of them.

A Russian friend of mine once warned me that he thought another Russian in our party was a KGB agent. He thought this because the man in question had nursed a single beer all evening long while the others at our table had put away pint after pint of Guinness. "Only a KGB agent would pass up the opportunity to drink so much foreign beer," my friend told me seriously.

All this notwithstanding, you don't *have* to drink with the Russians if you really don't want to. They may prod and pressure you at first to join them in multiple bottoms-up toasts. But if you look closely, you'll see that often the Russians themselves are not really draining their glasses each time. A tiny sip for each toast will do the trick.

In any case, it's better not to get drunk if you can't hold your liquor. Drinking yourself under the table will only make you look foolish. The Russians will think less of you for it.

Americans Have an Advantage

In the cultural interplay of business negotiations, Americans have a distinct advantage over other nationalities, for the Russians genuinely *like* us. All things being equal, they would rather do business with you than with any Japanese, Korean, German, or Britisher on the block.

"The Russians have an affinity for Americans," says Blavatnik. "They see the two countries as equals, with many similarities. Both countries are world powers, both are big countries. Both peoples are very friendly, both are big thinkers who are like to do things on a big scale, whether in business or pleasure."

A Common Frontier Spirit

The affinity perhaps runs a little deeper than that. It's probably no accident that our two countries became the first to conquer space, for both America and Russia are frontier nations, imbued for long centuries with a *pioneer spirit*. For Russia, the frontier was Siberia, its earliest settlers the unruly Cossacks, whose rude and violent temperament mirrored that of our cowboys and mountain men. Far from cities and governments, the settlers of both frontiers evolved a strong sense of self-reliance, a love for personal liberty and a healthy disdain for aristocratic pretension.

Nations of Peasants

Both Russians and Americans seem to pride themselves on their "peasant" origins. In their popular and folk culture, they glorify the humble, and skewer the proud. The Russians would no doubt love "Columbo," that bumbling, blue-collar detective who always manages to outthink the snooty, Beverly Hills swells. They would also love the drawling, down-home Ross Perot, that self-styled "mangy ol' cur-dog" who stole 20 million votes from the pampered politicos, pulling up to the presidential debates in a Hertz Rent-a-Car, while his opponents rolled in with lengthy motorcades of black limousines.

Deep in the Russian psyche lives a fairytale hero, "Ivan the Fool." Like Columbo, Ivan appears to be a bumbling peasant. But time and again, the "stupid" peasant outwits monsters, sorcerers, and arrogant knights. He has a secret power over his seeming superiors, a simplicity, a goodness, a God-like innocence.

In short, he's a very *American* sort of fellow. And he symbolizes all that is good, hopeful, and promising in the Russian people.

The Russian Tortoise
and the Foreign Hare

Pyotr Zrelov, one of the founders of Joint Venture Dialogue (see Chap. 10), once described to *Forbes* magazine a Japanese cartoon which had been shown to his Young Pioneer group when he was a child in the late 1950s. The Soviet Sputnik had just been sent into orbit, well in advance of the first American satellite. Russian pride was strong.

As *Forbes* described it, the cartoon "showed two teams trying to launch rockets: a high-tech, punctiliously organized group of athletic Americans and a scruffy, bewildered band of poorly dressed Soviets.

"The American team displayed split-second precision, flawlessly coordinated. The team leader pressed the button as the countdown hit zero. Nothing happened. Now to the Soviet team. People ambled about in confusion, some smoking, some not. No one had brought a match to launch the rocket . . . A team member, dispatched to get a match, returned an hour later with a bottle of vodka. Finally, someone found a match and held it to the fuse. Off went the rocket, climbing victoriously into the sky. Improvisation had won the day."

Something in that cartoon touched Pyotr Zrelov's imagination, inspiring him to go on to become one of Russia's preeminent business leaders today. Although made in Japan, that cartoon captured an essential element of the Russian self-image, which sees itself perpetually as the awkward tortoise who ultimately gets the best of the flashy foreign hare.

Don't Give Up on the Russians

It's more than just a quaint folk belief. Most Americans don't realize what an amazing feat the Russians achieved in space, producing comparable results to the Americans using *far more primitive technology*. Back in the 1970s, we mocked the Russians for their tin-can spaceships. But as commercial satellite launches evolved into big business in the 1980s, simplicity became an advantage, and suddenly we were startled to find the tortoise-like Russians pulling ahead.

After the Challenger disaster forced America to cancel most of its scheduled commercial satellite launches, the Russians stepped in to offer their services instead, undercutting world prices by a good $20 million per launch and achieving 90 successful missions per year with their kerosene-powered rockets, while our delicate, computerized space shuttle, crammed with intricate moving parts, microcircuitry, and expensive cooling systems to preserve its cryogenic fuels sat uselessly in the repair shop year after year after year.

The K.I.S.S. Principle

The Russians pulled off a similar feat in World War II, when they developed the T-34 tank. John Kiser III, whose company, Kiser Research, identifies and licenses advanced Russian technology in the West, regards the T-34 as a masterpiece of that classic engineering principle, "Keep It Simple, Stupid" or the K.I.S.S. principle.

In his book *Communist Entrepreneurs*, Kiser describes how the Russian tank, "crudely constructed with rough, unfinished castings, precision-machined only where absolutely necessary, and having cramped working conditions... nevertheless shattered German illusions of tank superiority. The German Mark III was better equipped with radios, was more comfortable, and had more sophisticated engineering, yet the Russians came out ahead on essentials."

Beyond the Russian Soul

As you work with the Russians, as you get to understand their strange, self-deprecating humor, their dogged pessimism, their morbid and fanatical temperament, their tormented history, their mysterious "Russian soul," never forget the T-34 tank or the Proton rocket. Never forget Ivan the Fool, with his idiot grin, his ragged clothes and his keen, unyielding mind.

For behind all the jokes and the putdowns of old mother Russia, the Russians still dream confidently of the day when once again that Russian tortoise will pull ahead of the shocked and astonished foreign hare. And he just might do it.

Russian Etiquette Tips

Russian culture is replete with folk customs and superstitions which Russians themselves often observe, but from which you as a foreigner are exempt. Everyone realizes that you don't know any better. For example, if you bring an even number of flowers to a friend's house, no one will be offended—even though many Russians would realize that even numbers of flowers are appropriate only for funerals.

However, Russians do observe certain basic niceties which differ significantly from ordinary manners in America. You will feel more poised and confident knowing and observing them. The more important of these follow:

- *Handshaking*: Russians take handshakes a bit more seriously than we. Generally, men (not women) will shake hands every time they meet, both when they meet and again when they part. In the winter, take off your glove before you shake someone's hand. Americans seldom do this, but Russians feel insulted when you offer them a gloved hand.

- *Chivalry to the Ladies*: American society is very confused right now about how men and women should behave around one another. Things are much simpler in Russia. A man treats a woman like a *lady*. If you kiss a woman's hand when you meet her and when you part, she will be flattered. She will not call you a sexist, nor will she sue you. If you don't feel comfortable with this Continental custom, a nice, quick bow will do. A man does not ordinarily shake hands with a Russian woman.

- *Don't Point Your Finger*: Americans love to point their fingers, but in Russia, it's considered rude. To point at another person or even to gesture too sharply toward them with your hands in any way carries a connotation of force or threat.

- *Don't Use Foul Language:* It is sometimes tempting to use colorful anatomical words and phrases in a foreign language, if you happen to know them. But don't try it in Russia. You're all too likely to use them at the wrong time and in the wrong company. Russians are much more squeamish about foul language than Americans, and still believe that you shouldn't use such words in the company of ladies.

- *Giving Gifts:* Russians give little gifts much more freely and spontaneously than most Americans. Whenever you visit a Russian's house, you should bring flowers and some little gift like a bottle of cognac. Foreign wines and liquors are usually appreciated more than Russian ones. It's nice to give other small gifts to friends from time to time such as art books, French perfume for ladies, and the like. In business, the best gift is something with your company name or logo on it like a fountain pen or cigarette lighter. That helps establish your position and shows that you care about your company. It also gives the recipient something to show off. Everytime he whips out his Acme Inc. fountain pen, he advertises to everyone around him that here's a man who does business with Americans. The best time to present your business gift is right away, as soon as you are introduced to your potential partner.

- *Take Off Your Shoes in the House:* Most Russians take off their shoes in the house. However, they realize that Americans don't usually do this, and will not be horrified if you forget. The best thing is to ask your host's preference when you come into his apartment.

- *Wash Your Hands Before Eating:* Most Americans are taught as children to wash their hands before eating. But, for some inexplicable reason, many stop doing it when they grow older, and spend the rest of their lives eating with dirty hands. Russians find this practice appalling, and with good reason.

- *Ask Before Taking Off Your Suit Coat in Meetings:* This is a minor point, but it's considered a little bit *nekulturno* (uncultured) to strip down to shirt sleeves in the middle of a formal business meeting. If you must, ask first. And take a cue from the others in the room. Some meetings are more formal than others.

- *Let Everyone Smoke:* If you have a serious medical problem being around cigarette smoke, you should probably try to stay within the borders of the United States. In Russia, as in most other countries of the world, people smoke like chimneys, anywhere, anytime, and certainly in business meetings. Although it's polite to ask permission before lighting up a cigarette, Russians may think you very odd and pushy if you deny them permission to smoke.

- *Sit in the Front Seat of a Cab:* Old Soviet notions of egalitarianism dictate that only stuck-up, capitalist snobs sit in the back seat of a taxicab, when there is a perfectly good, vacant seat up front by the driver. Communism is dead, but certain proletarian courtesies survive.

14

Russian Mind Games

How to Win Against Deceit, Treachery, Thievery, Bribery, Murder, and Other Russian Negotiating Tactics

We Americans love to share stories about the silly things that Russians have done in business. One of the all-time favorites in this genre concerns a large, multinational American corporation which was attempting to negotiate a barter deal. Part of the deal required the American company to sell Russian greeting cards in the United States, for which the Russians would receive part of the dollar profits. The problem arose when the Russians suddenly demanded not *part* of the profits, or even *all* of the profits. They demanded that they be reimbursed the *full retail price of the greeting cards*!

In most tellings, that's where the story ends. Everybody laughs. Those stupid Russians! Don't they understand about profit and loss? About overhead? Shipping costs? Did they really imagine that an American firm was going to agree to a deal that could only end up *costing* it money? Ha, ha, ha, ha, ha!

But guess what? The American company *did* agree to the Russians' terms. It had no choice. Only by agreeing could the Americans gain other, more vital concessions which they needed. The Russians had them over a barrel and knew it.

It's easy to see why Americans usually leave out this part of the story. It ruins the whole punchline. In the complete version, it's the Russians, not the Americans, who have the last laugh.

Masters of Intrigue

The Russians may not be schooled in the niceties of Western business practice, but they are masters of intrigue. Centuries of brutal despotism have forced them to perfect a devilish repertoire of strategems ranging from simple intimidation (as in the previous example) to deceit, treachery, thievery, bribery, and even murder in order to gain what they want.

In business negotiations, the Russians quickly size up your strengths and weaknesses and take ruthless advantage of them. You may not always understand their behavior, but don't assume that it is irrational. The most "senseless" Russian conduct is usually grounded in meticulous, cold-blooded calculation. Be advised that the Russians have a plan for you and your company. All too often, their plan works.

Fight Back and Win

If we believe that America offers a superior way of doing business, we will not prove this to the Russians by becoming their patsies. Even as we strive to be honest and fair, we must also be tough and wise. The Russians will adhere to our ways only if they see that our ways *work*.

In this chapter, I will outline a number of tough-minded negotiating principles by which you may fight forcefully for what is yours and *win*.

Treat the Russian Marketplace as a War Zone

It is said that the Japanese treat every business negotiation as a battle, which must end in clear victory for one side and abject defeat for the other. The Russians seem to operate from a similar premise. From the moment you set foot in Russia, consider yourself at war. The enemy might attack at any time, from any direction.

When my wife and I arrived in Russia in June 1992, we were already way behind schedule. Our two and a half-hour TV special about America was slated to air on the Russian Television Network in only three weeks. During that time, we had to shoot a 30-minute documentary on Russian-American business, produce a host introduction for the show, translate two existing American documentaries into Russian, and produce three promotional spots. Time was of the essence.

Yet, from the moment we landed, our Russian partners *deliberately prevented us from doing any work*. First, we were whisked off to the *dacha* (a cottage outside the city, usually rented, to which every self-respecting Russian repairs on the weekend) for two and a half days of drunken torpor. Subsequently, our every request for technical assistance was mysteriously denied. We clamored in vain for camera crews, for time in the editing room, for facilities and technicians to convert and translate into Russian the American programs we had brought with us. After a week of this runaround, our Russian partner announced that he was taking us back to the *dacha* for yet another round of "vodka therapy." The attack had begun.

The "Russian Culture" Scam

Throughout all these maneuvers, our Russian interpreter just kept telling us to relax. Nothing was amiss, he explained soothingly. We just needed to get used to Russian "culture." "When you're in Russia," he was fond of repeating, "don't expect anything to make sense." We asked him why we were expected to waste every weekend at the *dacha*. Our interpreter just laughed, "It's the Russian way!"

When we pointed out that further delays might destroy our chances of finishing the program, he lectured us: "This is how Russians do a three-week project. They spend the first two-and-a-half weeks talking about it. Then, at the last minute, they all scream and shout at each other and stay up all night and in the end it gets done."

It all sounded quite harmless and reassuring. And indeed, there was a certain truth in our interpreter's folksy observations. But as we were later to discover, our interpreter knew very well, even as he spoke these words, that there was far more afoot than mere "cultural" eccentricity. He was simply using "culture" as a smokescreen to mask the subtle machinations of his employer—our Russian partner—and to quell our rising suspicions.

In general, never accept "Russian culture" as an excuse for unprofessional conduct. More often than not, it is intrigue—not folk psychology—which lies at the root. The intrigue might be grand or petty. But its purpose is always to get the best of you and your company.

The Delayed-Attack Strategem

In *The Asian Mind Game*—a remarkably insightful book, in honor of which I have named this chapter—author Chin-ning Chu describes a 2000-year-old Oriental strategy, much used by modern Asian businessmen.

The ancient Chinese taught that a wise general will wear out his adversary by endlessly avoiding battle, forcing him to march over hill and dale, week after week, in fruitless pursuit, until sheer frustration and exhaustion forces the enemy to let down his guard. Only then will the wise general attack, when his psychological advantage is at a maximum.

The Russians practice a similar strategy. One American businessman flew to Moscow for a week with the intention of negotiating with several prospective partners. But one of his negotiating partners ended up dominating most of his time. The Russians spirited the American off to a remote *dacha*, and plied him with drink day after day. Each time the American tried to talk business, the Russians would shush him and pour out another round of vodka.

At the end of the week, the American dejectedly packed his bags to go home, certain that his trip had been a failure. Suddenly, the Russians started to negotiate. Before he knew it, the American had closed a deal with them.

"They cornered me into a position where if I didn't sign a deal with them, I would have wasted the whole week and gone home with nothing. It really put a lot of pressure on me to come to terms immediately. It's a very effective strategy."

Petty Wars for Petty Gains

Henry Kissinger once observed that the reason academic infighting is so vicious is that the stakes are so low. The same dynamic seems to prevail in the Russian workplace. One of the main reasons that Americans fail to recognize Russian intrigue is that we can't figure out their motives. Sometimes the "prize" the Russians seek is so unbelievably petty that we cannot imagine they would go to such lengths to achieve it. But they would and they do.

Our Russian production crew practiced a particularly effective form of the *delayed-attack stratagem*. For three weeks, they blocked our every attempt to get any work done. For example, every time we showed up for a scheduled session in the editing room, we would discover that there had been a "misunderstanding," or a "bureaucratic snafu," by which our time slot had been "accidentally" given to someone else. Day after day passed in this manner.

We clearly saw *what* the Russians were doing, but for the longest time couldn't figure out *why* they were doing it. After all, didn't they have as much of an interest as we in getting the job done? Not from their point of view. When we finally discovered the object of their machinations, we were floored by its pathetic shortsightedness.

Call Their Bluff

The Russians will wait until they think you're helpless before they bare their fangs. That's the time to dig in your heels and *fight*. More often than not, they'll back down if they see you really mean it.

Our Russian production crew waited until the last minute to show their hand. We were critically behind schedule, with only *two days* remaining before airtime. Suddenly, our Russian "producer" and "script editor" burst into the editing room. They announced that we only had *four hours* on the equipment. Earlier, they had told us we would have all day to work. "There's no time to waste," they said. "Don't argue. Just do what we say. We have to work fast."

The Russians then announced that the script I had written for the opening monologue was unacceptable. They had had the script in their possession for *two weeks*, but had never complained until now. The solution? Our Russian colleagues just happened to have already shot footage of *themselves* hosting the show on the grounds of the American Embassy. They suggested we use this footage rather than the introductory monologue I had written.

This was it. The Russians had jeopardized the entire project, delaying production up to the last second, and sabotaging any chance to produce a top-quality program, *just so they could force us to put them on the show!*

After a brief shouting match during which we made clear that we would not be bulldozed, the Russians withdrew. They seemed surprised that we had stood up to them. They also appeared to give in on every point. But we were soon to learn that they were only regrouping for their next attack.

The "Russian Bureaucracy" Scam

One of the favorite Russian ploys is to intimidate and mystify foreigners with the intricacies of the infamous Russian bureaucracy. The Russians played their final gambit on us only *24 hours* before airtime. When we showed up that Sunday morning at the Ostankino Telecenter, the guards refused to let us in. Ordinarily, our Russian partners obtained passes for us. They always seemed to get the passes they needed when they needed them. But on this day, they threw up their hands helplessly. "Foreigners aren't allowed in on Sunday," they shrugged. "What can we do?" We were finally allowed in later that afternoon. "Oh, it was difficult, very difficult," said our Russian script editor, as he handed us our passes. "We were lucky to get these."

My wife, Marie, was the only one who had been allowed in that morning. Once we were inside, she told us what the charade was all about. The Russians had been working since 7 a.m. on a news segment to be broadcast on the evening news. The segment was about our TV production. It featured the infamous footage of our Russian partners and production crew broadcasting from . . . guess where? The grounds of the American embassy.

The Russians seemed quite proud of themselves that day. They obviously thought they had "won." On the very last day of production, with the success or failure of our entire program hanging in the balance, the Russians had deliberately held up the works for almost eight hours just so they could perpetrate this petty coup.

Beware the Treacherous Interpreter

Time and time again, bruised and battered Americans returning from the "wars" in Russia will warn about treacherous Russian interpreters. The common wisdom is that if you don't speak Russian, hire your own interpreter. The interpreter provided by your Russian partner is little better than a spy in your midst.

Our interpreter was a very intelligent and able man—punctual, patient, friendly, an adept peacemaker at tense moments and vastly over-qualified for the position. But his ultimate fealty to our Russian partners proved a serious problem, especially during the final, nerve-wracking night of our editing process.

Although I can speak Russian passably, it was beyond my competence to directly supervise the rapid editing of Russian-language interviews. Our interpreter had to tell the video editor where to cut and splice. As time grew shorter and shorter, the video editor grew more impatient with our detailed instructions. We were taking too much time, he said. We were being too perfectionist.

Finally, the editor just stopped listening altogether. Ignoring our instructions, he began cutting off dialogue and overlaying images in all the wrong places, virtually at random. At a particularly critical moment, our interpreter sat stone-silent, refusing to transmit our orders until the editor had already performed an irreversible act of butchery.

When I called him on his behavior, our interpreter appeared exasperated with me. "We don't have time for all this nitpicking," he said. "What difference does it make anyway, these little details? Who's going to notice?"

Americans Are Naive

We discussed in the last chapter the curious cultural affinity which seems to exist between Russians and Americans. There is another reason, however, why Russians prefer working with Americans. They consider us to be prize suckers.

"The Russians think Americans are a little naive," says Vladimir Kononenko, an American film director who emigrated from Russia in 1976. "They feel that they can take advantage. And they will without blinking an eye."

According to Kononenko, Americans are too hesitant to call the Russians on their perfidy. "Americans are more delicate than other nationalities," he says, "more polite. They're afraid to be rude. The Germans, on the other hand, don't mind being rude at all."

Why the Russians Respect the Germans

Kononenko says that the Russians tend to respect the Germans more than other nationalities, because the Germans are such demanding business partners. "The Germans show they're not naive," he says. "They invest a lot of money in Russia, but they insist on getting what they pay for. They are very demanding and they're not always polite about it. The Russians understand that. They may hate it. But they respect it."

Management by Abuse

An alarming amount of nonsense has been written lately about the greater *egalitarianism* and *workplace democracy* that supposedly existed in Soviet industry. Many Russians are aware of this misconception, and will play upon it to manipulate naive Americans. They might tell you, for example, that, "You don't know how to work with Russians," if you're too rough on them.

Don't believe this line for a minute. No one is harder on the Russians than their fellow Russians. No matter how much they complain to your face, it's guaranteed that your Russian partners and employees are really amazed at your civility. They just aren't used to so much politeness.

John Francis recalls the brutal behavior of his two Russian partners toward employees. "When the staff comes in to work, they don't greet them, don't smile, don't even look at them," says Francis. At one point, Francis's City Looks hair salon held a three-day competition in which over 100 stylists competed for 24 positions. At the end of the three days, the two Russian ladies who managed the store had the job of telling the bad news to the losers.

"Those Russian girls just came out of their office crying and shaking, one after another," says Francis. "They just landed on them with both feet. They told them we don't want you, so get out."

Francis suggested to the ladies that they might be a little more tactful. "This is Russia," they countered. "These are Russian people. We know how to handle them."

Show Your Power

Vladimir Kononenko believes that your success in Russia will be largely determined by your performance in a brutal, but often subtle, contest of power and will. "The Russians must feel your power," he says. "You cannot just be passive with them. Set up your own rules and impose them on the Russians. Make them play *your* game, otherwise you'll end up playing theirs."

Before emigrating to the United States in 1976, Kononenko was a prominent film director in Russia. He returned to Russia to work on various film projects after 15 years of directing films and commercials in America. Equally fluent in the Byzantine rites of Russian intrigue and the cutthroat gamesmanship of Hollywood and Madison Avenue, Kononenko has developed a stern but effective philosophy for keeping the Russians under control. The following sections contain a few of his more important insights.

Don't Come to Russia Without an Extensive Rolodex

One of the first rules Kononenko learned was never to rely on a single Russian partner. You shouldn't even set foot in Russia without an extensive database of business contacts, even if you have to buy one! That way, you're never forced to dance to one person's tune.

In 1988, Kononenko cut a deal with Sovinfilm—the agency then in charge of foreign co-productions. As Sovinfilm's exclusive representative in the United States, Kononenko arranged with Kodak Pathé—a Paris division of Eastman-Kodak—to do a promotional film in the Soviet Union.

The trouble began almost immediately. After receiving multiple confirmations by fax, Kononenko obtained his visa, packed his equipment, and boarded a plane. During a brief layover in Amsterdam, he phoned his Russian partners.

The girl who answered the phone dropped a bombshell. "Can you postpone coming for a couple of weeks?" she asked brightly. "What are you talking about?" cried Kononenko. "I'm here in Amsterdam. I have a visa. I have your written invitation. I'm due in Moscow in a couple of hours. What should I do?"

"Just kill some time," suggested the young lady. "Play with the girls in Amsterdam."

Sovinfilm was going through a political shakeup related to Gorbachev's reforms. Until that was resolved, Kononenko had been put on ice. Luckily, Kononenko had a few choice phone numbers from his days as a Soviet director. Soon he had cut deals with three different film companies in as many different cities. He was still contractually bound to work with Sovinfilm, but he now had other suppliers and contacts to fall back on. "I learned my lesson very quickly with Sovinfilm," says Kononenko, "You cannot allow yourself to be subjected to their capricious behavior."

It was only after Kononenko had been in Russia for two months that he saw the full wisdom of making his independent contacts. After eight busy weeks of scouting locations, writing scripts, hiring talent, and preparing to shoot, Kononenko's associates in New York finally received a fax saying that Sovinfilm was ready to receive him. "I would have stayed in Amsterdam for two months waiting for their invitation!" he marvels.

You're On Your Own

When you run into serious problems with Russian partners—such as theft and extortion—don't expect anyone to help you. The police are notoriously corrupt, and will probably side with your Russian partner, especially if they're paid to stay out of it. Lawyers are of little use, since the laws change every minute, and are seldom enforced anyway. If you work for a corporation, don't go running to the home office. The reason they put you "on the ground" in Russia is so you would deal with sticky problems of this nature and take them off their hands. Even the American embassy will brush you off, telling you they don't get involved in business disputes.

In Russia, you're completely on your own. You must use cunning, craft and bluster to fight for what is yours. Kononenko found this out the hard way. For days, he tried unsuccessfully to claim the raw film stock which Kodak had sent to a Russian warehouse. Finally, a secretary told him the film had been taken by Surikov, the president of Sovinfilm. *Kononenko's own partner* had appropriated his film!

"I contacted Kodak in Paris. They just said, 'Too bad. What are we supposed to do?'" Kononenko realized then that if he wanted his film back, he would have to get it himself.

Show No Fear

Bluster and intimidation play a major role in Russian power plays. If the Russians sense that you're afraid, you'll get nowhere with them. Kononenko first tried to go "through channels" to get his film back. He asked his

Russian assistant director to go over Surikov's head and call the man's boss, acting in her official capacity as Kononenko's Russian representative. The idea flopped because the woman was intimidated by the prospect of confronting such powerful bureaucrats.

"She was afraid to talk to these people," says Kononenko. "She had been brought up with the idea that every boss is a big shot and you have to talk to them in a certain way. She kept on calling this guy's secretary, and she would just say, 'Excuse me, please,' very humbly. She would say, 'I'm from such and such studio.' She was afraid even to admit that she was calling on behalf of an American filmmaker. The secretary would sense her fear and would just snap at her, 'Who are you? Why are you calling?' The secretary would say 'Call back in an hour,' 'Call back in two hours,' and so on until the end of the day." Finally, Kononenko gave up on the woman. He decided to make the approach himself.

Russian Secretaries Don't Take Messages

In situations like Kononenko's, it's useful to know that Russian secretaries often don't take messages. A good technique for increasing the likelihood of getting your message through is the following:

> YOU: "Could you please tell Mr. So-and-So that I called?"
>
> SECRETARY: "Yes, of course. Good-bye."
>
> YOU: "But wait. Don't you want to know my phone number?"
>
> SECRETARY: (Exasperated sigh) "Yes, of course. What is it?"
>
> YOU: "Do you have a pen and paper to write it down?"
>
> SECRETARY: (Long pause) "Just a moment. I'll see if I can find one."
>
> YOU: (After she writes down the message) "Now, could you please read the message back to me?"

If she's still speaking to you after this ritual, it won't hurt to ask the secretary for her name. That way she feels a little more accountable.

Even after you get your message through to a Russian executive, you still have a battle on your hands to get a reply. However, "there are ways" to get through even to the most inaccessible Russian.

Use the Red Phone

In Soviet days, every Russian bureaucrat of any significance had a red telephone on his desk. This was the direct line which Communist Party *nomenklatura* used to network with one another. Party members carried around little red phone books containing every "red phone" number in town. Without these secret numbers, you couldn't get anything done.

The Communist Party is dead, but the network survives. In fact, you'll still see many red phones on the desks of Russian managers and executives. Even if the phone isn't physically red, you can rest assured that there are special phone numbers given out only to privileged insiders.

"If you call the special phone number," says Kononenko, "the person picks up and answers. But with the regular numbers, you just get a secretary. She always says the person you're trying to reach is in a meeting, on vacation, out at the *dacha*, or whatever. You'll never get to talk to him unless you have that special number."

Kononenko appealed to certain well-connected friends and obtained the secret phone number for Surikov's boss. When he got through on the first call, his Russian assistant director was shocked. "How did you get through?" she gasped.

Sometimes You've Got to Scream

In the American workplace, raising your voice can be the kiss of death. It marks you as "unprofessional," "erratic," "out of control," and other nasty things. The Russians have a far greater tolerance for human emotion. Indeed, showing strong emotion can often help your case.

"Don't be afraid to shout, if it's necessary," advises Kononenko. "Sometimes, that's the way to get things done. You cannot deal with Russians as if you are a corpse. They are very emotional. By showing them your emotions, you also show them you are a human being. That's why the Russians hate to deal with the Japanese. They have no facial movements. You never know what the guy is thinking. Russians hate that. They think the Japanese are too cold."

When Kononenko first broached his problem to Surikov's boss, the man laughed in his face.

"Surikov is just trying to survive," chuckled the bureaucrat. "You have to understand. He doesn't know what's going to happen to him tomorrow." But Kononenko let loose with a stream of angry and obscene invective. The assistant film director he brought with him shivered with fear. "She was terrified to hear me talking that way to such a powerful man," says Kononenko. But the official himself just kept laughing.

Create a Scandal

Finally, Kononenko resorted to the ultimate threat—*scandal*! He threatened to go to the Western press and tell the whole story. "How will you ever get foreigners to deal with you once they find out you act like this?" Kononenko challenged him.

The man kept on chuckling good-naturedly. But his laugh seemed a little weaker. "Okay," he finally said. "How much film do you need?"

Within hours, Kononenko had all the Kodak film he could use. He suspects it came from the same batch which Surikov appropriated in the first place.

An Undercurrent of Violence

Brute force has always played a major role in Russian "management" practice. Back in 1922, Felix Dzerzinsky, the infamous founder of the Soviet secret police, decided to investigate the famine then raging in the Volga region. It seemed strange to him that people were starving at a time when Siberian grain harvests were so abundant.

Dzerzinksy rode his private railway car to a small station 200 miles from Omsk. Noticing that a number of freight cars loaded with grain were sitting unattended on side tracks, Dzerzinsky ordered his car detached and left at the station. There, he lay in wait to see what would happen.

Days passed with no action. The grain just sat there. Dzerzinsky then asked the terrified station manager to telegraph Omsk and tell them there was an "urgent shipment" waiting to be picked up. Two days passed with no reply. Finally, he ordered the station master to telegraph that the dreaded Dzerzinsky himself was at the station waiting to be picked up. Incredibly, there was *still* no reply.

After waiting yet another 24 hours, Dzerzinsky had finally had enough. He hitched a ride on a passing train and rode into Omsk. There, he called a meeting of railroad managers. "What I want to know," said Dzerzinsky calmly, "is what became of those cables and why they were not answered."

After a long silence, one low-level official confessed that he had received the cables and pigeonholed them, as per standard office procedure. The man trembled with fear, certain that his life was about to meet with an abrupt end. But Dzerzinsky unexpectedly let the man go. Instead, he ordered the head of the department and his chief assistant to step forward.

"You are responsible for this office," he said. "It is you who will now be punished." Turning to the guards, Dzerzinsky commanded, "Take them out into the courtyard and shoot them."

As the shots resounded from outside the window, Dzerzinsky calmly informed the survivors of the meeting that from now on they would never know in which sidetracked freight car Dzerzinsky or one of his spies might be lurking. They got the message. Within a week, grain shipments began arriving regularly in the Volga region. The famine was over.

Of course, things have changed since the 1920s. Summary shootings are no longer officially sanctioned. But traditions run deep. A powerful undercurrent of violence and lawlessness still bubbles beneath Russia's veneer of civil calm. You must learn to be aware of violent threats, and to safeguard yourself against them. Don't be naive in Russia. You must be ready for anything.

Be Ready for Anything

After getting in a dispute with his Russian partner, one American businessman was physically attacked. Thugs broke into his hotel room, stole his money and all his possessions, and beat him to a pulp. This was the Russian's way of taking the uppity American down a peg. Such incidents are not unusual.

"Life is cheap in Russia," says another American businessman. "For $100 you can have anyone killed. For $10-$15 you can have a woman beaten up and raped."

This businessman tells how his Russian partner once hired gangsters to serve as bodyguards for a rock star the Russian was promoting. At a concert, the bodyguard got in an argument with the rock star and shot him dead. "But the guy was never arrested," says the American. "It was all swept under the carpet. He knocked off one of the leading rock stars in the country and got off scot free."

The Mafia Mentality

Most Americans who read the newspapers have learned that there is a "mafia" in Russia. But we have also gained a rather inaccurate view of what that means. We are told that the atmosphere in Russia today is "like Chicago in the 1920s," complete with "protection rackets" and "hit men." We are given to understand that Russia's freemarket reforms have opened the doors to an unprecedented crime wave, perpetrated by an underworld of sleazy new entrepreneurs.

In fact, the crime wave plaguing Russia today is more than 70 years old. It began with the Bolshevik Revolution. And its principal "dons" and "godfathers" are not new entrepreneurs, but high government and former Communist Party officials.

A Lawless Society

Many Americans imagine Communist Russia to have been a rigidly ordered state, where everything was done "by the book." In fact, it was more akin to Dark Age Europe. The Soviet Union was a lawless realm where local warlords stole with impunity, bullied the weak, exacted tribute, bribed police, tortured and imprisoned their enemies at will, and flaunted their ill-gotten wealth without fear of punishment.

For example, Party boss Sharaf Rashidov ruled Uzbekistan for 20 years in the brutal style of a Mongol khan. It is reported that one of his underlings kept a heavily fortified estate staffed literally by *slaves* and equipped with its own dungeon. With the collusion of top officials in Moscow, Rashidov "sold" millions of tons of non-existent cotton every year to the central government. Thousands of high- and low-level accomplices cooperated in falsifying harvest reports, doctoring account books, and running secret, black-market cotton farms of hundreds of thousands of acres. Rashidov even had Brezhnev's son-in-law, Yuri Churbanov (the first deputy minister of international affairs) on his illicit payroll.

For political reasons, Brezhnev's successors later cracked down on Rashidov's operation. But such sporadic shows of "reform," only concealed the deeper corruption which lay untouched at the core of Soviet power. For example, when a string of off-the-books factories and stores was uncovered in Georgia in 1972, the kingpin of the operation, Politburo member Vasily Mzhavanadze, was quietly let off the hook. He retired a millionaire.

The pilferage continues today. Some observers have estimated that as much as *$100 billion* has been illegally deposited in foreign bank accounts by corrupt Russian officials since 1991.

Corrupt from Top to Bottom

Such licentious behavior among the nation's rulers engendered a criminal culture which worked its way down to the lowest rungs of Soviet society. By some estimates, as much as 40 percent of Russia's food came to the consumer through black market channels during Communist days. Entire factories, stores, construction, and shipping companies operated freely outside the law, while the police and the KGB pocketed their cut of the loot and turned a blind eye. *Komsomolskaya Pravda* reported in 1988 that over 40,000 police officials were fired between 1985 and 1987 for corrupt acts ranging from fabrication of evidence to the taking and giving of bribes.

Virtually every citizen was involved. Motorists slipped a few rubles to the traffic cop rather than pay a fine. Factory workers stole raw materials. Laborers took on private construction jobs during their official work hours. Store clerks sold state-owned inventory to their friends. From the top to the bottom, the Soviet people acquired a sensible disdain for laws which they rightly regarded as fig leaves overlaying the shameless depredations of Soviet leaders.

The Pathological Workplace

Even Soviets who were not "on the take," were forced to practice deceit and fraud in order to survive the Soviet workplace. Workers conspired to cover for one another's gold-bricking. Division managers concealed information from factory directors, who in turn lied through their teeth to central planning officials.

For example, if a new machine was installed, the factory's management would underreport its performance to ministry officials so they could add 10 percent each year to show they were exceeding the five-year plan. If they fell short of the Plan, they would simply report fraudulent figures to make up the difference. Everyone knew that everyone else was lying. But as long as nobody got caught, everyone up and down the line was happy.

Watch Your Employees Carefully

As a result of this sordid history, Russian employees today often feel justified in stealing from their American bosses. To them, it's just another way of "working the system." Watch your employees carefully. They are geniuses at concocting larcenous and fraudulent scams of every kind.

Martin Lopata, the founder and former chairman of Sovaminco, at one point had as many as 32 luxury cars in his car service fleet. He began noticing that the cars were running up enormous mileage figures, far in excess of what would be expected from the normal business.

"I asked my Russian managers how many private car services I was really supporting," he says. Lopata ordered his managers to start checking the car mileage at the beginning and end of every day. They stared at him in horror.

"But if we do that," they objected. "We'll never get any drivers to work for us! This is just the way it's done!" The Russian managers had learned in their past jobs to wink at such employee pilferage. It was considered an acceptable perk of the job.

Protection Rackets

After a long absence from Moscow, Lopata once asked his Russian driver to take him to a certain cooperative restaurant he used to frequent. It was a trendy place with VCRs and TVs at every table, where you could watch bootlegged American videos. As you came in, you walked over a bridge, spanning a pond stocked with live trout. "You could point to a fish," Lopata remembers, " and they would catch it in a net and cook it."

But Lopata's driver sadly informed him that the unique restaurant was no more. The owner had refused to pay protection money to the "mafia." "First, they threatened him," relates Lopata. "Then they beat him up. The next time, they came in and machine-gunned him."

Many of Russia's new entrepreneurs seek to protect themselves from mafia racketeers by hiring private bodyguards. St. Petersburg restaurateur Alexander Rudenko reportedly retains 300 former KGB goons for that purpose.

But while the Western press has given wide play to such colorful tales, Russia's petty "protection rackets" form only the tip of a gigantic iceberg underlying the entire business structure of the CIS.

The Culture of Tribute

*"The ... underworld is not made up of
gangsters, drug peddlers, or white slavers.
The criminal world of [the Soviet Union]
includes store and restaurant managers and
directors of state enterprises, institutions,
collective and state farms ... the ruling
district elite acts in the name of the Party as
racketeers and extortionists of tribute, and ...
it is the criminal world per se who must pay
through the nose to the district apparat."*
                                    KONSTANTIN SIMIS
              *Former Soviet Ministry of Justice lawyer.
              From his book, USSR: The Corrupt Society*

A recent article in *Izvestiya* revealed that Vietnamese prostitutes routinely travel to Russia on multiple-use visas issued by Russian municipal agencies, while Russian prostitutes and pimps fly to Vietnam on official passports from the Russian Ministry of Foreign Affairs.

The story only touched on that huge, gray area where the "rackets" overlap with the Russian government itself. Just as it did in Soviet days, the Russian system operates on the medieval principle of "tribute." Traditionally, tribute is money which a vassal pays to his lord in return for which the lord refrains from killing him. In Russia, disco owners, whorehouse managers, and restaurateurs pay tribute to racketeers. But the racketeers themselves must pay their own tribute to high-level police and government officials.

The amounts of money are staggering. It is estimated that over $100 million was paid to Russian officials during the first half of 1992, just to facilitate illegal exports of oil and other commodities. Comparable figures would certainly be found in other areas of the economy.

This is the real "protection racket" in Russia. Foreign businessmen in Russia are rarely threatened by petty, mafia punks. But business deals, licenses, access to public utilities, and the like are routinely held for ransom by the grand "seigneurs" of Russia's bureaucratic baronies. One way or another, if you do business in Russia, you will eventually be asked to pay tribute.

How to Tell When They're Hinting for Bribes

Russian officials do not usually demand bribes in an obvious way, according to Kononenko. "They'll throw little hints," he says. "They'll say, well, it's very difficult to get this done. It will take three days for one guy to sign some documents, and maybe there's some other guy who won't sign at all. When they start talking like that, they're usually asking for a bribe."

The Problem with Bribery

Just in case you weren't aware, the Foreign Corrupt Practices Act forbids any American to bribe a foreign official or company executive. It would be nice if that were the end of the matter. It's against the law, so "just say no."

Unfortunately, you will run into serious difficulties trying to do business in Russia if you "just say no." I'm not saying it's impossible. Just extremely difficult. Unless your Russian partner is so powerful or so highly placed in the government that he can impose his will through fear and force, you're probably going to be forced to confront this moral dilemma sooner or later.

Everybody Lies

Bribery is one subject that Americans love to lie about. I don't know how many times American businessmen have assured me that they have never used bribery in Russia, only to relate later, in some unguarded moment, a sordid tale of graft and corruption in which they figured as key players.

In conducting the interviews for this book, I heard many versions of the disingenuous *"just say no"* philosophy.

"If you don't offer, they won't ask," said one entrepreneur primly.

"You just have to find honest people to deal with," explained another.

"Just say no. That's all it takes," offered a third.

"They're all lying," says one unusually candid entrepreneur "They're being dishonest with you. To get something done in Russia, you have to pay off every link in the chain."

"It runs the gamut," explains another American, "from having to give a crane operator a bottle of vodka so he'll lift some materials to the third floor of a building to just out-and-out cash payments to people."

How to Bribe Without Bribing

One American businessman recommends a simple technique for overcoming the ticklish complexities of bribery and American law. "You just hire Russian subcontractors and let them worry about it," he says. "They bring you a budget, they tell you how much money they need to get the result, and that's what you pay them. If part of that money goes for bribes, you tell them you don't want to know about that. That's their problem. You just pay them the fee and they get the job done."

It is unclear whether this technique truly absolves you from guilt under American laws. But apparently it is widely practiced among foreign businessmen in Russia.

Partnerships as Tribute

Sometimes the grand seigneurs of Russia demand far more than a mere bribe. They ask for a hefty chunk of your business. Very often, a foreigner will negotiate a deal to invest in a particular property, say, a tractor plant, and even go so far as to sign a contract. Suddenly, out pops some other ministry or government agency. "Wait a minute," they'll say. "You can't sign a contract with those guys. They have no legal authority. This tractor plant falls under our ministry, so you have to cut a deal with *us*."

Property titles and lines of authority are often sufficiently vague that two or more such entities may unexpectedly spring out of the woodwork before the deal is finally sealed. Sometimes, a rigorous document search conducted by a professional law firm will reveal such claims to be spurious. But at other times, you will have no choice but to pay your "tribute," dividing up the pie among the various clamoring *seigneurs*.

Theft by Bureaucracy

At times, you may have to defend your "fief" against the most dangerous and predatory warlord of all—the government. Lopata found this out the hard way when the Moscow City Government confiscated his chain of stores illegally.

It all started innocently enough. One day, a high-placed government minister brought his daughter around to Lopata's company, Sovaminco. To please her powerful father, Sovaminco's Russian manager hired her as deputy director of sales. Effectively, she was now in charge of running Sovaminco's chain of 14 hard-currency stores and copy shops in Moscow.

License to Steal

Trouble started almost immediately. The woman began offering wine, cigarettes, and beer in the stores for hard currency. This was illegal, since the stores were licensed only as copy centers and newsstands. She also began taking bribes from suppliers to stock their products in the stores.

"We caught her taking one of our Mercedes buses out of the country," says Lopata, "and bringing it back filled with VCRs and computers which had been given to her as bribes. I tried to fire her, but her father wouldn't allow it."

Not only was the woman's father a prominent minister, but her mother was a member of the Moscow City Council, which controlled every hotel in which the Sovaminco stores were located. Lopata was impotent.

The Sting

Encouraged by her successes and her apparent immunity, the woman became more brazen every day in her usurpation of authority. "She decided that the stores were really her personal fiefdom," says Lopata.

In 1991, Lopata fell ill. He turned out to have a benign brain tumor which required immediate surgery. It was while Lopata was recuperating from the operation that the Russians made their move.

"I got a series of faxes saying we're losing the stores in Moscow," says Lopata. "The City of Moscow is taking the stores."

The Conspiracy

What had happened, as Lopata later discovered, was that the woman had gone to the city government and convinced them that the foreigners were making too much money from Sovaminco. She then offered her own services. She knew all the secrets to running the stores. She was the one who managed them day to day. She had all the contacts with the suppliers. Why not take over the stores and make her general director? Then the city of Moscow can take 95 percent of the profits, instead of the 15 percent it's been getting. Throw Lopata 5 percent to keep him quiet. The City Council went for the plan, according to Lopata.

While Lopata was under the surgeon's knife, Moscow city officials visited Sovaminco's Russian general director, Alexei Morozov. It was a stickup. They gave Morozov an ultimatum: Sign over ownership of the stores immediately or face arrest and prosecution for illegal sales of wine, liquor, beer, and cigarettes. Terrified, Morozov signed on the spot.

"It was completely illegal," says Lopata. "There was no board meeting, nothing."

Lopata, now retired in Huntington Beach, California, estimates that he lost over a million dollars from the seizure of his stores.

Don't "Go Native"

Some Americans have been driven to desperate acts by the impotence of Russia's legal system. They respond to lawless Russian behavior with lawlessness of their own. Needless to say, this course is not recommended.

One American entrepreneur (who prefers to remain anonymous) tried for months to take legal action against his crooked Russian partner. Mr. X—as I shall refer to the American henceforth—had discovered 18 million rubles in his company's bank account which had no business being there. Investigation revealed that his Russian partner had borrowed a huge sum of money from another bank in the company's name, and had been using it as a private slush fund. In addition, the Russian had used company funds to buy a Mercedes and a Volvo for two of his friends and had loaned $30,000 to another.

An attorney himself, Mr. X attempted to sue his Russian director. But he quickly discovered that Russian courtrooms were enemy territory for foreigners. His first day in court flopped when the court refused to accept either his passport or his company's domestic or foreign registration as identification. Mr. X then spent weeks trying to obtain proper documents from obstructive Russian notaries, all to no effect.

Desperate Measures

In desperation, Mr. X hired two beefy Russians in the street for $20 apiece and launched a raid on his own office. While Mr. X's Russian director shouted and swore, his hired "muscle" emptied the office, loading up desk drawers and file cabinets on a truck outside.

Next, Mr. X typed up a flyer saying he needed an apartment for storage purposes and would pay the owner $100 per month. He didn't have to hand out many of them before Mr. X found himself the proud owner of a brand new office with an unlisted address—totally illegal, but at least temporarily secure.

In his secret hideaway, Mr. X pored over the confiscated records. The documents told an incredible tale of corruption. Among other horrors, Mr. X found bank withdrawal slips bearing the names of people who hadn't worked for his company in over a year. Such payment vouchers were supposedly invalid without Mr. X's counter-signature, but the Russian director had apparently gone ahead and forged it.

Even with this abundance of incriminating evidence, Mr. X was unable to obtain legal remedies. The bank refused point blank to provide him with copies of the missing records. The clerk at the City procurator's office informed him snootily that his office dealt only with "serious crimes," not petty "business disputes."

At last, Mr. X resigned himself to a stalemate. To this day, he continues operating his business from its new, secret address. Needless to say, his business is hardly thriving.

When in Doubt, Use a Russian Lawyer

In many ways, Russia's lawyers are its unsung heroes. Day after day, they battle quietly to introduce due process into Russia's savage bureaucracy. Indeed, some commentators point to Mikhail Gorbachev's law degree as one of the driving forces behind his passion for reform. Unlike the Bolshevik streetfighters and Stalinist executioners who preceded him, Gorbachev understood that law must take precedence over brute force.

As with Gorbachev himself, Russian lawyers prove most useful and effective not at interpreting the letter of the law, but at finagling their way around it. Western law firms have learned to rely upon local attorneys in their Russian practice.

"We wouldn't consider creating a Russian company in Russia without the help of a Russian lawyer," admits John Morton of Hale & Dorr. "They know how to get things done."

"For example, if you try to register a company in Russia, good luck. There are so many bureaucratic obstacles, notary seals, all sorts of fuzzy things the law doesn't talk about. The notary will ask you for things you never imagined. He might refuse to accept your passport as proof of identity and ask for a birth certificate instead. Who travels with their birth certificate? The whole process can take a month. But a Russian lawyer can take care of it right away, sometimes I don't want to know how."

Any Western law firm with an office in Russia can provide referrals to reputable Russian attorneys. See App. B for listings.

Don't Sue, Negotiate!

For all the reasons stated previously, you're better off not wasting your time with the Russian court system. There are really only two ways to deal with business disputes. The first is to build into your original contract a requirement that all disputes be resolved through international arbitration. The second is to simply *negotiate*.

Naturally, the lack of legal recourse puts you at a disadvantage in any serious dispute. But if you're dealing with honest partners, you should be able to work out a satisfactory solution. The real horror stories in Russia come from Americans who have unknowingly hooked up with thugs and gangsters. And, as one American attorney puts it, "Even in America, if you find yourself having a business dispute with Al Capone in a private room, and he says, 'I'm stealing $1000 whether you like it or not,' you'd better check your life insurance policy before threatening to call the FBI."

Choosing the right partner is thus your best, and perhaps your *only*, insurance against unpleasant brushes with Russia's corrupt legal system.

Use KGB Power

Obviously the best way to check out a partner for possible unsavory connections would be to gain access to his secret KGB file. "Impossible!" you say. But is it? Don't be too sure.

The mecca for out-of-work KGB spooks these days is a company called "Alex," Russia's first full-fledged detective firm. For a fee, they'll do everything from finding missing persons, investigating criminal cases, and running background and credit checks on negotiating partners to conducting sensitive market research. These guys are good at what they do. And talk about *inside connections!* Alex also provides hefty bruisers in camouflage fatigues for bodyguard and security duty. See App. B for contact information.

Don't Be a Hypocrite

Too much talk about Russian corruption can sometimes turn Americans' heads. We tend to wax overly self-righteous on this subject, and the Russians notice it. They are fully aware that American businessmen are not always angels themselves.

Exercise a little restraint when you start feeling the urge to get up on a soapbox and lecture the Russians on their lack of a "Judeo-Christian ethic." Americans who go to Russia feigning shock at such things as business partners who welsh on debts, suppliers who negotiate in bad faith, or even criminals who run protection rackets are rightly despised by the Russians as liars and hypocrites. The plain fact is that we are not shocked by such things, because we have them here too, in great abundance. Moreover, all too many American "entrepreneurs" have left behind them a trail of atrocities in Russia, with which the Russians are painfully familiar, even if you are not.

For example, a New York businessman recently was alleged to have taken a 10-million-ruble downpayment from a Russian entrepreneur for a shipment of Western beer and video products which he never delivered. "Shipping difficulties" were at fault, he claimed. However, the American did *not* offer to return the 10 million rubles. That same American also conducted a Moscow trade show, then allegedly welshed on the $50,000 fee to the Russian exhibition organizer.

Certainly, the infamous "Russian Mafia" which is fast taking root in New York City's Brighton Beach has found no shortage of criminal accomplices, bribe-able officials, and lackadaisical police as it forges a multibillion-dollar empire of Medicare and insurance fraud, dope dealing, gasoline bootlegging, and murder right in the heart of America's greatest metropolis.

None of this means that we should become any more tolerant of Russia's far more severe corruption. It just means that we should tell the truth about ourselves and not pretend to be something we are not.

A Happy Ending

Far be it from me to end this book on such a negative note. Americans do need to understand the worst that they will encounter in Russia. But if we conceive of the Russians as a mass of criminal conspirators, we do ourselves and the Russians a dreadful disservice.

Russia abounds with good and upright folk. If we who sojourn in their land adhere to a high standard of integrity, quality, and service, the best Russians will be more than eager to cast aside old ways and learn from us. Those of us with sufficient humility will no doubt discover that the Russians have a great deal to teach us as well.

Daily Survival in Russia

Whether you're a salesman, an entrepreneur or a high-level corporate officer, you're eventually going to come face to face with the hard realities of daily life in Russia. Even if you only travel there for a couple of weeks a year, a little inside information will help you enormously in making that time productive and pleasant.

Daily survival in Russia is not as hard as it used to be. At least for foreigners. A profusion of well-stocked, hard-currency shops and private restaurants now feeds a consumer subculture that is almost Western in its sophisticated demand. Hotels are fast coming up to Western standards. Come equipped with plenty of dollars, Deutschmarks or British pounds, and you can live like a king in Russia.

MOSCOW IS THE HUB

Moscow is still the nerve center of Russian commerce and the logical first stop for most foreign business travelers. As the largest and most cosmopolitan of Russia's cities, Moscow provides a good "compression chamber" for acclimating yourself to the Russian way of life. Most of the information in this appendix pertains specifically to that city.

Following are some valuable pointers on travel, lodging, shopping, food, entertainment, medical and emergency services, local transportation, and more—including listings of relevant contacts, services, and organizations.

This appendix is reprinted from the "Moscow City Guide," compiled by Karen Johnson and Lindy Sinclair, and updated bimonthly in *Moscow Magazine*, Moscow's preeminent, glossy city publication, available in English as well as Russian.

To subscribe, send a fax to Moscow (7-095-973-21-44) with your signature and credit card number, including expiration date, name, address, country, and zip code. Subscription rates (including postage) are as follows: U.S. and Canada—$56 per year; Europe—$45; other countries—$65.

If you'd rather pay cash, you can transfer the relevant amount directly to

Moscow Magazine through Bankers Trust Company in New York. Request that the money be transferred to Tokobank (in Moscow) for JV Moscow Illustrated Press 345022#001, Bank No. 04-162-680 chips UID 313093. After wiring the money, promptly inform the magazine by fax or at the following address: 10/1 Maroseika, Stroyenie (Bldg.) 2, 101000 Moscow, Russia.

If all this seems a little complicated, you might try giving a call to *Moscow Magazine*'s Dutch partners in Haarlem, The Netherlands. Phone: (023) 319-423, Fax: (023) 323-589. •

Travel and Lodging

Visas. If you plan to go to Russia, your first step is to get a visa. Although there are such things as *tourist visas* and *individual visas* you will have the most freedom and the least complications if you apply for a *business visa*.

First, you need a sponsor. That's an officially registered Russian business enterprise, joint venture, or government organization, which is willing to fax you a letter of invitation. The letter should explain the purpose of your visit ("for negotiations" usually does the trick), the cities you will be travelling to, and the expected duration of your stay.

Next, you obtain a visa application from the Russian embassy or consulate, or from your travel agent. Send it to the Russian embassy, along with two passport-sized photos, a photocopy of the first two pages of your passport and the letter of invitation from your sponsor. The visa should be issued within two weeks.

Russian Embassy
1125 16th St., N.W.
Washington, DC 20036

Tel.: (202) 628-6412, 628-7551, 628-7554.
Consular Dept.: (202) 332-0737

Russian Consulate (San Francisco)
2790 Green St.
San Francisco, CA 94123
Tel.: (415) 922-6644, 922-6643

Russian Consulate (New York)
9 East 91st St.
New York, NY 10128
Tel.: (212) 472-4732

Tip. On the application, be sure to add a few days to the beginning and end of your projected stay. Sometimes the Russians wait until the last minute to issue visas. Also, you might decide to prolong your stay in Russia for a few days. If you get caught at the airport trying to leave Russia with an expired visa, customs officials will sting you for a hefty fine, which was $250 and rising the last time I checked.

If you don't have a sponsor in Russia, don't worry. There are several travel agencies, bed and breakfast services and visa services specializing in East-West travel, who can arrange this for you. They have operatives in Russia who will issue such letters for a fee. In fact, this is probably the easiest way to go. The agency will handle all the paper work. You just fill out the forms, pay the fee and wait for your visa. Some of these organizations are listed here.

Travel Agencies

Barry Martin Travel
19 West St., Suite 3401
New York, NY 10004
Tel.: (212) 422-0091
Fax: (212) 344-1997

Commonwealth Travel Network
D.N. Young & Associates, Inc.
207 W. Ascension St.
Gonzales, LA 70737

Tel.: (504) 644-8605
Fax: (504) 644-1663.
Their motto: "If you're paying full fare, you're paying too much."

Margo's International Travel Service
1812 Irving St.
San Francisco, CA 94122
Tel.: (415) 665-4330 or
(800) 33 MARGO
Fax: (415) 665-4942
Telex: 340649.
Margo's also arranges U.S. visas for your Russian associates to visit you here.

Rahim Travel
12 South Dixie Hwy.
Lake Worth, , FL 33460
Tel.: (800) 556-5305
Fax: (407) 582-1353

Russia Travel Bureau
225 East 44th St.
New York, NY 10017
Tel.: (212) 986-1500
Fax: (212) 490-1650

Tour Designs, Inc.
616 G St., SW
Washington, DC 20024
Tel.: (202) 554-5820
Fax: (202) 479-0472

Visa Services

Visa Advisors
1930 18th St., NW
Washington, DC 20009
Tel.: (202) 797-7976

Trans-World Visa Service
P.O. Box 22068
San Francisco, CA 94122
Tel.: (415) 752-6957

Register your Passport on Arrival. Technically, you are supposed to register your passport at UVIR (Soviet Visa and Registration Office) within 72 hours of your arrival in Russia. This is done automatically if you stay at a hotel. You also go to UVIR to extend your visa and apply for an exit visa, if you are a long-term resident.

Gird up your loins (the crowd can be very aggressive) and head over bright and early to 42 Chernyshevskovo Ulitsa, tel. 207-01-13, 02-39. Open 10 a.m. to 6 p.m., it closes for lunch from 2 to 3 p.m. and Wednesday is a day off.

Bed-and-Breakfast Services. This is an increasingly popular alternative to Russia's expensive hotels. The following bed-and-breakfast services can arrange your travel, visa, and set you up in a comfortable apartment, all in one convenient and inexpensive package.

American International Homestays
Route 1, Box 68
Iowa City, IA 52240
Tel.: (319) 626-2125
Fax: (319) 626-2129

Cultural Access Network
Box 4410
Laguna Beach, CA 92652
Tel.: (714) 497-6773
Fax: (714) 497-6809

East-West Ventures, Inc.
P.O. Box 14391
Tucson, AZ 85732
Tel.: (800) 648-7304

Home and Host
2445 Park Ave.
Minneapolis, MN 55404
Tel.: (612) 871-0596
Fax: (612) 871-8853
Telex: 940 103 WU PUBTLX BSN

I.B.V. Bed and Breakfast Systems
13113 Ideal Dr.
Silver Spring, MD 20906
Tel.: (301) 942-3770
Fax: (301) 933-0024

International Bed and Breakfast
P.O. Box 823
Huntington Valley, PA 19006

Tel.: (800) 422-5283
Fax: (215) 663-8580

Pioneer East/West Initiatives
88 Brooks Ave.
Arlington, MA 02174
Tel.: (617) 648-2020

Apartment Rentals. Nowadays, everyone and his *babushka* wants to rent his apartment to you—for big bucks. Check the classified ads in the (English-language) *Moscow Times*. Rental agencies can also make the search easier, although laws change daily and prices probably do, too. In Moscow, try one of the following rental co-ops:

Astoria: Tel. 229-2300, Elex: Tel. 932-4969, Express: Tel. 227-5827

Medservice: Tel. 288-5875, 281-4805, Raznoservice: Tel. 246-95-87, 328-13-77

Avangard: Ul. Byelomorskaya, Tel. 455-92-10

Moscow Hotels

Aerostar: 37 Leningradsky Prospekt, Korpus 9, tel. 155-50-30

Akademicheskaya Hotel 1: Leninsky Prospekt, tel. 238-09-02

Akademicheskaya Hotel II: Donskaya Ulitsa, tel. 238-05-08

Belgrad: Smolenskaya Ploshchad 5, tel. 248-16-43 (see Zolotoye Koltso)

Cosmos: Prospekt Mira 150, tel. 217-07-85, 217-86-80

Intourist: Ulitsa Gorkovo 3/5, tel. 203-40-08, Izmailovo Tourist

Complex: Izmailovskoye Shosse 69a, tel. 166-01-09

Leningradskaya: Kalanchovskaya Ulitsa 21/40, tel. 975-30-08/ 32

Marco Polo Presnaya: Spiridonyevsky 9, tel. 202-03-81

Metropol: 1-4 Teatralny Proyezd, tel. 927-60-00, 00-02, 60-96

Mezhdunarodnaya I and II: Krasnopresnenskaya Nab. 12, (I) tel. 253-23-82, (II) tel. 253-27-60/1

Molodyozhnaya: Dmitrovskoye Shosse 27, tel. 210-93-11, 45-65

Moskva: Okhotni Ryad 7, tel. 292-11-00

Novotel: Sheremetyevo Airport 2, tel. 578-94-07/8

Orlyonok: Ulitsa Kosygina 15, tel. 939-88-44, 939-88-53

Penta: Olimpisky Prospekt 18/1, tel. 971-61-01

Pullman/Iris: Korovinskoye Shosse 10, tel. 488-80-80, 80-00

Rossiya: Ulitsa Razina 6, tel. 298-54-00

Savoy: Rozhdestvenka 3, tel. 929-85-00

Slavyanskaya/Radisson: Berezhkovskaya Naberezhnaya 2, tel. 941-80-20

Ukraina: Kutuzovsky Prospekt 2/1, tel. 243-30-30, 28-95

Zolotoye Koltso: Smolenskaya Ploshchad 5, tel. 248-67-34 (formerly the Belgrad I).

Airlines. In case you need to call an airline for any reason in Moscow, don't look around for a phonebook. You won't find one. The following are the Moscow numbers for major international airlines.

Aeroflot: Leningradsky Pt. 37, tel. 155-09-22, 156-80-16

Air France: Korovy Val 7, tel. 237-23-25

Air India: Korovy Val 7, Kor. 1, tel. 923-98-40

Alitalia: Ul. Pushechnaya 7, tel. 923-98-40

ANA: Mezhdunarodnaya 2, room 825, tel. 253-15-46

Austrian Airlines: Krasnopresnenskaya Nab. 12, Floor 18, tel. 253-82-68

British Airlines: Krasnopresnenskaya Nab. 12, Floor 19, tel. 253-24-92

Continental Airlines: Kolokolnikov Per., tel. 924-90-50

Czechoslovak Airlines: Ul. 2-Brestskaya 21/27, tel. 250-45-71

Delta: Krasnopresnenskaya Nab. 12, Floor 11, tel. 253-26-58

Finnair: Proyezd Khudozhestvennovo Teatra 6, tel. 292-87-88

Iberia: Krasnopresnenskaya Nab. 12, Floor 14, tel. 253-22-63

Interflug: Ul. B. Spasskaya 12, tel. 280-72-33

Japan Air Lines: Kuznetsky Most 3, tel. 921-64-48

Jugoslav Airlines: Kuznetsky Most 3, tel. 921-28-46

KLM Royal Dutch Airlines: Krasnopresnenskaya 12, Floor 13, tel. 253-21-50

Korean Air: Hotel Cosmos, room 1629, tel. 217-1627

Lufthansa: Olimpisky Prospekt 18/1, tel. 975-25-01

Malev: Proyezd Khudozhestvennovo Teatra 6, tel. 292-04-34

SAS: Kuznetsky Most 3, tel. 925-47-47

Swissair: Krasnopresnenskaya Nab. 12, Floor 20, tel. 253-8988

TWA: Berezhkovskaya Nab. 2, American Business Center, tel. 941-81-46

Departure and arrival information for international flights from Moscow can be obtained by calling Sheremetyevo (airport) II, tel: 578-75-18, 578-78-16.

Moscow Airport Tips

1. Sheremetyevo and Vnukovo airports are hard to reach by taxi unless you are willing to offer lots of rubles. If you don't speak Russian, your chances of paying anything but hard currency are slight.

2. At Vnukovo and Domodyedovo airports, look for the special Intourist lounge — both are on the airport's right-hand sides.

3. Turn up for the registration for domestic flights early, otherwise Aeroflot may sell your seat out from under you.

4. Domestic flights: Don't miss your flight announcement 20 minutes before take-off, since foreigners are put on the plane in a group, either first or last.

5. Try not to check your luggage. A lot goes astray. Most pilfering takes place on flights out of the country.

Moving Services. **Allied Pickfords** can pack, ship, and forward, from anywhere in the CIS to just about anywhere in the world. Call 243-76-09. **Mr. Berg** now has a man in Moscow. Call Boris Ivanov at 140-65-71. Or try the Finnish **John Nurminen** at 430-78-61/48 or the German **Klingenberg** at 434-24-14.

Local Transportation

Air Charter. The **Ministry of Civil Aviation** can charter a plane to fly almost anywhere for hard currency. Telex 412297 MOWR-TSU for the **Department of Charter Flights**, or the **Cargo Transport Division**, telex 411-969. The Dutch **AEC** can also get you a plane: tel. 250-99-74; fax 251-15-38.

Driving Tips. This guide will make your transition from the metro to a Mercedes a bit easier.

Accidents: Call your embassy right away. Grab a witness, fill out the forms, and call the GAI accident registration bureau, Prospekt Mira 5, tel. 923-53-73.

Buying a car: The **Spetsavtotsentr UpDK**, Kievskaya Ulitsa, Dom 10, sells vehicles for hard currency. Or buy a brand-new cheap Soviet car in Helsinki (or Stockholm) and have it shipped or drive it in. For a tax-free car from Denmark, call Stefan Bert at 292-51-10. Foreign cars are also sold by **Sovintravtoservice**, 2/1 Institutsky Per., tel. 299-77-73.

Car insurance: Getting your car insured is not mandatory, but recommended. If you pay rubles, you will be insured for rubles. The price per year is roughly 10 percent of car value. Visit **Ingosstrakh**, Pyatnitsa Ul. 12, tel. 231-16-77.

Car phone: The Finnish-Soviet joint venture **AMT** will install a Nokia car phone complete with mounting and all the gadgets for $3000. Base monthly charge is $50, plus costs per call. Call 941-30-92 or 941-10-50.

Car registration: Again, the **Spetsavtotsentr UpDK** is the place. You'll have to pay tax, the sum of which is calculated from the volume of the car cylinders—in cubic centimeters.

Car rental: **Intourist** (tel. 215-61-91) and some foreign hotels offer both Western and Soviet cars, with or without driver. Or call the **InNis** joint venture for a Nissan—from $51 daily. They have a great chauffeur service starting from $16 per hour: tel. 927-11-87 (perfect for 5 a.m. trips to the airport). Another good service is **Autosan**, their smallest car rents from $13/hour: mini vans from $24/hour. Call 280-36-00. Try also **Business Car**: they offer new Toyotas with or without chauffeur and a 24-hour service. Call 233-17-96 or, office hours, 231-82-25.

Intourservice offers van service or chauffeured limousine service: Tel. 203-00-96; limousine price is $20/hour; the stretch limos are equipped with VCR and a soft-drink bar. Other rental services include **Mosrent**, tel. 248-02-51; **Rozec:** 241-53-93: 241-78-10: and **Hertz:** 448-80-35.

Car repair: Try the **Tekhtsentr** at Kuntsevo, which specializes in Volvo and Toyota repairs. Also there is the joint venture **Volvo Moscow Service Center MTDS**, which delivers spare parts and accessories and hires Hertz rental cars. Ul. Gorbunova 14, tel. 448-00-35. **ABC Opel** specializes in Opels but will repair any European car. Parts are for hard currency, labor in rubles. Call 181-04-07. The Italian-run **Nefto-Agip** station on Leningradskoye Shosse will also do minor repairs for rubles: and has a hard currency shop that sells a variety of motoring paraphernalia. **Stockmann's** on Lyusinovskaya 70/1, tel. 954-82-34, sells auto parts and will place orders for you. Or visit the **UpDK-run Saab service** on Volgogradsky Pr. 177, tel. 379-62-45, or the **GlavUpDK** workshop on Kievskaya Ul. 8, tel. 240-20-92.

Driver's license: For accredited foreigners call 249-98-54, the price is just 133 rubles. For non-accredited residents, call 923-27-25 and ask for Victor Fomichev.

Gassing up: Most Soviet cars take only 73 or 93 octane, while foreign cars usually run on 95. Vouchers for this type of gas can be purchased for hard currency at your embassy. Ask around for the *zapravka* in your area.

Seatbelt: **GAIshniki** (Russian highway patrolmen) will fine you if you are *sans* seatbelt. Wear it anyway if you want to stay alive.

Tow truck: A car-breakdown station is at Varshavskoye Shosse 87, tel. 240-20-

92. There's a 24-hour emergency service station at Novotyzansky Per. 13, tel. 267-01-13. (*Attention*: Tow trucks will now cart your car away if you are illegally parked.)

Traffic violations: Those happy *GAIshniki* really perk up when they can pry rubles out of foreigners for real or imagined traffic violations. If you don't ask for a receipt, the fine is cheaper—the money goes straight into his pocket. If the *GAIshnik* is without a badge, you can ignore him—he's just moonlighting.

Driving Do's and Don't's. Driving is chaotic in Russia and everyone has a dramatic tale to tell. We recommend the following:

1. Don't turn left when forbidden, even if that means driving ten kilometers out of your way. Wait for a U-turn sign.

2. Use your horn only in emergency.

3. Use your headlights only at night outside the city. Otherwise use parking lights.

4. Observe speed limits: 90 km on highways, 60 on large streets, less on side/smaller streets.

5. Right turn on red light is illegal.

6. Drive in left lane only if right is not free or you are in a *zil* (*chaika* or ambassadorial vehicle).

7. Report minor accidents immediately to the GAI and keep records of all documents prepared by militia, witnesses, etc. If the accident is serious, call your embassy immediately.

Cab. Unlike in the West, you cannot just hail a cab in Moscow and climb in. Destination and the all-important price must be negotiated first. When a cab (or private vehicle looking to earn some extra rubles) stops, state your destination and promise between 30 and 75 rubles. Be prepared to pay more. You ought to get where you want to go. Gypsy cabs are best avoided at night. Women should never enter a taxi that has more than one person in it already.

Also, you can reserve a taxi by calling 927-00-00 or 927-21-08 (24 hours) around one hour's notice is needed: 227-00-00 or 227-00-40 (9 a.m. to 6 p.m.) for advance booking (one to seven days).

Tickets (Train or Plane). Airline tickets are sold to tourists only in hard currency, and prices are as expensive as anywhere else in the world. Call the airlines directly or try a travel agent. Train tickets are no longer the bargain they used to be—in fact, it is cheaper to fly. If you must get a ticket, go to **Intourist** at Ulitsa Petrovka 15. For Aeroflot tickets, try the **Aeroflot** counters at most foreign hotels.

Interrepublican Visas. To find out what you need or don't need to visit certain areas call the following embassies and representations:

Azerbaijan: Ul. Stanislavskovo 16, tel. 229-16-49

Armenia: Armyansky Per. 2, tel. 924-12-69

Belarus: Ul. Maroseika 17, tel. 924-70-31

Estonia: Sobinovsky Per. 5, tel. 290-50-13

Georgia: Ul. Paliashvili 6, tel. 290-69-02

Kazakhstan: Christoprudny Blvd. 3a, tel. 208-98-52

Kirghizstan: Ul. Bolshay Ordynka 64, tel. 237-48-82

Latvia: Ul. Chaplygina 3, tel. 925-27-07

Lithuania: Ul. Pisemskovo 10, tel. 291-16-98

Moldova: Kuznetsky Most 18, tel. 928-54-05

Tajikistan: Skaterny Per. 19, tel. 290-61-02

Turkmenia: Per. Aksalova 2, tel. 291-66-36

Ukraine: Ul. Stanislavskovo 18, tel. 229-28-04

Uzbekistan: Pogorelsky Per. 12, tel. 230-00-76

Translation and Interpreting

Translation Services. T r a n s l a t i o n services are available through **Intourist** or through local, privately run agencies. Your hotel service desk may also be able to help you find someone. Also try **Acme Russian-American Translation Services** (tel. 430-38-73 or fax 289-54-38) or Katyusha, Semyonovskaya Nab. 2/1, tel. 360-08-74, fax 360-63-17: IP Interpret, 1st Kadashevsky Per., tel. 231-10-20. In St. Petersburg, try **Astrelle**, Vasilievsky Ostrov, 2nd line, House 25, 199053 Leningrad tel. 218-72-18. (I personally recommend a little outfit called **Russtrade, Ltd.**, headed by Andrey Kravtsov, a former Air Force major with intelligence training in English. Address: 16, 1st Tverskoy-Yamskoy Per. #41, Moscow, 125047. Tel: 123-11-06, Fax: 310-70-65. R.P.)

Language Lessons. There are scores of places in Moscow that offer Russian language lessons (individual and/or courses) usually for hard currency. Try **IP Interpret**, tel. 231-10-20. **MARCH-INTENSIV** offers one-to five-month Russian courses at all levels. Call 928-12-69 or fax 921-12-40 for more information. Or try the language center at the **Mezh**, which teaches Berlitz-style

courses; call the service bureau at 253-27-62.

Daily Needs

Cleaning Services. When asked how they get their suits dry cleaned, most people sheepishly reply they wait for a trip to the West. Alternatives? The **Savoy** charges around $25 for each garment; the **Mezh** isn't much better. Try the joint venture **Visa**, 25 Alabyana near Sokol metro (tel. 198-16-79). They offer for rubles dry cleaning and laundry services and have a reputation for reliability. They can even do on-the-spot jobs.

Laundry. Getting your clothes washed can be a problem. If your hotel does not offer laundry services, the floor women in the hotel will be only too happy to oblige for a gift or an appropriate sum of rubles. Or try one of the *Prachechnaya Samoobsluzhivanniya* laundromats.

There is one on Leninsky Prospekt near Gagatin Square, one on Vavilova Ul. and one on Ul. Krasikova. Try also **Visa**, a small enterprise that offers laundry, dry cleaning and mending services. They are speedy and reliable. Call 198-16-79 or drop by, 25 Alabyana Ul. near metro Sokol.

Tailoring. Do you miss Saville Row? Call **Johnny Manglani** for a fitting. He can make everything from a summer linen suit to a silk dress. Pick a pattern and the material and the Hong Kong office will do the stitching. Call him at 255-10-89 or leave messages at 202-49-19 and 291-91-09. Or telex (51859 SWAMI HX) or fax (852-366 9680) in Hong Kong.

Hair. Need a snip off here and a bit off there? Head over to the international hotels and get their salons to do the deed. Call the **Mezh** at 253-23-78. They take bookings in the mornings. Try also the **Metropol**, tel. 927-60-02, or head up to the **Intourist Hotel**'s eleventh floor (tel. 203-15-89), or the **Yves Rocher** salon on Tverskaya (tel. 923-58-85) if you can get through. The hottest new hair-stylists in town are at **City Looks Salon,** an American franchise located at Chernishevska 2/1, Stroyeniye 1, 101000 Moscow. Tel: 928-70-84, 928-72-35. They take rubles or hard currency.

Exercise. The **Chaika** sports complex at Kropotkinskaya Nab. 3/5 offers a pool and athletic facilities for hard currency. Call 202-04-74 or 246-15-44. The **Penta Hotel** on Olimpisky Prospekt has a small pool and state-of-the-art workout facilities: call 971-61-01 to inquire about membership. The **Slavyanskaya Radisson** has opened its health center too, call 941-80-27 for details.

The **International Women's Club** offers aerobics classes. Contact your embassy for details; for dance classes in English or French, try the **Isadora Duncan Center**; call 479-54-78 or 284-63-96. For a communal fun run, hook up with the **Hash House Harriers**, a group of foreigners who meet once a week, usually on Sundays at 2:15 in front of the Ukraina Hotel. The $2 charge covers after-run beer. Call 280-54-93 for details. The Indian embassy has a great squash court, open to anyone for a fee. Call: 297-08-20. You might try the American Embassy, but their membership requirements are very exclusive. It's worth calling to see if you qualify. Tel: 252-24-51.

Film Developing. Although the quality may not be great, a few places do offer a reasonable developing job. On the second floor of the **Mezh** is a **Kodak** counter (hard currency: tel. 252-06-40). The **Fuji Film Center**, Novy Arbat 25 also offers a hard currency service. If you don't mind waiting one month, try the **Zenith** store near Sokolniki metro or the photo studio on 23 Ulitsa Gertsena, tel. 291-50-77.

Key Cutting. Yes! There is a *metal-remont* shop that has the blanks, the expertise and the means to make you an extra set of those clunky keys for your Russian apartment. Head over to 2 Ulitsa Shabolovka, near Oktyabrskaya Ploshchad. They ought to be able to make a set in a few hours.

News. It can be frustrating obtaining hard news here, especially when most newspapers that limp into Sovaminco Shops and hotels are already senior citizens. What to do? Watch CNN and subscribe! The *International Herald Tribune*, fax Paris 46 370-651, tel. 33 1-46-379-300. *Financial Times*, fax Frankfurt 49-69-722-677, tel. 49-69-75980. *The Wall Street Journal*, fax Netherlands 31-45-714-722, tel. 45-71-3777. To subscribe to Newsweek, contact Information Moscow, Leninsky Prospekt 45/426. For subscriptions to the English-language business weekly *Commersant*, call 941-09-00; for the English language *Moscow News*, call 229-81-86. There are plenty of papers to be had from kiosks in hotels—the Penta and Metropol are always well-stocked. For rubles, try the **Troyka Press** kiosk to the left of the Metropol Hotel; they sell *The Economist, Paris Match, Time* and lots of Western newspapers just a day or two old.

Medical and Emergency

Medical Services. Being sick in Moscow is no fun. And if you're seriously ill, it can be dangerous. A doctor is always on call in hotels, but if you are very ill, don't mess around. Contact a foreign doctor. Medicine here has a bad reputation for a good reason. Emergencies may well require evacuation, so be sure to have med-evac insurance. For a med-evac contract, call **Delta Consulting** (240-99-99, 240-23-07, fax 241-70-88), SOS (Telex 423939) or **Euro-Flite** (358-0-174455; fax 358-0-822624).

Embassies generally only accept staff and their families for treatment, so if you need a doctor, try the following:

Open to any foreign resident or visitor, The **American Medical Center** is a Western-style family practice. Their wide range of services includes 24-hour emergency service with on-call doctor and nurse as well as coordination of medical air evacuations. Diagnostic services include X-rays and a lab facilities. The center also has a pharmacy that sells medications as well as Western products, ranging from contact lens cleaner to toothpaste. Individual, family and corporate plans available. Near the Mezh Hotel, the clinic's address is 3 Shmitovsky Proezd, tel. 256-82-12, 256-83-78. **The Medicine Man** is a pharmacy in cooperation with **Ciba-Geigy**. Payment in cash and credit card. Ul. Tscherniakhovskovo 4, tel. 155-70-80, 155-87-88. Or try the out-of-the-way but well-appointed **Sana Medical Center**, staffed by Russian and foreign specialists; Ul. Nizhnaya Pervomaiskaya 65, tel. 464-12-54 or 464-25-63, fax 464-45-63, and telex 412240 SANA SU, open Tuesday–Sunday. It does not offer after-hours help, but has a pharmacy and an optician. Foreign residents and diplomats are welcome at **UpDK's** polyclinic for emergency treatment, x-rays, and tests on 4 Dobrininsky Pereulok. Call 237-39-04 for house-calls, 237-53-95 for emergency. A doctor can be at your door in half an hour, day or night. Some even speak English. Tourists can go to **Borkin Hospital** at 2-Botkinsky Proyezd 5, Korpus 5, tel. 255-00-15, but we only recommend it as a very last resort.

Medicine.   There are plenty of places to find foreign-made medicine: try the **American Medical Center's** pharmacy (listed previously) or **Unipharm** at Skaterny Pereulok 13, tel. 202-50-71. **Sana**, the French-Soviet hospital, also has a good pharmacy. The **Intersectoral Research and Technology Complex Eye Microsurgery** and the West German **Seidel Medizin GmBH** offer Western medicine for currency and can order medicine from abroad, 59a Blvd., tel. 905-42-27. Open Mon.-Fri., 10 a.m. to 5:30 p.m. For a central location go to the **Apteka** on Ulitsa Tverskaya. The hard currency outlet on the second floor features very reasonable prices. There is also the Swiss joint venture **The Medicine Man** at Cherniakhovskovo 4 (tel. 155-70-80, 155-87-88) who are in cooperation with **Ciba-Geigy**. Or try **Visa** at Poklonnaya 6 (tel. 249-78-18, 249-94-29).

Dentist.   **Medical Interline**, a Belgian-Swiss-Italian-Hungarian-Russian joint venture, can take care of all your dental problems with its multilingual staff and Western equipment. Intourist Hotel, Ulitsa Tverskaya 5, room 2030, tel. 203-86-31. The **Dental-Beiker Dental Clinic** on Kuznetsky Most 9, will fiddle with your teeth, but accepts money only by bank transfer (tel. 923-53-22). If you need to go to a Russian dentist, take your own needles.

Optical.   The **Sana Medical Center** offers eye exams, frames and lenses, as well as everything from pharmaceuticals to a check-up and a medical evacuation. Address: Ul. Nizhnyaya Pervomaiskaya 65, tel. 464-12-54, 464-25-63, 10 a.m. to 9 p.m., Tue.-Sat. and 10 a.m. to 5 p.m. on Sundays. For contact lenses (soft only) see **Optic Moscow**, an American joint venture located at Arbat 30 (tel. 241-1577, open 10 a.m.-7 p.m.). They provide consultations and stock cleansing materials.

Vet. For general information, call 112-74-21. The **Cat Lover's Society** will also do referrals; call 488-72-11. Two very good vets will do house calls; call Dr. Tatiana Yakubina at 301-05-04 ($20 a visit) or Dr. Alexander Kusmin at 142-01-05. If you need to have your pet fixed, visit the spiffy little co-operative **Vet Clinic Center** on Tsvetnoi Bulvar (#10/1). They provide anesthetic and do a quick, professional job for rubles. Tel. 921-65-65. Open weekdays 9 a.m.-8 p.m., Saturday 9 a.m.-8 p.m. Sunday and holidays, 9 a.m.-3 p.m.

Emergency and Important Numbers

Fire: 01

Police: 02

Ambulance: 03

Gas leak: 04

Local information: 05

Information for dialing cities within former USSR: 07

Moscow info: 09

Time: 100

Telegrams: 927-20-02

The **U.S. Embassy operates a 24-hour emergency hotline** at: 230-20-01, 230-26-10, 252-18-98. The normal embassy number is: 252-24-51, x52, x53, or 252-24-59. Address: Novinsky Bulvar 19/23, Moscow, 123242. (**Commercial Office:** 248-20-01, Fax: 231-21-01).

MOSCOW SHOPPING GUIDE

Shopping Moscow-style is a challenge. Just keep in mind that there are three lines—one to look at the goods, one to pay the cashier, one to collect your precious keepsake. Keep your elbows sharp, the temper tantrums down to a dull roar, and rejoice in the fact that it may take an hour, but it only costs ten cents. Happy hunting! (*All items are sold for rubles unless otherwise noted.*)

Food Shopping

Fast Food. These establishments will cater or deliver directly to your door for hard currency.

McDonald's: 200-16-55. Charges $5 delivery fee for takeout orders less than $50

Pettina: 286-52-17. Finnish hamburgers at their best; sodas and bland chicken sandwiches. Deliver daily (10 a.m. to 11 p.m.)

TrenMos: 245-12-16. Caters American sandwich-type items

Astro-Pizza: 245-12-16. It doesn't deliver, but you can call in a pick-up order

Pizza Hut: The Tverskaya Pizza Hut (229-20-13) offers free delivery of pizzas, beer, and soft drinks for dollars. They take cash only. You can also call in an order for pick-up at either branch (Kutuzovsky branch: 243-17-27)

Stockmann's
Credit cards only.
Zatsepsky Val 4/8
open Monday–Sunday 10 a.m.–8 p.m.
No lunch break.

Extremely well-stocked, this Finnish store carries everything from lettuce and avocadoes to beef patties and fish sticks. Non-food items include booze, foreign newspapers and magazines and some toiletries, knives, napkins, cleaning supplies, and auto accessories. The staff are helpful and you can rely on deliveries. (They always have eggs.)

Intercar

Hard currency only.

Peking Hotel, Bolshaya Sadovaya 5/1

Open Monday–Friday 10 a.m.–8 p.m., Saturday–Sunday 11 a.m.–7 p.m.

No lunch break.

The cheese counter at this German joint venture (prices are in DM) will make your eyes pop. Stock up also on wursts, homemade breads, fresh gingerroot, UHU glue, Italian pasta, toothbrushes, drain cleaner, papayas and ice cream cakes. Supplies, though, can be hit and miss.

The Irish Store

Hard currency only.

Ulitsa Novy Arbat 19, second floor

Open Monday–Sunday, 9 a.m.–8 p.m.

No lunch break.

A joint venture with the Irish firm Aerianta, this Western-style department store and supermarket features wide aisles, food, cheap alcohol, electronic equipment, some clothing and even a pub to celebrate great victories, like finally tracking down white housepaint. Selection is limited (lots of beans, biscuits and cheddar), but you don't have to be a linguist to distinguish powdered sugar from granulated. Avoid shopping on Saturday afternoon—the line is frustratingly long.

Tino Fontana

Hard currency only.

Mezhdunarodnaya Hotel

Krasnopresnenskaya Nab. 12

Open Monday–Saturday 10 a.m.–9 p.m., Sunday 10 a.m.–2 p.m.

Lovers of Italian food are in for a treat. This grocery store stocks lovely comestibles from the sunny south. Browse the dried pastas, and pick up bottled water, frozen shellfish, some very nice wines or toothsome biscotti.

Sadko

Hard currency only.

Bolshaya Dorogomilovskaya Ul. 16

Open Monday–Saturday 10 a.m.–8 p.m., Sunday 10 a.m.–6 p.m.

Lunch break 3 p.m.–4 p.m.

Cheaper than Stockmann's and more centrally located, Sadko has changed character over the years. Less gourmet, cheaper grog, sensible cheese and kilos of Swiss chocolate abound. As do the crowds. Best to go in the mornings and avoid weekends.

Julius Meinl

Hard currency only.

146 Leninsky Prospekt (Dom Turistov)

Open Monday–Saturday 10 a.m.–8 p.m.

Sunday 10 a.m.–6 p.m.

Yes, 146 Leninsky, this is a long way to go for Gummi Bears! But if you live in the area, this supermarket is no doubt a Godsend. Plenty of groceries, some fresh fruit and vegetables, lots of grog, and great Australian and German sweets.

Intermarket

Hard currency only.

Malaya Bronnaya Ul. 27/14

Monday–Sunday 10 a.m.–8 p.m.

No lunch break.

A dinky little supermarket that stocks all sorts of Dutch treats. The prices are very competitive and they have a large stock of delicious cheeses, not to mention salamis, bread, grocery items and plenty more. When everyone discovers the joys of Bitter Koekjes the shop will be packed to the rafters.

Cafe Confectionery

Hard currency only.

Metropol Hotel, main entrance and then ask for directions.

Open Monday–Saturday approximately 10 a.m.–8 p.m.

Life is improving. Now you can enjoy the delicious pastries of the Metropol's French chef outside breakfast hours. This very pretty cafe with friendly staff offers delicious coffee, tea, hot chocolate, and liqueurs and a magnificent array of pastries. And best of all, you can buy them by the box to take home.

Baku Livan

Ulitsa Tverskaya

Open Monday–Sunday 11 a.m.–10 p.m.

No lunch break.

Line too long at McDonald's? Head over to this joint venture where, for rubles, you can buy take-out hamburgers, shawarmas and wonderful falafel. And on the ground floor of the restaurant is a hard-currency counter brimful of exquisite bakhlava, truffles, and pastries. Payment is by weight. An elegant chocolate cake costs around ten dollars.

Lavish Co-op

Bolshaya Sadovaya 3, Korpus 6

Open Monday–Saturday, 8 a.m.–8 p.m.

No lunch break.

Tucked into the courtyard of an apartment block just down from the Peking Hotel, this small bakery sells fresh, tasty lavash, a flat Georgian bread. Bring a bag, and buy the dough (tyesta) to use as a pizza crust, or take away a freshly baked slab.

The Bakery

Olympic Penta Hotel

Olympisky Prospekt 18/1

Open Monday–Sunday 7 a.m.–10 p.m.

This is the trick—you leap out of bed at 7 a.m. on Sunday morning, head over to The Bakery, drool over their amazing selection of pastries, buy a dozen, race back home, brew a perfect pot of Earl Grey tea, and bingo: no matter what dastardly deeds you have committed all week, you are FORGIVEN!

Gastronom #20

Ulitsa Bolshaya Lubyanka 14

Open Monday–Saturday 8 a.m.–9 p.m., Sunday 8 a.m.–7 p.m.

No lunch break.

Affectionately called the "KGB Gastronom," as it is situated just behind the massive edifice of KGB headquarters. And surprise, surprise! This state food store *just happens* to be quite well stocked—unlike every other state food store in town. A chocolate counter, a butter counter that now sells only champagne, and a fish counter (that should be avoided like the plague it probably spreads) all pale insignificance beside the cooperative stall at the back of the shop. Sieves! Colanders! Vegetable steamers! Clever Tupperware-esque containers! They don't turn up all at once, of course. That would make it too simple. So you need to be a regular browser. It pays in the end.

Coffee. For those in need of a fix, you're in luck. Cafes serving strong and sickly or thin and weak are all over the place. For good espresso call in at the **Cafe Metropol**, open daily or **Cafe Lux** at Petrovsky Passage, 10 Ulitsa Neglinnaya. If you are on the Arbat, look out for the **Columbian Cafe** down from the Praga restaurant. And for "office supplies," give the **Montana Coffee Traders** a call at 252-06-71: they offer over a dozen flavors and deliver to your office free.

Alcohol. Every gastronom these days seems to have counters of champagne just waiting for someone with enough rubles to snap them up. If sickly sweet bubbly isn't your thing, try these options: At restaurants, buy a few extra bottles from your waiter. Or try one of the hard-currency grocery stores, or one of the many **Beriozkas** (in most hotels and a few other locations throughout the city). You can buy Georgian wine or a case of imported beer from **Pizza Hut**; or pick up a bottle of Lebanese wine from the hard-currency counter at the **Baku/Livan** restaurant, 24 Ulitsa Tverskaya. Two services will deliver for hard currency: **Intourservice** has an impressive selection of whiskeys, gins, liqueurs and wines you can order by the case; a case (12 bottles) of vodka (1 liter) costs 122.40 hard rubles; a case of Cotes de Duras Red (6 bottles) 52.20 hard rubles. Call 287-39-81 or 287-08-88, Monday to Saturday. Delivery within 48 hours; payment by credit card, cash, or account. Ask for their catalogue.

Farmers' Markets

Tsentralny Market
Tsvetnoi Bulvar 15

Weekdays till 6 p.m., Sundays till 4 p.m.

The most expensive farmer's market in Moscow—and the best stocked. High-quality fruits and vegetables can be found in great quantities, flown up from the south by enterprising businessmen. The roses are hideously expensive, but beautiful. Walk to the back to the meat section and pick up a whole piglet or hunk of beef, or go to the dairy building for honeycomb, farmer's cheese, and sour cream.

Cheryomushkinsky Rynok
Lomonosovsky Prospekt 1

Most seasoned market shoppers will tell you this *rynok* (market) has the best atmosphere—more relaxed than Tsentralny, although the prices are almost the same. Along with the usual food—meat, veggies, fresh and dried fruit and pickled goods—this market also sells painted wooden eggs, shawls, and *matryoshka* dolls.

Danilovsky Rynok
Ulitsa Mytnaya 74

Yes, that strange UFO perched in the middle of the highway is actually a market. You'll find one-stop shopping here, as the meat, sour cream and vegetables are all on sale in the same hall. The quantities are not as impressive as at Tsentralny, but occasionally they stock more eclectic products, such as Lithuanian cheese, home baked rolls, dried chiles and attractive plants, seeds, and flowers.

Department Stores

TsUM—Central Department Store
Ulitsa Petrovka 2

Open Monday–Saturday 8 a.m.–9 p.m.
No lunch break.

One of Moscow's largest stores. TsUM does get crowded. But there are bargains. Sometimes you'll spot fine amber or coral jewelry. You'll always see an endless supply of kitsch. Or pick up a Central Asian rug, a fur hat, or a slide projector. The trend towards renting out cooperative counters inside the state store ensures a good selection of jeans, jackets, shoes, jewelry, samovars, and accessories.

GUM–State Department Store
Krasnaya Ploshchad 3 on Red Square

Open Monday–Saturday 8 a.m.–9 p.m.

No lunch break.

Bathed in beautiful pastel colors, GUM is a visual heaven if not a shopper's paradise. A tourist mecca for all, you can find plenty of clothes, ugly ties, sheets, household goods, records and a passel of souvenirs.

Petrovsky Passage
10 Ulitsa Petrovka

Open Monday–Saturday 9 a.m.–8 p.m.

No lunch break.

"Passage" is going hard currency and upmarket. New kids on the block include Sony, Honda, Triumph, a great Shaffer stationery shop, Kodak and plenty more. Items for sale range from Chinese electronics to Russian souvenirs, couture, fur coats and cotton sheets.

Clothing Stores

Kalinka Mode
Hard currency only.

Profsoyuznaya Ulitsa 15

Open Monday–Friday 11 a.m.–8 p.m., Saturday 11 a.m.–6 p.m.

When you don't expect perfection (and let's face it, this isn't Paris), then you have to admire stores like this. They are trying hard and they have good things to offer. Friendly staff can lead you to the bargains among the racks of bright summer skirts, lovely Italian cardigans, jeans for kids and fun checked dresses. They also have shoes you could imagine yourself wearing.

Benetton
Credit cards only.

Prospekt Marksa, Hotel Moskva, and GUM,

First Line

Open Monday–Saturday 10–8 p.m.

No lunch break.

The small outlet adds a dot of color to the large gray People's Deputies Hotel. The bigger outlet adds a splash to the windows of the First Line of GUM. In this clean, light store are the trademark stacks of bright cotton or lambswool shirts, skirts and pants. The Russian staff is courteous to foreigners and icy to non-credit-card carrying people (read "Russians"), whom it heads off at the door.

Salentini
Hard currency only.

Ulitsa Tverskaya Yamskaya 26

Open Monday–Saturday 10 a.m.–8 p.m.

Lunch break 2–3 p.m.

You'll find slick Italian fashion at this store—for a price. It's worth a visit if you want to buy denim outfits for children and jeans and jackets for yourself. Other clothes on offer are overcoats, skirts, blazers and a small selection of Italian shoes (of course) for around one hundred dollars a pair.

Michel
Hard currency only.

Ulitsa Druzhinnikovskaya 11

Open Monday–Friday 11 p.m.–2 p.m.,
3 p.m.–8 p.m.

Alain Manoukian used to have a bou-
tique here, but another French store has
popped up in its place–and this one has
plenty to tempt an expense account wal-
let. Great splashy outfits, sensible blazers (around $300) and daring jackets;
skirts are plentiful and start at around
$80. The mens' clothes department
isn't huge, but it is well selected.

Rifle Jeans

Hard currency only.

10 Kuznetsky Most

Open Monday–Saturday 10 a.m.–7 p.m.

Lunch break 2–3 p.m.

Crowded and crazy Italian store,
stocking jeans, skirts, jackets, cordu-
roys, dress shirts and sweatshirts. The
prices are very reasonable. 35 or so
dollars can get you a pair of straight-leg
women's jeans. Some kids' sizes too.

Dom Mody/Zaitsev Showroom

21 Prospekt Mira

Open Monday–Saturday 10 a.m.–7 p.m.

Lunch break 1:30–2:15 p.m.

The ruble 'exhibition fee' to enter the
Slava Zaitsev showroom is a worthwhile
investment if only to browse through the
designer's creations. Winter coats seem
to be Zaitsev's specialty. They are most
original. The selection of women's
dresses is fairly small and, naturally, the
sizes are limited, but the clothing is stylish
and generally well made.

Dom Mody

Smolensky Bulvar, above Smolenskaya-
Filevskaya metro.

Open Monday–Saturady 10 a.m.–7 p.m.

Lunch break 1–2 p.m.

Racks of Russian designer wear (all
for rubles) are scattered about the mirrored showroom. The clothing is fairly
attractive, but there is little variety and
a very limited assortment of sizes. Still,
if you're lucky, you can pick up a nice
dress, coat or jacket.

Stationery and Office Supplies

Stockmann Fashion and Office Store

Credit cards only.

Leninsky Prospekt 78/8

Open Monday–Sunday 10 a.m.–8 p.m.

No lunch break.

A shop in the wrong category? Well,
the office supplies at the Stockmann are
truly wonderful. That doesn't mean I
didn't note the rest of the sprawling
premises—men's, women's and a small
section of children's fashion. It's just
that the chance to buy display books,
xerox paper, diskettes, Windsor and
Newton ink and everything else was too
tempting. They have a good cafe as well
to make the trip out here worth it.

Shkolnik

Leninsky Prospekt 21

Open Monday–Thursday 10 a.m.–7 p.m.

Friday 10 a.m.–6 p.m.

Lunch break 2–3 p.m.

There are plenty of such stores dot-
ting the city, but this one seems to be
the best. Chockful of writing paper,
notebooks, pens, and some art supplies,
you will always leave with some goodies.

Film and Electronics

Fairn and Swanson

Hard currency only.

Leninsky Prospekt 78

Open Monday–Saturday 10 a.m.–8 p.m.

No lunch break.

A row of televisions greet you as you stride into this hard-currency store located out on Leninsky. Everything you expect from an electronic store is here— all the name brands, all the products, plus a little more—spice racks, kitchen goods, coffee filters, knives, very cheap scissors. Barbie dolls, Lego and Levis are also here. Best bargains are to be had in the form of little ovens, great for the office. Plenty to choose from, around one hundred dollars. If you don't want to travel that far to shop, they also have an outlet at the Mezh.

Moskva

Hard currency only.

31 Kutuzovsky Prospekt

Open Monday–Sunday 10 a.m.–8 p.m.

Lunch break 3-4 p.m.

Walk under the red neon sign and step into an Aladdin's cave of electronic treasures. If you are in need of almost any electronic appliance—from faxes, computer printers to hair dryers—this store has a huge range. You can also pick up good, sensible Italian underwear, overcoats, jewelry and children's toys.

Fuji Film Center

Novy Arbat 25

Open Monday–Saturday 10 a.m.–9 p.m.

Separate counters here for developing Fuji film, in hard currency and rubles. The quality is not bad, but don't entrust your wedding photos to them. The biggest drawcard is the price. Around seven dollars for a role of film. They offer one-hour and overnight services (the prices vary for both), and have a small section selling drinks, cigarettes, and snack food.

Souvenirs and Knick-Knacks

Yantar (Amber)

Gruzinsky Val 14

Open Monday–Saturday 10 a.m.–7 p.m.

Lunch break 2-3 p.m.

Some secrets can't be kept forever— and this one is a beauty. Genuine amber, straight from Lithuania, a huge selection, and all for rubles. Shipments do vary, and, judging by the baubles decorating the sales ladies, you can see they get first pick. The biggest array is of necklaces, but they also have rings, bracelets and some truly horrible wall decorations. Around 400 rubles will get you a long strand, less for rings. Warning. If you tell your friends in the West about this shop, you'll spend all your Saturdays buying amber by the armful to send home.

Russkiye Souveniry

Kutuzovsky Prospekt 9

Open Monday–Saturday 11 a.m.–8 p.m.

No lunch break.

In this crowded store, one section sells overpriced jewelry; the others usually have beautiful lacquer boxes, silverware, small clay sculptures, brightly knitted socks and Central Asian hats. Everything is for rubles and the pace is bustling.

Beriozka

Ukraine Hotel, Kutuzovsky Prospekt 2/1

Second floor

Open Monday–Sunday 9 a.m.–2 p.m., 3 p.m.–8 p.m.

At first sight, the prospects don't look promising—a gloomy little cave of stock with too many staff and too few customers. But if, all of a sudden, you need a bottle of wine for a party and the line at the Irish Store is snaking out into the street—come in here! The prices are very competitive and they offer lots more than just grog. Pick up good dictionaries, guide books, a large selection of pretty scarves, porcelain, crystal, watches, and electrical appliances.

Izmailovsky Stadium

By Izmailovsky Park metro

Weekends only; from around 10 a.m. till sundown.

Make a day of it: this open-air flea market is full of treasures, from the usual souvenirs—such as *matryoshka* dolls, painted boxes and Russian scarves—to sterling-silver cutlery sets, art books, leather jackets, candlesticks, toys and even military jackets, belts and caps. You will need to bring plenty of rubles, as there is an enormous amount of stock and you'll find you want to buy it all.

Shopping on the Street

Kiosks. The best bargains to be had from these chaotic little capitalistic enclaves are at Kuznetsky Most for Western cosmetics and perfumes. Kutuzovsky Prospekt and Krasnopresnenskaya Ulitsa for clothes, booze, and juice, Kievsky Vokzal for cassettes, shoes, knick knacks, and clothes and the numerous kiosks along Novy Arbat for just about everything else.

The Moveable Markets

They are popping up all over the place—groups of people trying to make a few rubles by selling their treasures. The biggest ones are outside Christian Dior on Ulitsa Tverskaya for cosmetics and women's clothes and Detsky Mir for children's toys. But beware, those markets are illegal. So do like the sellers do. Keep a lookout for the militsia as you hand over the money.

DINING OUT IN MOSCOW

As in the West, much of your business will be conducted in restaurants. You should be familiar with the many dining options available in Moscow.

The author's personal favorite is **Tren-Mos**, at 21 Komsomolsky Prospekt (245-12-16). Insiders call it the "Rick's Place" of Moscow, a networking heaven for Muscovite movers and shakers. In this elegant, Casablanca-like haunt, celebrities, diplomats and corporate executives socialize to the strains of honky-tonk piano music. The Humphrey Bogart of this establishment is New Jersey-born Jeffrey Zeiger, who works the tables continually, cellular phone in hand, judiciously dispensing inside gossip, kissing ladies' hands and making strategic introductions. Your clients and business partners will be suitably impressed when the owner of this pricey restaurant greets you like an old and honored chum. Just tell Jeff that Richard Poe sent you. You'll be an instant insider. The cuisine is all-American, prepared by a master French chef. Also, try Jeff's new **TrenMos Bistro** at No. 1 Ostozhenka (202-57-22), an airy, relaxing place, serving light foods, home-cooked pastas, pizza and the like. Includes an adjoining bar. It's less expensive than TrenMos, and just as hip. Jeff splits his time between the two restaurants.

The following mini restaurant reviews are selected from *Moscow Magazine*'s latest "Moscow City Guide":

Russian Cuisine

Arbat

Rubles.

Novy Arbat 29, tel. 291-14-03.

It's hard to concentrate on the food (which is truly dreary) in this huge, noisy room, when a scantily clad woman is gyrating with a hula-hoop. Wild floor show, lots of dancing, plenty of champagne. If you're out for raucous, tacky fun, this restaurant is for you.

Arkadia

Rubles.

3 Teatralny Proyezd, tel. 926-90-08.

Location, location, location. This place has it. Tucked in the alley directly across from the Metropol, this cooperative is a favorite with Russians who have rubles to burn. The sizable menu is larded with the stand-bys: *bliny* with caviar, mushroom julienne, *lobio*, Estonian cheese salad, chicken Kiev. Nothing to write home about, but all tasty and typical enough to take visitors to. Plenty of local alcohol.

Atrium

Major credit cards only.

Leninsky Prospekt 44, tel. 137-30-08.

The usually fixed menu features Russian nouvelle cuisine—typical *zakuski*, soup, meat cooked in earthenware pots, fruit for dessert. With its marble-columned rooms and elegant yet unpretentious post-modern decor, you might well be in Paris or Manhattan.

Boyarsky

Hard currency only.

Metropol Hotel, fourth floor, Teatralny Proyezd 1/4, tel. 927-60-89.

Fabulous High Russian Camp at this top-of-the-line dining spot includes a stuffed bear, serenades from the balcony, and mismatched pre-revolutionary silver. Cuisine is traditional Russian with a fanciful twist. Delectable *pirozhki* with vintage brandy sauce, divine caviar-stuffed trout. Expensive.

Cafe Margarita

Rubles.

28 Malaya Bronnaya. No reservations.

The renovations are slick. Now the dinky tables and chairs match the walls. Sitting for a long time is uncomfortable, but this is a rare place where you can wander in without a booking at lunchtime and be out again in half an hour. Mushrooms are the mainstay—as a soup or in a casserole with potatoes and sour cream. Try the Tashkent salad—its combination of egg, meat, and mayonnaise is a tasty change from the usual cucumber and tomato starters. Desserts are sticky and rich.

Cafe Viru

Rubles.

50 Ulitsa Ostozhenka, tel. 246-61-07.

Salads (the mayonnaise, not the lettuce kind), sandwiches, coffee, and cakes are the stock and trade of this "Estonian" cafe. Sometimes they offer hot food. Near Park Kultury metro, this is a hang-out for a hip crowd.

Dyen i Noch (Day and Night)

Rubles.

12 Kolomensky Proyezd, tel. 112-94-25.

Rated "Restaurant of the Month" by *Moscow Magazine*, Dyen i Noch features a live sex show, a chef who used to cook for the Central Committee, and superb Russian haute cuisine. Features the best, creamiest, cheesiest toasted mushroom julienne in Moscow. Also outstanding are the crab in claret and creamed chicken crepe. Champagne, wine and vodka are for rubles, but a little circulating cart is loaded with hard-currency alcohol and cigarettes.

Druzhba

Rubles or credit cards.

Krasnopresnenskaya Nab. 12, Expocenter, tel. 255-29-70.

Small and cozy, this cooperative doubles as an art gallery, with floor-to-ceiling paintings. Banquets resemble medieval feasts, with suckling pigs lying prone among lavish dishes of caviar, heaps of elaborate salad bouquets and sparkling intoxicants.

Kropotkinskaya 36

Hard currency and major credit cards.

Ulitsa Kropotkinskaya 36, tel. 201-75-00.

Moscow's first co-op restaurant has a romantic, cozy downstairs with violinist, and a gilded, formal upstairs. The menu reads like a primer of Russian cuisine. Quality varies, but the *shchi* (cabbage soup), *bliny*, mushroom pie, and stuffed carp are usually well-rendered. Home-made gelato, Georgian, French, and Californian wines available.

Olimp

Rubles.

Embankment behind Luzhniki Stadium, tel. 201-01-48.

From outside, this long, low restaurant bedecked with strings of colored lights resembles a roadside rib joint in the US. The snazzy inside is unique—as is the sizzling musical revue. Tasty *pelmeni* and reasonable *dolma*. Alcohol (nasty Moscow bottled cognac and wine

stuff) is for hard currency. Bring wads of rubles.

Razgulyai

Rubles or hard currency.

Ulitsa Spartakovskaya 11, tel. 267-76-13.

The paint job (one room is blue and white, the other red, black, and gold) at this cellar restaurant makes you think you've stumbled into an enormous Russian souvenir. *Borscht, pelmeni,* and cutlets are nice renditions of Russian favorites. Sweet Soviet champagne and wine available. Loud and vibrant gypsy sextet on Fridays and Saturdays.

Rossiya

Rubles or hard currency.

Hotel Rossiya, Ulitsa Razina entrance, tel. 298-29-81.

Two words: the view. From the twenty-first floor of one of the largest hotels on the planet, you can survey St. Basil's and Red Square, and, if your eyesight is good, you can watch the changing of the guard at Lenin's Mausoleum. Loads of champagne and vodka, but the food is strictly industrial.

Strastnoi 7 .

Major credit cards.

Strastnoi Bulvar 7, tel. 229-04-98.

This gleaming chrome-touched restaurant is a good place to lounge over a quiet meal. The kitchen does a fine job with Russian cuisine: no surprises, but no major disappointments either. Wide selection of liquor, including Stella Artois beer. A favorite with businesspeople, who often drop some cash at the classy affiliated art gallery.

Taganka Bar

Rubles and hard currency.

V. Radishchevskaya 15, tel. 272-43-51.

Crowded, cramped, and ornate, with a cave-like atmosphere. Best loud entertainment in town. Albino frogs in the lobby aquarium, jazz bands, gypsy singers, and a nimble contortionist. *Zakuski* include pickled garlic, nuts, meat dishes, and lavish sauces. Try an entree if you have room. Watch the vodka. They have been known to serve moonshine.

U Margarity

Daytime: Pay rubles for food and hard currency for alcohol.

Night: Hard currency for everything.

Ulitsa Ryleyeva 9, tel. 291-60-63.

Unwind to the plaintive strains of a violin at one of the little tables grouped about a small fountain. Quality varies dramatically and the menu is limited, but this restaurant occasionally boasts delicacies you'll find nowhere else: smoked spring chicken, pheasant sauced with black cherries. Call to find out.

Vyecherni Siluett

Hard currency.

Taganskaya Ploshchad 88, tel. 272-22-80.

White-satin panelled walls and green-and-white lattice make this tiny restaurant look like a cross between a coffin and a garden party. The food is Russian, fussily prepared. Dishes include caviar, crab salad, broiled squash and cheesy chicken. The grape torte is luscious. Very pricey, this spot is frequented by *very* chic Russians.

Moosh

Rubles.

Ulitsa Oktyabrskaya 2/4, tel. 284-36-70.

This small Armenian co-op is not for the faint-hearted. Pictures of national martyrs deck the crimson walls, which also display old rifles. On a good night, the painfully loud music rouses the clientele to their feet to perform traditional dances and propose drawn-out toasts. Stand up for the anthem. The food, tasty but oversalted, includes *dolma* and mutton. Vodka and cognac.

U Pirosmani

Rubles for food; Hard currency for alcohol.

Novodyevichy Proyezd 4, tel. 247-19-26.

White-washed walls and beamed ceilings are the setting for Georgian specialties such as *hachapuri*, *lobio* and *satsivi*. Many of the hard-working waiters speak English, but this place is so popular they are always harried. Georgian wine flows, as diners enjoy the sounds of violin and piano or gaze out at the splendor of the sixteenth century Novodyevichy Convent.

Victoria aka Hard Rock Cafe

Rubles.

Zelyoni Teatr, Gorky Park, tel. 237-07-09.

Owned by rock-star-cum-producer Stas Namin, this is a favorite hangout of musicians, particularly heavy metal types. Action starts late. The Russian-Armenian dishes are simple but appetizing. Located in the basement of the Green Theater, deep within Gorky Park. (Don't walk alone after dark!)

Central Asian Cuisine

Yakimanka

Rubles or credit cards.

B. Polyanka 2/10, Str. 1, tel. 238-88-88.

The foreign business and academic crowd rubs shoulders with homesick Central Asians at this Uzbek restaurant as the lively band plays the latest Russian hits over and over again. The food mingles Mediterranean and Oriental influences—stuffed grape leaves, giant dumplings and *plov*. Some nights it can be genuinely tasty.

European/American

Arlecchino

Major credit cards.

Druzhinnikovskaya Ulitsa 15, tel. 205-70-88.

Everything in this sleek, pink-black-and-parquet restaurant is flown or trucked in from Italy. Professionally prepared Italian cuisine, although quality can vary. Risottos are good, and the array of tempting pastas includes a fine farfalle with gorgonzola. Plain pork and veal dishes satisfy plain palates. Italian wines.

Brasserie

Hard currency.

Penta Hotel, Olimpisky Prospekt 18/1, tel. 971-61-01.

This massive restaurant has shipboard decor (portholes, rope, and wavy blue walls), a Russian folklore floor show and a global village menu: tomato soup with puddles of fresh cream, assorted lettuce salad with goat cheese croutons, borscht with caviar, meaty duck breast with soy sauce and ginger, and rib-eye steak. One vegetarian dish, *moussaka*, is as heavy and oily as you get in Greece. Portions are hefty. You may not need the pastry cart.

Lazania

Hard currency (cash only).

Pyatnitskaya Ulitsa 40, tel. 231-10-85.

Set in a scenic neighborhood across the river from the Kremlin, Lazania makes a valiant attempt at preparing Italian food. The signature lasagna is disappointing, but, considering they are made with local ingredients, the other dishes are quite respectable. Homemade rolls, pasta and pastries are delightful touches. Popular with the well-groomed.

Peter's Place

Hard currency.

Ulitsa Chkalova 72, tel. 298-32-48.

Life-size toy soldiers guard this Dutch joint venture restaurant, which is more elegant than it sounds (don't come in jeans) although it has touches of whimsy: Liza Minelli and Peter the Great dine in one corner in frozen splendor. Food is Russianized European. Salade nicoise leans towards the native diced variety. Stuffed crepes, although tasty, are simply huge *bliny*. Handy to the Taganka Theater and open until midnight, stop by for a post-show supper. Or hit the shoebox-sized bar—open until 4 a.m.—for beer and dancing.

Potel et Chabot

Hard currency.

Hotel Mezhdunarodnaya, 2nd level, tel. 253-23-87.

Saccharine murals and harpists, draped in bedsheets set the scene in this fancy French restaurant. Luckily, the food is not so cloying. Rich and cheesy onion soup, soothing Dieppoise fish stew with lobster chunks, tender sauced veal chop, and lamb cake. For dessert, plump for the luscious Iced Nougat. Expense-account, dark-suited clientele.

Savoy

Hard currency.

Rozhdestvenka 3, tel. 929-86-00.

Classical restaurant with attentively prepared formal cuisine, and luxurious, opulent interior. Try the mouth-watering borscht, the refreshing cold salad of marinated pork, or perch fillets with dill butter. Or splurge on the reindeer tenderloin in flaky pastry. Ideal for elegant dinners. Prix-fixe business lunches are around $30.

Tino Fontana

Hard currency.

Hotel Mezhdunarodnaya, 3rd floor, tel. 253-22-41.

This restaurant towers over others in the city—at least in terms of price. Packed with those on expense accounts, it serves standard Italian cuisine—*pasta e fagioli*, sizzling *escalope pallanese*, and pasta dishes, including a flavorful fettuccine with wild mushrooms. Most ingredients are imported from Italy, and food is prepared by Italian chefs. Try the mousse or sumptuous *tiramisu*.

Asian

Mei-hua

Rubles and hard currency.

Ulitsa Rusakovskaya 2/1, Stroyenie 1 (next door to Rusalka Cafe), tel. 264-95-74.

This inconspicuous co-op (no sign, just a half-hidden doorbell) has the city's best Chinese food. The lazy Susans are laden with tasty appetizers: beef in orange sauce, sweet-and-sour cucumbers, spicy carrots. Entrees are small but entrancing: crunchy deep-fried chicken, tender barbecued pork, spicy pork with peanuts. Steaming jasmine tea and Dutch beer for $3 a can.

Peking

Ruble and hard currency rooms

Ulitsa B. Sadovaya 1/2, tel. 209-18-65.

A favorite with Moscow's hip lunch crowd, this state joint has the most extravagant, Hollywoodesque interior in town. The kitchen reflects the vagaries of Sino-Russian politics. After a long break, real Chinese chefs preside over the woks. The Peking duck is a treat. Connoisseurs of Chinese food will probably be disappointed, but unfussy fans go away pleased.

Sapporo

Hard currency.

12/14 Prospekt Mira, tel. 207-82-53.

This four-story restaurant in a restored mansion off the Garden Ring is the most entrancing new entry on the dining scene. Feast on delectable sushi, tangy miso soup, delicate tempura, and sukiyaki that is heaven in a bowl. The top floor hosts the city's only karaoke bar, where, for $3 a song, you can serenade the room as you sing along with a video disc. Even if you can't carry a tune, the fun is infectious.

ENTERTAINMENT AND RECREATION

Nightlife. If you're a culture vulture, a stint in Moscow is heaven: fabulous theater, concerts, opera, and ballet at very off-Broadway prices await you every evening. If you're not that type, you're stuck. There's little that sizzles in the capital. **Night Flight**, a hard-currency club, is open 9 p.m. to 5 a.m. Ul. Tverskaya 17, tel. 229-41-65. The hotels with the loudest nightlife are the **Intourist, Cosmos,** and the **Mezh. Inflotel**, the floating hotel berthed right by the Mezh Hotel, has recently opened the **Medussa** night club, which gets jumping with live music at 11:30 p.m. and with exotic and erotic dances at 12:30.

Stas Namin's **Hard Rock Cafe**, also known as **Viktoria** (located in Zelyoni Teatr in Gorky Park, tel. 237-07-09), is open late, but recent shootings appear to have deterred customers. The nightclub at **Peter's Place**, a Dutch joint venture restaurant near the Taganka Theater, stays open until 4 a.m.; the bar has a Friday Happy Hour from 6 to 7 for those who want an early start, tel. 298-32-48, Chkalova 72.

For the young and wild at heart, Moscow's swingin'est scene can be found at **Ulissa**, which comes into being every Friday and Saturday night, when the hockey rink at **Olimpisky Stadium** is transformed into a den of quintessentially Russian iniquity. Ulissa features casine gambling, erotic dancers, a huge dance floor, and much much more. (Office) Luzhnetskaya Naberezhnaya, 24 VOND, Moscow, 201-09-76, 201-00-61. Fax: 247-10-60.

Bars. Things are looking up for those who crave a quiet (or noisy) ale. Our favorite is **Savoy Bar**, where the waiters are friendly, you can dose up on CNN and order light meals. Also good are the **Spanish Bar** at the Hotel Moskva and the **Shamrock Pub** in the Irish House (which has raucous Irish singing on weekends and games nights during the week).

The **Bierstube** at the Penta Hotel, open from 11 a.m. to 1 a.m. has great draught beer and serves up German pub food. The **Artist's Bar** at the Metropol (open daily from 3 p.m. to 1 a.m.) is good for a formal drink. For a stand-up cold beer, try the bar in the **In Vino** Restaurant on the third floor of the Ukraina Hotel. The shipboard bar on the **Alexander Blok** (the floating hotel moored in front of the Mezh Hotel) has a happy hour from 5 p.m. to 7 p.m. and good river view. Try also the British joint venture pubs: the **Brown Bear** at the Expocenter by the Mezh or the **Galaxy** near the Cosmos (2 Selskokhozyaistvenny Per.). The latter is dead until about midnight, when a young, blackmarket crowd comes in for drinks and darts. The **Cosmos Bar** at the hotel of the same name is very sleazy.

If you are determined to punish yourself, there's always the **Hotel Belgrad**, the various **Hotel Mezhdunarodnaya** watering holes (which tend to be cavernous and bleak) and the perennial tourist favorite and prostitute pick-up, the patio bar in the Intourist Hotel.

Cinemas. Whether or not you speak Russian, you can still enjoy the local cinema scene. If you can't understand the chatter (for virtually all films are dubbed), at least you can get a kick watching the mouths move out of synch with the noise. Check your local newspapers for showtimes. Many films are foreign, but usually decades out of date.

Cosmos: Prospekt Mira 1, tel. 283-86-67,

Khudozhestvenny: Arbatskaya Pl. 14, tel. 291-55-98,

Espace Mir: Tsvetnoy Boulevard 11, tel. 200-96-96,

Moskva: Mayakovskaya Ploshchad 2, tel. 251-72-22.

Novorossisk: Zemlyanoi Val 47/24, tel. 297-54-92.

Oktyabr: Novy Arbat 42, tel. 202-11-11.

Povtornovo: Ul. Gertsena 23, tel. 202-49-42.

Rossiya: Pushkinskaya Ploshchad 2, tel. 299-01-41,

Strelya: Ul. Smolenskaya-Sennaya 23-25, tel. 244-09-53.

Casinos. The city has a casino for every taste and every pocketbook. For ruble gambling try the foreign-run **Bombay**. Entrance fee is 150 rubles; 50 rubles goes to charity, the other 100 you get back in the form of chips. Pleasant environment, minimum bet is 50 rubles. Rublyovskoye Shosse 61, tel. 141-55-04.

The **Savoy Hotel** has an elegant, full-scale casino for hard currency only. The **Leningradskaya Hotel** near Komsomolskaya Square has roulette and blackjack tables, as well as a restaurant and bar. Despite the dollar fee to get in, the action goes on late into the night. Call 975-19-67 for information.

The two-story **Casino Royale** is the largest in town. Located in the Hippodrome, both floors have bars, and there is a restaurant for a pre-gambling feed. You can play blackjack, roulette, stud poker, and punto banco—daily from 8 p.m. to 4 a.m.—for U.S. dollars only. Call 945-14-10. The Casino Royale also has slot machines, as do the Cosmos, **Intourist** and the **Mezh**. The **Alexander Blok** berthed across from the Mezh Hotel, also offers a casino and bar (tel. 255-93-23). Open until 4 a.m.

Theater Tickets. Nabbing a ticket to a cultural event is not always easy. The cheapest way is to buy a ticket at a kiosk or at the venue's box office before the event. Or try to get one through a hotel Intourist office for hard currency. The main lobby of the Metropol plays host to **IPS Theater Box Office**, which can provide you with good seats to popular events: call 927-67-29 or 927-67-28. Try also the scalpers outside before the event. You may get lousy seats, though!

Your Ready-Made Rolodex

A Complete Directory of Essential Business Contacts

The "club" of Western businessmen active in Russia is still relatively small and chummy. Everyone seems to know everyone else. To break into this club, you need a jump-start. That means *contacts*, both Russian and American.

I won't attempt to provide a comprehensive listing of every consultant, business service or successful Russia-preneur in existence in this appendix, but the names and numbers listed in the following pages should meet most of your initial needs. Many entries in this appendix are reprinted from *Moscow Magazine*'s "Moscow City Guide." Other information was provided by the U.S. Department of Commerce, the author's personal databases, and other sources.

Telecommunications

Calling Russia. Your first experience with the Russian system will probably be a phone call from the United States to Moscow. Dial 011-7-095 and then the local number. Most Russian phone numbers have seven digits, like our own. But sometimes they don't. If you're dialing a number with fewer than seven digits, try "rounding it off" by adding zeroes to the end. Sometimes it works. Other times it's not necessary. Don't be dismayed if a recording tells you that, "The number you are dialing cannot be reached at this time in the country you are calling." Just keep trying. It's not unusual to have to keep redialing for 20 minutes before you get through.

The proper way to answer the phone in Russia is "Ah-LYOH"—their pronunciation of "hello." Sometimes, more rudely, Russians will simply say "SLOOSH-ayu"—"I'm listening."

Calling from Russia. When in Russia, book an international call through the operator by dialing 8, waiting for the dial tone, then 194 or 196; problems or cancellations: 8-190. The operator will ask you to set a specific time for your call, which may be up to 24 hours later. If you don't speak Russian, have someone else make the call. If the operator hears a foreign language, she may say, "There's something wrong with the line. I can't hear you," and hang up. This can be very frustrating after you've spent the last 10 minutes trying to get through. The international operator's line is almost always busy.

Another alternative is to dial direct between midnight and 9 a.m. and on weekends; just dial 8, wait for the tone, then 10, country code, and number. If you call from a hotel, you will be charged hard currency: from a private apartment, rubles.

The Press Center, Zubovsky Blvd. 4, near metro Park Kultury, has 17 booths operated by the **Combellga** satellite network. Telephone and fax communications are immediate. Payment is in cash or by credit cards. Journalists need only flash their press card to get in. Others must dial 244-95-59 or 243-35-75 for an appointment.

Another expensive but effective way to call direct is to use a **Comstar** telephone booth. This Russian-British joint venture has 25 locations in the city; tel. 979-16-92, 210-09-62. You can pay with JCB, Amlix, or Visa, or buy a phone credit card from the cashier. Try also **Alphagraphics** at 50 Ulitsa Tverskaya, which has direct international phone lines—hard currency, of course; tel. 217-10-85.

Moscow Cellular Communications provides a direct dial cellular phone service. Sales office: 297-77-83.

For a ruble call, go to a major post office. The **Central Telephone and Telegraph** at 7 Tverskaya Ulitsa has international telephone lines; go early to avoid long delays. There is also a direct automatic line to Canada, the United States, and Eastern Europe. Telegrams are a cheap alternative, and can be sent from any major post office.

Faxing from Russia. Alphagraphics Printshops of the Future, Ul. Tverskaya Yamskaya 20; tel. 251-12-15, has a fax machine. They charge $10 per page for the first two pages, $6 for each page after that and $8 per minute for the phone charge. For more competitive prices, use the fax service at the **Savoy** hotel—only $4 per page to Europe and $11 per page for the United States. **IP Interpret** (tel. 231-10-20) offers international fax service for rubles.

The **Comstar Business Center** in the Passage Department Store (10 Petrovka Street, 3rd Floor, room 301; tel. 924-08-92, 924-13-85) comes highly recommended. They have international pay phones, faxes, telexes and E-mail.

Electronic Mail. Many companies use E-mail to communicate between United States and Russian offices. It's cheap, convenient and reliable. With an E-mail account, you can also send and receive telexes from your PC—a great boon in a country where fax machines are scarce and telexes still the preferred mode of business communication. The following E-mail services are popular among Western businessmen:

Compuserve: PO Box 20212, Columbus, OH 43220; tel. (800) 848-8990.

Infocom: tel. (800) 441-0926. In Moscow; tel. 925-12-35/40-93.

Sovam Teleport: 3278 Sacramento St., San Francisco, CA 94115; tel. (415) 931-8500, fax (415) 931-2885. In Moscow: tel. 229-96-63 or 229-34-66.

Sprint: 12490 Sunrise Valley Drive, Reston, VA 22096; tel. (800) 736-1130. In Moscow: tel. 201-68-90.

Courier Services

Don't use the Russian mail system. At best, your letter will take over a month to arrive. At worst, it will get lost. Fax or telex is your best bet. But if you must send a package, use one of the following express mail services.

BMT Courier Service—Hotel Mezhdunarodnaya 2, Rm 940, Krasnopresnenskaya Nab. 12; tel. (7-502) 253-29-40.

Delta Airlines—tel. (800) 638-7333. In Moscow: Floor 11, Krasnopresnenskaya Nab. 12; tel. 253-26-58, -26-59, Telex 413089. *Note:* Moscow only.

DHL Express Mail—tel. (800) 225-5345. In Moscow: Ulitsa Vesnina 1, Olympic Penta Hotel; tel. 201-25-85, 971-61-01, fax 201-24-90. In Kiev: c/o Soyuzvneshtrans, 3 Pochtovaya Square, 252076 Kiev; tel. (36-1) 157-69-92, fax (36-1) 157-69-81. In Odessa: c/o Soyuzvneshtrans, 7, Primorsky Blvd., 270026 Odessa; tel. (36-1) 157-69-92. *Note:* Serves Alma Ata, Baku, Kiev, St. Petersburg, Moscow, Odessa, Tbilisi, Vladivostok.

Federal Express—1st Floor Sovincentr, 3rd Entrance, Krasnopresnenskaya Nab. 12, 123610 Moscow; tel. (70-95) 253-1641, (In U.S.) (301) 953-3333, fax (70-95) 253-904. Cities served: Domodevo, Kaliningrad, Kaunas, Kazan, Kharkov, Khimki, Kiev, Lyubertsky, Lobnya, Minsk, Moscow, Mytischi, Podolsk, Pushkino, Riga, Schiolkovo, St. Petersburg, Tallinn, Troitsk, Vidnoe, Vilnius, Zelenograd, Zhelezno-dorozhny, Zhykovsky

United Parcel Service—15A Bolshaya Ochakovskaya, 119361 Moscow; tel. (70-95) 430-6373, (In U.S.) (800) 346-0106. telex 413089. Cities served: Khabarovsk, Moscow, Odessa, St. Petersburg, Tashkent, Vladivostok.

U.S. Postal Service—Just call your local U.S. post office and ask for Express Mail International Service. *Note:* Serves Alma-Ata, Arkhangelsk, Achkhabad, Baku, Bichkek, Brest, Dnepropetrovsk, Donetsk, Dushanbe, Irkutsk, Khabarovsk, Kharkov, Kaliningrad, Kaunas, Karaganda, Kazan, Kiev, Kishinev, Krasnodar, Krasnoyarsk, Lvov, Minsk, Moscow, Nakhodka, Nizhny Novgorod, Novgorod, Novosibirsk, Omsk, Odessa, Perm, Petropavlovsk-Kamchatsky, Riga, Rostov-on-Don, Saratov, Samara, St. Petersburg, Tashkent, Tallinn, Tbilisi, Tcheliabinsk, Tyumen, Vilnius, Vladivostok, Yakutsk, Yaroslavl, Yerevan, Yuzhno-Sakhalinsk.

For Shipping Heavy Cargo

Sea-Land Service, Inc.—(Edison, NJ) tel. (908) 494-3131. In Moscow; tel. 292-50-57, fax 292-50-57, telex 413205 USCO SU. Contacts: Richard Nicholson, Charlie Grant, Sima Gorovkovsky. *Note:* Ships large cargoes by sea, truck and rail. Lands at both European and Far East ports of the former Soviet states.

Office Space

Like other European countries, Russia imposes strict controls on construction in its historic downtown areas. The result is a chronic shortage of office space. Nevertheless, the savvy business pioneer can find surprisingly comfortable and modern office facilities by going through Western firms which specialize in providing office space for Western businesses.

Swatstroi—a Canadian-Russian joint venture, can set you up with first-class office suites in prime locations. Call 921-41-29 or fax 921-50-59. The joint venture **BBC** (**BIG Business Center**) offers fully serviced, Western-standard offices on Oktyabrskaya Square. Facilities include parking, tri-lingual receptionists and secretaries, international phones, computer rental, and conference rooms. Call Managing Director Vadim Nikitin at 237-51-95 or fax 234-53-95. Try also The **Radisson Hotel/American Trade Center** (tel. 941-80-20) or the Technopark—a snazzy new space located in VDNKh—the old scientific-industrial exhibition ground which was the Soviet answer to Disneyworld's Epcot Center; tel. 229-46-78.

U.S. Real Estate Companies in Russia. Real estate development is one of the hottest businesses going in Russia. Many of the following U.S. companies are heavily involved in developing Western-quality office buildings.

A&A Relocations-Russia Ltd.—Staropansky Pereulok 4, 107066, Moscow; tel. 923-78-13, fax 117-60-01, telex 412387 ATS SU. Contact: Sharon O-Brien. *Note*: Real estate and relocation services.

American International Corporation—2 Berezhkovaya Nab., Hotel Radisson/Slavyanskaya, Moscow, Moscow, tel. 239-37-96, 941-66-43, 941-66-44, fax 230-22-16, 230-23-18. **Contact:** Vladimir Draitser (Executive Vice President). **In U.S.:** One Park Plaza, 6th floor, Irvine, CA 92714; tel. (714) 852-7303, fax (714) 852-7302, telex 984193 HQIRVI, **Contacts:** Paul Tatum (President), Bernard Rome (Chairman of Executive Board). *Note*: Develops high-tech office complexes for Western businesses. Manages Radisson/Slavyanskaya Business Center, which includes 430 hotel rooms, 120,000 sq. ft. of office space, multimedia center, etc.).

Belgian Investment Group—(JV Big Steel) Mail Box 42, 117049 Moscow; tel. 237-51-95, fax 234-53-95, telex 411663

OMEGA. **In U.S.:** P.O. Box 2145, Winter Park, FL 32790; tel. (407) 647-2402, fax (407) 629-69-92. **Contacts:** Vadim Nikitine, Sr., Vadim Nikitine, Jr. *Note*: Rents out office suites and mini-suites to Western businesses.

Hines Interests—Leninsky Prospekt 146, Moscow; tel. 434-26-66, 434-14-55, 434-05-50, 434-35-20, fax 434-34-10. Contact: William L. Knopick (Director of Marketing). *Note*: Represents new UpDK building "The Park Place."

Interstroy—(Russian-American-Turkish JV), Kuznetsky Most 1/8, Moscow; tel. 450-51-15, 450-91-34, 292-51-21, fax 259-67-86. **Contacts:** Sergei Frolov, Alexander Somov. **In U.S.:** Design & Construction Technology (DCT) Ltd., c/o Marino Industries, 400 Meuchen Road, P.O. Box 358, South Plainfield, NJ, 07080; tel. (908) 757-9000, fax (908) 753-87-86. **Contacts:** Leslie L. Beach (President), Dave Geovanis (Marketing Manager: 908-757-0422). *Note*: Real estate development, international construction in joint ventures with U.S. companies).

Perestroika Joint Venture—Malaya Bronnaya 15B, 103104 Moscow; tel. 299-70-13, fax 290-34-80, telex 411742. **Contacts:** Cameron F. Sawyer (Acting General Director), Miles Jones (Director of Leasing), Jonathan Sparrow (Leasing Manager), Tracy Kwiker (Director of Marketing), Cindy Green-Fisher (Chief Financial Officer). **In U.S.:** The Worsham Group, 1605 Chantilly Drive, Suite 200, Atlanta, GA 30323; tel. (404) 634-1615, fax (404) 633-7128.

Putnik Joint Venture—Bolshoi Strochenovksy Pereulok No. 22/25 Moscow; tel. 236-44-93 (office), 291-20-93 (home), fax 202-43-59, telex 414724 BARD SU. **Contact:** John Reuther.

Rosinka—Leningradsky Prospekt 39, Soviet Army Sports Center, Swimming Pool Building, Room 22, Moscow; tel.

213-29-07, fax 213-29-07. **Contacts:** Christopher Senie (Director General), Nadezhda Serebryakova (Office Manager). **In U.S.:** Senie Kerschner International, 125 Main St., Westport, CT 06880; tel. (203) 226-1223, fax (203) 454-7890. **Contact:** Noland Kerschner (Vice President).

Office Phone Systems

The Finnish company **Nokia** is a good place to go for a Western phone—they also handle installation and service. Call them at 201-3079/83. Or try **Comstar** at 209-91-30: this British-Soviet joint venture can get you both phone systems and a local or international line (a hellish venture through official government channels). They offer installation and maintenance as well.

Siemens is another good bet for phone systems and installation; call 230-08-10, 230-08-21, or 230-07-32.

The **Combellga** satellite network offers international telecommunications by connecting your apartment or office. For inquiries, call 243-3575/78 or 244-9559.

Copying Services

Whether it's copies, faxes, new business cards or passport photos, your best bet is:

Alphagraphics—Printshops of the Future at Ulitsa Tverskaya Yamskaya 50; tel. 251-12-08, 251-12-15, fax 230-22-07, 230-22-17. AlphaGraphics also offers copy services in its bookstore at the Kosmos Hotel; tel. 217-00-81, 217-10-85, fax 281-95-51. It's expensive but speedy. Also try the following:

Comstar Business Center—Ulitsa Petrovka 10, Rm 301; tel. 924-08-92.

Hotel Savoy Business Center—Ulitsa Rozhdestvenka 3; tel. 929-37-80.

Rank Xerox Reprocenter—Ukraina Hotel, Kutuzovsky Prospekt 2/1; tel. 243-30-07, 243-12-90.

Radisson/Slavyanskaya Hotel Business Center—Berezhkovskaya Naberezhnaya 2.

Computers and Computer Supplies

The American franchise **Computerland** is going to save your life in Moscow, if you need to buy a PC, a printer or computer accessories in a hurry. It offers reasonable prices and warranties. Located in the Orlyonok Hotel, Ulitsa Kosygina 15, 117586 Moscow; tel. 939-81-28, fax 930-78-20. **Contact:** Oleg Matveev. Service Center: tel. 243-72-86, 298-11-02. **Contacts:** Andrei Malyshev, Oleg Ovchinnov. In U.S.: **Computerland/MBL International** (Secaucus, NJ); tel. (201) 865-7900. **Contact:** Eileen Exeter (Director of Marketing). Or check out the **SuperShop**, Astrakhansky Pereulok 5.

Another U.S. franchise, **MicroAge**, caters to especially to businesses, offering IBM and Hewlett-Packard peripherals, and providing service, supplies and support. Balaklavsky Avenue 3; tel. 316-21-11 or 316-21-18. Hard currency only. **Wang** has also moved in, offering a variety of equipment and services. Call 112-33-24/34-11/12-44 or pay them a visit at their business complex at VDNKh (building 1, unit 17, 18).

Security Systems and Guard Service

Theft, burglary, hijacking, kidnapping and extortion are rampant in Russia. If you set up a business there, you'll need the help of professional guards and reliable security systems. Many Russian businessmen hire active policemen or intelligence agents for protection. But this can lead to ticklish conflicts of interest, especially when your business itself operates on the fringes of the law—as most are forced to in Russia. You're better off sticking with private guards, who have no official connections. They can be hired in Moscow and St. Petersburg for anywhere from R4000 to R9000 per month, while burglar and fire alarm systems might cost as much as R100,000.

The **Moscow City Soviet Executive Committee** offers both guard service and burglar alarm systems (Lyublyanskaya Ulitsa 16; tel. 971-05-89). **Ello Industries, Inc.**—a diversified American company based in Secaucus, NJ—maintains its own private security force several hundred strong. For $15 per guard per hour, Ello will hire them out as guards, uniformed or plainclothes, armed or barefisted, as you prefer. Call 299-99-75. In the U.S.: (201) 865-2100. For a reliable—but expensive—guard service try **Alex**, a Russian company which provides great strapping fellows dressed to intimidate in full camouflage (tel. 255-29-01, 265-47-39, 263-27-01); to order a bodyguard directly, call 318-12-06. Alex also provides full-fledged detective services. Its staff of ex-KGB spooks really knows its business. **In the U.S.**, call (800) 354-2015, (207) 354-2015, fax (207) 354-0242. Address: **Alex-USA Ltd.**, PO Box 127, 26 Knox St., Tomaston, ME. Contact: David J. Bowman.

For alarm systems and the like, try **Star Progress**, (tel. 248-44-58, fax 230-26-01), for hard currency only. The Finnish company **Oy Esmi Ab** is the largest company manufacturing and marketing electronic and security products in Moscow. It offers burglar alarms

for offices and apartments, security monitoring, door intercoms, fire alarms and extinguishing systems; tel. 238-55-20, 238-53-41 and fax 341-50-18. **Medservice**, a German-Soviet joint venture, installs steel doors; tel. 288-58-75, 281-48-05. **Intermarket**, a home security store located by Patriarch's Pond (Ulitsa Mitskevicha 12), carries locks, safes and electronic security systems, and offers office security as well. Call 291-76-55. And the Dutch **AEC** will also install steel doors and alarms (tel. 250-99-74, fax 251-15-38).

Money and Banking

Changing Money. Banks in major hotels (such as the Rossiya, Belgrad, Mir, Molodyozhnaya, Kosmos, Penta, Metropol, or the Ukraina) or the American Express office are the best places to change your hard currency into rubles. Bring your passport, lots of patience, and your customs declaration form with you.

To get hard currency, try **Dialog Bank**, which offers a speedy money wire service from your bank in the West (for a small commission). Call them at 941-84-34, 941-83-49.

Or try **American Express** (21a Sadovo Kudrinskaya; tel. 254-43-05, 254-44-95, open 10 a.m. to 5 p.m., lunch break 12:30 to 1:30 and Novy Arbat 32, open daily 9 a.m. to 7 p.m., lunch break 1-2 p.m.). They give U.S. dollars in exchange for your American Express Traveler's Checks and a hefty fee, or will let you get money off your AmEx card — if you can write them a bank check.

If you plan to leave the country with the money, ask for a *spravka*.

Credit Cards. If you lose a card, call your bank in the States immediately and cancel it. Don't bother with the police. They won't know what to do. You can also call these numbers in Russia:

American Express: 245-25-50, 253-99-03, 254-17-95. (In St. Petersburg: 311-52-15.)

VISA: Call the Credobank credit card department at 131-92-92 (24 hours).

Intourcreditcard: 284-39-55 (closed weekends).

Often, you will be asked for your passport or picture ID when using your card—especially at hard-currency stores. At restaurants, don't write tips on your credit card—your waiter will never receive the money. Leave cash.

Russian Banks Authorized to Make Hard Currency Transactions

AKIB NTP Menatep,* Manezhnaya Pl. 7, Moscow; tel. 202-85-56

AvtoBank, Delegatskaya Ul. 11, Moscow; tel. 973-32-16

AvtoVAZBank, Komsomolskaya Ul. 97, Togliatti; tel. (8480) 24-65-35

Bazis Bank, Shosse Entuziastov 7, Moscow; tel. 362-69-68

Centrocredit, Pyatnitskaya Ul. 31, Moscow; tel. 231-75-81

Credit-Moscow, Tverskaya Ul. 7, Moscow; tel. 201-90-67

Credo-Bank, Kutuzovsky Prospekt, Moscow; tel. 249-77-82

DialogBank, Staropansky Per. 4, 103012 Moscowg; tel. 921-91-04, fax 923-65-56

ElexBank, Malyi Sukharevsky Pereulok 12, Bldg. 2, Moscow; tel. 208-67-03

Kuzbassotsbank, Kirovskaya Ul. 17, Kemerovo; tel. (3842) 26-57-45

Help Bank, Presnenskay Val 27, Moscow; tel. 166-80-19

Inkombank,* Nametkina Ul. 14/1, 117420 Moscow; tel. 332-06-99, fax 331-88-33

Innovations Bank, Chaikovsky Ul. 24, St. Petersburg; tel. (812) 234-26-89

International Economic Cooperation Bank,* Ul. Mashi Poryvaevoi, 107078 Moscow; tel. 975-38-61, 204-77-22, 29, fax 975-22-02

International Investment Bank, Ul. Mashi Poryvaevoi, 107078 Moscow; tel. 975-40-08, 204-73-11, fax 975-20-27

Moscow Business Bank,* Ul. Kuznetsky Most 15, Moscow; tel. 921-85-82, 924-02-37, fax 230-21-24

Moscow International Bank, Proyezd Khudozhestvennovo, Teatra 6, Moscow; tel. 292-07-09, 98-73, fax 975-22-14

Moscow Interregional Commercial Bank, Leningradsky Prospekt 9, Moscow; tel. 250-21-95

Mytischi Commercial Bank, Novomytischinsky Prospekt 30/1, Mytischi, Moscow Region; tel. 196-55-06

NGS Bank, Zhitnaya Ul. 14, Moscow; tel. 239-15-08

Petrovsky Bank, Ruzovskaya Ul. 8, St. Petersburg; tel. (812) 292-18-88

Priovneshtorgbank, Griboyedov Ul. 24/5, Ryazan; tel. (0912) 79-0561

Promstroibank,* Mikhailovskaya Ul. 4, St. Petersburg; tel. (812) 110-49-09

Resurs-Bank, Tretya Parkovaya Ul. 24, Moscow; tel. 306-78-55

Russian Federation Savings Bank, St. Petersburg Branch, Nevsky Prospekt 38, St. Petersburg

Russian National Commercial Bank, Myasnitskaya Ul. 26, Moscow; tel. 262-26-69

Sankt-Peterburg Bank, 70/72 Fontanka Embankment, St. Petersburg

Stolichny Bank, Pyatnitskaya Ul. 72, 113095 Moscow; tel. 233-58-92, fax 237-29-93

Tekhnobank, Bolshaya Gruzhinskaya Ul. 56, Moscow; tel. 254-79-35

Telebank, Znamenka Ul. 13, Bldg. 3, Moscow; tel. 291-87-06

TokoBank,* Sushchevskaya Ul., 8/12, 103030 Moscow; tel. 972-95-04, fax 200-32-96

UralVneshTorgBank, Generalskaya Ul. 7, Yekaterinburg; tel. (3432) 57-38-75

VneshEkonomBank-St. Petersburg,* Gorokhavaya Ul. 4, St. Petersburg

Yugmebelbank, Ul Kuznetsky Most 15, Prospekt Sholokhova 30, Rostov-on-Don; tel. (8632) 53-97-85

Russian State Banks

Central Bank of Russia, 117049, Zhitnaya Ul. 12; tel. 237-59-95

Bank of Foreign Economic Affairs of the USSR (Vnesheconombank SSSR), 107078, Novokirovsky Prospekt, 15/13; tel. 246-45-33, telex 411919 WTPRO SU

Bank of Foreign Trade of Russia (Vneshtorgbank RSFSR), 103031, Kuznetsky Most Ul., 16; tel. 928-71-16

Moskovsky Industrialny Bank, 109147, M. Kalitnikovskaya Ul. 7; tel. 270-51-02

Republican Bank of Russia, 103473, Semyonovskaya Ul. 40; tel. 281-03-49

U.S. Banks and Financial Firms in Russia

Batterymarch Financial Management (Joint Venture), Merzlyakovsky Pereulok No. 8, 121814 Moscow; tel. 290-29-52, 290-59-18, 203-33-96, fax 200-42-56, telex 411089 OMNIA. **Contacts:** Paul Rugo (Managing Director), Joel Barber (director), Richard Sobel (Director).

Bear Stearns & Co., tel. 936-29-24, fax 936-29-24. **Contact:** Mark Bond (Vice President).

DialogBank, Staropansky Pereulok 4, Moscow; tel. 921-91-04, fax 923-65-56, Radisson/Slavyanskaya Hotel, Ground Floor, Business Center; tel. 941-84-34, 941-84-24, fax 923-65-56. **Contacts:** Peter Derby (President), Alexander Goncharov (Assistant Vice President), Sanya Zezulin (Vice President/International Banking Division), Betsy Cohen (Vice President/Credit Card Services and Branch Manager). **In U.S.: Management Partnerships International (MPI)**, 440 S. LaSalle St., Suite 3300, Chicago, IL, 60605; tel. (312) 431-3550. *Note*: Handles corporate accounts and currency exchange. Offers VISA card.

Bank of America, 555 California St., San Francisco, CA 94104; tel. (415) 622-2073. **In Moscow:** 123610, Krasnopresnenskaya Nab. 12, Kv. 1605; tel. 253-70-54, 19-10, telex 413189 BOFA SU.

Chase Manhattan, One Chase Manhattan Plaza, 14th Floor, New York, NY 10081; tel. (212) 552-4676, Contact: Guy Buyske, VP. **In Moscow:** Krasnopresnenskaya Nab. 12, Office 1709, Moscow, Russia 123610; tel. 253-28-65, fax 230-21-74, telex 413912 CHASE SU.

*Russian banks in correspondent relationships with American banks. As follows: Inkombank (Citibank, Banker's Trust); Menatep (Citbank); Promstroibank (Citibank, Banker's Trust); Vnesheconombank (Citibank, Chase Manhattan, Marine Midland, Banker's Trust); International Economic Cooperation Bank (Chase Manhattan); MosBusiness Bank (Banker's Trust); Tokobank (Banker's Trust).

Newstar, Ulitsa Tverskaya 6, Suite 65; tel. 292-50-57, fax 292-50-57, telex 413205 USCO SU. **Contacts:** Richard Nicolson, Joseph Crowley, Leslie McQuaig, Dr. Vadim Levitan. **In U.S.:** 801 Pennsylvania Avenue, Suite 815, Washington, DC 20004; tel. (202) 508-3484, fax (202) 628-5986, telex 6732321. **Contact:** Arnold Sherman. *Note*: Merchant bank-business advisory firm.

Investment Services

Russian State Committee for Managing State Property, Moscow; tel. 291-47-65. Anatoly Chubays, Chairman. Disposes of all state property in Russia.

WorldTrade Executive, Inc., P.O. Box 761, Concord, MA 01742; fax (508) 287-0302. Extensive database on Russian firms available for privatization.

Balatep, Moscow; tel. 924-66-62, 923-81-51, fax 924-73-46. Offers co-financing of privatization projects in rubles.

Ecorambus, Moscow; tel. 212-56-79, 214-88-35, fax 213-26-29, 212-73-84. Specializes in scientific programs, experimental technologies, intellectual property.

Surgut Merchandise and Commodities Exchange, Moscow; tel. 312-34-00, 312-33-69, 311-64-42. Brokerage and privatization services in oil, gas, wood, fish.

First All-Siberian Investments Company, Novosibirsk; tel. (38232) 23-5932.

U.S. Law Firms in Russia

Adams & Reese, Lex International, Ulitsa Pushkinskaya 4/2, #1B, 103009, Moscow; tel. 925-84-30, fax 925-99-92.

Contact: Alexander Minakov. **In U.S.:** 430 One Shell Square, New Orleans, LA 70139; tel. (504) 581-3234, fax (504) 566-0210, telex 584426, **Contact:** Joseph C. Lemire (Partner).

Coudert Brothers, Coudert Brothers/IPATCO, Ulitsa Petrovka 15, Kv. 19-20; tel. 924-58-93, 923-93-30, fax 230-26-28, telex 413310, 413329, 413267 IPATC SU. **Contacts:** Mr. Zimmerman (President of IPATCO), Nancy Minneman, Richard Dean (Head of Representation, Wash. D.C.), A. James Redway (Resident Head of Office), S. Adam Deery, Marilyn McHugh, Jeremy Huck (Office Manager). **In U.S.:** 200 Park Avenue, New York, NY 10166; tel. (212) 880-4400, fax (212) 557-8137, 557-8136, telex 666764, **Contact:** Douglas R. Aden

Baker & McKenzie Bolshoi Gnezdnykovsky Pereulok 7, 103009 Moscow; tel. 200-61-67, 200-61-86, 200-49-06, fax 200-02-03, Telex: 413671. **Contacts:** Paul Melling (Head of Representation), Arthur George (Partner), Carol Patterson (Attorney), Mark Borghesani (Attorney), Kurt Montgomery (Office Manager), Diane Dowling, Irene Stevenson, Sarah Rhodes, Yuri Temochov. **In Kiev:** tel. 294-64-41. **Contact:** John Hewko (Attorney). **In U.S.:** 815 Connecticut Ave., NW, Washington, DC 20006-4078; tel. (202) 452-7012, fax (202) 452-7074, telex 89552, **Contact:** Eugene Theroux.

Chadbourne & Parke (Chadbourne, Hedman, Raabe & Advocates USSR—Finnish-Austrian-American JV), Maxim Gorky Nab. 38, 113035 Moscow; tel. 231-10-64, fax 233-52-98. **Contacts:** Robert Langer, Mark Hamlen (Administrative Director). **In U.S.:** 30 Rockefeller Plaza, New York, NY 10112; tel. (212) 408-5100, fax (212) 541-5406, telex 620520, **Contact:** Robert E. Langer. Clifford Chance—Yuzhinsky

Pereulok 15A, 103104 Moscow; tel. 973-24-15, fax 973-23-36. **Contacts:** William Knowles, Dr. Susanne Heger, David Scott, Marina Kasatkina, Maryann Gashi-Butler. **In U.S.:** (New York, NY); tel. (212) 750-1440.

Cole, Corette & Abrutyn, Ulitsa Usacheva 35, 119048 Moscow; tel. 245-50-42, 245-57-18, fax 245-57-18. **Contacts:** Jane V. Tarassova, Timothy Stubbs. **In U.S.:** 1110 Vermont Ave., NW, Washington, D.C. 20005; tel. (202) 872-1414, fax (202) 296-8238, (202) 872-1396, telex 64391, **Contact:** Edward H. Lieberman.

Hale and Dorr, Ulitsa Novoryazanskaya 36, 107066 Moscow; tel. 261-95-17, fax 923-65-56. **Contact:** John P. Hupp. **In U.S.:** 60 State St., Boston, MA 02109; tel. (617) 526-6235, fax (617) 526-5000, **Contact:** John Morton (Senior Partner).

Leboeuf, Lamb, Leiby & Macrae, c/o Okobank, Korovii Val 7, Entrance 1, Suite 13, 117049, Moscow; tel. 230-13-87, 230-16-55, fax 230-13-86 (manually activated), telex 413056 OKOMO SU, **Contacts:** James Mandel (lawyer), Rebecca Griffin (Insurance consultant), Lisa Wilson (paralegal). **In U.S.:** 520 Madison Avenue, New York, NY 10022; tel. (212) 715-8000, fax (212) 371-4840, telex 423416, **Contacts:** John I. Huhs, Eugene R. Sullivan, Jr.

Steptoe and Johnson, Maly Levshinsky 7, Kv. 3, 119034 Moscow; tel. 201-40-73, Satellite tel. 7-502-220-2220, fax 201-40-73, telex 413205 USCO SU, **Contacts:** Randy Bregman (lawyer), Scott Derby, Jean Platt. **In U.S.:** 1330 Connecticut Ave. NW, Washington, DC 20036; tel. (202) 429-3000, fax (202) 429-3000, telex 98-2503, **Contact:** Sarah Carey

White & Case, Ulitsa Tverskaya 7, Moscow; tel. 201-92-91, 201-92-92, 201-92-93, 201-92-94, fax 201-92-84. **Contacts:**

John Erickson, Alexander Papachristou, Timothy Power. **In U.S.:** 1155 Avenue of the Americas, New York, NY 10036; tel. (212) 819-8200, fax (212) 354-8113, telex 126201. **Contact:** Daniel J. Arbess

Shearman & Sterling, c/o JV MOST, Ulitsa Obrucheva 34/63, 117839, Moscow; tel. 333-90-70, fax 420-22-62. **In U.S.:** 599 Lexington Avenue, New York, NY; tel. (212) 848-4000, fax (212) 848-7179, telex 667290 WUI. **Contact:** Phillip Dundas. **In U.K.:** St. Helen's, 1 Undershaft, London, EC3A 8HX; tel. 44-71-283-9100, fax 44-71-626-1211. **Contact:** Steven M. Glick.

Vinson & Elkins, Ulitsa Vorovskovo 21, 121069 Moscow; tel. 291-34-29, 202-84-16, 202-68-74, fax 200-42-16, 202-68-74. **Contact:** Linda Sgoman (Permanent Representative), John Walter Van Schwartzenburg, Jay Cucelif, H. Don Teague. **In U.S.:** Houston, TX; tel. (713) 758-2222.

U.S. Accounting Firms in Russia

Arthur Andersen & Co., Ulitsa Novoriasankaya 40, 107060 Moscow; tel. 298-64-56, 298-64-57, fax 265-33-41, telex 911580 ARAND SU. **Contacts:** Hans Jochum Horn, Mikhail Kislyakov, Steven Willoughby, Valery Lapov, Sergei Bogdanov, Florence Bachelard, Bonnie-Jeanne Gerrety, Steven Sandweiss, Jim Marlatt, Lisa Gialidini. **In U.S.:** 33 West Monroe St., Chicago, IL 60603; (312) 580-0033.

Ernst & Young, Podsosensky Pereulok 20, 103062 Moscow; tel. 297-33-22, fax 227-09-93. **Contacts:** George Reese (227-19-59), Richard Lewis, Tim Bloomfield, Michael Motby, Stuart Thom, Jonathan Gilbanks. **In U.S.:** East European Division, 787 7th Ave., New York, NY 10019; tel. (212) 830-6000, fax (212) 977-9358, telex 7607796

Coopers and Lybrand, Ulitsa Tchepkina 6, Moscow. tel. 281-94-66, telex 413258 NWBMO SU. **Contacts:** Richard Robinson, John Pendlebury, Wayne Nash, Stanely Root, Andrey Balashov, Sergei Shibaev. **In U.S.:** 1251 Avenue of the Americas, New York, NY; tel. (212) 536-2000

Deloitte Touche (JV—DRT Inaudit), Vtoroi Samotyochny Pereulok, Dom 1/23, 103473; tel. 281-55-20, 281-50-73, 281-49-08, fax 971-64-19, **Contacts:** Partner in charge: William Potvin, Jim Driscoll, Mark Bond, William Touche, Olga Peterson, Julia Zagachin, Piers Hemy. **In U.S.:** World Trade Center, New York, NY; tel. (212) 669-5000

Price Waterhouse, Bolshoi Strochnovsky Pereulok 22/25; tel. 237-59-02, fax 230-29-36, telex 414724 BARD SU. **Contacts:** Sue Shale (Head of Representation), Byron Ratliff (Director, Petroleum Service), Kevin Crawford (CPA, Audit Manager), Allan Cooper (Director, Business Development), Mike Hackworth (Senior Manager, Corporate Finance), Barbara Duvoisin. **In U.S.:** Southward Towers, 32 London Bridge St., London SE1 9SY; tel. (1) 407-8989, fax (1) 378-0647, telex 884657/8, **Contact:** Bruce Edwards, Allan, Cooper, Bridget Gough (in Moscow)

U.S. Consulting Firms in Russia

Acquest, Biltmore Towers, 500 S. Grand Avenue, Suite 2050, Box No. 1, Los Angeles, CA 90017; tel. (213) 627-2424, fax (213) 627-6943, telex 49604804 ACQ LSA. **Contact:** Peter Guttridge

ASET Consultants, Inc., Ulitsa Vernadskovo, d. 33, kv. 153, 117331 Moscow, tel. 138-05-04, 201-50-21, fax 201-72-47, telex 412230 MPSM SU. **In U.S.:** 8350 Greensboro Dr., Suite 805, McLean, VA 22102; tel. (703) 790-1922, fax (703) 883-1305, telex TWX 510-660-8023. **Contact:** H. Randall Morgan.

Consultex/Consult America (Accredited), Ulitsa Usievicha, 8A, 125319 Moscow; tel. 155-75-71, fax 155-78-03, telex 413-205 USCO UR E-Mail/telex 612163 SMail. **Contacts:** Peter A Huchthausen, Andrew P. Sundberg, Alexander V. Kouznetsov.

Bain & Company (Joint Venture "BainLink"), Scherbakovskaya Ulitsa 40/42, 105187 Moscow; tel. 369-26-43, 369-59-48, fax 369-59-47. **Contacts:** James Allen (Consultancy Director), April Demuth (Consultant). **In U.S.:** tel. (617) 572-2000. *Note:* Bain-Link has a cooperative arrangement with OPIC (Overseas Investment Corp.) to offer new-to-market' consulting services to businesses entering the former Soviet states.

Davis, Graham & Stubbs, 370 17th St., Suite 4700, Denver, CO, 80202; tel. (303) 892-9400. **Contact:** Gary Hart.

Hale and Dorr (see "Law Firms")

McHugh & McCaffery Moscow, Staropansky 4, 107066 Moscow; tel. 924-96-55, 921-84-12, fax 265-57-14. **Contacts:** Robert W. Van Genderen (Director of Marketing).

Satra Corporation, 11/13 Tryokhprudny Per., 103001 Moscow; tel. 299-91-64, telex 413129 SATRA SU. **In U.S.:** 645 Madison Ave., New York, NY 10022; tel. (212) 355-3030, fax (212) 758-6366, telex 225747. **Contact:** Ara Oztemal (president).

Phargo Group (Canadian), 133 Young St., Toronto, Ontario M5H 1G4; tel. (416) 360-6003, fax (416) 360-7942.

Contact: Geoffrey Carr-Harris (president). In U.S.: 369 Wayside Rd., Portola Valley, CA 94028; tel. (415) 851-2102, fax (415) 851-2353.

Price Waterhouse (see "Accounting Firms")

D.N. Young & Associates, Inc., Hotel Mezhdunarodnovo II, 12 Krasnopresnenskaya Nab., Suite 1603, 123610, Moscow, Russia. tel. 253-16-03, fax 253-18-14. In U.S.: 731 Eighth St., SE, Washington, DC 20003; tel. (504) 644-8605, fax (504) 644-1663. Contact: David N. Young (president).

Vitas Corporation, 11/13 Tryokhprudny Per., Moscow; tel. 299-67-23, fax 200-02-50. Contact: Tom Laurita (Head of Representation). In U.S.: tel (212) 355-3030. 645 Madison Ave., Suite 1001, New York, NY 10012. Contact: Dr. Victor Golant, Corporate Vice President.

Vneshconsult (Russian firm), VDNKh, Pavillion 4, Moscow; tel. 181-42-94, fax 181-41-33, telex 411418

Franchising in Russia

Brownstein, Zeidman &Lore, 1401 New York Ave. NW, Washington, DC, 20005; tel. (202) 879-5730. Contact: Philip Zeidman.

International Franchise Association, 1350 New York Ave., Suite 900, Washington, DC, 20005; tel. (202) 628-8000. Contact: Robert Jones (Director of International Affairs).

U.S. Trading Companies in Russia

Argus Trading Ltd., Per. Sadovskikh 4, kv. 12, 103001 Moscow; tel. 209-70-71, 209-78-43, fax 200-02-07, telex 248209

ARGS UR. In U.S.: 6110 Executive Boulevard, Suite 502, Rockville, MD 20852; tel. (301) 984-4244, fax (301) 984-4247, telex 248209 ARGS UR. Contacts: Michael Rae, Boris Hadshi.

ASI, 730 Fifth Ave., 19th Fl., New York, NY 10019; tel. (212) 247-6400, fax (212) 977-8112. Contact: Len Blavatnik.

California Western Technology, Dimitrova 24, President Hotel, Moscow; tel. 239-39-76, fax 239-38-75, 230-22-16. Contacts: Andrei Lefebvre (President), Joseph Gerakos (Senior Vice President), John Lingle (Marketing Director), Marcus Montencourt (Commercial Director). Type of business: Trading and finance.

Cargill, Radisson/Slavyanskaya Hotel, Room 3006, Berezhkovskaya Nab. 2, 121059 Moscow; tel. 941-82-78, 941-83-73, 941-67-73 (mobile), fax 941-82-60, telex 612269 CARMS SU, Contacts: Juels Carlson (Vice President/Head of Representation), Tatyana Kabalkina (Executive Assistant). *Note*: Trades cotton, wheat, other agricultural products.

Chilewich Corporation, Kursovoi Pereulok 9, Apt. 2; tel. 202-19-04, 203-51-92, 202-17-40, fax 200-12-15, telex 413211 CHILW SU. Contact: Alexander Heydel (accredited representative), John Vinnik (accredited representative). Type of business: Trades in agricultural commodities and food products.

Diomides, Inc., Ulitsa Bryanskaya 12, Apt. 128, Moscow; tel. 240-64-30. Contact: Robert Stubblebine (Vice President).

Ello Industries, Inc., 255 Route 3 East, Suite 213, Secaucus, NJ, 07094; tel. (201) 865-2100, fax (201) 865-7996. Contacts: Mark Lysnyansky (President), Gary Kelly (General Counsel/Director of Business Development).

EXI International, Ltd., Ulitsa Schukinskaya, 12-1, 123182 Moscow; tel. 190-77-72, fax 943-00-26. **In U.S.:** 109 West 11th St., Suite 1100, Kansas City, MO 64105; fax (913) 649-8379, (816) 474-0619.

Gemini Management Group, Krylatskiye Holmy 1, 450, Moscow; tel. 415-94-19, fax 415-94-19, TOT-GEMINI, GEMINI-TOT Development Corp., **Contacts:** Edward Shevyrjov (Representative), Marshall D. Sokol (Managing Director). **In U.S.:** 6861 Elm Street, Suite 400, McLean, VA 22101; tel. (703) 821-1601, fax (703) 821-1605. Type of business: Trade and investment, business education and training programs, trade delegation management.

Polo International, Timura Frunze Sh. 18, Q. 15, 119021 Moscow; tel. 245-30-34, fax 310-70-60. **Contact:** Kevin Fortin.

Sibir, Inc. USA, Peking Hotel, Room 502, Moscow; tel. 209-09-02, telex 411661. **Contact:** Paul Grimsley (Moscow Director). **In U.S.:** 7929 Jones Branch Drive, Suite 320, Mclean, VA 22102; E. Paul Griffith (President).

The Upjohn Company, 2 Chistoprudny Bulvar, Apt. 45, 101000 Moscow; tel. 928-67-68, 924-60-34, 941-64-53 (mobile), fax 975-22-42. **Contacts:** Alexandre A. Boltenko (Senior Resident Representative), U.S. East European Development, Inc., 66 Leninsky Prospekt #30; tel. 137-00-03, fax 133-43-35. **In U.S.:** 7910 Ivanhoe Avenue #25, La Jolla, CA 92037; tel. (619) 453-51-58, fax (619) 297-53-39. **Contacts:** Sam Safaroff (President), Anne Rifat (Vice President, U.S. Operations), Tufan Safaroff (Manager).

Zig Zag Venture Group Ltd., International Trade Center, Krasnopresnenskaya Nab. 12, Office 504, 123610 Moscow; tel. 253-13-65, fax 253-93-83, telex 411636 AGENT SU. **Contact:** Michael Cliff (Chairman). **In U.S.:** 254 Fifth Avenue Penthouse, New York, N.Y. 10001; tel. (212) 725-6700, fax (212) 725-6915, telex 49602662. **Contact:** Victor Bondarenko (President).

Chambers of Commerce— By Republic

Armenia. Chamber of Commerce and Industry of the Republic of Armenia, 375033 Yerevan, Ul. Alevardyana 39; tel. 885-56-53-58, telex 243322. Contact: Ashot L. Sarkisyan (Chairman)

Azerbiajan. Chamber of Commerce and Industry of the Republic of Azerbaijan, 370601 Baku, Ul. Kommunisticheskaya 31/33; tel. 892-39-85-03, Contact: Kamran Asad Ogly Guseyon (Chairman).

Belarus. Chamber of Commerce and Industry of the Republic of Belarus, 220843 Minsk, vul. Ya. Kolasa 65; tel. 0172-66-04-60, Contact: Uladzimier K. Lesun (Chairman).

Estonia. Chamber of Commerce and Industry of the Republic of Estonia, Toom-Kooli 17, Tallinn 200106; tel. 0142-444-929, fax 0142-443-656, telex 173254, Contact: Peeter Tammoja (President).

Georgia. Chamber of Commerce and Industry of Georgia, 380079 Tbilisi, pr. I. Chavchavadze 11; tel. 8832-23-00-45, fax 8832-23-57-60, telex 212183, Contact: Guram D.Akhvlediani (Chairman).

Kazakhstan. Chamber of Commerce and Industry of Kazakhstan, 480091 Alma-Ata, pr. Kommunistichesky

93/95; tel. 3272-62-14-46, fax 3272-62-05-94, telex 25-12-28.

Kyrgyzstan. Chamber of Commerce and Industry of the Republic of Kyrgyzstan, 720300 Bishkek, UL. Kirova 205; tel. 3312-26-49-42, telex 251239, Contact: Karchinb Y. Ivanovich (Chairman).

Latvia. Latvian Chamber of Commerce, Bribas bul., Riga 226189; tel., 0132-228-036, fax 0132-332-276, telex 161111

Lithuania. Chamber of Commerce and Industry of the Republic of Lithuania, Algirdo 31, Vilnius 232600; tel. 0122-661-450, fax 0122-661-550, telex 261114, Contact: Jonas Povilaitis (Chairman)

Moldova. Chamber of Commerce and Industry of the Republic of Moldova, 277012 , Kishinev, ul. Komsomolskaya 28; tel. 0422-22-15-52, Contact: Vasily D. Gandrabura (Chairman).

Russia. Chamber of Commerce and Industry of the Russian Federation, 103684, Moscow, Ul. Ilyinka 6; tel. 923-43-23, fax 230-24-55, telex 411126.

Tajikistan. Chamber of Commerce and Industry, 734012 Dushanbe, ul. Mazayeva 21; tel. 3772-27-95-19, Contact: S.K. Sufievich (Chairman)

Turkmenistan. Chamber of Commerce and Industry, 744000 Ashkabad, ul. Lakhuti 17; tel. 3662-5-57-56, Contact: Lidia N. Osipova (Chairman)

Ukraine. Chamber of Commerce and Industry, 252055 Kiev, ul. Bolshaya Zhitomirskaya 33; tel. 044-212-29-11, fax 044-212-33-53, telex 131379, Contact: Aleksey P. Mikhailichenko (Chairman)

Uzbekistan. Chamber of Commerce and Industry, 700017 Tashkent, pr. Lenina 16a; tel. 3712-33-62-82, Contact: Delbart Yu. Mirsiaadova (Chairman).

Commodity and Stock Exchanges

Alisa Commodity Exchange, 117334, Leninsky Prospekt 45; tel. 137-65-14, 137-65-21, 137-00-06, fax 137-65-25.

Moscow Central Stock Exchange (MCSE), 103009, Ulitsa Granovskovo 5, Kv. 37; tel. 229-76-35.

Moscow International Stock Exchange, 125047, 1 Tverskaya-Yamskaya, Ul. 46, 251-03-92, 251-27-01.

Russian Commodities and Raw Materials Exchange (RCRME), 103070 Moscow, Ul. Myasnitskaya 26; tel. 262-80-80, fax 262-57-57.

St. Petersburg Stock Exchange, Ul. Skorokhodova 19; tel. 232-55-00, 232-18-86, fax 232-18-86.

Foreign Trade Organizations— By Republic

Armenia. Armentorg (Foreign Trade Organization), 375010 Yerevan, Pl.Respublika, Dom Pravitelstva, Contact: R.A. Sarkisyan (General Director).

Azerbaijan. Azerbintorg (Foreign Trade Organization), 370004 Baku, Ul. Nekrasova 7; tel. 892-93-71-69, telex 212183.

Belarus. Belarusintorg, 220084 Minsk, vul. Kollektornaya 10; tel. 0172-29-63-08, telex 220010, Contact: Viktor V. Andryushin (General Director).

Estonia. Estonian Small Business Association (EVEA), Kuhlbarsi 1, Tallinn 200104; tel. 0142-431-577, fax 0142-771-675, telex 173254.

Georgia. Gruzimpex (Foreign Trade Organization), 380018 Tbilisi, pr. Rustavelli 8; tel. 8832-93-71-69, telex 212183, Contact: D.A. Verulishvili (General Director).

Kazakhstan. Kazakhintorg (Foreign Trade Organization), 480091 Alma-Ata, ul. Gogolya 11; tel. 3272-32-83-81, telex 251238, Contact: A.M. Kyrbasov (General Director).

Latvia. Interlatvija (Foreign Trade Organization), Komunaru bul. 1, Riga 226010; tel. 0132-333-602, telex 161149.

Lithuania. Association of Lithuanian Businessmen, Pylimo 4, Vilnius 232001; tel. 0122-614-963, Contact: Arvydas Barauskas (President).

Moldova. Moldimpex (Foreign Trade Organization), 277018 Kishinev, Botanicheskaya ul. 15; tel. 0422-55-70-36, Contact: V.D. Volodin (General Director).

Russia. (see separate section entitled: "Authorized Russian Exporters")

Tajikistan. Tajikvneshtorg (Foreign Trade Organization), 734051 Dushanbe, pr. Lenina 42; tel. 3772-23-29-03, Contact: Yu. G. Gaytsgori (General Director).

Ukraine. Ukrimpex (Foreign Trade Organization), 252054 Kiev, ul. Vorovskovo 22; tel. 044-216-21-74, fax 044-216-29-96, telex 131384, Contact: Stanislav I. Sokolenko (General Director).

Uzbekistan. Uzbekintorg, 700115 Tashkent, pr. Uzbekistani 45; tel. 3712-45-73-13, Contact: Al Ikramov (General Director).

Authorized Russian Exporters

Export of energy and strategic raw materials is the hottest business in Russia today. Even if you are not now directly involved in such trade, the following Russian exporters can be valuable contacts for you. They have the money, the clout, and the contacts to get things done. And you never know when a trainload of nickel ore might come in handy to break the stalemate in some complex countertrade negotiation.

Commodity Groups

1. Crude oil, including gas condensate.

2. Petroleum products, oils, and other products of high temperature distillation.

3. Natural gas, oil gases, and gaseous hydrocarbons.

4. Electricity.

5. Pit coal, including charge, coke, and semi-coke.

6. Commercial timber, sawn timber, wood pulp, and cardboard.

7. Non-ferrous metals, raw materials for their production, rare and rare-earth metals, including secondaries, their alloys, powders, intermediate products, rolled stock of non-ferrous metals, scrap and waste metals.

8. Pig iron, rolled stock of ferrous metals including square billets, steel piping, ferrous alloys, scrap, and waste of ferrous metals.

4. Electricity.

5. Pit coal, including charge, coke, and semi-coke.

6. Commercial timber, sawn timber, wood pulp, and cardboard.

7. Non-ferrous metals, raw materials for their production, rare and rare-earth metals, including secondaries, their alloys, powders, intermediate products, rolled stock of non-ferrous metals, scrap and waste metals.

8. Pig iron, rolled stock of ferrous metals including square billets, steel piping, ferrous alloys, scrap, and waste of ferrous metals.

9. Mineral fertilizers, ammonia, methanol.

10. Inorganic acids.

11. Furs.

12. Grain.

13. Ground oil-cake.

Agrokhimexport, 2 Ulitsa Gretsevetskaya, Moscow 119900; tel. 203-50-33, fax 200-12-16, Telex 411678. (Licensed for commodity group 9 and 10 listed above)

Atomenergoexport, 18/1 Ovchinnikovskaya Naberezhnaya, Moscow 113324; tel. 231-80-14, 220-14-36, fax 230-21-81, telex 411397. (Licensed for commodity groups 2, 5, and 8)

Avtopromimport, Piatnitskaya St. 50/2, Moscow; tel. 231-81-26, fax 231-33-18, telex 411961. Specializes in automobiles.

Avtoeksport, 21 Ulitsa Malaya Pirogovskaya, Moscow 119435, tel. 203-06-62, fax 202-60-75, telex 112651. (Licensed for commodity groups and 2, and 7)

Dalintorg, 16a Nakhodkinsky Prospekt, Nakhodka, Maritime Kray, 692904; tel. 4-39-70, fax 4-45-17, 4-48-93, telex 213853 DITORG. (Licensed for commodity groups 5, 6, 8, and 9)

Exportles, 13/15 B. Kiselnyy Pereulok, Moscow 103755; tel. 921-28-09, fax 928-99-30. (Licensed for commodity group 6)

Exportkhleb, Smolenskaya-Sennaya Pl. 32/24, Moscow tel. 244-12-47, fax 253-90-69, telex 41145. Specializes in bread products.

Energomashexport, 25 Bezbozhnyy Pereulok, Block A, Moscow 129010; tel. 288-84-56, fax 288-79-90, telex 411965. (Licensed for commodity groups 5, 7, and 8)

Gazeksport, 20 Leninsky Prospekt, Moscow 117071; tel. 230-24-10, fax 230-24-40, telex 411987. (Licensed for commodity group 3)

Gammakhim, 32/34 Smolenskaya-Sennaya, Moscow 121200; tel. 244-21-81, fax 244-21-81, telex 411297. (Licensed for commodity groups 2, 9, and 10)

Interles, 3/2 Gogolevsky Bulvar, Moscow 121019; tel. 290-62-60, fax 230-25-48, telex 414763. (Licensed for commodity group: 6)

KAMAZ, 4 Ulitsa Akademika Rubanenko, Naberezhnaya Chelny, Tatarstan 423810; tel. 53-10-02, telex 412658. (Licensed for commodity groups 8, and 9)

Karelvneshtorg, Petrozavodsk 185028, Lenina St. 19; tel. code 8-81400, then 73-502. Specializes in Karelia region, bordering Finland.

Maritime Kray Union of Consumer Societies (Kraypotrebsoyuz), 3 Ulitsa Mordovtseva, Vladivostok 690000; tel. 22-53-70, fax 22-25-60, telex 213441. (Licensed for commodity groups: 8, and 9)

Mashinoimport, 32/34 Smolenskaya-Sennaya, Moscow 121200; tel. 244-33-09, fax 244-38-07, telex 411231 MIM. (Licensed to export commodity groups 2, 5, 6, 7, and 8)

Metallurgmash, 2 Slavyanskaya Ploshchad, Moscow 103718; tel. 924-80-92, fax 220-71-70. (Licensed for commodity group 8)

NAFTA-Moscow, 32/34 Smolenskaya-Sennaya, Moscow 121200; tel. 253-94-88, fax 244-22-91. (Licensed for commodity groups 1, and 2)

Neftekhimeksport, 31 Ulitsa Gilyarovskovo, Moscow 129832; tel. 284-86-14, fax 288-95-84, telex 411615 NEXT SU. (Licensed for commodity groups 2, 3, and 9)

Novoeksport, 33 Ulitsa Arkhitectora Vlasova, Moscow 117393; tel. 128-07-86, fax 128-16-12, telex 411204 NEKS. (Licensed to export commodity groups: 2, 5, 6, 7, 8, 9, and 11)

Oboroneksport, 18/1 Ovchinnikovskaya Naberezhnaya, Moscow 113324; tel. 220-17-48, fax 233-02-72, 233-18-13. Licensed to export commodity groups: 2, 6, 7, and 8)

Prodintorg, Smolenskaya-Sennaya Pl. 32/34, Moscow, tel. 244-20-60, fax 244-26-29, telex 411206. Specializes in meat and meat products, vegetable oils, milk and dairy products, sugar, and cigarettes).

Promsyryeimport, 13 Novinsky Bulvar, Moscow 121834; tel. 203-05-77, fax 203-61-77, telex 111824. (Licensed to export commodity group 8)

Raznoimport, 18/1 Ovchinnikovskaya Naberezhnaya, Moscow, 113324; tel. 220-12-16, fax 200-32-19, telex 112613. (Licensed to export commodity group 7)

Rostekhexport, 18/1 Ovchinnikovskaya Naberezhnaya, Moscow 113324; tel. 220-14-87, fax 233-07-86. (Licensed for commodity groups: 2, 5, 6, 7, 8, and 11)

Rosvneshtekhimpeks, 22 Olimpiysky Prospekt, Moscow 129110; tel. 151-26-01, fax 151-37-81, telex 411001. (Licensed for commodity groups 2)

Rosvneshtorg, 8/5 Ulitsa Barrikadnaya, Moscow 123242; tel. 254-80-50, fax 254-95-76, telex 411060 ROSST SU. (Licensed to export commodity groups 2, 5, 6, 7, 8, 9, and 10)

Selkhozpromexport, Ovchinnikovskaya Naberezhnaya, Moscow 113324; tel. 220-16-92, fax 921-93-64, telex 111446. (Licensed to export commodity groups 2, 5, 6, 8, and 9)

Soyuzpromexport, 32/34 Smolenskaya-Sennaya, Moscow 121200; tel. 244-47-68, fax 244-37-93, telex 411268. (Licensed to export commodity groups 5, 7, 8, 9, and 10)

Sovintorg, 4 Pereyaslavsky Pereulok, Moscow 129872; tel. 284-13-04, fax 975-23-07, telex 112419 ARTUS. (Licensed for commodity groups 2, 5, 6, 7, 8, and 9)

Sovkabel, 5 Shosse Entuziastov, Moscow 111112; tel. 362-96-45, fax 274-00-76, telex 411024 SCAB. (Licensed for commodity group 7)

Soyuzvneshles, 18 Ulitsa Lesteva, Apt. 11, Moscow 113162; tel. 954-20-58, fax 954-53-40. (Licensed for commodity group 6)

Spetsvneshtekhnika, 21 Gogolyevsky Bulvar, Moscow 119865; tel. 201-49-49, telex 411957, code OKPO 02839132. (Licensed for commodity groups 2, 6, 7, 8, 9, and 10)

Soyuzplodimport, 32/34 Smolenskaya-Sennaya, Moscow 121200; tel. 244-22-58, fax 244-36-36, telex 411262. (Licensed for commodity groups 12)

Soyuznefteexport, Smolenskaya-Sennaya Pl. 32/34, Moscow; tel. 253-94-88, fax 244-29-91, telex 411147. Specializes in oil and gas.

SovBunker, 14/9 Ulitsa Novoslobodskaya, Bldg. 7, Moscow 103030; tel. 258-91-22, fax 288-95-69, telex 411134. (Licensed for commodity group 2)

Sovtranzit, tel. 244-39-51, fax 230-28-50, telex 411266 Specializes in transport and shipping.

Tekhnoeksport, 18/1 Ovchinnikovskaya Naberezhnaya, Moscow 113324; tel. 220-17-82, fax 230-20-80, telex 111200 YuT. (Licensed to export commodity groups: 2, 5, 6, 7, 8, 9, and 10)

Tekhnopromimport, 18/1 Ovchinnikovskaya Naberezhnaya, Moscow, 113324; tel. 220-12-18, fax 230-21-11. (Licensed to export commodity groups 5, 6, 7, and 8)

Tekhnointorg, 64 Ulitsa Pyatnitskaya, Moscow 113836; tel. 231-26-22, fax 230-26-42, telex 411200. (Licensed to export commodity groups 6, 7, 8, and 9)

Tekhmashimport, 19 Trubinkovskiy Pereulok, Moscow 121819; tel. 202-48-00, fax 291-58-08, telex 411194, 411113. (Licensed to export commodity groups 7, 8, 9, and 10)

Tekhnopromeksport, 18/1 Ovchinnikovskaya Naberezhnaya, Moscow, 113324; tel. 233-05-28, fax 233-33-73, telex 411158. (Licensed to export commodity groups 2, 4, 5, 6, 7, and 8)

Tyazhpromexport, 18/1 Ovchinnikovskaya Naberezhnaya, Moscow 113324; tel. 220-16-10, fax 230-22-03. (Licensed for commodity groups 2, 5, 6, 7, and 8)

Tsvetmetexport, 25/31 Serpukhovskoy Val, Moscow 113191; tel. 954-36-88, fax 954-38-93, telex 412238 TSVET SU. (Licensed for commodity groups 7, 8, 9, and 10)

Uralvneshtorg, 1 Oktyabrskaya Ploshchad, Yekaterinburg, 620031; tel. 51-75-53, fax (3432) 58-99-56. Specializes in the Ural region.

Vneshintorg, 5 Ulitsa Marksistskaya, Moscow 109147; tel. 271-24-44, fax 274-01-02, telex 411250. (Licensed for commodity groups 2, 5, 6, 8, 9, and 10)

Vneshstroyimport, 6 Tverskoy Bulvar, Moscow 103009; tel. 290-03-76, fax 973-21-48, telex 411250 SVSI. (Licensed for commodity groups 2, 5, 6, 7, 8, 9, and 10)

Vneshles, 10 Ulitsa Ostozhenka, Moscow 119034; tel. 201-75-80, fax 928-43-96, telex 111478 TULLVneshles. (Licensed for commodity group 6)

Vneshpromtekhobmen, 9 Vasnetsova Pereulok, Moscow 129090; tel. 284-72-41, fax 284-73-95. (Licensed for commodity groups 2, 5, 6, 7, 8, and 9)

Vneshposyltorg, Marxistskaya St. 5, Moscow; tel. 271-05-05/10-20, fax 274-01-02, telex 411250 Specializes in package deliveries into/out of Russia.

Vostokintorg, First Krasnogvardeisky Proezd, Exhibition Complex EXPO-CENTR; tel. 205-60-55, fax 253-92-75, telex 411123. Specializes in machinery, commodities and finished products, including textiles, construction materials and foods from Central Asia.

Zarubezhtsvetmet, 19 Ulitsa Novy Arbat, Moscow 121911; tel. 203-86-65, fax 203-41-01, telex 412314 CARAT SU. (Licensed for commodity groups and 7, and 8)

Main Administration for Cooperation and Cooperatives of the Russian Federation Ministry for Foreign Economic Relations, 18/1 Ovchinnikovskaya Naberezhnaya, Moscow 113324; tel. 220-17-29, fax 233-12-49. (Licensed for commodity groups 2, 5, 6, 7, 8, 9, and 10)

Yekaterinburg Commercial Society, 41 Prospekt Lenina, Yekaterinburg; tel. 55-00-44, fax 55-69-12. (Licensed for commodity groups 6, 7, and 8)

Appendix C

Resources

Publications

Russia Business Survival Guide (Book)

Edited by Paul E. Richardson
Russian Information Services
Montpelier, VT (1992)

No business traveler in Russia should be without this indispensable handbook. Packed to the hilt with practical, easy-to-reference travel and business information, it provides detailed ratings of Russian hotels, information on local transportation, and a colorful, custom-created Moscow street map. It tells you how to get a visa, how to change currency, reviews customs regulations and other business legislation, provides tips on Russian business etiquette, and more. The yellow and white pages at the back contain over 4000 listings of Moscow businesses and state organizations, including names, addresses, phone, fax, and telex. *This feature alone is worth the price!* Also available from Russian Information Services is *Where in St. Petersburg*, containing yellow and white-page phone directories and other information for that important city.

Russia Business Survival Guide: $24.50

Where in St. Petersburg: $13.50

($3.50 for shipping and handling, and $1 for each additional item)

Order by phone: 1 (800) 639-4301 or (802) 223-4955

Order by fax: (802) 223-6105

Order by mail:
Russian Information Services
89 Main St. Suite 2
Montpelier, VT 05602

Yellow Pages Moscow (Book)

Edition 1992–1993

Commissioned by Moscow City Telephone Network

Published and Distributed by Claudius Verlag Hannover

With 421 info-packed pages, *Yellow Pages Moscow* boasts more than 27,000 listings, including phone, fax, and addresses for commercial, industrial, and government enterprises, including foreign companies and joint ventures! This is the *only official Moscow yellow-page directory* commissioned by the Moscow City Telephone Network in an *exclusive agreement* with the German publisher Claudius Verlag Hannover. Of course, nothing in Russia is perfect. Many listings found in the *Russia Business Survival Guide* (the second most complete Moscow phone directory) are not found in *Yellow Pages Moscow*, and many other important businesses cannot be found in *either* directory. *Yellow Pages Moscow* isn't complete, but it's the best available at this time.

Yellow Pages Moscow: $45

Order by phone: (800)4-MARVOL or (800) 462-7865

(310) 553-6100

Order by fax: (310) 553-9340

Order by mail:
  Marvol USA
  1925 Century Park East
  Tenth Floor
  Los Angeles, CA 90067

Buying a Business in Russia:
A Handbook for Westerners Interested in the Russian Privatization Process (Book)

By Youry Petchenkine, Ph.D.
D.N. Young & Associates, Inc.
Washington, DC (1993)

An incredibly detailed and authoritative guidebook on how to take a Russian company private. Tells you how to choose a likely takeover target, evaluate its assets, navigate the bureaucracy, and more. Thorough updates on recent legislation. Lists over 2000 Russian enterprises approved for privatization.

Buying a Business in Russia: $189 (AmEx accepted)

Order by phone: 1 (800) USA-4842

Order by mail: D.N. Young & Associates
  731 8th Street, S.E.
  Washington, DC 20003

Who's Who in Russia? (Software)

DOS Version 1.1

D.N. Young & Associates
Washington, DC (1993)

Find potential partners and business opportunities by searching this PC database containing over 25,000 state and private enterprises, joint ventures, and key Russian decision makers. Performs 1561 industry-specific searches, including foreign joint ventures, Russian banks, commodity exchanges, brokers, insurance agencies, and more.

Who's Who is Russia? $499 (AmEx accepted)

$69 for quarterly updates

Order by phone: 1-800-USA-4842

Order by mail:
  D.N. Young & Associates
  731 8th Street, S.E.
  Washington, DC 20003

Soviet Business Law, Vols. I-II:
Institutions, Principles, and Processes (Book)

By Christopher Osakwe
Butterworth Legal Publishers
Salem, NH (1992)

Just how *do* you go about terminating a Russian employee? What maternity rights does a Russian woman have at her workplace? And how do you go about suing that supplier who stiffed you? You'll find all the answers here. Professor Osakwe has written the book on Soviet business law. This monumental, two-volume work covers everything from contract law and settlement of business disputes to banking and tax statutes. Comes in looseleaf format, with periodic updates provided.

Order by phone: (603) 898-9664

Order by mail:
  Butterworth Legal Publishers

90 Stiles Road
Salem, NH 03079

East-West Executive Guide: A Monthly Legal and Strategic Guide Covering East-Central Europe, Russia, and the Commonwealth Republics (Newsletter)

Senior Editors: Alexander Marquardt, Esq., Rogers & Wells, & John H. Morton, Esq., Hale and Dorr

Co-Publishers: Gary A. Brown, Esq. & John F. Dunlop

Probably the most authoritative monthly newsletter on the subject of East-West commerce. Each issue is crammed with detailed information from the top experts in the field, with an emphasis on the practical and the "how-to." Readers will find latebreaking reports on new privatization programs, changes in banking regulations, export financing opportunities, foreign investment laws, Russian companies up for auction, and more—well in advance of the crowd. A subscription to *East-West Executive Guide* will make you an instant insider.

East-West Executive Guide: $576 per year. Payable by check or money order, in U.S. dollars only.

Order by phone: (508) 287-0301

Order by fax: (508)287-0302

Order by mail:
WorldTrade Executive, Inc.
P.O. Box 761
Concord, MA 01742

Russian Business Reports (Newsletter)

Published by Russian Information Services, Montpelier, VT
Faxed to your office every week, direct from Moscow, this newsletter gives you the lowdown on political and economic developments, sometimes *months* before *The Wall Street Journal* gets wind of them.

Russian Business Reports: $495 per year.

Order by phone: 1 (800) 639-4301 or (802) 223-4955

Order by fax: (802) 223-6105

Order by mail:
Russian Information Services
City Center
89 Main St., Suite 2
Montpelier, VT 05602

Interflo: Foreign Trade & Investment News of the Former Soviet Republics (Periodical)

No human being can possibly keep up with the ocean of raw business data pouring out of the former Soviet states every month. Let Interflo do the job for you. Each month, it gives a comprehensive summary of business news from the CIS, published in both Western and Russian newspapers, magazines and television news reports. Articles are boiled down to convenient, one-to- five-line abstracts, for easy scanning. For a small fee, Interflo will mail you the full text of individual articles. Also includes important government proclamations and government-issued economic data, as it comes out.

Interflo: $142 per year.

Order by phone: (201)763-9493

Order by mail: Paul Surovell/Publisher
Interflo
P.O. Box 42
Maplewood, NJ 07040

PlanEcon Report (Periodical) Next to the CIA, no one has more inside dope on economic develoopments in the CIS and Eastern Europe than PlanEcon. Their Report comes out 25 to 30 times per year.

PlanEcon Report: $1400 for one year.

Order by phone: (202) 898-0471, fax (202) 898-0445.

Order by mail:
 111 4th St. NW, Suite 801
 Washington, DC 20005-5603

BISNIS: Business Information Service for the Newly Independent States (BISNIS), U.S. Dept. of Commerce. The government is on your side! BISNIS is a one-stop shopping' data service provided free of charge by the U.S. Commerce Department for U.S. companies doing business in the former Soviet states. When you call the BISNIS line, specialists will answer your questions on trade and investment in the CIS. They will send you, free of charge, incredibly detailed, up-to-the-minute marketing reports on specific industries and regions of the CIS, leads on trade opportunities and partners, new legislation, etc. Ask them about other BISNIS services. Call (202) 482-4655 or fax (202) 482-2293

Mail:
 BISNIS
 Room H-7413
 U.S. Department of Commerce
 14th St. and Constitution Ave., NW
 Washington, DC, 20230

Background Reading

Red Tape: Adventure Capitalism in the New Russia

By Bill Thomas and Charles Sutherland
Dutton/Penguin Books
New York, NY (1992)

A lighthearted travelogue of the business scene in Russia.

Bear-Hunting With the Politburo: A Gritty First-Hand Account of Russia's Young Entrepreneurs—And Why Soviet-Style Capitalism Can't Work

By A. Craig Copetas
Simon & Schuster
New York, NY (1991)

A horrific compendium of everything bad about Russia's new entrepreneurs. Contains some useful historical background, but doesn't offer much hope, inspiration, or empathy.

Cutting the Red Tape: How Western Companies Can Profit in the New Russia

By Mark Tourevski and Eileen Morgan
The Free Press/A Division of
 Macmillan, Inc.
New York, NY (1993)

A basic primer for doing business in Russia. Includes extensive lists of important industrial and commercial organizations in various republics, with names, addresses and phone numbers. Also offers negotiating tips, legal insights, advice on choosing a Russian partner, and more. Very informative, if a little dry.

Rubles and Dollars: Strategies for Doing Business in the Soviet Union

Edited by James L. Hecht
Harper Business/A Division of
 HarperCollins
New York, NY (1991)

In-depth discussion of the Soviet business scene, circa 1989 to 1990. A lot has changed since then, but the essays in this book still provide a wealth of useful background on the country and its economy. Includes chapters on industrial management, investment in the Soviet Far East, financing joint ventures, Russian culture, and more. Out of print, but available through libraries.

Notes

Chapter 1

Onassis quote. Wynn Davis, *The Best of Success: A Treasury of Ideas*, Great Quotations Publishing Company, Lombard, IL, 1988, page 262. "... $75.5 million, according to the U.S. Commerce Department." "Best Prospects for Trade and Investment: 1992," page 2, U.S. and Foreign Commercial Service, Moscow. (202) 482-4655. "... **Russia's GNP declined 20-25 percent in 1992?**" Russia Battles Inflation with Financial Controls, NYT, 1/21/93, page A7, "Russia's Days of Shock Therapy Are Over" NYT 12/16/92, page A10. "... **5 percent of total production now comes from the private sector.**" RusDataDialine—BizEkon News, 4/2/92 (from BIZNES KHRONIKA, pages 1, 3). "... **substantial debts in Latin America.**" "Ruble Convertibility, Fighting Corruption, Privatization—Marshall Goldman Reports on Progress," *East/West Executive Guide*, 9/92, Vol. 2, No. 9, page 30. "... **a phenomenal 9100.**" UN Economic Commission for Europe (UNECE) Secretariat, Geneva, Switzerland. "**Graham Allison and Grigory Yavlinsky quote.** Graham Allison and Grigory Yavlinsky, *Window of Opportunity: The Grand Bargain for Democracy in the Soviet Union*, Random House, New York, 1991, page 38.

Chapter 2

"... **to leave the party.**" John Toland, *Adolf Hitler*, Random House, New York, page 922. "... **even *getting* rice.**" Akio Morita, *Made in Japan*, Penguin Books, New York, 1988, pages 2, 53. "**Japanese exports became world-competitive in many categories within ten years.**" Rafael Aguayo, *Dr. Deming: The American Who Taught the Japanese About Quality*, Simon & Schuster, New York, 1991, page 6. "**The Russians were 'dead!'**" Alan Bullock, *Hitler: A Study in Tyranny*, HarperCollins, New York, 1991, page 393. "... **never gave in till the last extremity.**" Benson Bobrick, *Fearful Majesty: The Life and Reign of Ivan the Terrible*, Paragon House, New York, 1987, page 108. "... **world price for aluminum has been cut in half.**" "The Coming Commodities Glut," *East-West Executive Guide*, 7/92, Vol. 2, No. 7, page 25. "... **'dumping,' on the part of Russia and other CIS states.**" "Raw Materials: Too Cheap and Too Valuable," *Delovie Lyudi*, 11/92, No. 28. "... **slashing his prices below market rate.**" Burton W. Folsom, Jr., *Entrepeneurs vs. the State*, Young America's Foundation, Reston, VA, 1987, page 92. "... **state-of-the-art centrifugal methods.**" Op.cit. "... **upped its harvest by 50 percent.**" Bill Thomas and Charles Sutherland, *Red Tape: Adventure Capitalism in the New Russia*, Penguin Books, New York, 1992, page 184. "... **and its billions in outstanding farm** loans." James Dale Davidson & Sir William Rees-Mogg, *Blood in the Streets,* Simon & Schuster, New York, 1987, pages 174-175, 179-180. ". . . 'best fighter aircraft in the Luftwaffe.'" *Interflow: A Soviet Trade News Monitor,* 5/92, page 12 (from Frankfurter Allgemeine, 4/16). ". . . ruthlessly reject any item which fell below quality standards."** Hedrick Smith, *The Russians,* Random House, New York, 1976, page 312. ". . . strident in their demands for government protection."** *Interflo: A Soviet Trade News Monitor,* 4/92, page 18 (from *The Washington Post,* 3/20/92)

Chapter 3

". . . something *Time* called a 'creeping coup'"** "Counterreformation," *Time,* 9/28/92, pages 52-54. ". . . live like pigs."** Michael Mandelbaum, "Coup de Grace: The End of the Soviet Union," *Foreign Affairs,* 1991/92, Vol. 71, No. 1, pages 181-182. **Kissinger quote.** Henry Kissinger, "Clinton and the World," *Newsweek,* 2/1/93, page 46. ". . . confiscated Anaconda Copper."** "Chile's Economy Roars as Exports Take Off in Post-Pinochet Era," *The Wall Street Journal,* 1/25/93, pages A1, A8. ". . . returned confiscated companies to their owners and lowered trade barriers."** *Ibid.* ". . . the fastest-growing in Latin America."** *Ibid.* ". . . Red China and Singapore as 'models' for the developing world."** "Is Singapore a Model for the West?" *Time,* 1/18/93, pages 36-37. "Why Global Investors Bet on Autocrats, Not Democrats," *The Wall Street Journal,* 1/12/93, page C1, C11. **"Before Yanaev could answer, the room erupted into laughter."** Michael Mandelbaum, "Coup de Grace: The End of the Soviet Union," *Foreign Affairs,* 1991/92, Vol. 71, No. 1, page 166. ". . . they also seem to harbor surprisingly little fear."** *Ibid.* **"There was no general strike."** *Ibid.,* page 182, **"His picture has adorned the cover of *Newsweek."*** "Risky Business: Can Capitalism Take Root in the Soviet Union?" *Newsweek* (International Edition), 7/16/90, No. 29. ". . . auctioned off a dozen apartments while tanks patrolled the streets outside."** "The Next Revolution: A Gold Rush on Apartments," *The New York Times,* 10/15/91." ". . . we understood best what was at stake."** *Ibid.* ". . . 4,273 PCs for every million people."** Zbigniew Brzezinski, *The Grand Failure: The Birth and Death of Communism in the Twentieth Century,* Macmillan, New York, 1990, page 36. ". . . bioengineering firms, architectural design houses, and steel mills."** James Dale Davidson & Sir William Rees-Mogg, *Blood in the Streets: Investment Profits in a World Gone Mad,* Simon & Schuster, New York, 1987, pages 143-153. **"Average firm size shrank dramatically during the '80s."** *Ibid.* ". . . *two-thirds* of those fast-growing new companies had fewer than 19 employees."** Wilson Harrell, "The Entrepreneurial Revolution—Its Impact on the Russian Economy," lecture given at Businesship Symposium, Moscow, October 29, 1990. ". . . lagging behind Taiwan, South Korea, Hong Kong and Switzerland."** Zbigniew Brzezinski, *The Grand Failure: The Birth and Death of Communism in the Twentieth Century,* Macmillan, New York, 1990, page 37." ". . . he first needed *glasnost.*"** Paul Zane Pilzer, *Unlimited Wealth: The Theory and Practice of Economic Alchemy,* Crown Publishers, New York, 1990, pages 19-20.

Chapter 4

Michael Adams quote. *Interflo: A Soviet Trade News Monitor,* 3/92, Vol. 11, No. 5, page 20. ". . . which enriched the British nation for many years."** Benson

Bobrick, *Fearful Majesty: The Life and Reign of Ivan the Terrible,* Paragon House, New York, 1987, page 148-149. ". . . so people could drum together as well as observe." Adam Hochschild, "Slow-Scan to Moscow," *Mother Jones,* 6/86, Vol XI, No. IV, page 28. "And his intelligence background gave him a chilling insight . . . " "S.F. Moscow Teleport—Electronic Detente," *Los Angeles Times,* 12/9/87. "Ah, a Californian!" *Ibid.* "What should you do if you see a snake in the road?" Eric Li, "Walk on the Wild Side: What I Learned from H. Ross Perot," *Success,* Vol. 38, No. 2, page 38. ". . . but decided that would ruin his Macintosh." "Macintosh Links Yanks with U.S.S.R.," *San Francisco Examiner,* 11/9/85. "The revellers sipped wine, nibbled hors d'oeuvres and talked of peace." Adam Hochschild, "Slow-Scan to Moscow," *Mother Jones,* 6/86, Vol. XI, No. IV, page 38. ". . . to plan emergency medical relief for Chernobyl victims in 1986." *Ibid.* "So if you copy everybody else on Wall Street, you're doomed to do poorly." "Securities Fund Shuns Wall Street's Fashions, Prospers in Hard Years," *The Wall Street Journal,* 5/28/75, pages 1, 23. ". . . the same weapons which crushed Saddam Hussein 15 years later." *Ibid.*

Chapter 6

". . . which should give some idea of the degree of confidence foreigners felt in Russia's future, back then." Judy Shelton, *The Coming Soviet Crash: Gorbachev's Desperate Pursuit of Credit in Western Financial Markets,* Macmillan, New York, 1989, page 162. James Dale Davidson & Sir William Rees-Mogg, *Blood in the Streets: Investment Profits in a World Gone Mad,* Simon & Schuster, New York, 1987, page 155. ". . . an immediate boycott against the renegrade state." *Op. cit.,* page 164, 166-169. "And everyone forgot there had ever been such a thing as Russian stocks and bonds." *op. cit.* ". . . a $500 million bond offering in the West." "Capitalist Tool," *Newsweek,* 6/1/92, page 4. ". . . the private plots are *40 times* more productive than state land." Hedrick Smith, *The Russians,* Random House, New York, 1976, page 266. ". . . it would escalate Russia's GNP to a staggering $26.8 *trillion.*" "Aggregate GNP of the Former Soviet Union, 1985-1996," PlanEcon, Inc., Washington, D.C. ". . . millions of dollars worth of Tsarist bonds in 1917?" Armand Hammer with Neil Lyndon, *Hammer,* Putnam, New York, 1988, pages 200-201. "Within three years, Hammer's profits soared into the millions." *Ibid.* ". . . the Asian Stock Exchange and the St. Petersburg Stock Exchange." *Delovie Lyudi,* 12/92, No. 29, page 26. ". . . and sell it out the back door to commodity traders." "The New Russian Revolution: The Transition to Markets in Russian and the Other Commonwealth States," Central Intelligence Agency, 6/8/92, page 3. ". . . similar computerized exchanges springing up across the CIS." *Interflow: A Soviet Trade News Monitor,* 7/92, Vol. 11, No. 9, page 34, (from *Forbes,* 6/8/92) ". . . according to the Russian Federation State Statistical Committee." *Delovie Lyudi,* 5/92, No. 23, page 29. ". . . formalized trade in vouchers has reached 3 million rubles per day and is rising fast." Youry Petchenkine, *Buying a Business in Russia,* D.N. Young & Associates, Inc., Washington, D.C., page 94-95. "Grain exports reached number one in the world." James Dale Davidson & Sir William Rees-Mogg, *Blood in the Streets: Investment Profits in a World Gone Mad,* Simon & Schuster, New York, 1987, page 154. ". . . some 20 percent of all vouchers sold to Czech citizens." "A Capitalist Free-for- All in Czechoslovakia," *The New York Times,* 4/12/92, page F10. "This database will be distributed via the Russian trade missions throughout the

· **world."** *Interflo: A Soviet Trade News Monitor,* 9/92, Vol. II, No. 11, page 32 (from Russian Television Network, 8/21/92).

Chapter 7

". . . while White Castle trailed behind at 167 stores." Franchising Goes Global," *World Link,* Jan./Feb. 1991, page 102. **"But over 95 percent of new franchises are still up and running after five years."** Michael E. Gerber, *The E-Myth: Why Most Businesses Don't Work and What To Do About It,* Harper & Row, New York, 1986, page 54. **"And the number grows every year."** "Franchise Fact Sheet," International Franchise Association, Washington, D.C. **". . . Subway Sandwiches and Salads will soon join the feeding frenzy."** "Fast Food Faces Slow Growth in CIS," *We,* 4/92, page 8. **"Many of them are ready to go into business, but not ready for full independence."** "McGoulash To Go: Franchising in Eastern Europe," *The Economist,* 4/6/91. **"Most U.S. franchisors would keep over from shock if a single advertisement generated so many attractive offers in the States."** *Ibid.* **". . . or they could be privatized by selling the individual units as franchises within a network."** Philip Zeidman, "Going Private Through Franchising," *World Link,* Jan./Feb. 1992, page 12-13. **"The scope of what has to be accomplished in the former Soviet republics makes speed an imperative."** "Philip Zeidman, "Franchising in the New Markets of Eastern Europe," *Eastern Europe Reporter,* 12/9/91, page 192.

Chapter 8

(P.100) "All the talk of a separate Ukranian people. . . is a recently invented falsehood." Alexander Solzhenitsyn, *Rebuilding Russia,* Farrar, Strauss and Giroux, New York, 1991, page 14. **(P. 118) ". . . there are 87 Alaskan-Siberian joint ventures. . . "** *Interflow* 6/92, Vol. 11, No. 8, page 15 (from *Christian Science Monitor,* 5/11/92). **(P. 119) "Such an economic policy. . . would assure collapse of the CIS."** *Plan Econ Report,* 3/27/92, Vol. VIII, Nos. 11-13, page 18. **Republic prognoses in general.** *Ibid.* **(P.130) ". . . poor mother embracing destitute daughter. . . "** *Ibid.,* page 38. **P. 132) ". . . 184 went to Armenia."** Bill Thomas and Charles Sutherland, *Red Tape,* Penguin Books, New York, 1992, pages 174, 179. **P. 135)** **"providing warm climate. . . and other entertainment"** *Op. cit.,* page 27.

Chapter 9

". . . U.S. West didn't, and is about to have its lunch eaten by tiny Plexsys Corporation." "It's Who You Know," *Forbes,* 7/6/92, page 46. **"Higher frequencies were reserved for military and civil aviation, said the Ministry."** *Ibid.* **"Vimpel tapped a few friendly shoulders at the Defense Ministry and gained special clearance for the restricted frequency."** *Ibid.* **". . . coming in the midst of Gorbachev's 1990 campaign for the presidency of the Soviet Union."** "Have I Got a Used Tank for You," *Business Week,* 3/12/90, page 108. **". . . coming in the midst of Gorbachev's 1990 campaign for the presidency of the Soviet Union."** "Soviet Prime Minister Angrily Answers Accuser: Ryzhkov in Tank-Sale Scheme," *The Washington Post,* 3/15/90, page A29.

Chapter 10

". . . employers were beginning to give them preference over the homegrown variety." "Lured by Zlotys, Ivan Plays the Model Migrant Worker," *The New*

York Times, 10/6/91, Section 1, Part 1, Page 1, Column 4. **"As far as alcohol, well, he didn't drink."** *Ibid.* **". . . 'my hero for the 20th century.'"** (MS page 224) "Little-Known Firm Has Become the Envy of Options Industry," *The Wall Street Journal,* 2/8/88, pages 1, 14. **". . . the young Bible student cum philosopher found his true calling—options and futures trading."** *Ibid.* **". . . that was really a door laid across two boxes."** *Ibid.* **". . . it quickly made him one of the world's richest men."** *Ibid.* **". . .** *guaranteed* **by the laws of mathematics."** *Ibid.* **". . . for up to 40 percent of total trading volume in global options markets."** *Ibid.* **". . . a rigorous enough test in a profession as money-mad as commodities trading."** *Ibid.* **"Ritchie kept five chefs on staff so employees could relax together over free meals."** *Ibid.* **". . . that there was no point in trying to get away from it."** Martin E.P. Seligman, *Learned Optimism,* Alfred A. Knopf, New York, 1991, pages 19-23.

Chapter 12

P. 190) ". . . rumored to be acting as proxies for foreign financiers." "The Buying of Hard Currency Accounts at Vnescheconombank," RusDataDialine, 5/28/92 (from *Nezavisimaya Gazeta,* page 2). **(P. 190) ". . . will start unfreezing hard-currency funds in July, 1993."** "Russian Bank to Thaw Cash," *The Wall Street Journal,* 12/21/92. **(P. 190-191) ". . . from 630 billion rubles. . . to 1.6 billion rubles five months later. . ."** *Interflo: A Soviet Trade News Monitor,* 8/92, (from *The Economist,* 7/18/92).

Chapter 13

(P. 200) "Their contempt for their own country proved more powerful than their physical senses." Mark Tourevski and Eileen Morgan, *Cutting the Red Tape: How Western Companies Can Profit in the New Russia,* Macmillan, New York, 1993, page 131. **P. 201) ". . . but humiliate ourselves before them, as Jacob did before Esau."** Benson Bobrick, *Fearful Majesty: The Life and Reign of Ivan the Terrible,* Paragon House, New York, 1987, pages 110-111. **(P. 202) ". . . a heavily guarded wing where women were concealed from the world."** *Ibid.,* pages 52-53. **(BP. 205)** "'It is not april Fool's day,' sniffed one indignant TASS official." "Elvis Spotted in Estonia!" *Time,* 10/23/89, page 52. **(P. 207) "Two Romes have fallen, but the third stands and a fourth there will not be."** *op. cit.,* page 76. **(P. 216) "Off went the rocket, climbing victoriously into the sky. Improvisation had won the day."** Esther Dyson, "High Risks, Distant Payoffs," *Forbes,* 12/11/89. **(P. 217) "The German Mark III was better equipped with radios, was more comfortable, and had more sophisticated engineering, yet the Russians came out ahead on essentials."** John W. Kiser III, *Communist Entrepreneurs: Unknown Innovators in the Global Economy,* pages 199-202.

Chapter 14

(P. 231) "Within a week, grain shipments began arriving regularly in the Volga region. The famine was over." Armand Hammer with Neil Lyndon, *Hammer,* Putnam, New York, 1987, pages 142-143. **(P. 233) ". . . as much as $100 has been illegally deposited in foreign bank accounts by corrupt Russian officials since 1991."** *Interflo: A Soviet Trade News Monitor,* 6/92, page 23, Vol. 11, No. 8 (from

Trud, 5/9/92). **(P. 233)** **"Komsomolskaya Pravda reported in 1988 that over 40,000 police officials were fired between 1985 and 1987 for corrupt acts ranging from fabrication of evidence to the taking and giving of bribes."** Zbigniew Brzezinski, *The Grand Failure: The Birth and Death of Communism in the Twentieth Century,* Macmillan, New York, 1990, page 72. **(P. 235)** **". . . while Russian prostitutes and pimps fly to Vietnam on official passports from the Russian Ministry of Foreign Affairs."** *Ibid.* 1/92, page 22, Vol. 11, No. 3 (from *Izvestiya,* 12/24/91). **(P. 235)** **"It is estimated that over $100 million was paid to Russian officials during the first half of 1992, just to facilitate illegal exports of oil and other commodities."** *Ibid.* 10/92, Vol. 11, No. 12, page 29 (from *Financial Times,* 9/23/92). **(P. 242)** **"That same American also conducted a Moscow trade show, then allegedly welshed on the $50,000 fee to the Russian exhibition organizer."** *Ibid.* 9/92, page 17, Vol. 11, No. 11 (*The Wall Street Journal,* 7/2/92).

Index

About the Author

Richard Poe has been covering the Soviet-American business scene for various magazines and newspapers since 1988. Formerly senior editor of *Success* magazine, he has most recently been involved in a number of television and print media ventures in Russia. Poe speaks Russian and travels frequently to the former Soviet states for business and pleasure.